D0876319

Statesmen in Disguise

Statesmen in Disguise

THE CHANGING ROLE
OF THE ADMINISTRATIVE CLASS OF THE
BRITISH HOME CIVIL SERVICE
1853–1966

GEOFFREY KINGDON FRY

B.Sc. (Econ.), Ph.D. (Lond.)
Lecturer in Politics, University of Leeds

MACMILLAN

London · Melbourne · Toronto

1969

JN
425
.F79
1969

© G. K. Fry 1969

Published by
MACMILLAN AND CO LTD
Little Essex Street London WC2
and also at Bombay Calcutta and Madras
Macmillan South Africa (Publishers) Pty Ltd Johannesburg
The Macmillan Company of Australia Pty Ltd Melbourne
The Macmillan Company of Canada Ltd Toronto
Gill and Macmillan Ltd Dublin

Printed in Great Britain by
ROBERT MACLEHOSE AND CO LTD
The University Press, Glasgow

73-411769

Contents

TO MY PARENTS

Preface

IN May 1967 I was awarded a Doctor of Philosophy degree by the University of London for a thesis entitled 'The Changing Role of the Administrative Class of the British Home Civil Service 1853–1965'. This book is an enlarged version of that doctoral thesis. The main material that has been added is that concerned with the written evidence that was submitted to the Fulton Committee on the Civil Service – appointed in February 1966 – during the first year of its existence, and which the individuals and organisations concerned were prepared to make available to me. The general argument of this book can be summarised in the following three hundred words.

'Although the nature of the convention of ministerial responsibility may be changing, under a system of parliamentary democracy, the Civil Service will always have to be subject to political control. This does not necessarily mean, however, that the Higher Civil Service should continue to be dominated by a separate Administrative Class seeing itself as specialising in "the awareness of ministerial responsibility". For that class's "all-rounder" tradition, its tendencies to give a low valuation to management, specialised knowledge, and "investigation . . . as preliminary to action", constitute attitudes more appropriate to the Service of a Regulatory State than that charged with administering the Welfare State and managing the economy. The central theme of this book is that the Administrative Class should be amalgamated with the Executive Class on the basis of a more specialised career structure: the leading grades of the merged class, together with the equivalent grades of the specialist groups, forming an integrated Higher Civil Service. The book traces the emergence of the Positive State and, against a historical background, an examination is made of its impact on the direct-entry recruitment and post-entry training arrangements of the Administrative Class, and the relationships of that class with the managerial Executive Class, and the leading specialist groups, before concluding that a more unified Higher Civil Service would provide the type of administrator needed by the modern State. It would, however, have to be an open hierarchy because, whereas a closed career Service may have been appropriate when the State itself largely stood aside from the rest of society, this is not the case in the era of the Positive State: the Service should exchange staff on a larger scale than at present with the local authorities, the public corporations, private industrial and commercial undertakings, and the universities.'

The author has received valuable help in developing this general argument into a doctoral thesis and then into a book. Every research student is, to some extent, dependent upon the quality, and the qualities, of his research supervisor. During the period 1962–6, when I was a post-graduate research student at the London School of Economics, I was very fortunate to have Professor H. R. G. Greaves as my research supervisor, and I take this opportunity of acknowledging my debt to him for his wise advice. Almost all of the doctoral thesis was completed at the L. S. E., but the finishing touches were applied to it, and it was converted into a book, during the first ten months following my appointment to the academic staff of the University of Leeds in October 1966. The advantage of working with Professor A. H. Hanson needs no elaboration, and I now express my gratitude for his advice. I owe even more to a fellow Lecturer at Leeds, James Macdonald, a former member of the Administrative Class. Mr Macdonald read all the many drafts of the book, and he proved to be an invaluable constructive critic of my work partly because of his fine command of the English language and partly because of his wider practical knowledge of the Civil Service.

I was a member of the Civil Service for about two years, and during that time I never advanced beyond the humble status of Executive Officer. At least when I was in its ranks, the Civil Service pursued the liberal policy of allowing those of its members who secured university places to take three years' unpaid leave to follow their chosen course of studies safe in the knowledge that they could eventually return if they wished to. I took advantage of these arrangements but, in the end, I chose to enter the academic profession which – although its salaries and promotion prospects compare very unfavourably with those of the appropriate classes of the Civil Service – seemed to offer rather more freedom. Although the Civil Service treated me very well, in writing this book I have not (consciously) held back from expressing my views about what I consider to be the problems of the Civil Service, and what I suggest are possible solutions to some of those problems.

From all the thousands of words that I have read about and around the subject-matter of this book, few gave me greater pleasure to read than the writings of Civil Servants. This is the case not only with those writers who can be said to be in at least broad agreement with some of the proposals advanced in this book – for example, Frank Dunnill and E. N. Gladden – but also those who would probably be opposed to them – for example, the late H. E. Dale, C. H. Sisson and Lord Bridges. Mr Sisson and Lord Bridges are still in a position to reply to my thesis and I hope that they will be given the opportunity to do so. Mr Sisson's writings come in for a good deal of criticism in this book, but this criticism is directed against the opinions that he expresses: it is not intended to suggest that his book is other than a very interesting and beautifully written piece of work. Similarly, I tend to disagree with some of the views expressed by Lord Bridges, but I recognise that he was the Head of the Civil Service for eleven years and that he had a lifetime's experience as a practical administrator and I welcome this opportunity of making clear my respect for his views.

In writing a book about the Civil Service, the outsider is heavily dependent upon cooperation from within the Service. I must make special mention of the help given to me by the Civil Service Commissioners and, to a lesser extent, by the Treasury. I must record, however, that I remain rather surprised at the lack of available statistical data about the Administrative Class of the Home Civil Service; hence, the motley collection of tables that comprise Appendix I of this book.

Two small technical points must be made about the content of certain footnotes. The first point is that references made to parliamentary debates since 1964 have been made to the Weekly

Hansard: this is important because the column numbers some-times differ from those given in the bound volumes which are published later. The second point is that I dealt with the written evidence of the Fulton Committee as it came out so that when that evidence comes to be published in bound form the page numbers may be different from those shown in my footnotes.

I also draw attention to the fact that I have dedicated this book to my parents, who have been a constant source of encouragement.

But, however much this book owes to other people's help and advice – and, as I hope I have made clear, it owes a good deal – there is only one person who must take responsibility for its con-tents: namely, myself.

The University of Leeds   G. K. FRY
August 1967

While this book was being prepared for publication, the Fulton Report on the Home Civil Service was published on 26 June 1968. My publishers considered that, although the Fulton Committee's terms of reference were much broader than those which I had followed in writing this book, readers would be interested in my views about the Fulton Report. While leaving Chapters 1–6 as they were when completed in August 1967, I have added a Post-script (pp. 361 ff.) to this book containing some observations about the Fulton Report. The form that the Postscript has taken, that of lengthy quotation from the Fulton Report, together with comment, was chosen not only in order to be as fair as practicable to the Fulton Committee, given that I found its Report to be an unimpressive piece of work, but also so as to make the reader less dependent than otherwise upon my interpretation of the Com-mittee's findings.

I take this opportunity of thanking my friend and colleague, Tom Nossiter, for helping me with the proofs for this book.

The University of Leeds   G. K. FRY
October 1968

Acknowledgements

THE Controller of Her Majesty's Stationery Office for general permission to quote from its publications.

The Treasury for permission to quote from material not normally made available to the general public.

The Civil Service Commissioners for permission to quote from their *Reports* and from certain recruiting material.

The Secretary to the Fulton Committee on the Civil Service for general permission, and to the following individuals and organisations for their permission to quote from evidence submitted to the Fulton Committee: Acton Society Trust, British Institute of Management, Civil Service Clerical Association, Confederation of British Industry, Professor B. R. Crick and Mr Thornhill, Dr A. F. Earle, First Division Association, Greater London Council, Institution of Professional Civil Servants, Labour Party, Liberal Party, Mr J. H. Robertson, Professor Peter Self, Society of Civil Servants and H.M. Treasury.

The Editor of *Public Administration* for general permission, and the following individuals for their permission to quote from articles published therein: Sir Charles Cunningham, Sir Maurice Dean, Sir James Dunnett, C. D. E. Keeling, Sir George Mallaby, Dr Henry Parris, D. E. Regan, Professor Kenneth Robinson, and Professor W. A. Robson.

The Editor of *Administration*, and Mr Seamus Gaffney for permission to quote from an article published therein.

The Editor of *The Listener* for general permission, and the following individuals for their permission, to quote from articles published therein: Harold Wilson M.P., Lord Bridges, Lord Helsby, Robert Nield, Ian Trethowan, Norman Hunt, and E. J. Hobsbawm.

The Editor of *The Political Quarterly* for general permission, and Professor W. A. Robson for his personal permission, to quote from articles published therein.

The General Secretary of the Institution of Professional Civil Servants for general permission to quote from material published in *State Service*.

The General Secretary of the Society of Civil Servants for general permission to quote from material published in *Civil Service Opinion*.

The General Secretary of the Civil Service Clerical Association for general permission to quote from material published in *Red Tape*.

The Editor of *The Times* for permission to quote from articles published in that newspaper.

The Editor of *The Sunday Times* for permission to quote from articles published in that newspaper.

The Editor of *The Economist* for permission to quote from material contained in that journal.

The Director of the Administrative Staff College at Henley for permission to quote from material connected with that institution.

The Director of the École Nationale d'Administration for permission to quote from material connected with that institution.

CHAPTER ONE

The Development of the Administrative Class and the Modern State since 1853

I   THE EMERGENCE OF THE POSITIVE STATE

THE bare minimum number of functions that the mid-nineteenth century British central Government could have been realistically limited to were four. First, the Government had the overall responsibility for the maintenance of internal law and order: hence, the primary responsibilities of the Home Office. Second, it attempted to ensure that the country was able to repel an external attack made upon her, and that she could also defend her overseas possessions: hence, the role of the Admiralty and the War Office. Third, it conducted the country's diplomatic relations with other sovereign states: hence, the duties of the Foreign Office. Fourth, it exercised a general control over the affairs of the country's Colonial Empire: hence, the responsibilities of the Colonial and the India Offices.

If the central Government had restricted its role to the performance of these four functions, it could have been correctly described as a 'law and order State'. Although the belief that 'Governments who governed least, governed best' was widespread in the ruling classes, particularly during the middle years of the century, the State never actually wholly stood aside from society as the theory of *laissez-faire* implied. Even in the economic sphere, where it came closest to observing that theory, the State did intervene to accord itself regulatory powers when public utilities showed themselves to be natural monopolies. The central Government also se cured regulatory powers to deal with abuses in working conditions in factories and mines, just as it came to supervise the local and private attempts made to ameliorate the social problems that the twin forces of industrialism and urbanism, unleashed by the take-off into self-sustained economic growth, had combined either to create or to illuminate.[1]

The prevailing prejudice of the period was that what could not be provided by private enterprise should, in the interest of personal freedom, be entrusted to either the local authorities or voluntary societies, rather than to the State. The major development in governmental activity during the nineteenth century, therefore,

[1] The following books were used among others to help to secure a background to the role of the State in the nineteenth century: Sir Ernest Barker, *The Development of Public Services in Western Europe 1660–1930* (1944); Asa Briggs, *Public Opinion and Public Health in the Age of Chadwick* (1946); Maurice Bruce, *The Coming of the Welfare State* (1961); Albert V. Dicey, *Lectures on the Relation Between Law and Public Opinion in England* (1905: 1962 ed.); Samuel E. Finer, *The Life and Times of Sir Edwin Chadwick* (1952); John S. Harris, *British Government Inspection as a Dynamic Process* (1955); Bryan Keith-Lucas, *The History of Local Government in England* (1958); Royston Lambert, *Sir John Simon and English Social Administration* (1963); H. J. Laski, W. I. Jennings, and W. A. Robson, *A Century of Municipal Progress* (1935); R. A. Lewis, *Edwin Chadwick and the Public Health Movement 1832–1854* (1952); Ephraim Lipson, *The Growth of English Society* (1949); Oliver Mac-Donagh, *A Pattern of Government Growth 1800–1860* (1961); Henry Parris, *Government and the Railways in Nineteenth Century Britain* (1965); Karl Polanyi, *Origins of Our Time* (1945); Roger Prouty, *The Transformation of the Board of Trade 1830–1855* (1957); Lionel Robbins, *The Theory of Economic Policy in English Classical Political Economy* (1952); David Roberts, *The Victorian Origins of the British Welfare State* (1960); Howard Robinson, *The British Post Office* (1948); William A. Robson, *The Development of Local Government* (1948); Adam Smith, *An Inquiry into the Nature and Causes of the Wealth of Nations* (1776: 1937 ed.); Eric Stokes, *The English Utilitarians and India* (1959); D. M. Young, *The Colonial Office in the Early Nineteenth Century* (1961).

The books were supplemented by the following articles: Lucy Brown, 'The Board of Trade and the Tariff Problem 1840–1842', in *English Historical Review* (1953); J. Bartlett Brebner, 'Laissez-Faire and State Intervention in Nineteenth Century Britain', in *Journal of Economic History*, suppl. VIII (1948); Doreen Collins, 'The Introduction of Old Age Pensions in Great Britain', in *Historical Journal* (1965); Valerie Cromwell, 'Interpretations of Nineteenth Century Administration: an Analysis', in *Victorian Studies* (1966); Jenifer Hart, 'Nineteenth Century Social Reform: A Tory Interpretation of History', in *Past and Present* (1965); E. P. Hennock, 'Urban Sanitary Reform a Century before Chadwick', in *Economic History Review* (1957); Royston Lambert, 'Central and Local Relations in mid-Victorian England: the Local Government Act Office 1858–71', in *Victorian Studies* (1962); Royston

took place in the sphere of local Government.[1] By 1890, local expenditure had increased to five times its 1820 level, and not only its volume but its character was radically altered. At the beginning of the century, the organisation of poor relief had been the largest single item of expenditure, but by 1890 it constituted only twelve per cent of local spending. The increased local expenditure had been made to pay for better road building, improved health and housing, and elementary education.[2]

In the social sphere, after 1834 and until the period of Liberal legislation after 1906, the central Government's role was the supervision of such local, and also voluntary, activities. At first, this supervision was exercised usually, but not always, through independent boards, such as the Poor Law Commission and the Board of Health. But, gradually, such activities came to be brought under direct ministerial control as the House of Commons, particularly after 1846, came to appreciate the potential of the doctrine

---

Lambert, 'A Victorian National Health Service: State Vaccination 1855–1871', in *Historical Journal* (1962); Bryan Keith-Lucas, 'Some Influences Affecting the Development of Sanitary Legislation in England', in *Economic History Review* (1954); Oliver MacDonagh, 'The Regulation of Emigrant Traffic from the United Kingdom', in *Irish Historical Studies* (1954); Oliver MacDonagh, 'Emigration and the State 1833–55: an Essay in Administrative History', in *Transactions of the Royal Historical Society* (1955); Oliver MacDonagh, 'Delegated Legislation and Administrative Discretions in the 1850s: a Particular Study', in *Victorian Studies* (1958); Oliver MacDonagh, 'The Nineteenth Century Revolution in Government: a Reappraisal', in *Historical Journal* (1958); Henry Parris, 'The Nineteenth Century Revolution in Government: a Reappraisal Reappraised', in *Historical Journal* (1960); David Roberts, 'Jeremy Bentham and the Victorian Administrative State', in *Victorian Studies* (1959); M. W. Thomas, 'The Origins of Administrative Centralisation', in *Current Legal Problems* (1950); Kenneth J. O. Walker, 'The Classical Economists and the Factory Acts', in *Journal of Economic History* (1941); F. M. G. Willson, 'Ministries and Boards: Some Aspects of Administrative Development since 1832', in *Public Administration* (1955).

[1] Even in the sphere of local Government there was reluctance among the governing classes to recognise the need for local gas and water monopolies: this is discussed by Herman Finer, *Municipal Trading* (1941) pp. 36–67.

[2] A. T. Peacock and J. Wiseman, *The Growth of Public Expenditure in the United Kingdom* (1961) p. 39.

of ministerial responsibility. From the outset, Ministers had been responsible for the activities of the Factories and Mines Inspectorates, which exercised regulatory control over industrial working conditions, while, after 1839, the Privy Council Committee on Education came to supervise the state grant made to voluntary societies.

The history of English education from the first state grant of £20,000, made in 1833, to the Balfour Act of 1902, provides an interesting example of the development of the social services in the nineteenth century. The initial state grant was made to two voluntary societies, and when it was increased in 1839, the administration of the grant was given to a Committee on Education which had Sir James Kay-Shuttleworth as its first Secretary, and he was able to develop a scheme of educational inspection and administration which was the necessary basis for future progress. A quarter of a century after the first grant, Parliament was voting an educational grant of £663,000 per annum. In 1870, the Forster Act added a system of state schools to the old voluntary framework, and control over them was given to a new local government organ, the School Board. The Forster Act did not introduce compulsory elementary education, though it empowered each School Board to require attendance by passing a by-law to that effect. By 1891, compulsory free elementary education was available for all. In 1900, the whole status of education was raised with the creation of a Board of Education whose President normally had cabinet rank, and very early in the board's history came the passing of the bitterly contested Education Act of 1902. Its architect was one of the board's Civil Servants, Robert Morant, who managed to capture the imagination and the political backing of the Prime Minister, Balfour, who steered the Bill through the House of Commons in the face of violent Liberal opposition led by the formidable Lloyd George. The Act made provision for rate aid to voluntary schools; but its major feature was that it abolished the School Boards, and placed the state system under the control of the education committees of the County and County Borough Councils. These local authorities were given the power to go beyond the elementary stage to provide secondary education, with a system of scholarships and free places being established for the most promising children.[1]

Just as the nineteenth-century central Government did not directly provide social services, so it also abstained from the provision of economic services, for the only business undertakings owned by the State were the Post Office, which was run largely as a source of revenue, and Military and Naval establishments, which supplied equipment to the Armed Forces. To this modest list could be added the State's responsibility for the conduct of commercial relations with other countries. The central Government did not, however, wholly observe Adam Smith's dictum that it was 'the highest impertinence and presumption . . . of Kings and Ministers to watch over the economy of private people'.[2] It did intervene to help to ensure minimum working conditions, and to protect the public when real competition broke down and monopolies emerged. An example of this occurred when the railways destroyed the competition of the canals and the turnpikes, and the Board of Trade, after 1840, came to exercise 'more or less minute control over the railway companies'.[3] The board had also

[1] See Ernest Barker, *The Development of Public Services in Western Europe 1660–1930* (1944) pp. 90–2. According to Kenneth Young, *Arthur James Balfour* (1963), Morant and Balfour 'both approached any problem with the same intellectual attitude' and their collaboration 'not merely produced a unique Education Bill but also forced it through the House and the country against the most fearful odds' (p. 206). An interesting account of the questions raised by the Education Act of 1902 was given by Eric Eaglesham, *From School Board to Local Authority* (1956). The controversial Morant has attracted a good deal of attention, not all of it as eulogistic as the biography by Bernard M. Allen, *Sir Robert Morant. A Great Public Servant* (1934), and the memories of him recorded by Violet Markham, 'Robert Morant. Some Personal Reminiscences', in *Public Administration* (1950). The ideal umpire in the debate about Morant was D. N. Chester, 'Robert Morant and Michael Sadler', in *Public Administration* (1950), the severely critical contributions to which debate being supplied by Michael Sadleir, *Michael Ernest Sadler 1861–1943. A Memoir by His Son* (1949), Lynda Grier, *Achievement in Education. The Work of Michael Ernest Sadler 1885–1935* (1952), and Sir George Kekewich, *The Education Department and After* (1920).

[2] Adam Smith, *An Inquiry into the Nature and Causes of the Wealth of Nations* (1776: 1937 ed.) p. 329.

[3] Sir Charles Trevelyan and Sir Stafford Northcote, *Report on the Board of Trade* (1854) p. 129. Henry Parris, *Government and the Railways*

acquired powers to 'watch over' and regulate the activities of the 'private people' running merchant shipping.[1]

The Board of Trade had, by the 1850s, become the government's department for private industry, and much has been made recently of its transformation during a period when the prevailing philosophy was supposed to be *laissez-faire*. The board's functions did add up to an impressive range of duties,[2] but one can still hold safely to the view that the role of the central Government in the free market or liberal economy was that of a referee or umpire. It either stayed on the touchline or mingled non-competitively with the competing entrepreneurs, imposing marginal restraints on their activities. The economy was dominated by the private capitalist, and the spirit of the period may well have been captured by *The Economist* in 1851, when it equated the unbridled pursuit of private gain with the national interest. It said:

> From the intimate connection between private enterprise and public welfare, it must not be concluded that the latter, which is the consequence of the former, not its impelling motive, should be made its object, and that private enterprise should, in consequence, be directed by public authority. That would extinguish it or leave it without a guide. Individual profit is its mainspring and governor. It cannot be interfered with except to misdirect or annihilate it. In fact, it ceases to be private enterprise when regulated or directed by public authority; and then it has no longer those limited and personal advantages in view which are its most infallible guides to success. The various bodies of directors now

---

in Nineteenth Century Britain (1965) is a beautifully written and original study which discusses state regulation of the railways during the so-called 'heyday of *laissez-faire*' and, indeed, takes the subject right up to 1914.

[1] Roger Prouty, *The Transformation of the Board of Trade 1830–1855* (1957) ch. III.

[2] The Board of Trade had made a significant contribution to the creation of the free market at home and towards the attainment of freer trade. In the process the board had shed some of its traditional tasks, such as the administration of the protective tariffs. In place of such functions, the board had become responsible for government statistics, for running a School of Design, for the registration of joint stock companies, but, above all, for the regulation of the two great transport industries, merchant shipping and the railways.

holding their half-yearly meetings, and to whose successful exertions in carrying out this great work thus far we do a willing homage, can only have a sense of their duties more vividly impressed on them by having the vast moral and social effects of their undertakings brought under their notice. [The journal concluded:] Of one thing they may be assured, that they will best promote the public interest by attending to the interests of their shareholders. All the advantages of their undertakings to the public spring from the hope of private gain, and whatever in the long run and permanently is for the advantage of the shareholders, will also be most for the interest of the public.[1]

The repeal of the Corn Laws in 1846 symbolised the nation's acceptance of the external application of the free market, Free Trade, which was not seriously questioned until the British manufacturers' advantage in comparative costs came to be eroded after about 1880. Both the internal free market and external Free Trade continued to dominate the economic system even into the early years of the First World War.

In the decade or so before the War the central Government began to extend its influence notably in the sphere of social insurance where the reforms that Bismarck had introduced in Germany in the 1880s provided examples that were sometimes improved upon. The Workmen's Compensation Act of 1897, revised in 1906, introduced industrial accident insurance, and an Act of 1908 introduced non-contributory old age pensions.[2] But it was Lloyd George's revolutionary National Insurance Act of 1911 that really marked the break with the State's largely regulatory past, for it introduced a centrally managed scheme of sickness insurance, with provision for unemployment insurance in certain industries.[3] Lloyd George had believed that it would be

---

[1] *The Economist*, 1 Sep 1951, p. 498: it was quoting its edition of 30 Aug 1851. I initially owed this reference to Political and Economic Planning, *Government and Industry* (1952) pp. 5–6.

[2] Barker, op. cit. pp. 75–6; A. J. P. Taylor, *Bismarck. The Man and Statesman* (1955) p. 202. A useful background to this topic was secured from an article by Doreen Collins, 'The Introduction of Old Age Pensions in Great Britain', in *Historical Journal* (1965).

[3] The passage of the National Insurance Bill was described by William J. Braithwaite in his memoirs edited by Sir Henry Bunbury, *Lloyd*

best to deal with all kinds of social insurance as a dovetailed entity, but he realised that it was not politically possible at that time.[1] His enlightened views on the subject came out clearly in a note he sent to his private secretary in 1911. He wrote:

> Insurance necessarily temporary expedient. At no distant date hope State will acknowledge a full responsibility in the matter of making provision for sickness, breakdown and unemployment. It really does so now, through Poor Law, but conditions under which the system had hitherto worked have been so harsh and humiliating that working class pride revolts against accepting so degrading and doubtful a boon. Gradually the obligation of the State to find labour or sustenance will be realised and honourably interpreted.[2]

In view of the acknowledgment of such responsibilities by the Churchill Coalition Government thirty years later, and the implementation of the appropriate measures of social legislation by the Labour Government after 1945, the staccato sentences of Lloyd George's note proved prophetic.

The Liberal Ministries of 1906–14, in which Lloyd George served, can be credited with other social advances, notably the introduction of Trade Boards for sweated industries and of Labour Exchanges in 1909. But the central Government still held back from the productive process in the economic sphere, and it even pursued a policy of 'Business as usual' during the early years of the First World War.[3] Circumstances eventually forced the State to take a more positive role in industry and commerce, as was later explained by the Director General of raw materials. He wrote:

George's Ambulance Wagon (1957). Further accounts of what Braithwaite described as 'the great adventure' that were found useful included: Bernard M. Allen, *Sir Robert Morant. A Great Public Servant* (1934); Lord Salter, *Memoirs of a Public Servant* (1961); Sir John Wheeler-Bennett, *John Anderson, Viscount Waverley* (1962); R. W. Harris, *Not So Humdrum* (1939).

[1] Thomas Jones, *Lloyd George* (1951) p. 39.

[2] Braithwaite, op. cit. p. 24.

[3] Samuel J. Hurwitz, *State Intervention in Great Britain 1914–1919* (1949) ch. 11. Hurwitz's excellent study provided a background to the economic and social policies either pursued or discussed by Governments both before and immediately after the First World War.

The growing intensity of the War, the enormous increase of the British armies, and the German submarine campaign against our merchantmen changed the situation radically. The Government requirements, on our own behalf and for our Allies, increased by leaps and bounds. To obtain any proportionate increase of supplies was a matter of immense difficulty and it became gradually evident that the task could not be left to undirected private enterprise. It was not possible to allow private importers to enjoy the almost unlimited opportunities which would have been open to them. Still less was it possible to permit the amount and character of the available supplies to depend upon their judgment, when any failure to make adequate provision would have had the most fatal consequences. From the beginning of 1916 onwards, the true character of the problem began to show itself.[1]

The result was the development of central government controls that came to affect, more or less completely, all the principal trades of the country. Practically all the metal and chemical trades came under the Ministry of Munitions; all food, feeding stuffs, as well as animal and vegetable oils and fats, came under the Ministry of Food; while merchant shipping came under a Ministry of Shipping. The War Office controlled wool and leather; the Board of Trade controlled practically all other industries, including railways, coal, timber, cotton, mineral oils, petrol, tobacco and paper. The controls themselves varied in character. In the more important cases they meant interference with the ordinary methods of supply and demand and with the adjustment of prices by economic laws. Beveridge later wrote that, under the stress of war, practical discoveries in the art of government had been made almost comparable to the immense discoveries made at the same time in the art of flying. The use of aeroplanes had not abolished the law of gravitation, but it had overcome or neutralised the law. In the same way, the controls which had successfully been carried out during the war had involved complete interference with the operation of economic laws. Beveridge asserted: 'We have learnt how to fix prices without stopping supply or production; we have largely neutralised during the War the mere power of

---

[1] *The Official History of the Ministry of Munitions: Raw Materials*, Cmd 788 (1920) p. 5. I initially owed this reference to Political and Economic Planning, *Government and Industry* (1952) p. 7.

the purse in obtaining the essentials of life; we have governed production, prices, wages, supplies and distribution by statutory regulations, and not by economic laws.'[1]

The later years of the war had seen the Government promising 'Reconstruction' afterwards, but the coming of peace saw a virulent and successful Press campaign launched against the Civil Service which seemed to aim at convincing the man in the street that, above all, the war had 'made the world safe for bureaucracy'. The economy-minded Geddes Committee was appointed with 'a roving commission to inquire into the social progress of the last fifty years, and to pronounce it evil wherever it does not serve the immediate ends of a business civilisation'.[2] The policy of retrenchment at almost any social cost was not completely successful in its destructive task, and among the new departments which were either created or survived the economy axe at the time were included the Department of Scientific and Industrial Research, and the Ministries of Labour, Transport and Health.[3] As might be expected, however, the inter-war period proved a relatively poor one for social reform, although some advances were made. Notable among these was Chamberlain's Widows, Orphans and Old Age Contributory Pensions Act of 1925 in the sphere of social insurance; while unemployment insurance was extended to a wider range of industries in 1920 and came to be based on a revised national system in 1934.[4] The most significant reform of the period was the Addison Act of 1919 which

> carried the Government into the business of housing. Later Acts carried it further. The building of houses with the aid of Government subsidies was one of the largest enterprises – certainly the

---

[1] Sir William Beveridge, *The Public Service in War and in Peace* (1920) pp. 4–6.

[2] H. J. Laski, 'The Civil Service and Parliament', an essay in the Society of Civil Servants' symposium, *The Development of the Civil Service* (1921) p. 21.

[3] D. N. Chester and F. M. G. Willson (eds.) *The Organisation of British Central Government 1914–1956* (1957) p. 25.

[4] Barker, op. cit. p. 77; and A. J. Youngson, *The British Economy 1920–1957* (1960) pp. 59–60 and 130.

largest collective enterprise – of the years between the Wars. It meant that the new Ministry of Health was in large part a Ministry of housing, and as such one of the most important departments of state. It helped to cover the outskirts of towns with municipal housing estates and to embellish the villages with the ubiquitous 'council houses' of the inter-War years, much criticised on aesthetic grounds, and insufficient in point of numbers for the need, but in general far better planned and equipped than the older houses for working class families which they supplemented or replaced.[1]

The Government's wartime machinery for controlling the economy was almost completely destroyed by the Press campaign against public expenditure: its only working legacy being the Railways Act of 1921 which amalgamated the railways into four large groups. Great publicity was given to the mistakes made by the State during its economic supremacy, although most of what blunders were committed had been the responsibility of businessmen who had been serving as temporary Civil Servants, but who were now leading the clamour to cut back the public sector and to introduce 'business methods' into what remained. The spirit that the State should not 'pay people for putting difficulties in the way of private enterprise' had triumphed by the middle of 1921.[2] But that year also marked the end of the post-war boom that had fostered the 'back to 1914' campaign. Ushered in was an economic depression which lasted until the operation of the Second World

[1] Charles Loch Mowat, *Britain Between the Wars 1918–1940* (1956) pp. 45–6.
[2] The general background to the immediate post-First World War years was secured from R. H. Tawney, 'The Abolition of Economic Controls 1918–1921', in *Economic History Review* (1943), Philip Abrams, 'The failure of social reform: 1918–1920', *Past and Present* (1963), and A. C. Pigou, *Aspects of British Economic History 1918–1925* (1947). Two books by Sir Stephen Demetriadi, *Inside a Government Office* (1921) and the largely repetitive *A Reform for the Civil Service* (1921), were examples of the call by former temporary Civil Servants for the introduction of 'business methods' into government departments. Beveridge, op. cit. pp. 7–8, commented adversely about such views. Youngson, op. cit. pp. 58–9, was also referred to: on p. 59 he quoted the demand of *The Economist*, 21 Dec 1918, p. 835, to end inhibitions upon private enterprise, which is repeated in the text.

War, and in which the rate of unemployment never fell below nine per cent and even rose above twenty-two per cent in the years when the impact of the Wall Street crash was most severely felt.[1]

The Governments of the inter-war period, whatever their political complexion, failed to solve the problem of mass unemployment. Within the limits imposed by their adherence to traditional policies of balancing the Budget, the Governments of the period, particularly those of the 1930s, did, however, make considerable

---

[1] Youngson, op. cit. p. 269. Besides Youngson's admirable survey, the following books and articles were used in order to secure a background about economic policy between the wars: Charles Loch Mowat, *Britain Between the Wars 1918–1940* (1956); A. J. P. Taylor, *English History 1914–1945* (1965); William Ashworth, *An Economic History of England 1870–1939* (1960); W. A. Lewis, *Economic Survey 1919–1939* (1949); J. M. Keynes, *General Theory of Employment, Interest and Money* (1936); Sir Roy Harrod, *The Life of John Maynard Keynes* (1951); Lionel Robbins, *The Great Depression* (1934); Sir Henry Clay, *Lord Norman* (1957); Andrew Boyle, *Montagu Norman* (1967); Sir Edward Bridges, *Treasury Control* (1950); Hugh Dalton, *Call Back Yesterday* (1953); John Raymond (ed.) *The Baldwin Age* (1960); A. C. Pigou, *Aspects of British Economic History 1918–1925* (1947); Samuel J. Hurwitz, *State Intervention in Great Britain 1914–1919* (1949); R. H. Tawney, 'The Abolition of Economic Controls 1918–1921', in *Economic History Review* (1943); J. M. Keynes, *The Economic Consequences of Mr Churchill* (1926); A. L. Bowley, *Some Economic Consequences of the War* (1931); L. S. Presnell, 'Lessons of the Twenties', in *The Sunday Times*, 27 June 1965; Symposium, '1931 Thirty Years After. Lessons and Legacies', in *The Economist*, 17 June 1961; Philip Snowden, *Autobiography* (1934); Colin Cross, *Philip Snowden* (1966); Pilgrim Trust, *Men Without Work* (1938); R. C. Davison, *British Unemployment Policy Since 1930* (1938); W. A. Morton, *British Finance 1930–1940* (1943); F. C. Benham, *Great Britain under Protection* (1939); Ernest Davies '*National Capitalism*' (1939); Sir Hubert Henderson, *The Inter-War Years and other Papers* (1955); Robert Skidelsky, *Politicians and the Slump. The Labour Government of 1929–31* (1967); H. W. Richardson, *Economic Recovery in Britain 1932–9* (1967); Derek H. Aldcroft, 'Economic Progress in Britain in the 1920's', *Scottish Journal of Political Economy* (1966); K. J. Hancock, 'The Reduction of Unemployment as a Problem of Public Policy 1920–29', *Economic History Review* (1962–3); H. W. Richardson, 'The Basis of Economic Recovery in Britain in the 1930's: a Review and a New Interpretation', *Economic History Review* (1962–3); Derek H. Aldcroft, 'Economic Growth in Britain in the Inter War Years: a Reassessment', *Economic History Review* (1967).

progress away from the free market and Free Trade towards the policies of what I propose to call a Positive State. By 1939, the process had clearly gone too far for that apostle of the liberal economy, *The Economist*, which lamented:

> Until the last decade or so it was the accepted doctrine among virtually all businessmen and perhaps more than half of the public that the State would intervene in the affairs of specific industries as little as possible. Complete *laissez-faire* went by the board decades ago, but until recently the tendency has been, at least among businessmen, to regard State intervention in industry as perhaps necessary, but if so a necessary evil. As a purely abstract proposition that would still doubtless be maintained. But in practice the attitude has changed. The change dates from the Great Depression and from its economic consequences in Great Britain, the protective tariff. Since 1932, the State has no longer appeared to industry solely in the guise of monitor or policeman; it has had favours to dispense. What is more, in addition to the concealed subsidy of a Customs duty, the State has begun to hand out specific subsidies in hard cash, from which agriculture has benefited most handsomely, but by no means exclusively. And, finally, in addition to tariff protection and cash subsidies, the State has in several cases lent its aid to the creation of legally enforceable determinations of minimum price and maximum output.[1]

However, the abandonment of Free Trade, the cheap money policy, the aid to special areas of very heavy unemployment, the attempts to rationalise and to lessen competition in agriculture and major industries such as coal and iron and steel,[2] only alleviated the problem of mass unemployment. A complete cure was rendered impossible because those who controlled or advised upon the Government's economic policy were unable to break away from the traditional conception of the Budget as being the same as household accounts, and to think in terms of resources instead of money symbols. As the Treasury, which was the major source of advice to the Government about economic policy, officially saw

[1] *The Economist*, 18 Mar 1939, p. 551. I initially owed this reference to Political and Economic Planning, *Government and Industry* (1952) p. 9.
[2] Youngson, op. cit. ch. IV.

its role as late as 1927 as being 'the department which, subject to the control of the Executive and the authority of Parliament, is responsible for the administration of the public finances of the country',[1] the failures in economic policy during the period were not surprising. The Treasury's traditions had, after all, been laid down during Gladstone's heyday when the main virtue to be looked for in a Treasury man was the ability to save 'candle ends', because public expenditure was ideally to be pared down to a bare minimum so that 'money should be left to fructify in the pocket of the taxpayer'.[2] Lord Bridges has since written: 'From about the 1920s onwards, the Treasury staff began to think of expenditure rather less in terms of the prospect of spending so much public money and rather more in terms of the employment of resources.'[3] No doubt some of them did, but the 'Treasury view' propounded to official committees still adhered closely to the balanced Budget concept, which ruled out such ideas as that increased expenditure on public works would benefit employment.[4] As late as 1938, for example, Sir John Simon in his budget speech showed the household accounts mentality when he asked the House to 'prepare itself' for the news that there was 'a deficit to be met'. As unemployment had been 9·5 per cent in 1937, and was running at the rate of twelve per cent in 1938, to modern eyes the prospect of a deficit would be welcome.[5] As Lord Bridges later wrote, it was true that the years between the wars were 'years of ferment in economic theory', and that 'until the end of the period there was very little agreement between economists on any course of action which could materially diminish the burden of unemployment'.[6] He could, with justice, have added that Keynes,

---

[1] Sir Thomas Heath, *The Treasury* (1927) p. 1.

[2] Sir Edward Bridges, *Treasury Control* (1950) p. 6.

[3] Bridges, op. cit. p. 8.

[4] Youngson, op. cit. pp. 254–5 and ch. VII generally. R. F. Harrod, *The Life of John Maynard Keynes* (1951) ch. X, contains a fascinating account of the duels Keynes had with the Governor of the Bank of England, Montagu Norman, and with the formidable Sir Richard Hopkins of the Treasury.

[5] House of Commons, *Official Report* (1937–38) vol. 335, col. 43; Youngson, op. cit. p. 269.

[6] Bridges, op. cit. p. 12.

who had found an answer to unemployment in his *The General Theory of Employment, Interest and Money* (1936), had delayed the acceptance of his ideas by his apparent love of fierce controversy almost for its own sake.[1] Nevertheless, there was no excuse for the Treasury's policy of clinging so closely to orthodoxy, and its reputation was diminished by its record during the inter-war period.

Once the Second World War had begun in earnest, the State rapidly assumed the control over the economy that total war demanded. Most of the major economists were recruited into the Civil Service, and their close proximity to each other, and to the Treasury generalists, may well have helped towards the readier acceptance of the Keynesian doctrine. The results of the new approach were in evidence by 1941 when the first National Income White Paper was published, and in his budget speech of that year, Kingsley Wood used the national income figures to discuss 'the inflationary gap', and thus began the modern system of managing the economy.[2]

Armed with this new approach, the Coalition Government published a White Paper on Employment Policy in 1944, in which it accepted as one of its 'primary aims and responsibilities the maintenance of a high and stable level of employment after the War'.[3] It rejected 'a rigid policy of balancing the Budget each year regardless of the state of trade', and it recognised that 'in the past the power of public expenditure, skilfully applied, to check the onset of a depression has been underestimated'. It was admitted

[1] This is a personal view of the man revealed in Harrod's biography. An example of his attitude that is of particular interest in this context is given by Harrod where he writes of Keynes's belief that 'there wasn't any place but Cambridge where one could learn economics' (p. 322); and Harrod believed that Keynes's attitude may have been responsible for the growth of a gulf between the thinking in Cambridge and at the London School of Economics that was to prove detrimental in the inter-war years (p. 323).

[2] House of Commons, *Official Report* (1940–1) vol. 370, ed. 1308. The background to these developments was outlined in an article by Richard Stone, 'The Use and Development of National Income and Expenditure Accounts', in D. N. Chester (ed.) *Lessons of the British War Economy* (1951).

[3] Cmd 6527 (May 1944) p. 3.

that the whole idea of pressing forward quickly with public expenditure when incomes were falling had previously encountered strong resistance from people who were accustomed to conducting their private affairs according to the very opposite principle. The Government had now realised that such resistance could be overcome if public opinion could be 'brought to the view that periods of trade recession provide an opportunity to improve the permanent equipment of society by the provision of better housing, public buildings, means of communication, power and water supplies, etc.'. Public investment was now to be used directly as an instrument of employment policy, and this meant not only the capital expenditure undertaken by the central Government, but also that of the local authorities and the public utility undertakings. In the past, such capital expenditure had followed the same trend as private capital expenditure and had tended to accentuate the peaks and depressions of the trade cycle. In the future, government policy, if the need arose, was to be directed to correcting that sympathetic movement.[1]

In the sphere of social security, with its acceptance of the Beveridge Report of 1942, the State acknowledged 'a full responsibility in the matter of making provision for sickness, breakdown and unemployment'. The report advocated a comprehensive insurance scheme which covered unemployment, industrial injuries, sickness and old age,[2] and it also made provision that 'in the limited number of cases of need not covered by social insurance, national assistance, subject to a uniform means test, will be available.'[3] The report further recommended: 'Medical treatment covering all requirements will be provided for all citizens by a National Health Service organised under the health departments, and post-medical rehabilitation treatment will be provided for all persons capable of profiting by it.'[4] Beveridge realised that what was proposed for unified social security sprang out of what had been accomplished

---

[1] Cmd 6527, para. 77, p. 25; para. 65, p. 22; and para. 62, p. 21.

[2] Sir William Beveridge, *Social Insurance and Allied Services*, Cmd 6404 (1942) para. 30.

[3] Ibid. para. 19 (x).

[4] Ibid. para. 19 (xi).

by building up that security piece by piece. His scheme retained the contributory principle of sharing the cost of security between the three parties – the insured person, his employer (unless self-employed) and the State. It retained and extended the principle that compulsory insurance should provide a flat rate of benefit, irrespective of earnings, in return for a flat contribution from all. Beveridge considered that the proposed scheme was 'in some ways a revolution, but in more important ways it is a natural development from the past'.[1]

Although the only major social advance which could be directly credited to the Coalition Government was the far reaching Education Act of 1944, the achievement of that Government, by pledging its successors to pursue full employment policies and to introduce and maintain comprehensive social security schemes, was to ensure that post-war British society would be radically changed for the better compared with that of the inter-war period. The electorate doubly ensured that this would be the case by decisively rejecting the government party of the 1930s, the Conservatives, at the polls and electing a Labour Government in 1945 with a substantial majority. That Government proceeded to implement the Beveridge social insurance proposals, and it also dramatically extended the area of influence of the State over the economy, not only by introducing a massive scheme to subsidise agriculture, but also by embarking on an ambitious nationalisation programme. The Bank of England was brought under public ownership, and the management of the coal, gas and electricity industries, the railways, road haulage, the airlines, and the iron and steel industry was placed in the hands of public corporations which were semi-independent of ministerial control. The Labour Government's chosen means of managing the economy also proved very controversial, for although initially there was little choice but to retain the rigid system of wartime controls, the Government failed to remove them once the period of inevitable shortages had passed, thus freezing the economy into its existing pattern, which hindered economic recovery. Despite its general and genuine

---

[1] Ibid. para. 31.

achievements, including the then novel one of having normally maintained full employment, the Labour Government proceeded to pay the electoral price for being associated with a period of austerity, having their majority reduced to a barely workable margin in 1950, and being defeated at the 1951 election. This latter achievement in defeat may be partly explained by fears, naturally exploited by Labour spokesmen, that a Conservative electoral success would mean the destruction of the Welfare State and a return to the mass unemployment society of the 1930s. In fact, the only dismantling done by the Conservatives was of Labour's negative economic controls, from which they reaped electoral benefits. Even in the disputed sphere of the nationalised industries, only iron and steel and road haulage were partially denationalised. So, as early as 1953, both major political parties had demonstrated in office, in peacetime conditions, that they accepted that the State had a positive role to play in a modern society.[1]

[1] The verdict on the record of Labour economic planning after the Second World War is purely personal but to secure a background about it and the early years of the Churchill Government after 1951, the following books were consulted: John Jewkes, *Ordeal by Planning* (1947; rev. ed. 1968); A. A. Rogow and Peter Shore, *The Labour Government and British Industry* (1955); Political and Economic Planning, *Government and Industry* (1952); Hugh Dalton, *High Tide and After* (1962); Colin Cooke, *Stafford Cripps* (1957); G. D. N. Worswick (ed.) *The British Economy 1945–1950* (1952); Michael Sissons and Philip French, *The Age of Austerity 1945–51* (1963); Joan Mitchell, *Crisis in Britain 1951* (1963); J. C. R. Dow, *The Management of the British Economy 1945–1960* (1964); A. J. Youngson, *The British Economy 1920–1957* (1960); Andrew Shonfield, *British Economic Policy Since the War* (1959); Norman Macrae, *Sunshades in October* (1963); Samuel Brittan, *The Treasury Under the Tories, 1951–1964* (1964). On nationalisation particular reference was made to the following books: W. A. Robson, *Nationalised Industry and Public Ownership* (1960); A. H. Hanson, *Nationalisation: A Book of Readings* (1963); R. F. Kelf-Cohen, *Nationalisation in Britain. The End of a Dogma* (1961); Michael Shanks (ed.) *The Lessons of Public Enterprise* (1963). It was not suggested that the use of public corporations was a novelty as regards the post-war Labour Governments of 1945–51, for the Liberals had created the Port of London Authority in 1908; and during the inter-war period the Conservatives had created the Central Electricity Board and the British Broadcasting Corporation (1926), the London Passenger Transport Board (1933) and the British Overseas

With the Welfare State and the full employment economy established, the 1950s ought to have been a period in which the country's institutions were thoroughly re-examined in the light of the changed role of the State. The country's constitutional machinery had been devised during the era of the Regulatory State and, not surprisingly, it was now in need of a radical overhaul. The balance between the legislature and the Executive had shifted markedly in favour of the latter over the previous century, but there was as little interest in parliamentary reform as there was in improving the efficiency of the Executive. The terms of reference given to the Royal Commission on the Civil Service that was appointed in 1953 illustrated the spirit of the times. For the commission was restricted to the examination of pay and conditions of service, and precluded from considering such questions as structure, recruitment, training and promotion procedures.[1]

Airways Corporation in 1940 (Youngson, op. cit. pp. 62–3 and 132). By the Coal Act of 1938, the Chamberlain Government had nationalised mining royalties, an obvious 'prelude to the nationalisation of the coal mines after the War' (A. J. P. Taylor, *English History 1914–1945*, 1965, p. 406). On returning to power in 1951, the Conservatives, as is noted in the text, did de-nationalise iron and steel and road haulage in 1953; but they also created yet another public corporation by the Atomic Energy Act of 1954, largely through the efforts of Lord Cherwell (Lord Birkenhead, *The Prof. in Two Worlds*, 1961, pp. 278–9, 281–2 and 298–316).

[1] The Royal Commission on the Civil Service (chairman: Sir Raymond Priestley) of 1953–5 was appointed 'to consider and to make recommendations on certain questions covering the conditions of service of Civil Servants within the ambit of the Civil Service National Whitley Council, viz: (a) whether any changes are desirable in the principles which should govern pay; or in the rates of pay at present in force for the main categories – bearing in mind in this connection the need for a suitable relationship between the pay of those categories; (b) whether any changes are desirable in the hours of work, arrangements for overtime and remuneration for extra duty, and annual leave allowances; (c) whether any changes are desirable within the framework of the existing superannuation scheme.' (*Report*, p. 1) The Priestley Commission devoted chapter III of their report to a consideration of the limitations imposed by their terms of reference, saying that those terms 'have been drawn more narrowly than those of the Tomlin Commission' (ibid. para. 54), that is the previous Royal Commission on the Civil Service (chairman: Lord

Ironically, the commission was appointed during the centenary year of the radical Trevelyan–Northcote Report, which had laid down much of the basis upon which the modern Civil Service was organised. The most appropriate manner in which to mark that centenary would have been to set up an official inquiry of similar scope, armed with modern methods of independent research, which could have thoroughly examined the question of whether or not the revolution that had taken place in the role of the State over the previous century had been matched by a revolution of similar proportions in the Public Service. If not, what sort of Service did the Positive State really need and, most important of all, what sort of leading administrators? It was not until 1966 that, with the appointment of the Fulton Committee on the Civil Service in February of that year, an investigation of this type was undertaken, after no less than four inquiries into different aspects of Civil Service management and performance had helped to foster a climate of opinion markedly unfavourable to the existing arrangements.[1] These arrangements will now be considered at greater length, with particular reference to the Administrative Class, the governing class of the Home Civil Service, and against the

---

Tomlin) of 1929–31. The Priestley Commissioners complained that their terms of reference made 'no mention of a variety of matters such as structure, grading, complementing and their relationship to the size of the Civil Service; nor are we called upon to make recommendations about recruitment, training, and promotion procedures. Though we have not felt debarred from enquiring into these questions, we have found it extraordinarily difficult to examine and advise upon the pay rates of an organisation so complex as the Civil Service without the opportunity of making positive proposals on these intimately related matters.' (Ibid. para. 55.)

[1] The results of the four inquiries referred to were published in the following reports: the *Sixth Report from the Select Committee on Estimates* (1957–8) concerning Treasury Control of Expenditure, together with the Treasury's reply which is contained in the *Seventh Special Report from the Select Committee on Estimates* (1958–9); the Report of the Plowden Committee, *Control of Public Expenditure*, Cmnd. 1432 (1961); the *Fifth Report from the Select Committee on Estimates* (1963–4) covering Treasury Control of Establishments; and the *Sixth Report from the Select Committee on Estimates* (1964–5) concerning Recruitment to the Civil Service.

background of the preceding account of the advent of the Welfare State and the managed economy, and of the historical development of the Service which will be traced in the second part of this chapter, and what follows is a consideration of those subjects which were excluded from the terms of reference given to the last Royal Commission on the Service. This consideration has the advantage of being able to take account of the written evidence which was submitted to the Fulton Committee in its first year of working.

II ADMINISTRATORS, MANAGERS AND 'STATESMEN IN DISGUISE'

Although the role of the mid-nineteenth-century State was a modest one, it was nevertheless true that:

> The Government of the day could not be carried on without the aid of an efficient body of permanent officers, occupying a position duly subordinate to that of Ministers who are directly responsible to the Crown and to Parliament, yet possessing sufficient independence, character, ability and experience to be able to advise, assist and to some extent influence, those who are from time to time set over them.[1]

---

[1] *Report on the Organisation of the Permanent Civil Service* (1853) p. 3. Recent research by Jenifer Hart, 'Sir Charles Trevelyan at the Treasury', in *English Historical Review* (1960) provides 'confirmation for the view that Northcote's part in preparing the main Report was a minor one' (p. 108). Northcote's ambitions lay in the political sphere, and he became involved in the Civil Service reform movement because of his connection with W. E. Gladstone, who saw it as 'my contribution to Parliamentary reform' (John Morley, *The Life of William Ewart Gladstone*, vol. I, 1903, p. 511). Northcote eventually rose to be Chancellor of the Exchequer and being 'rather a stiff Conservative' he did little to aid the cause of Civil Service reform in later years. His biographer said of Northcote that 'No man was ever less speculative' (Andrew Lang, *Life, Letters and Diaries of Sir Stafford Northcote*, vol. I, 1890, p. xiv), but as he secured the second best degree in his year at Oxford and achieved high status in his chosen career, he could hardly have been very stupid. Nevertheless, the main driving force behind the revolutionary Organisation Report was

It was the object of the Organisation Report of 1853, written by Sir Charles Trevelyan, the highest-ranking official at the Treasury, with the aid of an aspiring politician, Sir Stafford Northcote, to secure an even greater degree of efficiency among the 'body of permanent officers'. The reformers wanted to see created a largely self-sufficient career Civil Service that would train its own administrators so that they could, on merit, hold the highest positions in the Service, instead of, as at the time, having often to fill them from outside its ranks. They advocated a more unified Service, with its work subjected to a more satisfactory division between intellectual and mechanical duties, with its direct entrants recruited by open competitive examinations, and not by patronage, and with promotion within the Service being on the basis of merit in place of seniority. Trevelyan and Northcote had designed a Service which could be realistically seen as being politically anonymous, for the Civil Servants received their initial appointments independently of Ministers. Indeed, the full doctrine of ministerial responsibility, that each Minister was responsible to Parliament for the conduct of his department, and that the act of every Civil Servant was by convention regarded as the act of his Minister, was not universally accepted until the Trevelyan–Northcote reforms came to be slowly implemented after 1870.[1]

Sir Charles Trevelyan, who was at the head of the Treasury between 1840 and 1859. Macaulay described him as 'a most stormy reformer', and the portrait he drew of him was almost that of a fanatic (Sir George Otto Trevelyan, *The Life and Letters of Lord Macaulay*, vol. 1, 1888, pp. 384–5). As Sir Charles Trevelyan was the major author of the Organisation Report, contrary to the usual 'shorthand' description of it, hereinafter it will be referred to as the *Trevelyan–Northcote Report*.

[1] The definition of ministerial responsibility is that of Sir Ivor Jennings, *The Law and the Constitution* (1959) pp. 207–8. The view expressed in the text accords with the findings of Professor S. E. Finer, 'The Individual Responsibility of Ministers', in *Public Administration* (1956) p. 380. Other articles used concerning this topic: Gerald E. Aylmer, 'Place Bills and the Separation of Powers: Some Seventeenth Century Origins of the "Non-Political" Civil Service', in *Transactions of the Royal Historical Society* (1965); Edward Hughes, 'Sir James Stephen and the Anonymity of the Civil Servant', in *Public Administration* (1958); G. R. Kitson-Clark, ' "Statesmen in Disguise". Reflections on the History of the Neutrality of the Civil Service', in *Historical Journal* (1959).

Presumably, Graham Wallas had this in mind when he described the creation of the Civil Service along the lines of the Organisation Report as 'the one great political invention in nineteenth-century England.'[1] It may well have been, but the value of political, like any other, inventions depends on when they are applied, and the application of the Trevelyan–Northcote proposals proved to be a very lengthy process. Following Chadwick's dictum that 'For the due efficiency and working of the chief measures proposed for the improvement of the Public Service, it is essential that they should be conducted, not on separate and independent departmental arrangements, but on the general scale of the Service',[2] it would not be sensible to consider the process by which the Organisation Report's principles were put into practice as having been even partially completed before 1920. Although open competitive recruitment to the general classes of the Service, those dealt with in the Trevelyan–Northcote Report, eventually came to provide a bond of unity on that side of the Service, the bond of having 'entered by the same gate and of being of the same vintage, or perhaps a year or less in bottle than Smith of the department across the road',[3] the Service of even the immediate pre-First World War period was not integrated but departmentalised. Indeed, a contemporary administrator compared it with a 'University with separate Colleges as in Oxford or Cambridge, as distinct from an integrated University like Manchester – without even the measure of unity that is given in the former case by University Professors and institutions'.[4] When the Permanent Secretary to the Treasury, Sir Warren Fisher, could write in 1930: 'Until relatively recent years the expression "Civil Service" did not correspond either to the spirit or to the facts of the organisation so described',[5] it was realistic to consider that, while the implementation of the Trevelyan–Northcote reform programme began as early as 1870,

[1] Graham Wallas, *Human Nature in Politics* (1938 ed.) p. 249.
[2] *Papers relating to the Reorganisation of the Civil Service* (1855) p. 187.
[3] Sir Edward (later Lord) Bridges, *Portrait of a Profession* (1950) p. 10.
[4] Lord Salter, *Memoirs of a Public Servant* (1961) p. 37.
[5] Sir Warren Fisher, *Written Statement submitted to the Tomlin Commission* (1930) para. 3.

it could not be seen as being much more than partially completed until half a century later.

This time lag had one important consequence. The 'political invention' of an autonomous career Civil Service may well have been appropriate in the heyday of the Regulatory State when the central Government itself largely stood aside from the rest of society; and it may have been relevant in the 'golden age' of the doctrine of ministerial responsibility that lasted from about 1870 until the Liberal reforms after 1906 began to widen the scale of departmental duties and to reintroduce non-ministerial boards. But, in the inter-war period, although no Government openly recognised the change, the State began to assume positive and constructive duties besides its traditional functions, and the need became not a closed Civil Service, but one which was open for some interchange of staff with those in the fields administered, and those who had expertise in the increasingly complex subjects dealt with by departments. Ironically, the leading Civil Servants in the Service that Trevelyan and Northcote had sweepingly, and to some extent misleadingly, condemned were often experts in the general fields that their departments dealt with: Chadwick and Sir Rowland Hill being obvious examples. To have such experts in the Service with outside reputations, who could be associated with particular policies, was incompatible with a totally non-political Service, and the introduction of a career Service, where in the most important part of which, for reasons that will be examined, such technical expertise tended to be frowned upon, consolidated the doctrine of ministerial responsibility. So that, when the Service faced relatively simple duties, among its leading administrators were men who would now be called technocrats, whereas when its duties became complex, the men who held the equivalent posts tended to pride themselves on not being specialists in the subject matters concerned, but in 'the awareness of Ministerial responsibility'.[1]

---

[1] C. H. Sisson, *The Spirit of British Administration* (1959) p. 13. This last phrase is Sisson's: as will be clear from the frequent references made to his views throughout this book, he would deplore any move towards technocracy.

The same bias towards the non-specialist was to be seen in the reforms of the Service that took place in the immediate post-First World War period. For the greater degree of integration that followed from them was carried farthest on the generalist side of the Service, particularly with regard to the Administrative Class, which was the direct descendant of the 'intellectual' half of the simple division of labour made by Trevelyan and Northcote, and whose position as the ruling class of the Service was both confirmed and consolidated. However, the various types of specialists that the Service had come to need because of its increasingly complex duties remained organised in small departmental groups with inferior salaries and career prospects compared with their generalist counterparts. The explanation for this situation, advanced by Sir Warren Fisher, in 1930, was that 'all the regular types of Civil Servants have been in existence for generations', whereas 'these experts are relative innovations'.[1] Fisher seemed to have forgotten how recently the generalist side of the Service had been refashioned to assume its existing form, but there was something to be said in favour of the general point that he was making. After all, at the time that Trevelyan and Northcote had written of the need to make 'a proper distinction between intellectual and mechanical labour',[2] the departments, although they liked to treat their functions as needing specialisation, really only faced relatively simple administrative and clerical duties in most cases, and in the other instances their leading administrators, often drawn from outside the Service, supplied what specialisms were needed. Many of those who entered the higher ranks of the Service in late career from other professions were lawyers, and indeed the legal profession constituted the only numerous group of specialists needed in the departments of the Regulatory State. They prosecuted offenders against the existing legislation and advised about its working and the form of future regulations; while the actual task of seeing that the law was observed fell to the various inspectorates that reviewed conditions

---

[1] *Tomlin Evidence*, question 18,780. The inter-war position of the specialist groups, their present role and the place of the expert in the modern Service are topics discussed in fuller detail in chapter 5.

[2] *Trevelyan–Northcote Report* (1853) p. 17.

in factories, mines and schools, and to the medical inspectors of the Local Government Board. The Office of Works employed a few surveyors in connection with their responsibilities for government buildings, and the duties given to the Board of Agriculture led to the need to employ veterinary surgeons, but even as late as 1900, the number of specialists employed in the Service could be described as very small and the varieties as very few. The widening of the functions of the central Government, a process that was particularly marked after 1906, eventually led to the recruitment of 'a large and increasing army of specialists concerned with almost every form of human endeavour and drawn from almost every profession'.[1] Yet, the proper assimilation of this 'army' into the Service did not take place until after the Second World War, about a quarter of a century after the comparable stage had been reached on the generalist side of the Service. The tendency to keep the technical expert at arm's length was not a surprising development as such experts were seen as 'relative innovations' in the Service, but in view of the nature of the duties that came to face the Service, it was nevertheless a very unfortunate one.

The increasing complexity of the functions that were accorded to the central Government was also reflected in the more sophisticated division of labour that became needed on the generalist side of the Service. When the Trevelyan–Northcote reforms were implemented after 1870, their simple two-tier structure was at once modified, for although an 'intellectual' class or Upper Division and a mobile Lower Division emerged, the purely 'mechanical' work was assigned to temporary writers. By 1890, the structure

[1] Sir Francis Floud, 'The Sphere of the Specialist in Public Administration', in *Public Administration* (1923) pp. 117–18. The close link between the Bar and the Civil Service was made clear by Sir Algernon West, *Contemporary Portraits. Men of My Day in Public Life* (1920). For example, Thomas Farrer, who was called to the Bar, was employed in the Board of Trade in the preparation of the Merchant Shipping Bill of 1849. In West's view: 'His services in the preparation of that measure and its passage through Parliament were very great, and led to his appointment to the Board of Trade as Permanent Secretary' (p. 81). The permanent headship of the Home Office until the 1880s was filled from outside from the Bar: for example, both Adolphus Liddell and Godfrey Lushington entered that department after legal careers (pp. 168–9).

had been further modified, for what were now called the First and Second Divisions were supported by classes of Assistant and Boy Clerks. Even this structure had its departmental variants, and one particularly important development was that in certain departments work that was judged to be of a quality falling between that of the First and Second Divisions, normally supply work, accounting and auditing, was assigned to small, self-contained, separately recruited departmental classes. These were grouped together in 1906 to form an Intermediate Class, so that by 1914 there was really a four-tier structure on the generalist side of the Service. It was headed by the small, largely university-educated First Division, followed by an Intermediate Class limited to certain specialised duties, then a Second Division which was seen as performing 'the central region of work in the Public Service', with the fourth tier consisting of Assistant Clerks, Boy Clerks and typists.[1] Much has since been written about the achievements of

[1] The historical development and the current structure of the generalist side of the Service were adequately described in the *Fourth (Majority) Report of the Royal Commission on the Civil Service* (chairman: Lord MacDonnell) 1914, ch. I (pp. 5–24) and ch. III (pp. 28–43). The complexities of the structure were emphasised in the *Interim Report of the Reorganisation Committee of the Civil Service National Whitley Council* (chairman: Sir Malcolm Ramsay) 1921, para. 65. There were about 2500 Boy Clerks who entered the Service by a comparatively simple examination between the ages of fifteen and sixteen; and on attaining the age of eighteen they had to leave the Service unless they had succeeded in a special examination for entry to the Assistant Clerks Class or achieved success in one of the open competitions. The Assistant Clerks Class numbered over 3000 and it was recruited solely from the Boy Clerks: there were certain supervising posts within the class, while there were opportunities of special promotion to the Second Division 'on ground of exceptional merit'. The Second Division numbered about 4000 and occupied 'the central region of work in the several public departments' and constituted the largest class in the Service. Admission to it was by open competitive examination with the age limits placed at seventeen and twenty. The Second Division clerks had opportunities of promotion to some 800 staff posts and severely limited chances of advancement to the First Division. The Intermediate Class was 'of quite recent growth. It was designed to cover ground for which the qualifications of the First Division were unnecessarily high, those of the Second Division, as a body, scarcely adequate.' Candidates for the open competition had to be between 18 and 19½. The class numbered about 1250, of

the Reorganisation Committee of 1920–1 in rationalising this structure, but their contribution was, in fact, rather modest. As regards the Administrative Class, as the First Division was now known, all the committee eventually did was to approve the *status quo*, for the major changes in that class's career pattern and conditions of service followed from the various reforms that were associated with Sir Warren Fisher's appointment as Head of the Civil Service in 1919, not from the work of this committee.[1] The initial analysis made by the committee, however, suggested something more radical, for they described the Executive Class, which they had formed by merging the Second Division and the Intermediate Class, and the Administrative Class as sharing 'the work

---

whom about 500 had entered by the intermediate examination and the rest had been recruited from the Second Division by selection of the more competent of that class who were already serving in the departments where the new class was introduced (*MacDonnell Minority Report, 1914*, paras 15–18).

[1] The 1919 reforms are discussed later in the text, but it is worth while elaborating the point about the contribution of the Reorganisation Committee. The MacDonnell Commission had not been divided about either the role or the separate existence of the First Division: they were divided about its new name, with the *Minority Report* favouring 'Junior Secretarial Officers', and the *Majority Report* successfully advocating 'Administrative Class' (*Minority Report*, paras 28–30; *Majority Report*, ch. III, para. 38). The real debate was over the rest of the structure. The *Majority Report* wanted a Senior Clerical Class to replace the work done by the Second Division and the Intermediate Class and a Junior Clerical Class to cover the remainder of the work (ch. III, paras 18–27). The *Minority Report* wanted to have First Grade Clerks and Second Grade Clerks instead: the former corresponding 'almost exactly with the present Intermediate Class', and to be employed on a limited scale 'not in immediate juxtaposition' with the other classes, the Second Grade Clerks covering the lower work (paras 31, 34–7, 70). The Gladstone Committee came down in favour of the Minority Report's scheme (*Final Report*, 1919, paras 3, 5, 9, 12, 14, 15, 16, 52). All the Reorganisation Committee did was to merge the Second Division and the Intermediate Class into an Executive Class employed on the basis of the latter, while it divided the remainder of the work between a Clerical Class and a Writing Assistant Class. The *Reorganisation Report* was important, but some of its fame depends upon the fact that it represented 'the first occasion on which a body composed entirely of present or past Civil Servants . . . have been given the opportunity of framing a scheme for its reconstruction' (*Interim Report*, para. 4).

which is concerned with the formation of policy, with the revision of existing practice or current regulations and decisions, and with the organisation and direction of the business of Government'.[1] The committee did not, however, follow its own logic and recommend the creation of an amalgamated Executive–Administrative Class. It favoured separate hierarchies and, moreover, the restrictive definition of executive duties that it subsequently made led to that class being employed on the same basis as the pre-1914 Intermediate Class, limited to self-contained branches, rather than as a general service class like the former Second Division.[2] If there had to be a separate Executive Class, it would have been better to have served the best of both worlds, and created a service-wide managerial class embracing a range of specialisms. As it was, the 'general service' element came to be covered by a separate clerical hierarchy, initially created by the committee from the ranks of the former Assistant Clerks.[3] The Reorganisation Committee,

[1] *Interim Report of the Reorganisation Committee* (1921) paras 16–17.

[2] The Reorganisation Committee's definition of the Executive Class's duties as being those concerned with 'the higher work of supply and accounting departments, and of other executive or specialised branches of the Service' (*Interim Report*, para. 32), led to the class being employed on a very limited scale during the inter-war period. As to why the Executive Class was introduced at all, Sir John Anderson's evidence to the Tomlin Commission was interesting: 'I was a signatory of the Reorganisation Report and my understanding of the Executive Class was that the terminology was very closely related to the method of recruitment; that a separate Executive Class was recognised because the view was taken that there was work in Government departments of such a kind as to make it desirable to recruit direct to the Service at a particular point in the educational scheme of the country; to recruit people who had completed a secondary school education' (question 2173).

[3] The Reorganisation Committee had assigned to the Clerical Class 'all the simpler clerical duties' not given to Writing Assistants, while in addition they were seen as 'dealing with particular cases in accordance with well defined regulations, instructions or general practice; scrutinising, checking and cross-checking straightforward accounts, claims, returns, etc., under well defined instructions; preparation of material for returns, accounts, and statistics in prescribed forms; simple drafting and precis work. Collection of material on which judgments can be formed; supervision of the work of Writing Assistants.' (*Interim Report*, para. 24.) In normal times, direct recruitment was to be open, competitive written examination at sixteen to seventeen (ibid. para. 25); although the class was

far from unifying the generalist side of the Service, devised a structure of separate administrative, executive and clerical hierarchies, to be linked by an inter-class promotion machinery that, in practice, was only introduced with some reluctance.[1] It was not until 1947 that the executive and clerical hierarchies were merged, and that the potentialities of the open competition entrants to the Executive Class as 'most useful general purpose agents' were recognised.[2] But, although certain administrative posts were regarded as executive, and the latter hierarchy now reached up to Under-Secretary level, the Administrative and Executive Classes remained separate. This was particularly unfortunate now that the Executive Class had a wider role, because the continued division between the classes meant the perpetuation of the divorce between the Administrative Class and management that the latter class's traditions had fostered. The small, compact and socially and educationally homogeneous Administrative Class had achieved integration before any of its potential rivals for the control of the commanding heights of the Service, and it imposed its scale of values on the Service it ruled. As will be seen, many of its attitudes were more appropriate to the era of the Regulatory State, when many of them were formed, than one in which

---

to be initially composed of Assistant Clerks and those Second Division clerks who could not be found executive posts (para. 70). The Reorganisation Committee had 'not contemplated that all offices will contain members of both the Clerical and Executive Classes', and that where the Executive Class was not employed there was to be a comparable clerical hierarchy (para. 36). The *Tomlin Report* made it clear that this was the normal structure in the inter-war years (para. 78).

[1] The *Reorganisation Report* (paras 22, 35, 39, 45, 51, 52, 63) made very clear its preference for inter-class promotion and it advocated central pooling arrangements to facilitate this. Although a limited competition for promotion to the Clerical Class from the minor and manipulative grades was introduced in 1928, other central machinery was not introduced until 1936. Sir Warren Fisher summed up the prevailing attitude by dismissing the idea of a central pool as 'complete nonsense' because it interfered with the responsibilities of heads of departments (*Tomlin Evidence*, questions 18,918–18,921).

[2] *Treasury Factual Memorandum to the Priestley Commission* (1953) para. 275.

the central Government had a positive and constructive role to play.

These attitudes and traditions, moreover, originated in a Service that was divided into departments which were small enough to be personally controlled by the Minister. Indeed, at the time that Trevelyan and Northcote wrote, and perhaps even at the turn of the century, many departments were not much more than Ministers' personal clerical establishments, and they only rose above that status when the policy decisions facing Ministers became not only more numerous but also more difficult.[1] In the Home Office of the 1880s, for example, almost every paper was handled personally by the Permanent Under-Secretary, and very often by the Home Secretary himself, and even Assistant Secretaries were expected to submit all their decisions for approval. Even as late as 1911, the Home Office was still small enough for the Permanent Under-Secretary to control his staff in a very personal way, as there were only just over twenty on the administrative side. Sir Harold Scott, who entered the Home Office that year, later wrote

---

[1] Lord Strang illustrated this point in describing the Foreign Office of the last century. He said that it was one measure of the relative simplicity and straightforwardness of foreign problems in those times that those who had the handling of them were so few: 'However competent and energetic the Foreign Secretaries of the Victorian era may have been by the standards of their time – and most of them were undoubtedly both – the fact that they were able to manage their business at all with a small and primitive departmental apparatus speaks for itself. They may not have felt either unhurried or unharassed; but they did contrive, and usually within the limits of a quite reasonable working day, to control personally the whole machinery of British external relations. They had scarcely any Civil Service advisers, and employed a clerical staff which would nowadays be regarded as totally inadequate – in methods and training, if not in numbers – for one major diplomatic mission.' Strang said that from 1900 onwards the increase in the pressure of the work brought about staff increases and changed methods. Nowadays, the Foreign Secretary in receiving advice wants a definite recommendation about action (Lord Strang, *The Foreign Office*, 1955, pp. 19 and 31). The size of the other departments, and the memoirs of those who served in them, suggests that the Foreign Office may have been a typical nineteenth-century department as regards the quantity and quality of work allotted to it: but without a full range of memoirs one cannot be entirely sure that this was the case.

that the Liberal legislation and the First World War brought many changes to both the Office and the Service, not least in the earlier responsibilities that were given to his generation and their successors. One result of the increased volume of work was that 'there was simply no time, as in pre-War days, to refer every decision to one's senior, you had to make up your own mind on the spot.' Although he was a Principal, Scott found that, as a matter of course, he was settling most of the matters which in the past had been put up to an Assistant Secretary.[1]

Without comprehensive sets of memoirs covering the whole range of departments, there is no way of knowing whether the Home Office was typical of the Service or not, but at least some doubts may be reasonably expressed about the need for a graduate Higher Division before, say, the 1890s. Indeed, such doubts were to be found in the comments made by contemporaries about the relevant proposals in the Trevelyan–Northcote Report. Sir James Stephen said that the Service needed not 'statesmen in disguise' but 'intelligent, steady, methodical men of business', and therefore did not need to recruit men from the cream of the university honours graduates.[2] Sir George Arbuthnot wrote that the report's recommendations proceeded 'from a misapprehension of the functions which the permanent Civil Officers of the Crown are required to discharge'. They could not

---

[1] Sir Harold Scott, *Your Obedient Servant* (1959) pp. 27–31 and 48. Scott wrote that the Home Office of 1911 was closer to the department of a hundred years ago than to a Ministry of today: 'As I discovered to my surprise, it still retained something of the grace, circumstance and leisure to which the young men who entered it from Oxford and Cambridge were accustomed in their comfortable Victorian homes, and office life was still influenced by the rhythm of the London season' (pp. 24–5). Sir Laurence Guillemard, *Trivial Fond Records* (1937) pp. 12–19, described the Home Office of the late 1880s in similar terms. That the Colonial Office of 1906 was also a very leisurely institution was made clear by Sir John Anderson, *Administrative Technique in the Public Services* (1949) p. 6. The general pace of work over the period was indicated by the fact that in the late 1880s the Cabinet found time to debate who should fill a Principal Clerkship in the Treasury (Sir John Kempe, *Reminiscences of an Old Civil Servant*, 1928, p. 142).

[2] *Papers relating to the Reorganisation of the Civil Service* (1855) p. 76.

in ordinary cases aspire to become statesmen, and to carry out systems of policy. Their humble but useful duty is, by becoming depositories of departmental traditions, and by their practical acquaintance with the working of those laws by which Constitutional jealousy has guarded the Civil administration, as they affect their own departments, to keep the current business in its due course; to warn Ministers of the consequences of irregular proceedings into which they might inadvertently fall; to aid in preparing subjects for legislation; and possibly to assist by their suggestions the development of a course of action.[1]

Such duties need not necessarily be mundane, and Sir Robert Giffen made it clear that the duties of the leading Civil Servants of the 1880s were comparable to those faced in similar posts in private enterprise. But he did draw attention to the 'great practical difficulty' of 'fitting the Upper Division into the whole Service', meaning that there simply were not enough posts of this level of responsibility in the Service to justify a separate division.[2] As to why the Upper or Higher Division was created and maintained apparently in numbers excessive for its duties, Robert Lowe, the architect of open competition, provided a clue when he said that departments thought it 'more gentlemanly' to have 'as many men as possible under Class I in order to elevate the office'.[3] Lowe admitted that he had originally been 'substantially in favour of having one class', namely the Lower Division, as being the most appropriate for the duties of the Service, but he had come to believe that, as with diplomats, 'you do not select perhaps the man who knows most of the business, but a certain amount of representation goes with the thing'.[4] The leading officials of the major departments were 'brought into contact with Members of Parliament and gentlemen of good education and position, and we

[1] Ibid. p. 411.

[2] *Royal Commission on the Civil Service* (chairman: Sir Matthew White Ridley) *Second Report* (1888) *Evidence*, questions 19,115, 19,123, 19,130 and 19,391. Giffen had had experience of working both inside and outside the government Service.

[3] *The Civil Service Inquiry Commission* (chairman: Sir Lyon Playfair) *First Report* (1875) appendix B, question 3134.

[4] *Select Committee on Civil Services Expenditure* (chairman: Mr Childers) 1873, *Evidence*, question 4451.

thought that if the competition were wholly limited to the second class, the Public Service would suffer for want of that sort of free-masonry which exists between people who have had a certain grade of education, and we thought it desirable to secure that'.[1] Sir Thomas Farrer, an early opponent of Lowe's ideas, later came to hold similar views because: 'Experience has led me to think that it is extremely desirable to have in the upper ranks of the Service men who have the *esprit de corps* of our public schools and our Universities, and who are able to hold their own, to speak what they consider to be the truth about their business; and able to deal with persons outside the office as gentlemen.'[2]

Prominent among the main objections to the introduction of open competition made by leading administrators at the time of the Trevelyan–Northcote Report were fears that people of low social origins might gain entry to the higher posts of the Services: there was a general feeling that such people could not be trusted to be the confidential advisers of Ministers.[3] 'The aristocratic or rather plutocratic character'[4] of the education demanded of entrants to the Upper or Higher Division and its successors ensured that, although they rarely came from the highest ranks of society, they at least had backgrounds that were reasonably acceptable to such people. The First Division came to be seen as a desirable career, not soiled with 'trade', where a man who considered him-

---

[1] Ibid. question 4397.

[2] *Ridley Evidence*, question 19,975.

[3] Edward Romilly, for example, baldly asserted: 'The great majority of the appointments will fall to the lot of those who are in the lower social position' (*Papers relating to the Reorganisation of the Civil Service*, 1855, p. 289). The Secretary of the Board of Trade, James Booth, shared this fear and added: 'The lower you descend in the social scale the less is the probability that the candidate for the Civil Service will possess those moral qualifications which I have already insisted on as being more important than the intellectual ones in the practical business of official life' (ibid. p. 133). In 1873, Adolphus Liddell revealed that one of the reasons why the Home Office had at first refused open competition was because clerks might be recruited 'who would give information out of doors from what they saw going on in the office' (*Childers Evidence*, question 4306).

[4] *Childers Evidence*, appendix 5, p. 292: the phrase was that of T. H. Farrer.

self a gentleman could conduct a life so leisured that, as late as 1911, the amount of work done in the higher reaches of the Home Office was dictated by the rhythm of the London season. In such an atmosphere, it was not surprising that one of the strongest, and most unfortunate, attitudes of our traditional ruling class was firmly implanted: namely, that of the amateur, the all-rounder or intelligent layman. The pre-entry education preferred was the 'liberal education' of the older universities in subjects of no direct practical relevance, and the men to model themselves on were the laymen justices of the peace, and the landowner taking the all-round view of how others were managing his estate.

Ironically, the unification of the Service was to lead to the strengthening of the all-rounder tradition, not the rejection of it that the gradual emergence of the Positive State warranted. The tradition had rather more limited scope in the departmentalised Service, and it certainly found no place in the Trevelyan–Northcote Report. The reformers of 1853 had envisaged the very highest positions in departments, but they did not advocate a versatile 'intellectual class': only the clerks employed on 'mechanical duties' were seen as being mobile between departments.[1] Arbuthnot expressed the prevailing opinion about the nature of the role of the leading Civil Servant when he said:

> To fulfil these duties with efficiency, it is necessary that, as a general rule, each man's experience should be confined to the special branch of the Service in which he is himself engaged. Such is the complicated character of our institutions, that, without such division of labour, no man could obtain that intimate acquaintance with details, and the bearing of those details upon general principles, which constitute the distinction between the permanent executive officers and members of the Government who are charged with the duty of administration.[2]

Forty years later the same attitudes were shown in the Treasury's reasons for rejecting the Ridley Commission's recommendation that uniformity of pay and grading should be introduced into the

---

[1] *Trevelyan–Northcote Report* (1853) pp. 7, 18–19, 22–3. Trevelyan made this point crystal clear in a note in *Papers relating to the Reorganisation of the Civil Service* (1855) p. 233.

[2] *Papers relating to the Reorganisation of the Civil Service* (1855) p. 411.

Upper Division. They argued that whereas it was appropriate for the Second Division clerks to be transferable 'according as the public interests require', the less homogeneous character of the work of the Upper Division made it 'not practicable to ensure general transferability'.[1] In 1913, the Permanent Secretary to the Treasury, Sir Robert Chalmers, gave a similar view: 'The Class I man is certificated to his office; the Second Division man is in the Service at large.'[2] Chalmers, drawing on his experience in the Inland Revenue, saw the administrator as not being 'such a proper subject for general service as the Second Division man', because his work was more specialised and transferring him between departments could not be done 'without a great waste of acquired power, because he would go to a place where his knowledge would be absolutely cancelled'.[3] But the Inland Revenue at the time was 'probably the most specialist department of the lot',[4] and may well not have been representative of the Service. Certainly, in the development of the Intermediate Class, one could see the First Division shedding what it saw as its more 'mechanical' duties, those thought to require specialised careers, and cutting down its range so that, despite the expansion of departments into very much more than Ministers' personal offices, the division could still see itself as the Ministers' personal advisers. Indeed, the Ministers' private office, not the various divisions with their increasingly difficult duties, remained the focal point of the First Division career. A cursory knowledge of them might suffice, but an early apprenticeship in the various implications of ministerial responsibility was essential. The latent cult of versatility became a reality as departmental barriers were weakened after the experience of the National Insurance adventure of 1911–12 in which young administrators from all over the First Division were attached to the Treasury to help with the passage and implementation of this

---

[1] *Paper showing the manner in which the recommendations of the Royal Commission with respect to the Civil Service has been dealt with* (12 Feb 1894) p. 8.

[2] *MacDonnell Evidence*, question 35,942.

[3] Ibid., question 35,944.

[4] This, at least, was Sir Warren Fisher's view: *Tomlin Evidence*, question 18,848.

bitterly contested social advance.[1] This episode and the effects of the First World War led to the First Division having greater 'elements of unity' introduced into its previously 'fragmentary' structure, but like the all-rounder tradition that was consequently strengthened, unification was also not a sudden development.

It could be traced in the development of the role of the Treasury from Trevelyan's time, and in the enhanced status and powers given to his successors as head of that department. Trevelyan had seen the Treasury as 'eminently a superintending office',[2] and as 'the proper supervising and controlling body in all matters which relate to the public establishments.'[3] Speaking of the whole range of government departments, Trevelyan considered it to be 'the duty of the Treasury to see that this extensive and complicated machinery is neither redundant nor deficient, and that it is maintained in good working order by the adoption of every well established improvement and the application of the requisite motive power'.[4] Successive committees and commissions came to advocate similar powers for the Treasury,[5] but in 1914 the MacDonnell Commission could still write: 'Whatever may be its indirect

---

[1] Lord Salter later wrote: 'It was interesting to see when the great test of the Civil Service came with the War a few years later, that a Civil Servant, whether of the First or Second Division, who had had the educative experience of work with the Insurance Commission, was regarded as a jewel beyond price by the departments which had to expand rapidly for the new tasks.' Salter said that the mobilisation of the best brains of the departments had 'profound consequences for the future development of the Civil Service'. In his view, the later unification of the Service was largely due to the personality of Sir Warren Fisher, who made his reputation during the Insurance episode (Lord Salter, *Memoirs of a Public Servant*, 1961, pp. 70–2).

[2] *Papers relating to the Reorganisation of the Civil Service* (1855) p. 427.

[3] *Second Report of the Playfair Commission*, appendix F, question 78.

[4] Ibid. question 79.

[5] For example: the *Third Report of the Childers Committee* (1873) paras 10 (6) and 10 (7); the *First Playfair Report* (1875) p. 23; the *Second Ridley Report* (1888) para. 19. The Treasury described the ineffective record of the Consultative Committee, that the Ridley Commission had hoped would give the Treasury greater control over establishments, in the first appendix to the *Fourth Report of the MacDonnell Commission* (appendix 15).

influence, the Treasury does not, in practice, exercise a sufficiently effective control over the organisation of departments unless the question of finance was concerned.'[1] The reason for this was, of course, that if the Treasury had attempted in earlier years to introduce organisational reforms into 'a department presided over by a Cabinet Minister', such an intervention 'would have led at once to very great friction, and practically would end by making the exercise of a control in that form impossible'.[2] But by 1914, the departments were very much more than Ministers' private offices, and the MacDonnell Commission rightly recommended the creation within the Treasury of 'a special section for the general supervision and control of the Civil Service', and which would 'watch over the general conditions and activities of the Civil Service with a view to its effective and economical employment; and make of its own initiative all enquiries that may be necessary to that end'.[3] The First World War intervened before these recommendations could be put into practice, but one of the effects was to accelerate the trend towards integration. The Haldane and Bradbury Committees, covering the same ground, endorsed and supplemented the MacDonnell proposals.[4] As a result, in 1919, an Establishments department was created in the Treasury under a Controller of Establishments, who ranked equally with the Permanent Heads of major departments, and who was Chairman of the Standing

[1] *MacDonnell Majority Report*, ch. IX, para. 96.

[2] *Ridley Evidence*, question 10,709. This statement by Sir Reginald Welby, the Permanent Secretary to the Treasury, was supported by Sir Algernon West, the Chairman of the Board of Inland Revenue, who said that it was 'quite impossible' to envisage the Treasury having the power to 'initiate reforms of organisation' (ibid. question 17,288). The pre-1919 position was summarised by Robert Lowe, who had told the Playfair Commission: 'The Treasury have a great deal of power in preventing people from doing things, but they have not much power in making them do things' (appendix B to the *First Report*, question 3120).

[3] *MacDonnell Majority Report*, ch. IX, para. 101.

[4] *Report of the Machinery of Government Committee* (chairman: Lord Haldane) 1918, paras 15–20; *Final Report of the Committee appointed to Inquire into the Organisation and Staffing of Government Offices* (chairman: Sir John Bradbury, with Warren Fisher a member) 1919, paras 13–22.

Committee of the Establishment Officers who were appointed in the leading departments. The Establishments department was charged with 'responsibility for questions of personnel and remuneration, the organisation of civil establishments and superannuation', and the Service, therefore, had the central staff organisation that real and lasting unity demanded, even though its early record proved to be undistinguished.[1]

The granting of a salary differential to the Permanent Secretary to the Treasury, compared with the other Permanent Heads of departments, when that post was created in 1867, was an early indication of the future importance of that position. Indeed, in 1872, the Chancellor of the Exchequer, Robert Lowe, defending the differential, said: 'The Secretary to the Treasury was not an Under-Secretary of State, he was at the Head of the Civil Service.'[2] However, despite the grandeur of this title, its holders did not initially, outside of the financial sphere, have wide powers to intervene in other departments' affairs. For example, the 'Head of the Civil Service' at the time that Lowe spoke, Sir Ralph Lingen, tried and failed in the late 1870s to persuade the leading departments to adopt the Playfair Commission's recommendations about grading and salaries.[3] Lingen's successors seemed to interpret their role restrictively, but nevertheless by the immediate pre-First World War period, the Permanent Secretary to the Treasury was recognised as the Prime Minister's logical choice as

[1] *Treasury Memorandum to the Select Committee on Estimates, Fifth Report* (1963–64), *Treasury Control of Establishments, Evidence*, para. 5, p. 1. The *Tomlin Report* had been faintly critical about the Treasury's record (paras 594–597); but the *Select Committee on National Expenditure, 16th Report*, 1941–2, was scathing in its criticism: 'In the period between the two Wars the response of the Treasury to the demand that expert knowledge and study should be brought to bear on the problems of departmental organisation was meagre in the extreme' (para. 56).

[2] House of Commons, *Official Report* (1872) vol. 210, col. 848.

[3] *Ridley Evidence*, question 20,211. Lingen asked Sir Lyon Playfair: With regard to those points in your scheme which have not been carried out they attach themselves, do they not, to the fact that there is no central controlling authority in the Civil Service analogous to what the War Office, the Commander in Chief's Office, or the Board of the Admiralty is in the naval and military services?' Playfair agreed (ibid. question 20,217).

an adviser on Civil Service matters.[1] This position was consolidated in 1919 on Sir Warren Fisher's appointment as Permanent Secretary to the Treasury and Head of the Civil Service, for it was emphasised that he had 'the duty of advising the Prime Minister in regard to Civil Service appointments', which meant 'all the more important appointments throughout the Service'.[2]

Not least because of the holder's forceful personality, both the description of Fisher's position as 'Head of the Civil Service' and the range of powers that accompanied it, provoked a political controversy of which there are still traces.[3] In answer to the critics,

[1] House of Commons, *Official Report* (1926) vol. 194, cols 331–2. The speaker was David Lloyd George.

[2] House of Commons, *Official Report* (1926) vol. 192, col. 519. The speaker was the Prime Minister, Stanley Baldwin.

[3] Concerning the controversy over the record of Sir Warren Fisher as 'Head of the Civil Service' during the years 1919–39, even the mild Lord Bridges has observed: 'I have no doubt that a great deal of the ferment and disputation arose out of Fisher's excitable ways and his habit of talking in an unguarded way about what he regarded as the demerits of those – quite a large number – whom he held in no high repute' (*The Treasury*, 1964, p. 175). Sir Warren Fisher, indeed, was a man with an 'obsession with personal quality as a factor in government', and he was convinced that 'in the 1930s Britain was desperately poor in such quality among her professional military and civil advisers'. Apart from Sir Maurice Hankey and Sir Robert Vansittart, Sir Warren Fisher 'was and felt himself to be a titan among minnows' (Donald C. Watt, *Personalities and Policies. Studies in the Formulation of British Foreign Policy in the Twentieth Century*, 1965, pp. 102–3 and 115). The most interesting legacy of Fisher's period at the head of the Treasury is 'the growth of a school of thought' which seeks 'to lay at Sir Warren Fisher's door the main responsibility for the policy of appeasing Germany, and of seeking to further this policy by illegitimate intervention into the running of the Foreign Office, which then by definition was part of the Home Civil Service' (ibid. p. 107). The views of this 'school of thought' are to be found in the writings of Lord Murray of Elibank, *Reflections on Some Aspects of British Foreign Policy Between the Wars* (1946); Sir Harry Legge-Bourke, *Master of the Offices* (1950); Frank Ashton-Gwatkin, *The British Foreign Service* (1950); and Sir Walford Selby, *Diplomatic Twilight 1930–1940* (1953). One notes that, in the relevant volume of his memoirs, Sir Anthony Eden (now Lord Avon) draws attention to two attempts by Sir Warren Fisher to intervene in Foreign Office matters. The first occurred in 1936 when Eden successfully prevented him from asserting a right of veto over ambassadorial appointments. The second occurred in late 1937 when the question arose about who was to succeed Sir Robert Vansittart as

(footnote 3, page 52, continued)
Permanent Under-Secretary at the Foreign Office. Eden records that Fisher
attempted to persuade him to appoint the Head of the India Office to that
position, but that he was 'firmly convinced that it made no sense to bring
someone who was inexperienced in international diplomacy into the most
responsible advisory position in the Foreign Office' (Lord Avon, *Facing
the Dictators*, 1962, pp. 319–20 and 521). Given the statements made in
Parliament about the powers accorded to the Head of the Civil Service,
as long as the Foreign Office was treated as part of the Home Civil Service,
Fisher's attempted interventions, at least in these instances, do not
seem to be 'illegitimate'. They could only be described as such if the
Foreign Service was a separate entity which, indeed, it became in 1945
as one of the so-called 'Eden reforms'. In the relevant part of his reminiscences, Eden does not make clear whether or not the desire to escape
from the sort of extraneous control over leading appointments that
Fisher attempted to exercise was one of the major factors in the Foreign
Service being made separate (Lord Avon, *The Reckoning*, 1965, pp.
257–8). As to whether or not Sir Warren Fisher was an advocate of the
appeasement of Nazi Germany, the writings of, and about, the arch-
anti-appeaser, Sir Robert Vansittart – who was at the head of the Foreign
Office between 1930 and the beginning of 1938 – have relevance.
Vansittart's memoirs are studded with warm references to Fisher's
support in his unsuccessful struggle to persuade the National Government
to face up to the implications of the Nazi menace. Vansittart's verdict on
Fisher was that he was 'a great Public Servant ignorantly traduced by
small fry', and described him as 'the best friend that I ever had in
adversity, less good in better days' (Lord Vansittart, *The Mist Procession*,
1958, pp. 350–1, 443, 507 and 510). Vansittart's memoirs, however,
'stop rather abruptly in 1936' and, taking up Vansittart's story, Ian
Colvin has pointed a less flattering picture of Fisher's loyalty during the
last year or so of Vansittart's period at the Foreign Office. Colvin argues
that by 1937 Fisher was suffering from 'an eclipse of influence' and that he
'found it expedient to associate his fortunes with those of the rising man
among the senior Civil Servants, Sir Horace Wilson'. Colvin records
that in May 1937 Fisher and Wilson attempted to persuade J. P. L.
Thomas, Eden's P.P.S. at the Foreign Office, 'to work behind the back
of his own chief' in order to 'lessen the damage that had been done by the
Foreign Office in general and by Vansittart in particular'. Thomas
refused to co-operate. Later, Fisher attempted to persuade Lady Vansittart
'to tell Van not to write these long papers for the Cabinet. They do not
like it and his predecessors did not do it. He is exceeding his functions.'
Fisher warned that Vansittart would not get his G.C.B. 'that way'.
When Lady Vansittart asked why he should want a G.C.B., apparently
'this guileless question about an honour to the fount of many honours
disconcerted Sir Warren'. When on a third occasion – at a lunch with the
Vansittarts – 'Sir Warren and Sir Horace betrayed their close communion
of ideas', Lady Vansittart 'warned her husband not to trust them, but he
found only good words to describe his two colleagues' (Ian Colvin,

the constitutional position of the Head of the Civil Service was defined in 1926 and 1942. On the first occasion, Stanley Baldwin said: 'The supreme head of all the Services of the Crown is the Sovereign. The ministerial head of His Majesty's Civil Service is the Prime Minister. The principal officer of that Service is the Permanent Secretary to the Treasury; that title was introduced in 1867 and the post has since carried with it the official headship of the Service.'[1] But as 'no formal instrument recording the fact appears then to have been issued', the critics of the powers given to the Head of the Civil Service, understandably, found it difficult to accept that all that had happened was that 'the position was explicitly reaffirmed in 1919 by the Government of the day as

---

(*footnote 3, page 52, continued*)
Vansittart in Office, 1965, pp. 145 and 147–8). Although Ian Colvin's researches cast doubt upon Vansittart's 'good words' about Fisher's steadfastness in supporting him in his fight against the National Government's foreign policy in relation to Nazi Germany, it is still difficult to see how 'the main responsibility for the policy of appeasing Germany' can be laid 'at Sir Warren Fisher's door'. Fisher was 'as virulently and obsessively anti-German as Vansittart himself'. Indeed, D. C. Watt has observed about Vansittart and Fisher: 'Their animus against Germany stemmed less from a hatred of Nazism as such than from a quasi-racialist conviction, not uncommon in their generation, of the peculiar and continuing wickedness of Germany, her unreliability and the uncompromising challenge to Western civilisation she represented. Both were prepared to compromise if need be with an aggressive Italy or Japan; with Germany there could be no compromise.' (pp. 85 and 102.) Unfortunately, Sir Warren Fisher rarely ventured into print, although one notes the vigorously anti-appeasement remarks made in part of the introduction to his article, 'The Beginnings of Civil Defence', in *Public Administration* (1948). Any real attempt at a general assessment of Sir Warren Fisher's career – and, of course, of his record in relation to the policy of appeasing Nazi Germany – must wait until the relevant archives are open to scholars. Although traditionalists are, of course, free to argue that Sir Warren Fisher was the exception to which any rule may occasionally be subject, one can observe that Fisher's actions in conducting himself as 'a kind of unofficial Minister of Defence' (Sir James Grigg, *Prejudice and Judgment*, 1948, p. 53), in so far as we are able to fairly evaluate them at this stage, do not seem consonant with the traditional interpretation of the convention of ministerial responsibility – the convention around which the role of the Administrative Class, which Fisher played a major part in helping to fashion, has been built.

[1] House of Commons, *Official Report* (1926) vol. 191, col. 2093.

part of the reorganisation of the 'Treasury'. In 1942, in answering
a debate on the subject, the Lord Chancellor, Viscount Simon,
repeated Baldwin's definition and carried it further by saying:

> Appointment as 'Permanent Secretary to the Treasury and
> Official Head of H.M. Civil Service' is made by the Prime
> Minister with the approval of His Majesty. The sanction of
> Parliament to appointments and titles in the Crown Services is
> not required. The function of the holder of the post is to direct,
> subject to Ministerial authority, the work of the Treasury, in-
> cluding that part of the Treasury's work which is concerned with
> the central oversight of the official machinery of Government;
> his duties in this regard include that of advising the Prime
> Minister and First Lord, after consultation with any other
> Minister concerned, on appointments to certain senior posts
> in the Service which require the Prime Minister's approval,
> namely, the Permanent Heads of departments, their Deputies,
> Principal Finance Officers, and Principal Establishment Officers.
> The holder of this post is, of course, in the exercise of his functions
> subject to the authority of the Government of the day and he has
> no powers independent of the Minister to whom he tenders
> advice and to whom he is responsible.[1]

There had, in fact, been nothing sinister about Fisher's appointment. The Lloyd George Coalition Government had become
convinced by 1919 that the problem of how to replace 'a most
extraordinarily rich crop of great Civil Servants' at the head of the
various departments who were coming up to retiring age, was to
escape from the limitations imposed by the departmentalism of the
existing Service, and to treat it as a whole for the purposes of
promoting to the highest posts.[2] Lloyd George himself later made
it clear that during the lengthy period that he was a Cabinet Minister, the powers accorded to the Prime Minister and his principal
adviser had always been of that order: what had happened after
the First World War was that they were formalised and made
explicit.[3] Nevertheless, Winston Churchill, in defending the 1919

---

[1] House of Lords, *Official Report* (1941–2) vol. 124, cols 193–4.

[2] House of Lords, *Official Report* (1942–3) vol. 125, cols 284–91; the
speaker was Lord Geddes who had been President of the Board of Trade
in that Government.

[3] House of Commons, *Official Report* (1926) vol. 194, cols 331–2.

arrangements in 1927, was unconvincing when he argued that 'Ministerial opinion is what rules in these matters.'[1] For it was doubtful if either the Prime Minister or the Chancellor of the Exchequer, to whom Churchill ascribed such control, would have the time or perhaps even the interest to challenge seriously the views on promotions and appointments put forward by a man at the head of a unified career profession, the Administrative Class, which dominated the highest posts of the Service.

The extent of that dominance during the inter-war period was indicated by a description made of the Higher Civil Service of 1938 by one of its former members, Harold Dale. Defining that body as consisting of all posts in the Civil Service of Assistant Secretary status and above and their equivalents, Dale estimated that out of a total of about 550 no less than 500 were occupied by members of the Administrative Class: the others being filled by between twenty and thirty lawyers and a similar number of other specialists.[2] Therefore, apart from the legal profession, the specialist groups were poorly represented in the inter-war Higher Civil Service, and the Executive Class was entirely absent. The channels of official advice to Ministers were monopolised by the Administrative Class, and it was regrettable that its unification, symbolised by the terms of Fisher's appointment and marked by such essential advances as the standardisation of the class's grading and salary structures,[3] led to the strengthening of the all-rounder tradition. Fisher treated the Treasury as 'a sort of clearing house of general staff',[4] thus fulfilling Trevelyan's ambition of that department being 'a staff corps' recruited from 'the whole of the Civil Service'.[5] Given the central role of the Treasury, such a development was,

[1] House of Commons, *Official Report* (1927) vol. 208, col. 94.

[2] H. E. Dale, *The Higher Civil Service of Great Britain* (1942) p. 16. Dale had risen to the rank of Principal Assistant Secretary, that is what would now be called Under-Secretary, in the Ministry of Agriculture and Fisheries.

[3] Uniformity of salaries followed from the recommendations of the *Asquith Committee of 1920–21* which was appointed to 'advise as to the Salaries of the Principal posts in the Civil Service'.

[4] *Tomlin Evidence*, question 18,787.

[5] *Second Report of the Playfair Commission* (1875) appendix F, questions 79–80.

to some extent, welcome. Fisher's policies with regard to the qualities to be looked for in candidates to fill the senior appointments
across the Service were of more questionable value. The all-
rounder tradition was sadly in evidence as Fisher made it clear
that, in recommending the appointment for a Permanent Secretary's post, the range of qualities looked for did not need to include
a wide knowledge of the subject matter that comprised the duties
of the department concerned. This was because: 'A man who has
been running one of these huge businesses under inconceivable
difficulties can run any of them.'[1] In Fisher's eyes, the Permanent
Secretary was a general manager: 'They are not experts. Let us
guard ourselves against the idea that the permanent head of a
department should be an expert; he should not be anything of the
kind.'[2] Not even in a department that was very largely technical,
in which category Fisher duly placed his former department, the
Inland Revenue, asserting: 'If you ask my folk there, I hope they
would say I was not a bad fellow, but I think that they would also
say that I knew very little about their technicalities.'[3] Changing
about between unrelated jobs was thought to be no problem,
because the type of Permanent Secretary he had in mind was 'a
man of such breadth of experience that he will soon find himself
picking out the essential points; and, remember, there is a great
deal to be said for a fresh eye'.[4] The man 'who has travelled is
far less rigid than the man who is *in situ*; and, as I say "musical
chairs" keeps them alive; and that is to the advantage of the departments and of the Government Service'.[5] There was some truth in
Fisher's statement that his view of the role of a Permanent Secretary did not represent a serious departure from the old conception.
He believed: 'The old view used to be, so far as they had a view,
that they should put up the man serving in the department; he
would not necessarily be the technician of the department, almost
certainly he would not be; so that there is no real change except
that you have broadened your field of selection.'[6] No doubt the
previous Permanent Secretaries, and their fellow administrators,

---

[1] *Tomlin Evidence*, question 18,809.   [2] Ibid. question 18,805.
[3] Ibid. question 18,848.   [4] Ibid. question 18,852.
[5] Ibid. question 18,556.   [6] Ibid. question 18,847.

had maintained amateur attitudes even to the duties that they un-convincingly argued needed departmental specialisation. Never-theless, there had been an important change of context. When administrative work had been relatively simple and homogeneous it had been treated as if it needed departmental specialisation; whereas, now it had become complex and might well need more specialisation, it was thought of as being homogeneous. The man who had experienced 'musical chairs' might be a better general manager for it, but it could at least be doubted if he could com-bine that role with that of policy adviser in complex fields from which he had hitherto been excluded.

Fisher's reign as Head of the Civil Service ended in 1939 but, although by the time that Sir Edward Bridges had attained that position in 1945 the responsibilities of the central Government had been substantially widened and the tasks of its administrators made considerably more difficult, the Bridges era, which lasted until 1956, was marked, if anything, by a strengthening of the all-rounder tradition. Bridges, in a series of lectures and writings of superb intellectual quality, stressed the virtues of the 'intelligent layman' in administration even in such potentially complicated spheres as Treasury control of expenditure. He preferred to see it exercised 'not by experts, but by laymen', and he argued that there was 'nothing odd about this' because: 'In practically all walks of life the expert or enthusiast in any particular field does not have the final word, but has to get the approval of some layman or lay body.' The Treasury official dealing with, say, education or defence was thus not an expert in either of these fields and would have had no prior intellectual commitment about the matters with which he is dealing, derived from a long period of service in the field or a professional connection with it. But given his general background and his experience of government service, he will start with at least the educated layman's knowledge of what happens in the field with which he is dealing.' He thus 'starts with a rather detached point of view', and the approach adopted was that 'of common sense and all-round experience'. This system of control by intelligent laymen meant that a Treasury official was 'rarely left for many years on the control of one type of expenditure. He will move from one job to another carrying with him the increased experience of how public business is carried on and how to grasp the essentials of new proposals after a short experience of them.'[1]

Versatility was the hallmark of Bridges's ideal administrator:

> The first time a man is told to change from work which he has mastered to a new job, he may feel that the special knowledge he has acquired is being wasted. He may grudge the labour of mastering a new job, and may even wonder whether he will be equally successful at it. But when a man has done five jobs in fifteen years and has done them all with a measure of success, he is afraid of nothing and welcomes change. He has learnt the art of spotting what points are crucial for forming a judgment on a disputed question even when he has the most cursory knowledge of the subject as a whole.[2]

Bridges correctly anticipated that outsiders would 'get the impression of a man who can see round corners and through brick walls', and he admitted:

> It all sounds rather like black magic, but as with most pieces of magic the explanation is quite simple, once you know it. I am told by those who are good linguists that when you have learnt above five languages, the sixth, seventh and eighth become quite easy to master and the ninth and tenth are child's play. It is as though the essence of all syntax of language had got into their blood stream.

Bridges believed that something rather like this was true of many administrative problems:

> Nearly every problem bears a family resemblance to something which the experienced administrator has handled before. To him it is not some entirely new problem which he is asked to solve at short notice: it is the old wolf in a new-look sheepskin. Something in the shape of the thing strikes him as familiar. His experience tells him where the point of entry will probably be found; or warns him of the difficulties ahead which others, without his training, would not see.[3]

---

[1] Lord Bridges, *The Treasury* (1964) pp. 51–3.

[2] Sir Edward (later Lord) Bridges, *Portrait of a Profession* (1950) pp. 22–3.

[3] Sir Edward (later Lord) Bridges, 'Administration: What is it? And how can it be learnt', an essay in A. Dunsire (ed.) *The Making of an Administrator* (1956) pp. 14–15.

Bridges also made clear the powerful position of the leading Civil Servant, emphasising the difficulty of drawing a proper distinction between policy and day-to-day administration, and the major part played in framing policy by administrators:

> It is indeed precisely on these broad issues that it is the duty of the Civil Servant to give his Minister the fullest benefit of the storehouse of departmental experience: and to let the waves of the practical philosophy wash against ideas put forward by his Ministerial master.[1]

The leading Civil Servant was not lacking in opportunities to use his position of influence for, as Bridges wrote:

> The experience of anyone who has worked in Whitehall is that there is an early stage in any project when things are fluid; when, if you are in touch with those concerned and can get hold of the facts, it is fairly easy to influence decisions. But after the scheme has been worked on for weeks and months, and has hardened into a particular shape and come up for final decision, then it is very difficult to do anything except approve it or throw it overboard.[2]

It is not difficult to imagine the experienced administrator, one whose leading attributes Bridges had described as 'a sense of timing' in such matters,[3] intervening 'when things are fluid' to steer policy along the lines that he considered best.

Although even the classic definition of the duties of the Administrative Class gave it a potential managerial role in assigning to it the tasks of 'the coordination and improvement of Government machinery', and 'the general administration and control of the departments of the Public Service', as Bridges's lectures made clear the class always gave pride of place to 'the formation of policy'.[4] As one Principal recently wrote of his Administrative Class

---

[1] Sir Edward (later Lord) Bridges, *Portrait of a Profession* (1950) p. 19.

[2] Lord Bridges, 'Whitehall and Beyond', in *The Listener*, 25 June 1964, p. 1016.

[3] Sir Edward (later Lord) Bridges, 'Administration: What is it? And how can it be learnt', an essay in A. Dunsire (ed.) *The Making of an Administrator* (1956) p. 13.

[4] The classic definition being given in the *Interim Report of the Reorganisation Committee* (1921) para. 43.

colleagues: 'By training and inclination they are fitted to regard themselves as advisers to Ministers and to the small group of very senior officials who help to fashion Ministerial policies. This is, they feel, the essence of their function. This is where the excitements lie. This is the field where brilliance may be displayed and advancement won.' He asserted that 'proximity to Ministers and acquaintance with the highest questions of State are what really interest the great majority of them'.[1] A Permanent Secretary, Sir James Dunnett, came to very much the same conclusion:

> There is, I think, a tendency for the administrator to look at himself rather too exclusively as the man who advises the Minister on policy. I sometimes detect a view that quasi-diplomatic work is at the top of the scale so far as administrative work is concerned, and that more mundane tasks such as formulating and carrying out a road programme are what the Greeks would have called *banausos*, rather below the dignity of a gentleman.[2]

Another administrator, C. K. Munro, saw this attitude as colouring the whole outlook of the Administrative Class for, in his opinion, its members 'were not expected to have the qualities of push and go or the organising abilities necessary to drive any constructive undertaking through to success, and if they possessed them it did not tell particularly in their favour'. To the men who mattered most: 'Brains and power of expression both at the conference table and on paper were the qualities that counted, while the practical energy that gets things done and, more important still, the power to organise on practical lines were regarded as qualities of a lower order.' It once fell to Munro to interview a number of the ablest juniors in the Administrative Class, drawn from a variety of Ministries, and when he examined them on this matter: 'I was astonished to find how their selection and training had been influenced by this outlook. As administrators of the type required for regulative legislation they were first class material. But hardly one of them had any interest in organisation as such

[1] Frank Dunnill, 'The External Relations of the Administrative Class', in *Civil Service Opinion*, April 1964, p. 105.
[2] Sir James Dunnett, 'The Civil Service Administrator and the Expert', in *Public Administration* (1961) p. 227.

or regarded driving things along as being even remotely within his province.'[1]

Munro's feeling of astonishment cannot be shared when one recalls the historical development of the class, but one can certainly endorse his concern. As Dunnett has argued, the fact had to be faced that 'increasingly Government departments are doing very much more than advising Ministers. Many of them are, in effect, running big businesses. Clearly this is true of the Service departments. The Service departments are running very large businesses indeed. It is true of many other departments as well, for example, the Ministry of Supply.'[2] As Sir Oliver Franks concluded from his wartime experiences in that Ministry:

> The Administrative Civil Servant needed much more than analytic power and the ability to make proposals based on an analysis of the situation. He had to take a line, expound it, persuade and convince. He had to have the strength of will to take responsibility and not to lay it down until finally policies and plans had been translated into facts. When Government has positive and constructive policies in the sphere of economic affairs, an Administrative Class Civil Servant in a department dealing with economic affairs has management responsibilities which reach over beyond policy into execution.[3]

More recently, the Plowden Committee also emphasised the importance of such responsibilities, and they defined management as including:

> The preparation of material on which decisions are taken; the technical efficiency with which large operations of administration are carried out; the cost consciousness of staff at all levels; the provision of special skills and services (scientific, statistical, accountancy, O. and M., etc.) for handling particular problems, and the awareness and effectiveness with which these are used; the training and selection of men and women for posts at each level of responsibility.[4]

[1] C. K. Munro, *The Fountains in Trafalgar Square* (1952) p. 28.

[2] Dunnett, op. cit. p. 227.

[3] Sir Oliver Franks, *The Experiences of a University Teacher in the Civil Service* (1947) p. 12.

[4] The Plowden Group, *Control of Public Expenditure*, Cmnd 1432 (1961) para. 44.

Therefore, increased attention to management was needed not only in the 'big business' departments that Dunnett had spoken of, not merely in the departments dealing with economic affairs that Franks had talked of, not simply in the Establishment and Organisation divisions of the several departments, but throughout the range of activities which the Ministries carrying out the functions of the Positive State undertake.

The type of careers normally followed by the Administrative Class do not reflect the fact that 'increasingly Government departments are doing very much more than advising Ministers'. The Administrative Class's ideal administrator remains the 'intelligent layman', and it still sees its special role as 'the awareness of Ministerial responsibility'. These attitudes have not altered despite the fact that about forty per cent of the Administrative Class is now drawn from the Executive Class and the various specialist groups – compared with twenty-five per cent in 1931 – probably because direct entrants predominate among the holders of posts of Assistant Secretary status and above.[1] Although the Administrative Class no longer accounts for ten-elevenths of the posts at Assistant Secretary level and above in the Civil Service as it did before the war, in fact only about one-quarter, it still provides the majority of the posts of Under-Secretary rank or better, while thirty-three of the thirty-six posts of Permanent Secretary in status in the Service are filled by members of the Administrative Class.[2]

The whole tone of administration in the Service is still set by the Administrative Class. If that tone is to be changed – and the argument of the subsequent chapters of this book is that change is

[1] *Tomlin Report* (1931) para. 103; H.M. Treasury, *Civil Service Manpower* (1966) table 20. This latter table, which gives details about the Administrative Class by Method of Entry as at 1 Jan 1966, is Appendix I, Table 2 in this book: the remainder of that appendix contains further statistics about the Administrative Class.

[2] *Evidence presented by the Institution of Professional Civil Servants to the Fulton Committee on the Civil Service* (1967) para. 27. No precise statistics about the composition of the Higher Civil Service appear to be published, but those given in the *Treasury Factual Memorandum to the Fulton Committee on the Civil Service* (1966) for its component classes clearly indicate that the Administrative Class still has a majority of those posts of Under-Secretary status or better.

needed – the orientation of the leading administrators will have to be changed: and the only way of achieving this is by radically recasting the Civil Service. The initial step in that process should be the abolition of the separate Administrative Class. The artificial division between policy and execution that persists in the Civil Service would be ended by a merger between the Executive and Administrative Classes. This subject is examined in chapters 4 and 6, but at this point it can be said that an amalgamation of these two classes would enhance the status of management, and coupled with a rationalisation of the merged hierarchies, a greater emphasis on specialisation and a continuation of the recent trend towards more, and better, formal post-entry training, a more relevant type of administrator would be likely to emerge than at present. But to consolidate the generalist side of the Service, while leaving the specialist groups in their relatively underdeveloped state, would be to repeat the mistakes of the past. The specialist hierarchies need to be still further improved, and their status should be raised by making their posts of Assistant Secretary status, or better, part of a newly unified Higher Civil Service with the fused executive-administrative hierarchy. But, above all, the new Higher Civil Service needs to be open for interchanges of staff with public and private industry, the local authorities and the universities. Dunnett believed that without measures of this type there was a risk of departments becoming 'somewhat inbred and a little bit self-satisfied', and he recalled: 'The introduction of men of ability from other professions during the War and who have stayed on since, has given the Service, in the areas which have been strengthened in this way, a vigour and vitality which it might otherwise not have had.'[1] In the era of the interventionist central Government, it is essential that the Higher Civil Service should be an open hierarchy.

In place of the now outmoded all-rounder tradition, the leading Civil Servants will need to lean more in the future in the direction of technocracy. Lord Bridges may have been right in suggesting that there is a similarity between all administrative problems, but he was not necessarily correct in arguing that the best man to

[1] Dunnett, op. cit. p. 226.

tackle them was an administrator who had avoided special know-ledge in the appropriate field, or whose career was generally char-acterised by an absence of specialisms of any kind. Although basing recruitment on a certain type of 'good general education', and sub-mitting such entrants to an apprenticeship based on the assumption that administration is 'something only to be learned by doing it – like riding a bicycle',[1] ensures a remarkable uniformity of outlook in the Administrative Class, it does not follow that that outlook is all that is wanted. When it leads to a situation where members of the Administrative Class do not 'typically think of themselves as managers',[2] it is an outlook that ought to be discarded. The Service does not need a governing class devoted only to serving Ministers, because members of an integrated Higher Civil Service would develop the appropriate skills as an obvious part of their jobs. The service to Ministers, indeed, does not even really reflect the responsibilities of the vast majority of the members of the Administrative Class, although it does help to determine their approach to those responsibilities. Even though the situation varies, in many departments the Minister usually only has fre-quent contacts with administrators of Under-Secretary status or higher; that is, only one-fifth of the Administrative Class. It is not sensible to orientate the careers of Principals and Assistant Princi-pals to the role played at that level: the ceiling of even the average direct-entrants' career is the Assistant Secretary grade, members of which are bound to spend as much time, if not more, in dealing with the affairs of their divisions as in contacts with the Minister. The subject matter dealt with is now of such difficulty that know-ledge of the fields concerned ought to be demanded of the admini-strators concerned instead of being regarded almost as a residual consideration. Greater specialisation is surely the answer to greater complexity of duties, and it could well lead to two important and desirable developments. Firstly, although the parliamentary time-table will never permit a complete change of priorities, there will be a greater tendency to treat problems from a technological rather than a political standpoint. Secondly, administrators who

---

[1] C. H. Sisson, *The Spirit of British Administration* (1959) p. 29.
[2] Dunnill, op. cit. p. 105.

specialised more would establish closer relationships with the experts in the fields concerned. Knowing the field better might also enable them to break out more often from the encirclement of pressure groups to secure other and perhaps more disinterested advice. The administrator has to keep the subject matter down to manageable proportions, and if his actions are 'mere acts of recognition' and he has a 'deliberately commonplace vision',[1] into the field of vision or recognition ought to come wider sources of advice.

But whatever the shape of the Higher Civil Service of the near or distant future, the present finds the Administrative Class as 'the chief source of advice to Ministers on current Government business'.[2] Directly descended from the 'intellectual class' envisaged in the Trevelyan–Northcote Report of 1853, it still tends to relate its role to the trappings of ministerial responsibility, when the complex duties of the modern departments demand a wider outlook. The chapters which follow discuss the direct-entry recruitment and the post-entry training of the Administrative Class, and that class's intra-service relationships with the Executive Class on the one hand, and the specialist classes on the other, viewed in a historical context and against the background of the emergence of the Positive State, and in relation to the functions which the modern administrator has to be able to perform.

[1] Sisson, op. cit. p. 24.
[2] Civil Service Commission, *Administrative Group of Appointments* (1967) p. 9.

CHAPTER TWO

Direct-Entry Recruitment
to the Administrative Class

I OPEN COMPETITION IN PRACTICE 1870–1939

THE role of the leading Civil Servant in the departments of the
Regulatory State was a modest one compared with the complex
tasks that face the modern administrator. The departments of the
period were too small, and their duties were too simple, either to
create difficult managerial problems, or to demand the employment
of specialists other than small groups of lawyers and inspectors.
The contemporary administrators did not need to have qualities
of initiative, drive and organising ability: the work came to them,
thrown up by the working of the various regulations, and in
the form of the parliamentary needs of the Minister. The leading
Civil Servants of the period were the socially acceptable personal
aides of Ministers who, like themselves, led a leisurely existence
until the pace of political activity speeded up after the turn of
the century. Whether a graduate Higher or First Division was
really needed by the Service before the 1890s has already been
questioned.

Nevertheless, writing in 1853, influenced by Benjamin Jowett[1]

[1] At the time of the *Trevelyan–Northcote Report* Benjamin Jowett
(1817–93) was Fellow and Tutor of Balliol College, Oxford. His letter to
Trevelyan anticipating and rebutting probable objections to the proposal
for open competitive examinations, and outlining a possible scheme of his
own, was published with the report (pp. 24–31). Although Jowett did
not become Master of Balliol until 1870, as a leading university reformer
he was a well-known Oxford figure long before that which 'led to his
being consulted with regard to educational movements of a wider scope
such as that for opening to competition posts in the Home Civil Service
and in that of the East India Company'. Jowett later showed a 'life long
interest in the Public Service of India' (Evelyn Abbott and Lewis Campbell,
The Life and Letters of Benjamin Jowett, 1897, vol. I, pp. 185–6). Jowett

and the results of the period of self-reform at Oxford and Cambridge,[1] and by Macaulay's advocacy of similar measures for the Indian Civil Service,[2] Trevelyan and Northcote recommended that direct-entry recruitment to 'the superior situations' in the Service should be by centrally-conducted 'competing literary examinations', which would be 'on a level with the highest description of education in this country'.[3] The introduction of open competition, like the implementation of the other major principles of the Organisation Report, was a slow process. The Civil Service Commission was established as early as 1855, but, although its initial powers were extended by certain provisions of the Superannuation Act of 1859, for the first decade and a half of its existence the commission was called upon to administer a system of limited and permissive competition.[4] No real progress was made towards

---

was nothing less than 'one of the key figures of Victorian England, the mentor in chief of its golden age'. It is sad that to an increasing number of educated people his name means nothing, unless it reminds them of the celebrated quatrain which when it was first printed ran thus:

> 'First come I. My name is J-w-tt.
> There's no knowledge but I know it.
> I am Master of this College.
> What I don't know, isn't knowledge.'

(Geoffrey Faber, *Jowett: A Portrait with Background*, 1957, pp. 21–2.)

[1] The period of self-reform was described and discussed by John Roach, 'Victorian Universities and the National Intelligentsia', in *Victorian Studies* (1959); and in the historical introduction to the *Report of the Royal Commission on Oxford and Cambridge Universities* (chairman: H. H. Asquith) 1922.

[2] Macaulay's advocacy being contained in the *Report on the Indian Civil Service* (Nov 1854), which was reprinted in a collection of papers on *The Selection and Training of Candidates for the Indian Civil Service*, C. 1446 (1876): Jowett being a member of Macaulay's Committee which drew up the report. Trevelyan looked on Macaulay, his brother-in-law, as 'little less than an oracle of wisdom' (Sir George Otto Trevelyan, *The Life and Letters of Lord Macaulay*, 1888, vol. I, p. 427). Judging by the remainder of this biography, Macaulay was very much less than that.

[3] *Trevelyan–Northcote Report* (1853) p. 11.

[4] This is evident from the *Report of the Select Committee on Civil Service Appointments* (chairman: Lord Stanley) 1860. The Civil Service Commissioners complained to the committee: 'The competitive test frequently exists in name where it is not resorted to in fact' (ibid. p. xiii). The committee, which included Northcote and Lowe, was a dull and

the goal of open competition until after Gladstone became Prime Minister in 1868. His Chancellor of the Exchequer, Robert Lowe, was an enthusiastic Civil Service reformer, and at the end of 1869 he appealed to Gladstone: 'As I have so often tried in vain, will you bring the question of the Civil Service before the Cabinet today? Something must be decided. We cannot keep matters in this discreditable state of abeyance.' Gladstone encountered opposition when he raised the matter, but devised a neat compromise whereby all branches of the Service were thrown open to competition where the Minister concerned agreed.[1] The resulting Order in Council of 4 June 1870 introduced open competition into all the major departments except the Home Office, which relented in 1873, the Foreign Office and the Education Office.[2] By 1894, not, as will be seen, with complete accuracy, the Treasury felt able to say that open competition for the Higher Division was 'now the rule'.[3]

The form that the 'competing literary examinations' eventually took owed more to the scheme that Macaulay had drawn up for recruitment to the Indian Civil Service than to the plans that Jowett had outlined in a letter appended to the Trevelyan–Northcote Report.[4] Macaulay's theory that the best preparation

---

cautious body and could not raise the courage to follow its convictions. Though it was 'not prepared to advise the immediate introduction into the whole Civil Service of entirely open competitions, we would nevertheless recommend that the experiment first tried at the India House in 1859, be repeated from time to time in other departments' (p. xv); nothing was done along these lines. Chapter 1 of the *MacDonnell Majority Report* ('Historical Sketch of the Civil Service 1853–1912') paras 10–14, described and discussed the events of the period between 1853 and 1870.

[1] John Morley, *The Life of William Ewart Gladstone* (1903) vol. I, pp. 948–9.

[2] Civil Service Commission, *Orders in Council, Notices in the London Gazette relating to Examinations for the Home Civil Service, the Army, the Civil Service of India, etc.* (1909) pp. 6–10 and appendices II and III.

[3] H.M. Treasury, *Paper showing the manner in which the recommendations of the Royal Commission with respect to the Civil Service has been dealt with* (1894) p. 11.

[4] Jowett's scheme included a preliminary examination which tested 'the indispensable requirements of public offices generally' which were thought to be 'a thorough knowledge of arithmetic and book-keeping,

for an administrative career was 'a liberal education' rather than a relevant professional training, not only dominated the early history of what became known as the Class I examination, but still has a considerable influence in the present-day arrangements for Administrative Class recruitment. Macaulay believed that 'men who have been engaged, up to one and two and twenty, in studies which have no immediate connexion with the business of any profession, and of which the effect is merely to open, to invigorate, and to enrich the mind, will generally be found, in the business of every profession, superior to men who have, at 18 or 19, devoted themselves to the special studies of their calling'.[1] As the only subjects regularly taught in universities at the time were classics and mathematics, any examination scheme aimed at graduate recruitment into the Service would have to follow the pattern indicated by Macaulay. The Class I scheme that was introduced in 1870 contained a preliminary qualifying examination along the lines advocated by Jowett, but when that was dropped in 1895, the

---

and English composition'. Those who survived that hurdle then faced a literary examination based upon 'the best elements of higher education in England, without special reference to the wants of the public offices': not surprisingly, Jowett believed: 'The knowledge of Latin and Greek is, perhaps, upon the whole, the best test of regular previous education.' The most interesting part of Jowett's scheme was that where he discussed 'the special requirements of the higher departments of the public offices', which appeared to him to be 'chiefly two, viz., a knowledge of the principles of commerce, taxation and political economy in the Treasury, Board of Trade, and C.; of modern languages and modern history, under which last may be included international law, in the Foreign Office. In the offices which are principally offices of account, mathematical talent may with advantage, be insisted upon. Whether immediately wanted for the daily work of the office or not, all such attainments tend to give an official a higher interest in his employment and to fit him for superior positions' (Jowett, op. cit. pp. 26–8). Jowett seemed to be looking ahead to a time when the range of university studies available would be much wider than in 1853; and his latter remarks about the need for relevant pre-entry training have never been favoured in the Service as regards the Administrative Class.

[1] Report on the Indian Civil Service (1854) op. cit. p. 25. Ascribing its authorship to Macaulay is justified because his biography makes it very clear that he lived up to his aim of finishing it within a week, apparently without consulting the other members of the committee (G. O. Trevelyan, op. cit. p. 372).

competition came to consist of the Macaulay ideal of an examination in which the candidates could take any or all of the papers, none being obligatory, combined with provisions which penalised candidates found to be 'mere smatterers' in subjects they presented.[1] After 1906, a limit was set on the number of papers that a candidate could take by imposing a ceiling of total marks.[2] The successful candidates in order of merit chose which department they would enter,[3] and as the examination neither tested their aptitudes nor contained papers directly related to the subject matter of their future duties, this was as fair a system as any other.

Between 1870 and 1939, in normal peacetime conditions, from the standpoint of attracting the intellectual cream of at least the older English universities, the record of the Class I examination and its modified successor was one of outstanding success. Yet, at the time of the Organisation Report, the overwhelming majority of the practising and retired administrators disagreed with the reformers' assertion that 'it would be natural to expect that so important a profession' as the Civil Service 'would attract into its ranks the ablest and most ambitious youth of the country'.[4] Sir James Stephen, who had retired from the Service in 1847 to become Professor of Modern History at Cambridge, asserted: 'The prizes to be won are not worthy of the pursuit of such young men as I am constantly observing among the foremost of the competitors for academical honours.' He was convinced that no man of real mental power, to whom the truth was known beforehand, would 'subject himself to an arduous examination in order

---

[1] *Report of the Committee appointed by the Lords Commissioners of His Majesty's Treasury to consider and report upon the scheme of examination for Class I of the Civil Service* (chairman: Sir Stanley Leathes) 1917, paras 1–5. Macaulay's report had made it very clear that: 'Nothing could be farther from our wish than to hold out premiums for knowledge of wide surface and small depth. We are of the opinion that a candidate ought to be allowed no credit at all for taking up a subject in which he is a mere smatterer' (op. cit. p. 26).

[2] *Leathes Report*, op. cit. para. 5.

[3] As the *Third Report of the Select Committee on Miscellaneous Expenditure* (1873) para. 10 (1) put it, the successful candidates 'are allowed to elect in turn the particular department in which vacancies exist'. This system continued until 1939.

[4] *Trevelyan–Northcote Report*, p. 4.

to win a post so ill paid, so obscure and so subordinate. Or should he win it, no such man will long retain it.'[1] Stephen and the other critics were wrong in their gloomy forecasts for three main reasons. Firstly, in an age in which the upper classes scorned any connection with 'trade', an opening in the Higher Division of the Service had a certain social standing: as Sir John Kempe wrote, such posts were regarded as 'more respectable and less strenuous than those in institutions connected with trade, such as banks, insurance offices, and commercial firms'. To some extent the distaste among university graduates for a career in 'trade' lingered on until after the Second World War, although by then, and possibly as early as 1914, the pressure of work at the top of the Service was comparable with, if not more severe than, that in private industry and commerce.[2] Secondly, the Higher Division offered, and the Administrative Class still offers, a competitive starting salary and not the prospect of a long and poorly-paid period of professional training. At the time of the Trevelyan–Northcote Report, Herman Merivale wrote that parents chose vocations, not the graduates, and that they 'would urge their sons to a competition which, if successful, would relieve themselves of the necessity of supporting them through several expensive years, whatever the risk of disappointment and *taedium vitae* which they might entail in those sons'. Graduates of a later period may have been less in the hands of their parents, but without private means faced much

---

[1] *Papers relating to the Reorganisation of the Civil Service* (1855) pp. 75–6.

[2] Sir John Arrow Kempe, *Reminiscences of an Old Civil Servant* (1928) p. 38. Writing in 1941, and contrasting the Higher Civil Service of 1938 with that of 1898, H. E. Dale said: 'The chiefs of the Service are on the whole far harder worked and more constantly strained than they used to be. Forty years ago there were a few men in Government Offices who gave all their lives to their work; but they did it from choice, not from necessity.' By 1938 in contrast 'for most of the year, the permanent Heads of great departments and their principal subordinates can have little leisure'. The pressure of business 'on which they must bend their full attention scarcely ceases from the time they reach the office till they leave it: and often they take the papers home'. One of the causes of the drift into the private sector which Dale deplored was: 'The work is likely to be less in volume, and no more exacting of mental and nervous effort.' (*The Higher Civil Service of Great Britain*, 1941, pp. 192 and 196.)

the same financial considerations.[1] Thirdly, and perhaps most important, was the state of supply and demand in the careers market for graduates.

At the time of the Organisation Report it was unfavourable, as the Master of Marlborough made clear when he welcomed the report's proposals because they opened 'a new profession at the time when the old ones are overstocked'. In his opinion:

> That the difficulty of making a start in life increases every year, is painfully apparent to every schoolmaster and tutor who watches with any interest the career of those among his pupils who do not wish to enter Holy Orders, and have no private friends or connexions to bring them forward. Hundreds of young men, in every way qualified and deserving, would gladly accept such remuneration as the Government bestows on its Civil Servants.[2]

The situation was much the same half a century later for, as Lord Salter has written:

> To a young man who had achieved distinction at Oxford or Cambridge the range of careers open was very limited. The two fighting services were mostly recruited from young men who had made their choice earlier and did not go to the University; the Church attracted only those who had a special vocation for it; the Bar had some glittering prizes, but it was a highly hazardous profession for any except those who not only had the requisite talent but some personal connections, especially with solicitors, which would ensure them a fair start; industry was almost entirely recruited, for its most attractive posts, by family or personal influence – it did not welcome, and still less, as large industries now do, woo young graduates.

Salter concluded: 'The three great civilian Services' – the Home, Indian and Colonial Civil Services – 'which recruited through the

---

[1] *Papers relating to the Reorganisation of the Civil Service* (1855) pp. 316–17. Merivale was the Permanent Under-Secretary of State for the Colonial Office.

[2] *Papers relating to the Reorganisation of the Civil Service* (1855) p. 61. The educational interests generally were very enthusiastic: for example, the Headmaster of Harrow anticipated a 'great benefit' from 'the opening of a new profession to young men of liberal education' (p. 89). Some of the enthusiasm followed from Jowett's gross over-estimate of the number of annual vacancies that would need to be filled as T. W. Murdoch, the Chairman of the Emigration Board, pointed out (pp. 297–8).

joint examination each August had by far the strongest appeal to those who led in the honours schools.'[1] It continued to retain that appeal until 1939.

Of course, those who were successful in the pre-1914 style of competition by wholly written examination later came to insist on its superiority compared with later methods. Salter even maintained that the order of merit was directly related to administrative potential. He was greatly impressed by the fact that, 'Basil Blackett and John Anderson were actually first on their respective lists, and by the collective judgment of their colleagues twenty years later (and no human judgment is more nearly infallible) they would have been pronounced the best of their years'. Salter believed that it was no defect of the examination that 'such supreme talent should have had a slight advantage over genius with a touch of unorthodoxy', and he recalled that Keynes would have been first in his year but for the marks that he lost on economics.[2] Without doubting the merits of the particular examples quoted, the general subsequent success of those who headed the examination list was not surprising: they had the choice of departments, and in a sense the verdict of the examiners could be self-perpetuating. Salter was perhaps misguided in praising the examination for rewarding orthodoxy. Keynes's own comment upon his results was fitting: 'I evidently knew more about economics than my examiners.'[3] There were enough pressures towards orthodoxy in the Service the candidates entered, without holding out extra premiums for it in the method of entry.

At least one contemporary administrator, the former Permanent Secretary to the Treasury, Sir George Murray, was less than enthusiastic about recruitment by written examination. He said in 1912: 'While the men who are drawn from the Class I examination are, I think, very good for the purposes for which they are required for the first ten, or twelve, or fifteen years of their official life, I have at times been rather disappointed at finding how few of them emerge satisfactorily from the ruck and come out as really capable

[1] Lord Salter, *Memoirs of a Public Servant* (1961) p. 35.
[2] Ibid. pp. 35–6.
[3] Sir Roy Harrod, *The Life of John Maynard Keynes* (1951) p. 121.

heads of departments.' Murray had himself entered the Service by patronage, and predictably he believed that the difficulty 'in finding men to fill the highest places' in departments had not been experienced 'when the Civil Service was recruited in a rather different way'.[1] If this was the case, a possible explanation was that open competition may well have raised the average standard of the First Division, so that it became relatively harder for the potentially outstanding administrator to shine and to make an early escape from the routine duties of the division's lower grades. Academically, the quality of the direct entrants by open competition was very high: for example, the Warden of All Souls assured the Mac-Donnell Commission that the Service recruited 'the best that Oxford can produce'.[2] If there was difficulty in filling the highest posts, the fault may have lain 'in the system of training after entry, and in the conditions of subordinate service; it need not be with the competitive system'.[3]

Nevertheless, by the time that the MacDonnell Commission examined the Service in the immediate pre-First World War period, there was a strong case, which the commission partially recognised, for reforming that competitive system: as a result of its recommendations, a committee charged with that task was appointed in 1916, under the chairmanship of Sir Stanley Leathes.[4] The Leathes Committee found that the theory stated by Macaulay was constructed on the basis of facts which, by 1916, had either been greatly modified or no longer existed. When it was constructed

[1] *MacDonnell Evidence*, questions 1955, 1981–3, 1999–2001.

[2] Ibid., question 4447. The Warden at that time was Sir William Anson.

[3] *Leathes Report*, op. cit. para. 13.

[4] *The MacDonnell Majority Report* recommended (No. 22): 'A Committee composed of specially qualified persons should be invited by the Treasury to examine the suitability of the syllabus and methods of the Class I Examination' (ch. III, para. 50, pp. 42–3). The central tasks assigned to the Leathes Committee, which was appointed in 1916, were: 'To consider the report upon the existing scheme of examination for Class I of the Home Civil Service', and 'To submit for the consideration of the Lords Commissioners of H.M. Treasury a revised scheme such as they may judge to be best adapted for the selection of the type of officer required for that Class of the Civil Service, and at the same time most advantageous in the higher education of this country.'

there had only been one course of higher education in England, a course of classics and mathematics. It had been easy, therefore, to construct a competitive examination which would be equal for all trained competitors, and which would select the best man so far as an examination could distinguish the best. Since that time, however, subject after subject had been added to the list of university courses. Moreover, whereas in 1855 there had only been three teaching universities in England, by 1916 there were ten, besides university colleges. The history of Cambridge illustrated the general movement. In 1855 there were two triposes, the Mathematical and the Classical. It was necessary to obtain honours in the Mathematical Tripos as a condition of admission to the Classical Tripos. By 1916 there were eleven triposes at Cambridge, in each of which an honours degree could be obtained. The Commissioners had tried to adapt their examination to these changes by adding subject after subject to their list, until their schedule had contained thirty-eight different subjects.[1]

It could also be said that the main subjects of education in Macaulay's time were among those which lent themselves most readily to processes of written examination, with the results giving a relatively just distribution of numerical marks. Apart from the multiplication of subjects of self-contained university study, and apart from the great difficulty of evaluating performance in disparate subjects to a just standard by numerical marks, for instance in French as against philosophy, it could be argued that many of the more modern university subjects did not lend themselves to so exact a valuation of results as Greek translation and composition, or certain branches of mathematics. The syllabus in each subject had also to be generalised to suit the methods of a greater number of teachers and students all working in freedom and independence. It was probably inevitable that the syllabus would be better suited to some institutions and to certain groups of candidates than to others. Just treatment of all candidates was more difficult than it had been in the early days of the Civil Service Commission, and the task of devising a Class I examination had become far more complex than had been contemplated by Macaulay.[2]

[1] *Leathes Report*, para. 11.   [2] Ibid. para. 12.

By 1916, it could also be said that the faith in competitive examination was not what it had been twenty years before. Cambridge, its original home, had abandoned the strict order of merit in most of the public examinations. The Senior Wrangler and the other Wranglers were merged in the First Class, and there had been no senior classic for over thirty years. Examiners, whose attention had been directed to classification rather than to arrangement in order of merit, had come to see that the mere addition of numerical marks produced results not even in accordance with such justice as an examination was capable of dispensing. When numerical marks were applied not to one common schedule of subjects, but to the considerable number of combinations possible under the Class I scheme, the degree of approximation might well be still less. When subjects such as history, mathematics and natural science had to be brought to a common standard, that standard could not be accepted as fully reliable.[1]

The Leathes Committee correctly concluded that the Class I competition needed to be remodelled, and they outlined a two-part scheme, with what they called Section B being along the lines of the pre-1914 examination, with papers being set in what were considered to be the chief studies at university level. The committee placed on an equal footing 'the main schools' which they said were 'Classical languages, history and literature; Modern languages with history and literature; History; Mathematics; and the Natural Sciences'. Each grouping carried papers worth 800 marks, but as candidates were required to take papers in Section B of a total value of 1000 marks, all would have to offer papers outside their degree course.[2] The major reform made by the Leathes Committee was the introduction of a compulsory section into the scheme. This was called Section A and its total value was 800 marks which ensured that it would 'count substantially in the competition'.[3] Leathes had told the MacDonnell Commission that there ought to be a compulsory part in the scheme in which English was 'more extensively tested', and in which every candidate would be 'obliged to know something of a modern language'.[4] The

---

[1] Ibid. para. 14.   [2] Ibid. paras 20 and 36.
[3] Ibid. para. 36.   [4] *MacDonnell Evidence*, questions 417–18.

committee over which he presided correctly argued that 'all well-educated young men should be able to use the English language skilfully and accurately and to grasp its meaning readily and correctly'. A compulsory paper in English and an essay, both worth 100 marks, were therefore introduced, together with three further papers of the same value. The first dealt with 'modern subjects, social, political and economic; the second required the translation of a modern foreign language; and the third was intended to give a substantial advantage in the competition to those candidates who, by whatever means, had obtained and retained a sound knowledge of elementary general science. Section A was completed by a viva voce examination, a major innovation, which was worth 300 marks and which was seen as 'a test, by means of questions and conversation on matters of general interest, of the candidate's alertness, intelligence and intellectual outlook, his personal qualities of mind and mental equipment'.[1]

As the Leathes Committee's scheme governed direct-entry recruitment to the Administrative Class between the isolated competition of 1921 – regular normal open competitions were not resumed after the First World War until 1925 – and 1939, it merits a close examination. To some extent the Leathes scheme represented an advance on the pre-1914 system: but no real attempt was made to relate the recruitment process to either the duties that faced the successful candidate, or the different qualities needed in the administrator now that the heyday of the Regulatory

[1] *Leathes Report*, paras 22–9 and 36. The MacDonnell Commission had examined, but did not actually recommend, 'the institution of a viva voce examination' which had 'the object of ascertaining the candidates' general mental calibre, and the possession of those qualities of common sense, sound judgment, resourcefulness and resolution, upon which the written paper rarely gives assurance' (*Majority Report*, ch. II, para. 44). The commission called attention to evidence which had favoured the proposal (para. 45) without noting the volume of adverse comment. Leathes himself had told them that 'in theory' the introduction of a viva voce was 'quite excellent' (question 213) but he believed that 'the practical difficulties are very great' (question 130). By 1917, Leathes had changed his mind, while his belief that languages were a particular asset led him to advocate that those who could offer an 'extra numerum language' would have a possible hundred marks advantage over their rivals (*Report*, paras 28 and 36).

State had obviously passed. At a time when the Civil Service provided one of the few openings available to general graduates, the Leathes Committee kept rigidly to the old idea that the administrative competition should be 'a test of general rather than highly specialised ability and education',[1] and failed to encourage the development of studies which were either directly related, or formed a useful background, to the actual duties of the Administrative Class. Even if the committee was correct in asserting that candidates for the administrative competition should not be expected to 'study exclusively either politics, law, economics or philosophy', this did not justify them in placing candidates who had read such subjects at a disadvantage. The committee failed to live up to its promise to greatly increase 'the individual and collective weight of these studies'. Such useful background subjects as economic history, political organisation and public finance received only half the marks accorded to such subjects as Italian history and literature, and astronomy;[2] and the minor revision in the weightings that took place in 1937 did not alter this fundamental imbalance.[3] Regarding the compulsory section of the scheme, the committee was correct in saying that the ability to write good English was 'specially valuable for Civil Servants':[4] but, in the general context of their scheme they seemed to be placing more importance on the manner in which the administrator would present material than on the nature of its contents. The most radical departure from tradition, the introduction of the viva voce, proved to be the most controversial of the Leathes reforms. Its aims were admirable: it was to be 'a valuable corrective to the results of the written papers' because it would attempt to reveal qualities which 'cannot be tested by a written examination', yet which were 'useful to Public Servants'.[5] The Leathes Report

---

[1] *Leathes Report*, para. 11.   [2] Ibid. para. 36.
[3] Civil Service Commission, *Civil Service Examinations*, 1931 (pp. 10, 43–5) and 1937 (pp. 44–6).
[4] *Leathes Report*, para. 23.
[5] The committee believed: 'the marks assigned under this heading should be a valuable corrective to the results of the written papers, and should not infrequently help a useful man to success or save the State from a bad bargain' (*Report*, para. 29).

was, however, guilty of imprecision not only about the length of the interview, but also about the qualities that were to be looked for. Given the already evident change in the role of the State, some serious attempt ought to have been made to test the candidates' aptitudes for the increasingly varied types of work facing administrators, and to look for qualities such as organising ability and the sort of personal drive that carries policies through the execution stage. Complete precision was impossible, but the committee should have done better than to have singled out the ability to maintain 'nervous equipoise', and they should have charged future boards with a more specific role than asking questions about matters of general interest on which they considered 'every young man should have something to say'. Even allowing for the possibly inevitable difficulties involved in the initial working of what was an innovation, the record of the inter-war viva voce proved to be a sorry episode in the history of Administrative Class recruitment.

The Civil Service Commissioners themselves later admitted this. The board that conducted the interview consisted 'solely of the First Commissioner, who was Chairman, and University representatives. Apart from the Chairman, the interest of the Service as user was not represented at all; nor, with rare exceptions, was that of the general public.' The interviews were not even as long as the half an hour that Leathes had suggested to the Mac-Donnell Commission, being '15 to 20 minutes as a rule, and it was hardly possible for the Board to do more than form a general impression of the candidate's personality and interests. Time did not permit the probing of his underlying qualities of character, intelligence or ability.'[1] This had certainly not been the view that Leathes' successor as First Civil Service Commissioner, Sir Roderick Meiklejohn, had presented to the Tomlin Commission, for he believed that there were 'dozens of things you can find out from a young man in fifteen minutes'. Meiklejohn added: 'You may ask him almost anything which occurs to you to find out what his interests are, and how he reacts to other people and other things. It is as wide as we can make it. Of course, you ask him

[1] Civil Service Commissioners, *84th Report*, section XIV, paras 8–11; *MacDonnell Evidence*, questions 36, 159.

about his games and his sports; everything under the sun really.'[1] The interviewers were not in any case looking for administrative potential, for they concentrated instead on the candidates' 'general address, good manners, brightness, interest in various things and sympathy', the last word being a synonym for 'tact'.[2] The possibilities for social prejudice at such an oddly conducted interview were there, even though one of Leathes' main fears was the unlikely one that 'there might be too much sympathy for the rough diamond'.[3] The idea that there was social bias in the viva voce was dismissed as 'the most complete bunkum' by Sir Warren Fisher, who assured the Tomlin Commission: 'When I am looking at a fellow really I am not concerned with what his father was: I am concerned with what he is.'[4] Fisher's sentiments were admirable, but he was not on the interviewing board, anyway, not even being sure how long the interview lasted. There was a definite suspicion that the inter-war interview was a vehicle of social prejudice: a suspicion that still lingers, and for which the Service may still be suffering in recruitment.

This aspect of the inter-war viva voce, fortunately, did not prevent the later development after the Second World War of a method of entry into the Administrative Class which included a series of interviews. An important departure from the traditional

[1] *Tomlin Evidence*, questions 1367 and 1419. Meiklejohn believed that it was possible to estimate any man's or woman's personality in a fifteen minutes' interview (question 1388).

[2] *Tomlin Evidence*, questions 1081–4. Meiklejohn had such faith in the viva voce that he wanted to adopt for the administrative competition the Foreign Office system of the period, namely of using it to decide who sat for the examination (questions 1138–1159). The Tomlin Commission, in one of its braver moments, rejected this deplorable idea (*Report*, para. 255).

[3] *Tomlin Evidence*, question 22,378. The Tomlin Commission convinced itself that there were 'no grounds' for any suspicion that the interview offered 'scope for the display of class prejudice' (*Report*, para. 253). Meiklejohn's assurance: 'We try them on every side, intellectual and social characteristics' (*Evidence*, question 1377) suggests otherwise.

[4] *Tomlin Evidence*, questions 18,821–2. Fisher admitted that he did not know how long the interview lasted (18,717). He favoured 'anything from 30 to 40 minutes' (18,718), which was surely the bare minimum needed if the Interview Board was going to 'spend an appreciable time on each candidate' (*Written Statement*, para. 16).

literary competition had also been made in the Reconstruction examinations by which ex-servicemen were recruited into the Administrative Class after the First World War. The method used was described as 'competitive selection': the successful candidates emerged after surviving an initial sifting of applications by the Civil Service Commission, a qualifying examination and an appearance before a Selection Board.[1] Over 200 entered the Administrative Class by this method and it took several years before a similar number of entrants were secured by normal open competition.[2] Indeed, it is worth noting that although direct-entry recruitment from the universities by open competitive examination had been introduced as early as 1870, it seems very probable that at no time since have the direct entrants to the Administrative Class and its predecessors been drawn solely from that source. The careers of patronage appointees who had entered the Service before 1870 could well have lasted into the present century, while even in 1914 the leading administrative positions in the Boards of Education and Agriculture were filled by patronage.[3] The First World War had seen outsiders brought into the

[1] *Third Interim Report of the Gladstone Committee on Recruitment to the Civil Service after the War* (30 Oct 1918) paras 7–19.

[2] *Report of the Southborough Committee on ex-Service recruitment to the Civil Service* (1924), which stated (para. 31) that, as regards the Administrative Class, since the armistice over 200 ex-servicemen had been appointed to this class. For the five years 1925–9 the average number of open competition entrants per annum was about fifteen (*Tomlin Evidence*, question 1056); and as the annual average for 1930–8 was thirty-seven (*Civil Service Commission's Written Evidence to the Priestley Commission*, 1954, para. 20), it can be fairly concluded that it was not until the mid-1930s that the reconstruction intake was numerically equalled from 'normal' sources.

[3] The Board of Education unrepentantly recruited its 'Examiners' by patronage, maintaining rather unconvincingly that such posts were essentially different from those of the First Division. The MacDonnell Commission (*Majority Report*, ch. IX, para. 29) successfully recommended the abolition of the board's special recruiting arrangements, which were well described in the *Appendix to the 2nd Report* of the Commission (appendix XII, p. 533). The Board of Agriculture and Fisheries had already chosen to abandon its special examinations for 'Assistants to Heads of Branches' in favour of reliance on the Class I examination (*MacDonnell Evidence*, question 35,938).

Administrative Class: its cessation saw ex-service recruitment on a large scale, and the Second World War repeated this pattern.

II RECRUITMENT AND THE POSITIVE STATE: THE POST-WAR RECORD

The various pledges made by the wartime Coalition Government that its post-war successors would establish and maintain a Welfare State, and that they would ensure full employment by managing the economy, meant that when normal peacetime conditions returned, the direct-entry recruitment arrangements for the Administrative Class would have to be drastically remodelled. The whole recruitment process needed to be made more professional and more relevant. The Civil Service Commissioners needed, at the very least, as Professor Robson said in 1937, to 'devise a series of examination tests which would distinguish the cautious, negative, obstructive type of individual' from the 'positive, constructive, problem-solving, planning type'[1] for whom there was now an even more pressing need than before. The orientation of the recruitment machinery ought to have been away from the all-rounder towards the professional manager, and perhaps much more attention needed to be given to the subjects that had been taken by candidates at their universities as giving some indication of their interests as well as of their aptitudes. Although the overriding aim of the recruitment process had to be to secure the desired number of recruits of the right quality, two secondary, and not necessarily unconnected, aims ought to have been to widen the number of universities, the range of academic disciplines studied and the types of social background from which the recruits were normally drawn. There was also a need to get away

[1] William A. Robson, 'The Public Service', an essay in the collection edited by him, *The British Civil Servant* (1937) p. 21. Robson said that he could 'devise a series of examination tests which would distinguish the cautious, negative, obstructive type of individual from the positive, constructive, problem-solving, planning type for whom there is so great a need at present'.

from the idea that all direct-entry recruitment to the Administrative Class should take place at Assistant Principal level. The
majority of recruits ought to have continued to be attracted at
that level, but in the era of the Positive State a closed Administrative Class was inappropriate and outside recruitment from other
professions needed to take place at Principal and Assistant Secretary levels also. As one observer rightly said in 1944, the inflow
of men at those levels at a later stage in life 'would continually
freshen the Service, keep it in touch with the development of
administrative technique, maintain its intellectual communication with the larger world, and do a great deal to break down the
cloistered separateness of Whitehall, the "place apart" '.[1]

As recruitment to the Principal and Assistant Secretary grades
from outside the central Government sphere did not begin until
twenty years later, it will be gathered that the post-war reforms
made by the Civil Service Commissioners in their Administrative
Class recruitment machinery fell short of the ideals listed above.
Nevertheless, the changes made, although they did not go as far
as the changed role of the State demanded, did constitute a major
readjustment. Not the least spur to the Commissioners was the
fact that by the criterion that no direct entrant ought to be
recruited who was 'not capable of rising to the rank of Assistant
Secretary at least', researches showed that the Service had selected
too many comparative failures in its competitions between 1905–
1939. Whether they had entered by the pre-First World War open
competition, the post 1918 Reconstruction competitions, or the
inter-war system, an average of $13\frac{1}{2}$ per cent of the direct entrants
of each group had failed to rise above the rank of Principal. The
Commissioners came to believe that a more sophisticated method
of personnel selection could reduce the rate of failures 'perhaps to

---

[1] Temporary Civil Servant, 'Government Administration and Efficiency', in *Political Quarterly* (1944) p. 100. The writer convincingly
argued: 'I think it is a mistake to suppose that recruitment to the Civil
Service should take place exclusively at the age of 21, 22 or 23. The
Service needs a variety of experience, and there is no reason why it should
be deprived completely of the services of men who have proved themselves to be good at administration and few men have done that at 22'
(p. 99).

as low as 5%'.[1] The Reconstruction period that immediately followed the war proved to be a useful time for experiment. As the ex-service candidates had all had their education interrupted to some extent, the inter-war method of entry was inappropriate, and the Barlow Committee of 1944 recommended a competition along the lines of that used after the First World War, although without the rather arbitrary initial sifting of candidatures.[2] The Commissioners introduced into the selection process a stage consisting of a series of tests and interviews along the lines that had been used by the War Office to select army officers during the war.[3] When normal open competitions for the Administrative Class were resumed in 1948, besides an improved version of the inter-war competition, which was called Method I, the Commissioners introduced a modified version of the Reconstruction system, which they called Method II.[4] The Commissioners also

[1] *Ninth Report from the Select Committee on Estimates* (1947–8) *Evidence*, question 1858. The First Civil Service Commissioner, Sir Perceval Waterfield, observed: 'People who fail to rise above the rank of Principal ought not to have been recruited. One ought to be able to devise a technique which will exclude those people altogether' (question 1749).

[2] National Whitley Council, *Recruitment to Established Posts in the Civil Service during the Reconstruction Period* (chairman: J. A. Barlow) 1944. This report assigned three-quarters of the administrative vacancies in that period to ex-servicemen (para. 24), and outlined a possible scheme (para. 14). At the request of the Civil Service Commissioners, the committee referred to 'the possibility of introducing modern methods of selection, on the lines, for example, of the technique developed during the War by the Army through the War Office Selection Boards' (Civil Service Commissioners, *Memorandum on the use of the C.S.S.B. in the Reconstruction Competition*, 1951, para. 10).

[3] Sir Perceval Waterfield deserves the credit for introducing this innovation into Civil Service recruitment procedure, having adopted it 'after having visited half a dozen of the War Office Selection Boards, and reached the general conclusion that there was something we could adopt to our own purposes' (*Ninth Report from the Select Committee on Estimates*, 1947–8, *Evidence*, question 1861). The Civil Service Commissioners described how the Reconstruction Competition developed in their *Memorandum on the use of C.S.S.B. in the Reconstruction Competition* (1951) paras 13–17.

[4] After stating that candidates for Assistant Principal vacancies had to be at least twenty but under twenty-eight on the 1 August of the year in which they competed, the Civil Service Commissioners wrote about

(*footnote 4, page 85, continued*)

the means of direct entry to the Administrative Class in 1967: 'There are two distinct methods of selection, though the qualifying examination is the same for both, with a somewhat lower qualifying mark for Method I than for Method II. The examination consists of three papers: Essay, an English paper, and a General Paper. For Method II, which now produces about three-quarters of the successful candidates, the qualifying examination may be taken in London and some other large towns in January, April, or September. Candidates who reach the qualifying standard in the January examination are invited between February and May to attend the Civil Service Selection Board, where they have tests over two and a half successive days. This Board assesses the suitability of candidates . . . and recommends which candidates shall appear before the Final Selection Board. The Civil Service Selection Board stage for candidates who qualify at the April or September examination comes during the early summer and autumn. The Final Selection Board decides, in the light of the candidates' records, their performance in the earlier stages of the competition, and the Board's own judgement at interview, which candidates are to be declared successful. Candidates are normally told their results within three days of their final interviews.' Candidates applying by Method I 'may take the qualifying examination, held in London and some other large towns, in January or April. Those who qualify are called to interview in London between May and July, and also take written papers in optional subjects chosen from a list covering the main courses at Universities. This examination is held in London and other University towns in the first three weeks of July. In this Method the order of merit is determined by the total of the marks awarded for the interview and the optional subjects.' As regards academic qualifications, for Method II all candidates (except certain regular members of H.M. Forces and members of H.M. Overseas Civil Service) must have, or obtain in the year of entry, a University or C.N.A.A. degree or a Diploma in Technology: this must either (i) be a degree or diploma with first or second class honours, or (ii) a degree or diploma with third class honours, together with a further degree awarded after postgraduate study or research. For Method I no special qualifications are stipulated, but candidates 'would normally need to be of at least second class honours standard to have a reasonable chance of success'. Candidates who already have a first class honours degree (or Diploma in Technology), or a second class honours degree and a further degree awarded after postgraduate study or research, may apply at any time, and are normally exempted from the qualifying examination for Method II. Candidates with first class honours applying by Method I may be granted exemption from the optional papers if they obtain a high total of marks for the qualifying examination and the interview. Candidates may enter for the Administrative Class competition by either or both methods, but they may not take Method II more than once in a calendar year (Civil Service Commissioners, *Civil Service Posts for Graduates*, 1967, pp. 88–99). Method II, therefore, consists of three stages at each of which a candidate may be

remodelled the Final Selection or Interview Board compared with its much criticised pre-war predecessor. The First Civil Service Commissioner was still the Chairman, but on the board, which was now usually eight or nine strong, continuity of experience was also provided by regularly invited retired senior Civil Servants, normally three or four in number, and one woman member. The current user interest was represented by an invited serving Establishment Officer, while the remaining members were chosen in an attempt to represent the interests of the universities and the public. Three panels were created consisting respectively of university representatives and those of business and industry and the trade unions: the Commissioners tried to arrange that one representative of each panel was always present. The interview they helped to conduct usually lasted from forty-five to sixty minutes.[1]

The post-war Administrative Class recruitment record has been a mixed one. The Commissioners, now faced with strong competition at this level from an expanding academic profession and also from industry and commerce,[2] failed after 1953 in their primary

---

(*footnote 4, page 85, continued*)
eliminated. The first stage is a non-academic written qualifying examination; the second is a series of tests and interviews at the Civil Service Selection Board; and the third stage is an appearance before the Final Selection Board, which determines the result. 'Typically, some 40 per cent of those who sit any qualifying examination go to C.S.S.B., and of these about two-thirds to three-quarters go to the Final Board' (ibid. p. 121). Between 1948–57, Method I had the majority of the vacancies assigned to it, but since then it has rapidly become the less important means of entry. In 1963 the two methods of entry were brought closer together by a modification of Method I. An initial qualifying examination, identical with that for Method II, was introduced, and candidates who did not qualify in this were not allowed to sit the academic papers or attend the interview, the aggregate marks for which decides the final order of merit. The Interview Board is exactly the same in composition as Method II's Final Selection Board, and the interview lasts for a similar length of time (*97th Report of the Civil Service Commissioners*, p. 1).

[1] *84th Report of the Civil Service Commissioners*, section XIV, paras 8–11.

[2] One of the reasons why the Commissioners introduced Method II was because: 'With the increasing tendency of business firms to offer attractive jobs to University graduates, the Civil Service seemed likely to lose ground in competition with the business world if the Commissioners

aim of filling the Assistant Principal vacancies notified to them.[1]
Nevertheless, they could point to the apparent success of Method
II, without the introduction of which the overall recruitment
position might have been much worse. Method II proved to be
more attractive to candidates than Method I and, to judge from
departmental gradings of performance, it also produced fewer
failures in subsequent service.[2] Taking such gradings with the
probation statistics, the recruitment process as a whole produced
remarkably few failures,[3] although, as some Permanent Secretaries
were not slow to point out to the Priestley Commission, it did not
seem to produce enough potentially outstanding administrators.[4]
Reading the evidence of those leading Civil Servants, however,
one really wonders if the recruitment machinery, whatever the
improvements in its formal efficiency, was yet orientated towards
the needs of the Positive State. The type of person looked for was
still much the same as in the days of Leathes and Meiklejohn. The
departments kept asking the Commissioners for 'one or two more
people who we can put into a Minister's private office fairly soon'.

should continue to insist on all their candidates taking, in addition to their
degree examination, an arduous and exhausting series of written papers,
the result of which could not be known until the early autumn, while
their rivals were content with a much simpler method of selection, the
result of which would be known to the candidate within a few days'
(The Civil Service Commissioners, *Memorandum on the use of the C.S.S.B.
in the Reconstruction Competition*, 1951, para. 2). The competition from
the expanding academic profession has, however, proved to be the
severer (*Priestley Evidence*, question 314; *Sixth Report from the Select
Committee on Estimates*, 1964–5, *Evidence*, pp. 22–3).

[1] Appendix II, Table 1.

[2] *Sixth Report from the Select Committee on Estimates* (1964–5), *Evidence*, Memorandum by the Civil Service Commissioners, pp. 26–8. Appendix II, Tables 2 and 3.

[3] Ibid. The Commissioners concluded (para. 17, p. 28): 'The indications, judging both by the small number of probation failures and by departmental gradings of performance, are that the general standard of entrants has given satisfaction to departments.'

[4] For example, Sir Harold Emmerson (questions 2923–4), Sir Henry Hancock (3635, 3629–30), Sir John Maud (3948 and 4003), and Sir Godfrey Ince (3733). 'Dazzlers', apparently, were people who 'if they had gone into business or academic work they would have gone very near to the top' (Maud, 3948), and presumably showed such qualities very early; 'flyers', one assumes, are thought to be of comparable ability.

The Commissioners were not usually able to oblige because of a shortage of 'really outstanding candidates': 'outstanding' in this context referred to candidates who showed 'already in their early twenties just the right combination of intellectual and personal qualities for administrative work in the Civil Service. "General purpose all-rounders" might be a better description.'[1] To continue to make the all-rounder the ideal administrator instead of the professional manager was to invite much the same type of recruit as before and to deter other possible entrants. The recruitment net needed to be cast much wider than before, but instead, the typical Administrative Class recruit remained the man with a good arts degree from either Oxford or Cambridge, almost always drawn from a middle class, often upper-middle class, background. Before suggesting what either can or ought to be done about this, a brief review of the major features of the Administrative Class recruitment record is called for.

As the First Division Association, the Administrative Class's 'trade union', told the Priestley Commission: 'Before the War there were always more successful candidates with First Class Honours than others, but since 1948 there have been fewer.'[2] As there had also been a decline in the proportion of Firsts among the ranks of the successful candidates during the inter-war period compared with the immediate pre-First World War years,[3] the trend highlighted by the F.D.A. had been evident for some time. Recently available statistics show that about forty per cent of the successful candidates during the period 1948–56 had Firsts and the figure was thirty per cent for the period 1957–63.[4] It was perhaps

[1] *The Civil Service Commissioners' Written Evidence to the Priestley Commission* (1954) para. 22.

[2] *Written Evidence*, para. 8, p. 173.

[3] Tomlin Commission, *Appendix VIII to the Minutes of Evidence*, para. 90: the decline was from an average of eighty-five per cent over the years 1907–10, to sixty per cent in 1925–9. The Civil Service Commissioners attempted to minimise these changes in their evidence (questions 1064 and 1321: *Appendix XVIII to the Minutes of Evidence*, statement 1).

[4] *Sixth Report from the Select Committee on Estimates* (1964–5), p. 27 (para. 10) and p. 30, table C, appendix 11, table 7. All but about eight per cent of the successful candidates in the period 1948–63 obtained either a First, an undivided Second or an Upper Second Class Honours degree.

with this trend in mind that leading administrators bemoaned the lack of 'flyers' and 'dazzlers' among recent entrants. Dr Gladden even concluded that 'the overwhelming increase in the proportion of the Second Class Honours group among the successful candidates', compared with the pre-war period meant that the Administrative Class 'will find it less easy in the future to maintain its predominance over the rest of the Civil Service on the basis of outstanding intellectual brilliance'.[1] The Administrative Class is hardly under any intellectual threat from the present Executive Class, in whose ranks the percentage of graduates of any kind cannot be much more than one per cent, and some of the best members of which are, in any case, creamed off into the Administrative Class through the limited competition and by direct promotion. Both the F.D.A. and Gladden are surely taking the honours divisions rather too seriously, particularly as they are designed to indicate approximately academic ability and not administrative capacity, and it can be said that the trend of post-war administrative recruitment has been away from the evaluation of academic prowess towards an attempt to judge practical potential. In any case, comparisons over time can well be misleading because of the development of the university subjects studied, and because of the widening of the social catchment area of the students themselves, which may have made the university honours schools more competitive than in the past.

Although the apparent comparative shortage of 'flyers' and 'dazzlers' among the young members of the Administrative Class seems to have caused great concern in the ranks of its senior members, it may be doubted if they are particularly worried over the not necessarily unconnected trend of the maintenance of the dominance of the direct entry to the class by Oxford and Cambridge graduates.[2] The general attitude very probably still is, as

---

[1] E. N. Gladden, *Civil Service or Bureaucracy?* (1956) pp. 75–6.

[2] Ever since 1870, Oxford and Cambridge have provided the overwhelming majority of the successes in the Administrative Class open competitions. During the period 1905–14 their share of direct entrants was eighty-two per cent, and it was seventy-eight per cent during the years 1925–37, staying at the same level during the period 1948–56, and actually

the Warden of All Souls told the MacDonnell Commission, that the Oxford or Cambridge training is the best for administrative work because it involves 'contact with men and carrying through smoothly and effectively the business of a department which has social relations with a good many outside bodies and persons'. The life of the older universities, the college life, the competition of colleges, the management of college business, the constant interchange of ideas and conflict of minds in debate which went on there, in his view gave 'the best preparation for public life'.[1] Certainly, the experience of such a background would be a decided advantage in interviews conducted by people who valued it; while the Oxford and Cambridge practice of making their students, whatever their subject, write at least one essay a week is a very useful preparation for Civil Service examinations which have increasingly placed importance on good English.[2] Some, like the Leathes Committee, probably think that the explanation for the continued dominance of the Administrative Class entry by the residential universities is that they attract 'a great proportion of the ablest and best trained students', and: 'If the results of the

---

increasing to eighty-five per cent over the years 1957–63 (*Sixth Report from the Select Committee on Estimates*, 1964–5, *Evidence*, p. 27, para. 8). This latter figure has to be treated with some caution because if the period is subdivided, it can be seen that the worst years for the other universities were those between 1957 and 1960: thereafter, their successes have climbed steadily until in 1963 and 1964 they enjoyed a rather better proportion of successes than in the period between 1948 and 1956 (ibid. question 250). In 1965 'the proportion of successful candidates from Universities other than Oxford and Cambridge increased from 16 per cent in 1964 to 24 per cent' (*99th Report of the Civil Service Commissioners*, p. 4), and this percentage increased to thirty-five per cent in 1966 (*100th Report of the Civil Service Commissioners*, p. 8). Appendix II, Table 5 shows the period 1948–63 in detail.

[1] *MacDonnell Evidence*, questions 4423–4. Although maintaining that he did not regard 'the atmosphere of the older Universities as something exclusively desirable for a man to breathe' (question 4517), Sir William Anson admitted to the commission that he did 'attach a good deal of importance to the influence of the social life and the social atmosphere of the old Universities' (question 4514).

[1] Sir James Grigg, 'The British Civil Service', an essay in Joseph E. McLean (ed.) *The Public Service and University Education* (1949) p. 155. Grigg headed the Administrative Class list in 1913.

competition did not correspond to this fact something would be wrong with the competition.'[1] Such statements need an important qualification, but there is no denying the attractiveness of the open scholarship system in the days before the grants system; while more recently the Robbins Committee's evidence showed that at Oxford and Cambridge in 1961 thirty-nine per cent of the men and fifty-two per cent of the women undergraduates had secured three or more G.C.E. Advanced Level subjects with marks of sixty per cent or better, whereas at other universities only eighteen per cent of the men and fifteen per cent of the women had Advanced Level results of this standard.[2] But, of course, even such impressive statistics do not account for the older English universities securing in the region of four-fifths of open Assistant Principal vacancies in every period since 1905.[3] The particular strength of Oxford and Cambridge, where few would dispute their supremacy, both was and is in such subjects as classics and history and the arts side generally, and it has always been from such sources that most of the Administrative Class candidates and the successes have been drawn. The older universities have always had a larger proportion of students, compared with their rivals who could be classified as male 'general graduates', mainly arts men, meaning that they have taken an Honours course which has not specifically committed them to a particular profession or calling.[4] The male graduates of other universities are far more likely to have taken courses that really constitute professional training; while their arts faculties are more likely to contain much higher proportions of women students, not normally a plentiful source of administrative recruits. Adding in the factor of tradition, that the Oxford and Cambridge graduates perhaps see the

[1] *Leathes Report*, para. 18.

[2] *Sixth Report from the Select Committee on Estimates* (1964–5) *Evidence*, question 246.

[3] Ibid. p. 27 (para. 8).

[4] I arrived at this not particularly original conclusion after reading through the statistics for British universities given in the *Commonwealth Universities Year Book* (1965). Professor W. J. M. Mackenzie in his Memorandum to the Select Committee on Estimates, op. cit. (pp. 130–1, para. 13), stated the career choices facing the graduate with greater clarity.

Administrative Class as their preserve, with the right to be at the centre of things in Whitehall, the dominance of the older English universities appears to be less of a conspiracy than some seem to think.

Yet given the imperfections of the university system, the other universities must produce more 'general graduates' of the required standard than ever considered the Administrative Class as a career. As to why London graduates of this type do not enter, the Secretary of the Appointments Board has argued:

> probably the London student is more worldly than the Oxbridge student. He has to jostle with the rest of us in Tubes and so on and he has an awareness of life which is probably slightly different from that of the Oxbridge student. I think he tends to feel that if he has a good shot at industry and commerce he is the person who will get on and who can rough it with the rest.

The implication is that the London student feels that the Civil Service offers a sheltered monastic career.[1] The apparent sophistication of the London graduate is probably not reflected in the graduates of the civic universities, with their higher proportions of 'first generation' students, and the general distrust among their graduates of the 'corridors of power' and of the capital itself.[2] The Scottish universities have done relatively well in the administrative competition, and Professor Kelsall believes: 'one reason why the Scottish Universities are more successful than the English redbrick candidates is that their particular intonation is not regarded as being equally as damaging as that of candidates from, say, Bradford or Huddersfield. I think this makes quite a difference.'[3] It may well do, but where the Scottish record is much

---

[1] *Sixth Report from the Select Committee on Estimates* (1964–5) *Evidence*, question 508–9.

[2] W. J. M. Mackenzie, op. cit. p. 136. The excellent memoranda submitted by the Acton Society Trust to the Select Committee on Estimates contains a wealth of information about the attitudes of students at the University of Hull towards prospective careers in general and the Administrative Class in particular (ibid. pp. 194–219).

[3] *Sixth Report from the Select Committee on Estimates* (1964–5) *Evidence*, question 399. The record of the Scottish universities is shown in Appendix II, Table 5.

better is in Method I, where written papers predominate and where the social graces, or lack of them, cannot count for so much. However, it is probable that fears of social prejudice and a bias towards Oxford and Cambridge products in the selection machinery, may well deter 'general graduates' of comparable merit in other universities from applying for the Administrative Class.[1]

According to the Civil Service Commissioners, those who pointed 'to the preponderance of Oxford and Cambridge in the lists of successful candidates overlook the fact that members of these Universities are now drawn from a very wide social background'.[2] Many critics do, but the residential universities still draw their students from a much narrower range of social origins than the other universities,[3] and this has naturally been reflected in the social composition of the Administrative Class entry. The great majority of both candidates and successes are drawn from the families of the two leading occupational groups, and in more recent years there has been a further shift towards them. The records of competitors drawn from the lower reaches of the middle class and from all types of working-class home, are depressing, particularly in Method II, where one-half of the successes are drawn from the highest occupational group.[4] It is difficult to say whether or not the present selection processes favour Oxford and Cambridge graduates from upper-middle-class backgrounds. The reliance on written papers in Method I limits the scope

---

[1] Ibid. p. 194 (para. 7).

[2] *95th Report of the Civil Service Commissioners*, p. 3. The Commissioners' additional point that: 'These critics similarly neglect the contribution of London and the Scottish, Welsh and provincial Universities to the Scientific and Professional Classes of the Service' was also valid. But as these classes enjoy considerably less power than the Administrative Class, this neglect was forgivable.

[3] For example, of the male undergraduates entering Oxford and Cambridge in 1961 only thirty per cent had been to a local education authority maintained school compared with seventy-two per cent at other universities; and, while fifty-four per cent of the Oxford and Cambridge entrants had been to independent schools, this was only true of fifteen per cent of the entrants to the other universities (*Report of the Committee on Higher Education*, 1963, p. 80).

[4] *Sixth Report from the Select Committee on Estimates* (1964–5) p. 27 (para. 12): Appendix II, Table 9 refers.

for such bias, although one explanation of the Oxford and Cambridge dominance once put forward was that it was 'possibly due to most of the examiners being appointed from those Universities.'[1] That would open the door to cultural prejudice, despite the competitors' being known in the written papers only by serial numbers; but the examiners in fact seem to be drawn from representative sources.[2] The Method I interview and the central and last stages of Method II provide more obvious opportunities for bias. The well-rounded Oxford and Cambridge graduate seems to have an advantage in Method II with its series of interviews; but the official statistics show that candidates from other universities find the written qualifying examination the most difficult hurdle to negotiate.[3] The possibility of social prejudice in any interview process cannot realistically be ruled out. But, at least, unlike private industry, the Civil Service's recruitment methods are subject to public scrutiny, and there is some obligation to do justice to its Administrative Class candidates. One hopes that a member of recent Final Selection Boards, D. N. Chester, is right in asserting that polish and the social graces are only marginally a help to candidates.[4]

Another subject of continuing comment has been the predominance of classics and history graduates among the Administrative Class direct entrants.[5] Before the First World War, as Sir Stanley Leathes admitted, the Class I examinations were weighted in favour of the subjects studied at the older universities, particularly Greats at Oxford,[6] which the Leathes Committee later described as giving an unequalled 'coherent training', although it

---

[1] 'The Civil Service and its Critics', in *Political Quarterly* (1954) p. 300.

[2] At least, that is my view, having looked at the lists of examiners in successive reports of the Civil Service Commissioners.

[3] Appendix II, Table 10: these figures were supplied by the Civil Service Commissioners.

[4] *Sixth Report from the Select Committee on Estimates* (1964–5) *Evidence*, question 1104.

[5] Ibid. p. 27 (para. 9): Appendix II, Table 6 refers.

[6] *MacDonnell Evidence*, question 570. There can be little doubt, looking at his answers to questions 556 and 559, that Leathes personally regarded the Oxford 'Greats' man as the ideal First Division entrant.

had to be content to share with the classics course at Cambridge the description of 'the widest of University courses'.[1] In 1916, the Civil Service Commissioners said that in their opinion 'such subjects as language, literature and history, are, on the whole and for the most part of young men, the best preparation for the Higher Civil Service'.[2] Such subjects remained greatly favoured in the inter-war competitions, and they are hardly under-valued in the current Method I examination. The First Civil Service Commissioner, however, assured the Priestley Commission that an arts graduate is no longer considered the only satisfactory administrative direct entrant: 'The reverse is the case, but unfortunately the scientists and the engineers do not go in for the Administrative Class.'[3] The official statistics for the period since 1948 certainly bear out that statement, while another unfortunate feature they reveal is that over the period there has been a decline in the number of competitors and successes with degrees in economics and related subjects. Classics and history stand out prominently among the subjects taken by successful candidates since 1948,[4] and Professor Robson wrote in 1964: 'A large proportion of the most senior members of the Service still believe that a good Classics degree – meaning Greats, of course – is the finest preparation for the highest positions.'[5]

Practising administrators have not written a great deal about what is the best pre-entry academic training for administration, although Sisson did not conceal his preference for 'a liberal education' in subjects with as little reference to future duties as possible.[6] Sir James Grigg considered that a mixture of history

[1] *Leathes Report*, para. 18.

[2] The Civil Service Commissioners made the statement in a letter to the Treasury dated 25 July 1916 (*Leathes Report*, para. 8).

[3] *Priestley Evidence*, question 316. Sir Paul Sinker emphasised that he wished that 'more of them would come into the Administrative Class by the ordinary door' (question 318).

[4] Appendix II, Table 6 refers.

[5] William A. Robson, 'The Reform of Government', in *Political Quarterly* (1964) p. 208.

[6] Sisson favoured the recruitment of intelligent young men and women who had had 'a good non-vocational education' (C. H. Sisson, *The Spirit of British Administration*, 1959, p. 34). He made it clear that he

and mathematics was 'very nearly the ideal education in general as well as providing the best preliminary training for the Public Service'. Grigg, who had himself taken an 'unholy alliance' of mathematics and natural sciences, deplored the increased importance attached to law and economics.[1] Sir Henry Self, who had also taken mathematics and science, believed that the classicist was 'extremely good at advising on and reaching decisions on policy but he is less suited for an active department'. Self thought that the mathematician had 'a clear and proper appreciation of the position of an administrator: he works out conclusions and establishes them one by one', whereas the scientist tended 'to get absorbed in marshalling facts and cataloguing situations: I would say he was not good at reaching decisions'.[2] Probably many would agree with the views expressed by Lord Strang in 1964:

> Certainly it would be better if more established Civil Servants had an economic or scientific or technological background. I do not myself share the view that an Arts degree is, in itself, a better qualification for a Civil Servant than any other kind of degree. There has been too much talk about the two cultures. Any well educated man, with the requisite disposition, whatever academic discipline he may have followed, can be made into a skilled professional administrator. It is his education, not his speciality, that matters most.[3]

Another view would be that a liberality of education may not now be possible, and in selecting future administrators it might be best to concentrate on the group of subjects that constitute the most relevant 'general education': in the case of Government, the

---

preferred the British approach to the Continental system of attaching special importance to administrative law and economics, studies of the kind 'supposed, in our time, specially to promote an understanding of the works of government' (ibid. pp. 38–9).

[1] Grigg, op. cit. p. 155.

[2] Sir Henry Self, 'The Responsibility of the Administrator', an essay in A. Dunsire (ed.) *The Making of an Administrator* (1956), pp. 73–4.

[3] House of Lords, *Official Report* (1963–4), vol. 254, cols 607–8.

social sciences. Every administrator should have a grasp of economic and social history, and even Grigg believed that the leading Civil Servant ought to have read sufficient economics to be able to know what a professional economist is talking about.[1] However, given the present state of the market for 'general graduates', direct entrants to the Administrative Class will normally have served their degrees in other disciplines, making it more realistic to look to post-entry training to provide the necessary grounding in the social sciences.

The Administrative Class has therefore failed to greatly widen the number of universities, the range of academic backgrounds and the types of social origins of their direct entrants, and it has been roundly condemned on all these counts by outside critics. Such critics have not, however, found it easy to suggest ways in which the situation they condemn can be improved. Ironically, the development of Method II, the biggest post-war advance in Administrative Class recruiting, has seen candidates drawn from the families of the higher occupational groups doing exceptionally well, and part of the price of progress seems to have been to slow down any tendency towards the democratisation of the direct entry to the Class. Whether this is serious or not, of course, depends upon one's view. Herman Finer's opinion, expressed in 1937, was that if the composition of the Administrative Class included 'the memory of misery, hunger, squalor, bureaucratic oppression, and economic insecurity, perhaps a quality would be added to their work in the highest situations which could not fail to impress the Minister at a loss for a policy or an argument'.[2] In the more prosperous post-war period such sentiments have taken the form of calls for more leading Civil Servants with working-class backgrounds. While expressing general sympathy with such views, one can still observe that commentators who hold them perhaps tend to forget that leading administrators of working-class origins do not always maintain contact with or wish to represent those whom they have left behind in the educational race. By the age at which they reach a position of some influence, their parents

[1] Grigg, op. cit. p. 157.
[2] Herman Finer, *The British Civil Service* (1937) p. 94.

may well be dead, and what is probably their main link with their working-class past is severed.[1] One reason why so few direct entrants to the Administrative Class have been drawn from working-class backgrounds is that, despite all the talk of an educational revolution since 1944, the percentage of male university students whose fathers are manual workers has hardly changed at

[1] Kenneth Robinson, in discussing R. K. Kelsall, *Higher Civil Servants in Britain* (1955), made some interesting observations about Finer's views which he saw as being at least partly endorsed by Kelsall. Robinson argued that men who succeeded in entering the Higher Civil Service 'from much lower social strata may be just as likely to take the view that failure to rise is the result not of faulty organisation of society but of the defects of those who fail. The successful industrialists who rose from the humblest origins in the nineteenth century were not generally supposed to be those with the greatest regard for their work people, as much contemporary fiction shows. And, on the other hand, many of those who have enjoyed some of the advantages of inherited wealth (or even those obtained for them by severe sacrifice on the part of their "middle-class" parents) have been obsessed by a sense of social guilt. There is not really very much reason to suppose that the son of working-class parents, whether he enters the Administrative Class by open competition or promotion, will necessarily have greater regard to the interests of the workers than the child of middle- or upper-class parents' ('Selection and Social Background of the Administrative Class', in *Public Administration*, 1955, pp. 387–8). There is, obviously, something to be said in favour of Mr Robinson's arguments, although one doubts if 'social guilt' is as widespread among those who enjoy, or have enjoyed, social and educational privilege as the relevant sentence of Mr Robinson's comments suggests. As to the manner in which nineteenth-century industrialists drawn from the working class treated their employees, one can say that there were many attacks upon this kind of entrepreneurial behaviour in that century and that it is difficult to believe either that even most of such behaviour can be attributed to capitalists 'who rose from the humblest origins' or that many such industrialists did not treat their workers in an enlightened manner. Finer's general argument, to which Mr Robinson objected, was that if a substantial majority instead of a small minority of leading administrators had been drawn from the working classes, then the policies advocated by those administrators would be different because some of their formative years would have been spent in a different environment – the environment of the majority of the population. An Administrative Class whose direct entrants particularly were mainly drawn from working-class backgrounds would not necessarily have warm regard for those remaining in 'much lower social strata', but it is difficult to believe that, generally, they would not have a better understanding of working-class problems.

all since before the war.[1] It is probable that middle-class parents, allegedly suffering under the yoke of the Welfare State, have been more determined to ensure that their children take full advantage of wider educational opportunities than the less sophisticated parents farther down the social scale. Ideally, one would like to see an Administrative Class 'broadly representative of the various social and economic classes of the community',[2] but such a development is not likely until more working-class parents come to demand a better and longer education for their children.[3]

[1] The Robbins Committee wrote: 'In terms of father's occupation, almost three quarters (71%) of undergraduates in 1961–2 came from families of non-manual workers. Among these, most (59%) came from the professional and managerial group (18% from higher professional and 41% from other professional and managerial), and the remainder (12%) were the children of clerical workers. A quarter of undergraduates came from the families of manual workers: most (18%) coming from the families of skilled manual workers and few from semi-skilled (6%) and unskilled (1%) backgrounds. A higher proportion of women students (74%) than men students (69%) came from middle-class homes.' The committee noted: 'There was little change between 1928–47 and 1961 in the proportions of students at University coming from working-class backgrounds, in spite of the fact that the number of students at University had more than doubled during this period. In the case of women the proportion had risen from 13% in 1928–47 to 23% in 1961, but as regards men, there was little evidence of any change. Over this period, there seems to have been no significant change in the proportion of all members in the relevant age group having fathers in manual occupations' (*Appendix 2B to the Report of the Committee on Higher Education*, 1963, paras 14–15). The following books were also consulted about this subject: Jean Floud, A. H. Halsey and F. M. Martin, *Social Class and Educational Opportunity* (1957); A. H. Halsey, Jean Floud and C. A. Anderson, *Education, Economy and Society* (1961); Brian Jackson and Dennis Marsden, *Education and the Working Class* (1962); Peter Marris, *The Experience of Higher Education* (1964); and J. W. B. Douglas, *The Home and the School* (1964).

[2] William A. Robson, 'Bureaucracy and Democracy', an essay published in his collection, *The Civil Service in Britain and France* (1956) p. 14.

[3] Such a development was actually envisaged by Norman Macrae, *Sunshades in October* (1963). He argued: 'Nobody could possibly have foreseen that the growth in living standards in Britain, started off during Mr Butler's Chancellorship of 1952–55, would lead to the great and happy transformation of society which they in fact effected. Nobody can see where the next spurt will lead to. My guess is that the things which will be in high income elasticity of demand in most working-class homes will often be immensely desirable social things, like a better and longer education for their children' (p. 97). Macrae's

It is a reasonable forecast that never again will the Civil Service Commissioners enjoy the same situation as prevailed in the Edinburgh of Sir John Anderson's student days when it was regarded 'virtually as a *sine qua non* that its best scholars should take the Civil Service examination. Any boy considered of appropriate calibre for such a calling underwent very considerable pressure to do so from the University authorities, from his parents, and from his fellow students.'[1] Before the war, the Service 'did not attempt to go into the world to do any recruiting propaganda', and the Commissioners had been able to say to candidates: 'If you want to get into the Civil Service this is the way to do it, and if you like to come along we will examine you, otherwise we are not interested.'[2] In the post-war years, the Commissioners have had to enter the graduate market and sell their goods like anyone else.[3] The introduction of Method II, where the result can be declared before graduation, may have helped to prevent the Administrative Class's recruitment position from becoming worse.[4] The Commissioners have also moved away from the restrictive age limits

optimism is to be admired, and one hopes, justified: but there is obviously a difference between the acquisition of tangible consumer durables, and something intangible like the ensuring of maximum educational opportunities. The working class seem to have been slow to appreciate the relationship between educational opportunities and earning power. The trend towards earlier marriage, which is likely to be intensified by the balance against men in the marriage market, is not likely to encourage working-class children to put off the day when they actually start earning.

[1] Sir John Wheeler-Bennett, *John Anderson, Viscount Waverley* (1962) p. 15.

[2] *Ninth Report from the Select Committee on Estimates* (1947–8) *Evidence*, question 1706.

[3] *95th Report of the Civil Service Commissioners*, p. 1.

[4] This cannot, of course, be proved because there is no way of knowing how successful or otherwise using Method I as the sole means of entry would have been; but the statistics, particularly over the last decade when the restrictions upon the number of places assigned to Method II were removed, suggest that the introduction of Method II may well have helped Administrative Class recruitment. As to recent developments in Method II, there was a suggestion in 1965 that the Civil Service Commission was 'about to start continuous recruitment of Assistant Principals' (*Sixth Report from the Select Committee on Estimates*, 1964–5, p. 232). But what the Commissioners actually did decide to do was 'to increase the number of opportunities of entry during the year to the

imposed on candidates in the past, and the upper-age limit has now been raised from twenty-four to twenty-eight,[1] a change which has attracted more candidates with higher degrees.[2] The

---

Administrative Class by holding a supplementary Method II competition in September'. This competition was reasonably successful, and it was retained for 1966 (*99th Report of the Civil Service Commissioners*, p. 4). In 1966: 'For the first time Method II recruitment to the Administrative Class took place at three periods in the year, with a qualifying examination in January, April and September' (*100th Report of the Civil Service Commissioners*, pp. 8–9). These arrangements were maintained in 1967 (Civil Service Commission, *Administrative Group of Appointments*, 1967, pp. 1–2).

[1] This change was actually made in 1961 (*95th Report of the Civil Service Commissioners*, p. 2). Since 1956 there had been signs of a movement away from the traditional restrictive age limits. In the summer of that year, in order to fill vacancies left over from the 1955 open competition, a supplementary competition was held for which 'candidates had to be up to 2 years above the normal competition age limits, and to have a First Class Honours degree'. The aim of the competition was to offer a means of entry into the Administrative Class to people 'who had stayed on at Universities to do research or taken up other employment'. There was no written examination; short-listed applicants were given tests at the C.S.S.B. before going on to the Final Selection Board. All five successful candidates had been engaged in research or university teaching since graduation (*91st Report*, para. 13). Similar competitions were held in 1957 and 1959 (*92nd Report*, para. 16; *94th Report*, para. 15).

[2] The First Civil Service Commissioner, Sir George Abell, told the Select Committee on Estimates in 1965: 'The age limit for the Administrative Class is 28 and this broadens the opportunities for recruiting postgraduates.' Sir George said that the Commissioners 'have been active in trying to attract the attention of postgraduates but this is quite difficult'. He did, however, say that 'this is quite a promising field and we are getting a number of candidates from it' (*Sixth Report from the Select Committee on Estimates*, 1964–5, *Evidence*, question 238). In fact a feature of the 1965 Administrative Class results was 'the increase in the number of successful candidates who were postgraduate students'. There were sixty-six postgraduate applicants and seventeen successes, compared with forty-five applications and eleven successes in 1964; eight of the 1965 successes were from universities other than Oxford and Cambridge (*99th Report of the Civil Service Commissioners*, p. 4). In 1966 'the provision for exempting candidates with first class honours degrees from the qualifying examination in Method II was extended to those with second class honours degrees plus a higher degree. It is hoped that this concession will attract more of the larger number of students who now pursue postgraduate studies or research' (*100th Report of the Civil Service Commissioners*, p. 9).

Commissioners have also introduced as an experiment the despatch of individual letters to 'all new first class honours graduates, drawing their attention to the opportunities open to them in the Administrative Class', the initial response to which seems to have been reasonably promising.[1] Three times a year Whitehall visits are arranged by the Treasury which 'enable students to gain a view at first-hand of the machinery of Government and of the work of administrators in various departments', and which the Commissioners consider to be 'a valuable aid to recruiting'.[2] With, in their opinion, some measure of success, the Commissioners have attempted to improve their contacts with senior members of the teaching staffs of universities other than Oxford and Cambridge, in the hope that such academic staff will make aware to students, whom they consider to be 'promising material for the Civil Service', the opportunities which 'a career in the Government Service affords'.[3] Another development aimed at improving Administrative Class recruitment has been the creation by the Commissioners of a system of Liaison Officers, that is 'young serving members of the Class who maintain touch with their University or, in the case of Oxford, Cambridge and London, their particular College, and thereby help to foster an interest in the Service among undergraduates'.[4] However, the Liaison Officers are 'people up to their eyes in work in the departments', and the Commission can only hope to 'get hold of them for two or three days a year'.[5] In 1965, the Commissioners felt the need to strengthen the Liaison Officers scheme by appointing two Principals, one of whom concentrates on 'improving the response from Universities other than Oxford and Cambridge by fostering

[1] This experiment was begun in 1965 and the Civil Service Commissioners later commented: 'This letter produced some additional candidatures for the supplementary Method II competition in September; in addition, a number of those who responded expressed interest in the possibility of entry into the Service after completing their postgraduate work' (*99th Report of the Civil Service Commissioners*, p. 3).

[2] *99th Report of the Civil Service Commissioners*, p. 2.

[3] *100th Report of the Civil Service Commissioners*, pp. 7–8.

[4] *98th Report of the Civil Service Commissioners*, p. 4.

[5] *Sixth Report from the Select Committee of Estimates* (1964–5) *Evidence*, question 953.

contacts with the academic staff and the Appointments Boards'. In this work he is helped by the other Principal, who is engaged on duties 'connected with Administrative Class recruitment generally', while in addition being responsible for 'coordinating the work of Liaison Officers with individual colleges at Oxford and Cambridge'.[1] Although the Liaison Officers scheme is being persisted with, their tasks should really be taken over by full-time staff. The appointment of the two Principals may represent the belated beginnings of a move in this direction.

There have been temptations to tinker further with the present recruitment process and to hope that all will come right in the end, but it can be doubted if the major problems will be solved while retaining the present structure of the generalist side of the Service. Somehow the Service must attract more graduates. It will not do this without offering more than entry to the present Executive Class – which is the present entry which most graduates have to expect, allowing for the Special Departmental Classes.[2] The aim must be to attract the graduates who are not at present considered appropriate for the Administrative Class and who do not consider

[1] *99th Report of the Civil Service Commissioners*, p. 2.

[2] The Special Departmental Classes are: H.M. Inspectors of Taxes in Inland Revenue Department; the Cadet Grade in the Ministry of Labour; Assistant Postal Controllers in the Post Office. In 1965, it was hoped to fill about sixty, ten and fifteen posts respectively by the joint competition (Civil Service Commissioners, *Administrative Group of Open Competitions*, 1965, pp. 2 and 14–19). In 1965, however, recruitment to the Special Departmental Classes through competitions associated with those for the Administrative Class was 'still well below the needs of the departments concerned. The separate competition (without written examination) for posts of Inspector of Taxes gave better results, and steps have been taken to offer posts in the Ministry of Labour and the Post Office under similar arrangements' (*99th Report of the Civil Service Commissioners*, p. 5). Although Inspectors of Taxes continued to be recruited through the Administrative Group competition, since 1961 what was initially described as 'a supplementary form of semi-continuous competition' has been held for their recruitment in which 'There is no written examination; selection is based on tests and interviews at the Civil Service Selection Board and an interview before the Final Selection Board' (*95th Report*, p. 6). This continuous competition has been particularly successful and Ministry of Labour Cadets and Assistant Postal Controllers in the Post Office are now wholly recruited by this type of competition (*100th Report*, pp. 9–10).

the Executive Class appropriate for them. This must require the creation of an entry from which all the administrative jobs required to be performed by graduates can be filled. Many of such jobs which seem to the outsider scarcely distinguishable in type and responsibility, may at present be done in the one case by a member of the Administrative Class and in the other by a member of the Executive Class. The obvious solution is a structure which combines at least these two classes. This subject will be discussed in chapters 4 and 6, but for the present purposes it must be remarked that, to be worthwhile, the merged class will have to be more specialised than at present, certainly as regards broad groupings of departmental activities, for example, the social services; while there will also have to be specialisation of functions within these groupings, for example, Establishments work: although there will have to be a residue of the same type of administrators, the size of which will vary between departments, the general ideal should become the professional manager, not the all-rounder. The creation of a merged Executive–Administrative Class along these lines will obviously have implications for the direct-entry recruitment arrangements of the generalist side of the Service. The recruitment system on this side of the Service has failed to adjust itself to university expansion. There is a pool of ability to be tapped, but as has been said it can be doubted if the Civil Service Commissioners will be able to exploit it sufficiently unless all graduates enter the Service upon the same terms. All graduate entrants could come in at, say, the level of the present Executive Officer grade, receiving the same, and one hopes a greatly improved, amount and quality of post-entry training, and being assigned to specialised careers according to their interests and aptitudes. The decision about who would be most likely to fill the highest posts in the Service would become a function of personnel management within it, and not that of a selection process whose real efficiency from that standpoint must always be in doubt, not only because the Civil Service Commissioners 'do not follow up the careers of unsuccessful candidates',[1] but also because of the inherent difficulty of attempting to identify among

[1] *Priestley Evidence*, question 327.

candidates usually in their early twenties 'the pool from which the
next generation's Permanent Secretaries will be drawn'.[1]

The change in orientation away from the 'amateur' and the end
of the 'exclusiveness' of the Administrative Class might well
encourage more general graduates from universities other than
Oxford and Cambridge. If so, there would be some chance of
eventually changing the social balance at the top of the Service, and
of widening the range of university subjects normally studied by
those successful in the competitions. With more specialised careers
to offer, the Commissioners might find it easier to attract a broader
field of graduates than at present, because those graduates will be
able to see more clearly how their degrees will be directly useful
to them. For example, Social Administration graduates might
well be attracted to a career in the Ministry of Health or the Ministry of Social Security helping to administer the social services,[2]
but not the prospect perhaps of being placed somewhere less con-
genial and less obviously relevant to their interests. While not
neglecting the older provincial universities, the Commissioners
must make a special effort to attract the better graduates of the
newer universities where traditions will not yet have hardened.
The graduate recruitment net must be thrown wider because even
if it was desirable to maintain the Administrative Class as a separate
élite, those graduates who are thought to be attracted by such
status – by what Sir Laurence Helsby has called the 'mere fact
that it is difficult to get in'[3] – since at least 1953 have not been

[1] *Evidence presented by the Confederation of British Industry to the
Fulton Committee on the Civil Service* (1966) para. 14.

[2] The representatives of the University of Hull actually gave this
example in their evidence to the Select Committee on Estimates in
1965 (*Sixth Report*, 1964–5, *Evidence*, question 1027).

[3] *Sixth Report from the Select Committee on Estimates* (1964–5) *Evidence*,
question 829. It is interesting to note that in his evidence to the Priestley
Commission, Sir Paul Sinker, the then First Civil Service Commissioner,
after pointing to the competition for graduates, from industry and
academic life particularly, observed: 'Other people say that because the
Administrative Class has increased in size and more are taken in, it has
perhaps lost some of the prestige it used to carry. It used to be rather an
achievement to get into the Home Civil Service Administrative Class,
and it may be that it is less so than it was before the War' (*Priestley
Evidence*, question 314). Sir Laurence Helsby may be right in suggesting

coming forward in sufficient numbers to sustain that *élite*. It is to be hoped, however, that the sort of new structure outlined above would still prove attractive to the leading Oxford and Cambridge graduates. The firm guarantee of an Assistant Secretary post in the early forties could not be held out, but the Commissioners could still point to the excellent opportunities generally available at the top of the Service, and the prospect of more competition for them ought not to deter the right type of graduate.

Under the kind of changed régime discussed above, Method II would probably become even more dominant than at present. Indeed, despite its advantage of providing an avenue of entry with limited opportunities for social bias, Method I's eventual retention must now be in doubt, because the most recently available statistics clearly indicate that its appeal to candidates continues to decline.[1] While Method I is retained, the weighting accorded to the social sciences in the written part of this Method needs much improvement. The qualifying examinations now common to both Methods need revising. Too often the essays are of the 'What is truth?' variety, when they could well be more specific, dealing with such subjects as Britain's economic problems or the role of science and technology in modern society, subjects upon which 'every young man should have something to say'.[2] Method II's C.S.S.B. tests would have to be geared to more

---

that the 'exclusiveness' of the Administrative Class attracts certain graduates: on the other hand, it may repel others of comparable ability who may well be more numerous.

[1] The Civil Service Commissioners commented about the 1966 results: 'The number successful by Method II rose and the slight falling-off in the total of candidates found suitable was due to a further and sharp decline in the number of candidates competing by Method I, with only 16 successful candidates by this Method compared with 28 in 1965. The trend in favour of Method II is now very strong indeed. In the January 1966 qualifying examination 366 candidates sat for Method II only, no more than 31 for Method I only, and 143 for both Methods; in the April qualifying examination only 20 candidates sat for Method I only. Only 63 candidates took the optional academic papers in Method I in July – the lowest number in the long history of this examination' (*100th Report*, p. 9).

[2] The phrase is, of course, that of the Leathes Committee (*Report*, para. 29).

specialised careers, looking for the professional manager by probing for job aptitudes rather than working on the erroneous assumption that administrative work is homogeneous. It seems only a matter of time before the Commissioners will either have to insist upon candidates having had a relevant pre-entry training, or, at the very least, making clear their preference for such an academic background. Such a development, and indeed many of the other changes suggested above, need not necessarily be dependent upon the abolition of the separate status of the Administrative Class, although it can be doubted if the required change in attitudes can be achieved without reforms on that scale.

There have been welcome recent signs of rethinking about recruitment to the Administrative Class. Since 1959 there have been arrangements for outside recruitment to the Principal grade, usually from ex-members of the Armed Forces or Overseas Civil Service.[1] In 1964 it was announced that, in future, three Assistant Secretaries between the ages of forty and forty-five were to be recruited annually from candidates with specialised experience not normally available within the Service. A further development was that up to six Principals a year were to be recruited between the ages of thirty and thirty-five from people who have held responsible posts in industry and commerce, or at a university, or in some professional field: candidates with a knowledge of economic, industrial, commercial or financial matters, or a scientific or a technological education were placed at an advantage.[2] The early results of these competitions have been excellent, and further

[1] These competitions were 'designed to make up for the shortfall of acceptable Assistant Principal candidates in recent years and to provide opportunities for members of H.M. Overseas Civil Service and H.M. Forces whose careers had been cut short by changes in overseas territories or in defence requirements'. The competitions for 1959 and 1960 'were restricted to men and women in these categories', but that of 1961 was 'also open to others'. This latter condition was not applied to the 1962 and 1963 competitions and one of the two competitions held in 1964 (*Civil Service Commisioners, 94th Report*, para. 16; *95th Report*, p. 4; *96th Report*, p. 9; *97th Report*, p. 9; *98th Report*, p. 11). The competitions were conducted on the same basis as Method II.

[2] *Sixth Report from the Select Committee on Estimates* (1964–5) *Evidence*, appendix 13, p. 262.

arrangements have since been made for substantial outside recruitment to permanent posts in the Principal grade.[1] In 1966, these took the form of two separate competitions: one having age limits of thirty to thirty-six, and the other, which had more vacancies allotted to it, having age limits of thirty-six to fifty-two.[2] These measures were, however, thought unlikely to 'make good the immediate shortage' of Principals, and it was announced in 1965 that, in addition, 'a number of industrial and commercial organisations and the Universities have been asked to consider releasing able and adaptable people for temporary employment in the Civil Service. Those chosen will mostly be aged between 30 and 40 and they will serve as temporary Principals for about two

[1] The Civil Service Commissioners wrote in 1965: 'Three Assistant Secretary posts were offered during the year in accordance with the Government policy of bringing into the Service at this level people with specialised experience. There was a good field of applications, and appointments were made to the Ministry of Housing and Local Government, the Post Office, and the Ministry of Technology.' The Commissioners said: 'there was a serious shortage of Principals, partly because of earlier recruitment deficiencies at Assistant Principal level, partly because of the demands placed on Government departments and the creation of new departments; it was also felt necessary to bring outside experience into the Civil Service at this level. To meet this situation two open competitions were held for Principal posts covering together an age range of 30–52. The competitions attracted a very large number of candidates: the final yield was just under 70. Those successful have been drawn from a wide range of occupations including industry, journalism, University teaching, educational administration and scientific research, as well as the Armed Forces and the Overseas Civil Service. It may be of interest to note that, out of some 50 graduates amongst the candidates appointed or to be appointed, 26 were from Universities other than Oxford and Cambridge; 9 graduates had read economic or commercial subjects at University and 13 held degrees in scientific or technological subjects.' (*99th Report*, p. 4.)

[2] The Civil Service Commissioners wrote in 1966: 'In accordance with Government policy to bring into the Service people with valuable experience in other fields and to help make good the general shortage of Principals ten people between the ages of 30 and 36, forty-one between the ages of 36 and 52, were recruited as Principals. The latter competition, which was open also to members of the Forces and Overseas Civil Service, attracted over 1,600 applicants, of whom 220 were invited to tests and interview at the Civil Service Selection Board' (*100th Report*, p. 9).

years.'[1] These temporary entrants will probably bring 'valuable experience' into the Civil Service, but they will normally need the two years they are to be employed to secure sufficient experience of the environment of central Government to be successful Principals. An even greater reliance on permanent recruitment at Principal level, at least for the next few years of serious shortage would seem wiser than temporary secondments of this nature The question of late-entry recruitment at the higher levels of the Service was raised when in 1964 the then newly created Department of Economic Affairs recruited men from the private sector to highly-placed new posts as Chief Industrial Adviser and Industrial Adviser.[2] These posts were, however, not seen as normal Civil Service jobs, but as special jobs for the successful performance of which considerable experience of private industry was essential. Provided that practice has shown that such experience was imperative, and that the holders of the jobs concerned have not come to act as would ordinary Civil Servants, these appointments seem appropriate. Although it is too soon to comment fully upon recent developments, it can be said that a closed Administrative Class is inappropriate in the era of the Positive State, and that these developments show that this has been recognised as a question.

Wider changes in the structure of the generalist side of the Service could well lead to an improvement in the quantity and quality of its direct entrants. But, whatever advances either continue to be made or are in prospect with regard to direct-entry recruitment, little can be achieved without parallel progress in the sphere of post-entry training: until very recently, as will be seen, the Civil Service's record in that sphere was mediocre.

[1] House of Commons, *Official Report* (1964–5) vol. 717, written answers for 30 July 1965, cols 192–3.

[2] House of Commons, *Official Report* (1964–5) vol. 705, written answers for 26 January 1965, col. 141.

CHAPTER THREE

The Post-Entry Training
of the Administrative Class

I THE 'DO-IT-YOURSELF' CODE

IN view of the non-vocational nature of the university studies normally taken by its direct entrants, it might have been thought that the Administrative Class would place great emphasis on formal post-entry training for its Assistant Principals, and that it would also make provision for such training for higher administration later on in such entrants' careers. But, although the Administrative Class had become a largely self-contained and self-governing profession by 1920, the traditional outlook in its ranks towards formal post-entry training has always been unfavourable, and has remained so until very recently, despite the increased, and increasing, complexity of the duties assigned to the class. This attitude was eloquently summarised by Sir Stanley Leathes when he said in 1923:

> Indeed I was never trained myself as a Public Servant, except for a brief period of six weeks. I dropped my pilot as soon as I was allowed to do so, and learned my job by doing it. My training from that point has been continued on the Montessori system. I have played with my bricks on the floor until I believe that I partly understood their nature and properties. As for the qualifications necessary and desirable for a Civil Servant I should quote the time-honoured maxim '*non multa sed multum*', and bid him learn all about something rather than a little about many things. But my own practice throughout life has been exactly the opposite: my own training has been all that it should not have been; it happens to suit not only my temperament but my office; but I am a warning, by no means an example; and I should never preach my heresies.[2]

---

[1] Sir Stanley Leathes, 'The Qualifications, Recruitment, and Training of Public Servants', in *Public Administration* (1923) p. 343.

He was actually preaching the accepted doctrine about post-entry training, and as Leathes had reached the heights of Deputy Secretary, his attitude towards training would be more likely to be taken as an example than as a warning by an aspiring Assistant Principal.

Although the Reorganisation Committee had described the Assistant Principal as a training or cadet grade, only five of the twenty-one departments which employed that grade in the inter-war years had a formal training programme, and even in their case there was little attempt to do very much more than job rotation.[1] The experiences of Sir Maurice Dean were probably typical: 'I was sat down in a hideously ugly room with three or four colleagues, handed a bunch of files and told to get on with it. Such questions as I produced were answered, correctly or otherwise, by

---

[1] The exceptions were the Ministries of Health and of Labour, the Colonial and Dominions Office and the Post Office: only in the latter case does the training appear to have been taken sufficiently seriously (Harvey Walker, *Training Public Employees in Great Britain*, 1935, pp. 10–12). The Institute of Public Administration sponsored discussions about post-entry training in the Public Services in 1926, 1929, 1932 and 1938; and the report of one of its research groups, 'Post-Entry Training and Education in the Public Services', in *Public Administration* (1933) pp. 37–57, was a useful description and discussion of Civil Service training at that time. Some interesting proposals for reform were made by Sir Henry Bunbury, 'Problems of Training for the Public Service: The Civil Service', in *Public Administration* (1938). For the Administrative Class and 'selected members of other grades', Sir Henry envisaged 'a year of specialised training immediately after entry', possibly this could 'with some advantage be divided into two periods of six months, the latter being taken after a year or two of practical work'. The course would deal with both background subjects and techniques. As background subjects, Sir Henry suggested 'economics, economic history, public finance (including taxation), social science, constitutional law, comparative public administration, and the principles of organisation and management'. The major techniques he wanted to see studied were those of inquiry and research, statistical method and financial control (ibid. pp. 271–2). The various conferences held by, the research groups appointed by, and the articles published in the journal of the Institute of Public Administration about the need for post-entry training arrangements for the Administrative Class to be radically improved had little direct effect, but they may well have helped to build up a climate of opinion favourable to at least a measure of reform, a measure that indeed followed the *Assheton Report* (Cmd 6525) of 1944.

friends and colleagues and for the rest it was a matter of answering my own questions.' Sir Maurice recalled that he eventually 'dredged up' all or most of the requisite facts about such subjects as public finance and parliamentary procedure, and he observed: 'The time and energy involved in scratching together facts that could easily have been thrown together in a textbook, seemed to be wearisome and unnecessary. It is rather like compiling your own logarithm tables. It can be done and it sharpens up one's arithmetic marvellously, but it is better and quicker to buy the book.'[1]

The Assheton Committee, which reported on Civil Service training in 1944, said that it was generally true that 'neither inside nor outside the Service has there been much systematised post-entry staff training in peacetime'.[2] The committee considered that the post-entry training of the pre-war administrative entrant had been 'too much a matter of hit or miss, sink or swim.' Generally, the new entrant had been given a desk and left to look at papers, or to try his hand at dealing with them, as they came along, with such guidance as his immediate superior might give. Unfortunately his senior was often so hard pressed that he found it easier to do the work himself, where necessary, than to teach the junior his job. Such training as the new recruit received came from observing the work of others. This was not, however, because it had been found by experience that theoretical training or teaching was useless to him, but either because it had not been considered or because it had been assumed to be useless. The Assheton Committee thought such an assumption was mistaken: 'While administration can be represented as being primarily a matter of common sense, we believe that the real achievement of the balanced judgment which is the real meaning of common sense in this connection

---

[1] Sir Maurice Dean, 'The Public Servant and the Study of Public Administration', in *Public Administration* (1962) p. 23. This article was based on a lecture given by Sir Maurice at the University of Reading in December 1961. He was at that time Permanent Under-Secretary of State for Air, and he later held the post of Permanent Secretary at the Ministry of Technology before his retirement in 1966.

[2] *Report of the Committee on the Training of Civil Servants* (1944) para. 8. The chairman of the committee was Ralph Assheton.

can be hastened and facilitated by a well thought out training scheme.'[1]

The Assheton Committee drew up a possible training scheme for Assistant Principals, the most important innovations of which proved to be too ambitious for the tastes of the Administrative Class until the scheme was actually bettered in 1963. The committee also made modest provisions for training for higher administration, which the Administrative Class, in practice, improved upon in some respects. The scale of the facilities made available for training for higher administration remained open to criticism, while for almost twenty years after the Assheton Report, a mildly modified form of the 'do-it-yourself' code represented the post-entry training of the Assistant Principal.

II   THE POST-ENTRY TRAINING OF THE ASSISTANT PRINCIPAL

The Assheton Committee discussed at length the training needs of the Assistant Principal, saying that he needed a greater knowledge of facts on the one hand, and a better grasp of the implications of what he was doing on the other, than he had usually received through the pre-war version of the 'do-it-yourself' code. The committee said that the first could be acquired gradually by live work, supplemented by departmental training and informative lectures. The second, under the pre-war system, he was left to build up from the cases that came before him and the remarks of his superiors. The committee observed:

> If he is the right sort of recruit he does no doubt in time acquire a conception of Civil Service administration with its need for bringing into harmony the ideal and the practicable, the legally permissible and the politically possible, against which all his future decisions are consciously or unconsciously tested. But the process must be a slow one, since the examples which impress his mind come before him successively over a period of years and he has no

---

[1] *Report of the Committee on the Training of Civil Servants*, para 91.

framework of ideas into which to fit them. Such a framework can be supplied by courses of instruction at the beginning of his career.[1]

The Assheton Committee conceded that there was something to be said for the immediate plunge into day-to-day work of young people who had experienced a long spell of school and university life, and were above all anxious to do a job of work. They might well be discouraged by the prospect of a further period of tuition, and any scheme of training which ignored this fundamental and healthy psychological reaction would be seriously handicapped. The committee, however, considered that, from the long-term point of view, there were very formidable disadvantages inherent in the policy of leaving the recruit to learn his job by trial and error. They included not only delay in his becoming a fully effective member of the department, but also the risk of dissipating the enthusiasm with which he started on his first job. The committee wanted to avoid these disadvantages without raising the difficulties likely to be associated with a too lengthy or a too theoretical course of training. They recommended centralised training which

> would give the recruit the idea that administration means something more than taking a number of unrelated decisions on disconnected files: that what he is doing is to contribute to the formation or operation of a policy: that such processes are going on in many departments besides his own: that solutions, some good, some not so good, have been found for the difficulties they raise: that there are generally a number of alternative methods of operating a policy besides the one his department has chosen: and that his mind should be constantly on the alert to criticise or to justify.[2]

The committee rejected ideas presented to them about establishing a staff college or allowing the Assistant Principals to attend a university course in appropriate subjects, and said that they wanted the centralised course to be in the hands of the Civil Service under a Director of Training and Education.[3] They wanted the course to last for 'anything from 2–3 months requiring an average attendance throughout that period of about two days a week but possibly beginning with an intensive course, more or less

---

[1] Ibid. para. 92.　　　[2] Ibid. para. 93.　　　[3] Ibid. para. 96.

on a full-time basis, say, for the first fortnight and tapering away towards the end of the period'.[1] The object of the course was admirable, being 'to shorten the process by which the recruit forms his own administrative standards and to inculcate from the beginning of his service a professional approach'. It would familiarise him from the start with the various types of problems which arose in the Service, the factors which had to be taken into account in solving them, and the sort of solutions which had been found successful. The instruction was to take the form of reading and discussion classes, and lectures which would cover the following ground.

> [Firstly] an explanation of the functions of the various departments and their relations with the public. [Secondly] the financial and Parliamentary background of the administrator's work. [Thirdly] a study of the administrative machine, indicating the type of organisation through which Government departments have worked; the agents and mechanical devices at their disposal and the technique of orders, forms, codes of instruction, etc.; the internal organisation of a headquarters office and the use of the expert by the non-expert. [Fourthly] the study of the meaning of the term 'administration' with illustrations from large scale administrative schemes put into operation in the past, showing what circumstances the administrator has had to bear in mind, how he has obtained the necessary data for decisions; what considerations have led to the adoption of particular expedients, and how far and for what reasons they have proved successful or unsuccessful. [Fifthly] methods of securing the cooperation of the public in the operation of a policy. [Sixthly] the inculcation of high Civil Service standards; the need for a sense of urgency, and for accuracy and decision; avoidance of incomprehensible instructions and of the appearance of uncertainty of purpose, and the need for constant comparison of performance with the standard attainable.

The committee also wanted to see the course giving 'some training in methods of preparing and presenting statistics, and the logical principles underlying their interpretation'.[2] With this type of preparation for the job, the committee believed every bit of live work, however small in itself, would have 'more meaning for the recruit than it has at present, and his individual experience could

[1] Ibid. para. 97.   [2] Ibid. para. 98.

not fail to be more fruitful. Experience would of course still be, as it now is, the most important single influence in the development of his professional capacity'.[1] The committee considered that the fact that the direct entrant would already be assigned to a particular department would make the course practical instead of academic and greatly increase the vividness of his interest. The presence of other recruits attached to different departments would vary the angles of approach and make the discussions more lively in that comparisons could be drawn from the experience of the pupils. The committee saw the tuition as being provided by persons expert in training or teaching and partly by experienced Civil Servants able to impart the fruits of their experience.[2]

It is difficult to see how, in such a brief part-time course, the Assheton Committee's aims could be satisfactorily met. There is also the point that those aims did not go far enough in some respects. Remembering the type of university studies that the large majority of the direct entrants had followed, the inculcation of 'a professional approach' into them would, for example, need a much more comprehensive training in statistics than the committee contemplated, while, at the very least, there would also be the need to make good the committee's surprising failure to recognise the desirability of considerable formal instruction in economics. The committee were also being rather optimistic in hoping that from such modest beginnings might develop 'a centre which would serve as a clearing house of ideas for Civil Service administrators and a repository of schemes, successful and unsuccessful, which have been tried out in practice'.[3]

The committee wanted to see a departmental training programme running parallel with their scheme of generalised central training which would be given to all direct entrants. The new recruit was to be allocated to a branch, carefully chosen both for the nature of the work and for the tutorial ability of the superior officer, and he was to have 'a certain amount of practice on live work from the outset'.[4] On the completion of the centralised training, which would normally be about three months after entry,

<hr>

[1] Ibid. para. 99.   [2] Ibid. para. 100.
[3] Ibid. para. 101.   [4] Ibid. para. 102.

the administrative entrant would be available full-time in his department, and the committee believed that his training should be continued there, not only by doing live work under an experienced officer, but also by background training in the form of discussions and visits and by a carefully planned movement from job to job. The committee said: 'Every effort ought to be made to ensure that an Assistant Principal, before he reaches the stage of being considered for promotion to Principal, has as wide an experience as possible of his department. In general, he ought never to be left for more than two years in any one branch and, wherever possible, movement ought to take place at more frequent intervals than that.'[1] The committee emphasised the value gained by experience of work

> as a private secretary, whether to a Minister or to a senior official. In the former case, the young man and woman gains an intimate acquaintance with Parliamentary routine and grows accustomed to think of the reactions of policy upon Members of Parliament and the public whom they represent. An efficient private secretary service must be the paramount object but, subject to that consideration, the more Assistant Principals that can be given a period of such work the better.

The committee considered that the duration of each appointment ought to be limited to spread the value of this training more widely.[2] They also emphasised the importance of field work, saying: 'Given the existing system of recruitment and the type of responsibility for which the Assistant Principal is being trained, the leaders of the Civil Service in the future will be all the better fitted for their jobs if in their younger days they have seen the work of the department at its circumference as well as at its centre.' The committee added the sensible rider: 'It is essential, however, that they should be made to do a real job of work in the field and to shoulder actual responsibility, especially in the handling of the public. Visits and watching others work are not sufficient.'[3]

The Assheton Committee's enthusiasm for a greater measure of post-entry training for the Administrative Class did lead to some post-war improvements; but the regard in which formal

[1] Ibid. para. 104.   [2] Ibid. para. 105.   [3] Ibid. para. 106.

post-entry training was held fluctuated considerably over the years after the Assheton Report and a reasonable guide to its fortunes can be found in the status accorded to the Director of the Training and Education Division of the Treasury which was established in 1945. The Division's first Director was an Under-Secretary, but in the period of retrenchment of 1952–3, when training was singled out for specially severe cuts, this appointment became a Principal's post. The development of a more constructive attitude towards training over the next year or so saw the position made up to Assistant Secretary status at the end of 1955, and ten years later, in the post-Plowden era, the Director of the Training and Education Division had become an Under-Secretary once again.[1]

Looking at the training position in the mid-1950s, those parts of the Assheton Committee's recommendations that had fitted in well with the 'training-on-the-job' cult could be seen to have been fully implemented. The Assistant Principal was officially seen as undergoing training during the whole five years or so that he spent in that grade. After an initial training course in his department, the direct entrant was posted to a division where 'right from the start he is given some responsibility'. By far the most important part of his training was thought to be gained 'by moving from division to division at intervals of from 6 to 8 months ending up, if he has any luck, as a private secretary to a Minister or the permanent head of his department'.[2] Lord Bridges has stressed the value of early mobility and the need to choose jobs for their training potential, and he emphasised that he attached special importance to an Assistant Principal having private secretary experience. This was 'training on the job *par excellence* for from the vantage point of a private office, he will have a bird's eye view of his own department, he will see how his seniors go about their work, and

[1] The Report of a Working Party appointed by the Joint Committee on Training of the Civil Service National Whitley Council, 'Review of Civil Service Training since the Publication of the Assheton Report', in *Whitley Bulletin*, Nov 1964, pp. 156–9. The Chairman was S. P. Osmond, and this publication is hereinafter referred to as the *Osmond Report*.

[2] David Hubback, 'The Treasury's Role in Civil Service Training', in *Public Administration* (1957) p. 102.

get an insight into the relations, in the broadest sense, between the Executive and the Legislative'.[1] If the Assistant Principal belonged to a Ministry with a regional or local network he was likely to have spent about six months working in a local office. In addition to what was described as 'training by variety of experience coupled with responsibility', the Assistant Principal might also go on special short courses organised by his department, and he also had some opportunity of studying some administrative problem during a short visit to another country in Western Europe.[2]

But, whereas the Assheton Committee had recommended a two or three months' central course of initial training for Assistant Principals, until 1963 they only received what was called the Junior Administrative Course, given after a few months of service, and only lasting for two or three weeks. The object of this very brief course was 'to broaden the Assistant Principal's understanding of the machinery of Government and of the organisation of the Civil Service', and it was normally attended by between sixteen and eighteen Assistant Principals drawn from the various Ministries, together with one or two young foreign Civil Servants, generally from Western Europe. The speakers were mainly drawn from within Whitehall and included Ministers as well as senior Civil Servants, although some lectures were given by outside experts, usually a Town Clerk or a lawyer. Those attending the course worked in syndicates to discuss topical problems, and each was either a chairman or a vice-chairman of one of the syndicates, each of which had to produce a report. The course was officially seen as being designed 'to give an Assistant Principal his main bearings on a wide variety of subjects, so that if he ever has to tackle problems connected with any of them, he will at least have somewhere to begin'.[3]

The modesty of the Junior Administrative Course was approved of by Sisson, who said that it accorded well with the view that members of the Administrative Class were 'intelligent amateurs who

[1] Sir Edward Bridges, 'Administration: What is it? And how can it be learnt?', an essay in A. Dunsire (ed.) *The Making of the Administrator* (1956), p. 20.
[2] Hubback, op. cit. p. 103.   [3] Ibid.

form their judgments on the basis of experience rather than as a result of a prescribed course of theoretical training'.[1] Sisson recorded that the British administrator travelling abroad was 'shocked to discover that many countries are administered by men who read books about public administration. Such people were committing the crime of learning from books something one just does. It is rather like venturing into matrimony only after a course of Havelock Ellis which, for a healthy nature, should not strictly be necessary.'[2] Not all, however, shared Sisson's view that administration was 'something only to be learned by doing it'. Professor Robson was one observer who contrasted the 'three weeks of isolated talks' which constituted the Junior Administrative Course, and at which the Assistant Principal never had the chance of 'getting to grips with anything', with 'the three year course provided for recruits in the highest grades of the French Civil Service', which Sisson was indirectly referring to.[3]

The French system of post-entry training, conducted at the now famous *École Nationale d'Administration* has come to be increasingly admired in Britain and deserves a detailed note. As Professor Cassin has written: 'If France has long been a highly centralised country, its central administration has always been in compartments';[4] one of the major aims in establishing the E.N.A. in 1945 was an attempt to introduce a greater measure of unity into the Higher Civil Service. Previously, the *Grand Corps* and the departments had recruited separately, but in 1945 their individual examinations were abolished and replaced by two parallel examinations, success in which assured entrance to the E.N.A. One of these examinations was limited to Civil Servants of at least five years' seniority and the other was open only to university graduates:

[1] C. H. Sisson, *The Spirit of British Administration* (1959) p. 37. Mr Sisson is an Under-Secretary in the Ministry of Labour (since Apr 1968 the Department of State for Employment and Productivity).

[2] Sisson, op. cit. p. 28.

[3] William A. Robson, 'Recent Trends in Public Administration', an essay in the collection edited by him called *The Civil Service in Britain and France* (1956) p. 58.

[4] René Cassin, 'Recent Reforms in the Government and Administration of France', in *Public Administration* (1950) p. 184.

at first the annual vacancies were shared between them,[1] but in 1958, because of the continued failure of the group concerned to fill its quota successfully, the percentage of places reserved for serving officials was reduced to one-third.[2] Indeed, in 1958, the whole entrance examination system was remodelled,[3] so that for graduate candidates it now takes the following form. Candidates for admission to the E.N.A. are eliminated by successive stages, the first of which is the *épreuves d'admissibilité* which consists of five tests (four of which are compulsory and one of which is optional), the marks for which being weighted according to stated coefficients. The first test is an essay, for which six hours are allowed on a subject concerned with ¦the general evolution of ideas and of political, economic or social events since the middle of the eighteenth century (coefficient 6). The second test is an essay, for which four hours are allowed, on a subject concerning economics

[1] André Bertrand, 'The Recruitment and Training of Higher Civil Servants in the United Kingdom and France', an essay in William A. Robson (ed.) *The Civil Service in Britain and France* (1956) pp. 171 and 173.

[2] Henry Parris, 'Twenty Years of l'École Nationale d'Administration', in *Public Administration* (1965) p. 396. Later Dr Parris wrote: 'During the early years of the School, half the places (as compared with the present one-third) were reserved for serving officials, but it was found in practice difficult to fill them. Between 1946 and 1953, when the half and half rule was in force, only 330 civil servants entered, as against 418 graduates. At that period, the Director of the School saw signs of improvement in the civil service entry, and favoured the retention of the balance, both on social grounds and to meet the views of the civil service trade unions. Nevertheless, the proportion was subsequently reduced to one-third (as stated above).' Dr Parris also published a table which showed that 'it is proving difficult to fill even this quota' (ibid. pp. 401–2).

[3] As is noted later in the text, Dr Parris has rightly described the present E.N.A. entrance examinations as imposing specialisation in the social sciences but penalising any marked specialisation within them. However, he made it clear that: 'Before 1958, the situation was very different. Those who had passed the qualifying examination for graduates were required to state a preference for one of four groups of careers: general administration, public finance, social administration and foreign affairs. Three of the four tests in the classifying examination required answers in the chosen field. Successful candidates followed in the School a course of studies appropriate to the choice of career indicated. But at the end of the course, all graduates of E.N.A. were arranged in order of achievement, irrespective of the section in which they had been studying.

(coefficient 4). The third test is an essay, for which four hours are allowed, on a subject concerning the political and administrative institutions of France and other leading states as well as international institutions (coefficient 4). The fourth test is a translation into French, for which three hours are allowed, of a text in one of the following languages: German, English, Arabic, Spanish, Italian and Russian (coefficient 2). The fifth test is optional; it is concerned with either mathematics or statistics, and it lasts for four hours (coefficient 3). Those candidates who are declared successful in the *épreuves d'admissibilité* then face the *épreuves d'admission* which consist of five further compulsory tests, four of which are oral examinations, and three optional tests, once more with marks weighted according to stated coefficients. The first compulsory test is a conversation, lasting twenty minutes, with an examining board, having as its starting point a commentary made by the candidates during the space of ten minutes on a

---

The man (or woman) at the head of the list was allowed an almost unrestricted choice of all the vacancies. The situation could arise in which a candidate admitted originally because of proficiency in public finance, and having studied that subject in the School, would as a consequence of passing out near the top of the list, choose to be posted to the *Conseil d'État* because of its high prestige. Similarly paradoxical results ensued for those at the bottom of the list. A man who had specialised in public law, hoping for a billet in the *Conseil d'État*, would have had not the least hope of finding one if he came, say, seventieth in the list. He would probably have to console himself with a post in one of the social service departments which are lowest in prestige. Hence, it was found to be largely a matter of chance whether the specialised courses, intended to lead to specific careers, had in fact any relevance to the eventual postings.' Moreover, 'there was a growing interest in *polyvalence* for its own sake. It is not easy to find a concise English equivalent for this useful word as used metaphorically by the French, though "the quality of being equal to anything" is one long familiar and much admired in Britain, not least in British administration. One of the original aims of E.N.A. had been to create a body of Civil Servants, modelled on the British Administrative Class, who would be capable of being transferred from Ministry to Ministry at the highest level.' Accordingly, in 1958, both in order to escape from the revealed anomalies in the working of the four courses of instruction, and in pursuit of the new ideal of *polyvalence*, the teaching framework of E.N.A., as well as its entrance examination, was radically altered' (Henry Parris, 'Twenty Years of L'École Nationale d'Administration', in *Public Administration*, 1965, pp. 397–8).

text of a general character. Candidates have thirty minutes to prepare themselves for this commentary (coefficient 5). The second compulsory test is an oral examination, lasting thirty minutes, concerning social questions (coefficient 3). The third compulsory test is an oral examination, lasting thirty minutes, concerning, at the choice of the candidate, either administrative law or public finance (coefficient 3). The fourth compulsory test is an oral examination, lasting thirty minutes, concerning international questions (coefficient 3). The fifth compulsory test is one of physical exercises comprising running, the high jump, rope climbing, weight throwing and swimming (coefficient 1). The first optional test is an oral examination, lasting twenty minutes, in either one or two additional foreign languages (coefficient 1). The second optional test is an oral examination, lasting fifteen minutes, concerning, at the choice of the candidate, one of a wide choice of university subjects, including social psychology, sociology, biology, geology, general physics, industrial technology and human and economic geography (coefficient 1). The third optional test is an additional physical test, notably in either parachute jumping or the piloting of an aeroplane or glider (coefficient 2).[1] It is fair to say that 'the general character of the examination imposes specialisation in the social sciences but penalises any marked specialisation within them'.[2] As Sisson noted without enthusiasm, the vast majority of the direct entrants are drawn from the university law faculties or from other institutions 'which addressed themselves to the teaching of law or of such subjects as economics, sociology and political science'.[3] Before the war, the *Grand Corps* had drawn most of their direct entrants from candidates who had been educated at a private institution in Paris called *École Libre des Sciences Politiques* which combined legal studies with teaching in

[1] École Nationale d'Administration, *Concours d' Entrée et Scholarité* (1967) pp. 4–6. The entry tests for the officials' competition follow the same general pattern, although there are minor differences, notably that essay themes are related more to contemporary problems and questions of administration or public law (ibid. pp. 6–8; Séamus Gaffney, 'The École Nationale d'Administration of France 1945–1966', in *Administration*, 1966, p. 126).

[2] Henry Parris, op. cit. p. 397.

[3] C. H. Sisson, *The Spirit of British Administration* (1959), p. 44.

the social sciences. After the war that institution was nationalised and became the Institute of Political Studies of the University of Paris and at the same time, as well as in the following years, similar institutes were established in a number of provincial universities.[1] It still provides the most relevant preparation for the exacting E.N.A. entrance examinations: for example, of the sixty-two candidates who were appointed from the graduates' competition in 1964 no fewer than fifty had studied at the Institute of Political Studies of the University of Paris and twenty-one of these had a law degree as well.[2]

Although the French had never adhered to the Macaulay concept of 'a liberal education' as the ideal pre-entry training for administrators, up to 1945, as André Bertrand later wrote, the position as regards post-entry training had been the same in Britain and France. The young direct entrant, immediately after passing his entrance examination, had begun 'quite empirically and in the most haphazard way, to learn his job and its technicalities on the spot'. Taking into account the machinery of the entrance competitions, this practice could have been more safely

[1] Séamus Gaffney, op. cit. pp. 121–2.

[2] Ibid. p. 126. Dr Parris has observed: 'A study of the educational background of E.N.A. entrants shows that the establishment of provincial Institutes of Political Studies has completely failed to break the monopoly of *Sciences Po* – symbolically the Paris Institute has inherited the nickname of its predecessor, the *École Libre*. Moreover, twenty years after the decision to establish provincial Institutes, the preponderance of *Sciences Po* over all other sources of recruitment is growing, rather than diminishing. Between 1947 and 1951, its graduates took 43 per cent of all the places. By the period 1961–3, the proportion had risen to 67 per cent. The advice one would give to a school-leaver who aspired to high rank in the French Civil Service is clear and may be put in sporting terms. "Enrol at *Sciences Po*, and the odds will be five to one against. At any other Institute, they will be three times as great – almost as high as those against the valiant few who get into E.N.A. without any higher education at all".' Dr Parris considered: 'It is easy to see why the reforms of 1945 have not been more successful. For centuries, Paris has drawn to it the ambitious young from every part of the country. In the academic world, its magnetism acts on students and teachers alike. Benefiting from this force, *Sciences Po* has had no difficulty in maintaining the position held by its predecessor the *École Libre*, as the most effective institution for the student who wishes to enter the Higher Civil Service. Its full-time staff are supplemented by part-time teachers of the highest distinction from

continued in France, where most of the basic knowledge of the candidates in the field of social sciences had been carefully examined through various papers and viva voce. But in spite of this, it was in France, and not Britain, that a training school was established in 1945. The British Administrative Class remained addicted to the 'rule of thumb' and, until 1963, contented itself with what Bertrand described as 'departmental training of a very limited character', together with 'very remarkable but quite short intensive courses run by the Treasury'. On the other hand, the *Grande École* had been dear to French hearts since the Revolution, and, to the ranks of such great technical schools as the *École des Ponts et Chaussées* and the *École des Mines*, the French added the E.N.A., which aimed at giving their administrative cadets a thorough professional training extending over about two and a half years.[1]

At the time of writing the course of study is divided into two parts and extends over twenty-nine months altogether. The first twelve months consists of a *stage d'administration*, which is spent

---

other University institutions, from public life, and from the Civil Service. This reliance on part-time help, which could be a weakness is turned into a source of strength. Seminars conducted by Civil Servants, themselves often graduates of E.N.A., in subjects such as administrative law, the economics of planning, and international relations, are of especial value to students preparing for the School's entrance examination. These facts being widely known, a high proportion of those seeking careers in the Public Service enrol there. Moreover, the pre-eminence of the Paris Institute, as compared with those in the provinces, naturally drains talent from the latter, which are at an added disadvantage because of the relatively small number of part-time teachers available outside Paris. This magnet of the capital begins to act on the future higher Civil Servant from the provinces in many cases during his education, years perhaps before he actually enters the Service' (Henry Parris, 'Twenty Years of L'École Nationale d'Administration', in *Public Administration*, 1965, pp. 406–7). Of the graduate entrants to the E.N.A. during the period 1961–3, no fewer than 87·6 per cent had been educated at the Paris Institute of Political Studies. It is interesting to note that during that period, only 15·9 per cent of the serving officials who entered the E.N.A. had no higher education (ibid. p. 406).

[1] André Bertrand, 'The Recruitment and Training of Higher Civil Servants in the United Kingdom and France', an essay in W. A. Robson (ed.) *The Civil Service in Britain and France* (1956) p. 179.

away from Paris working under the guidance of a Prefect in the provinces. Bertrand believed that the *stage* developed the character and personality of the *stagiaires*, and gave them a wide insight into administrative problems, and allowed them to see how administrative affairs were actually handled in concrete cases, to understand local needs and the way that they could be met on the spot, and to discover the methods and procedures of administration.[1] Sisson found the sort of claims that Bertrand made for the initial *stage* 'even a little melodramatic', although he did not doubt its value. He made the point that a great deal depended on the attitudes of the men of the prefecture towards the *stagiaire*, and said that they were not always very helpful.[2] Given human nature, this would not be surprising, but no doubt experience has taught the E.N.A. which Prefects and Prefectorial staffs have enthusiasm for the *stage*, and which have not. At the end of the *stage*, the Prefect sends the E.N.A. a written opinion of the *stagiaire*, awarding him marks, which count in the final classification at the end of the course, for the manner in which the student has tackled his duties. In addition, before the end of the *stage d'administration*, the *stagiaire* has to write a *mémoire de stage* in the form of a twenty-five-to thirty-page essay on a specific problem which has been set for him at the commencement of the stage, and the marks awarded for which also count in the final classification.[3] Sisson believed that the Assistant Principal drafting private office letters was receiving a much more relevant training than he would by doing such exercises, and he dismissed the *mémoire de stage* as 'somewhat too abstract'.[4]

This was also Sisson's verdict on the cycle of academic studies which the cadets pursue at the E.N.A. during the first half of the second part of their course. By means of these studies, Bertrand saw them as being able 'to broaden, deepen and systematise in an administrative approach, various elements of knowledge that they had previously acquired and, in many cases, applied in actual administrative life during the previous year'. At the same time, the cadets were receiving 'a professional training designed to

[1] Ibid. p. 180.
[2] Sisson, op. cit. pp. 46–7.
[3] Gaffney, op. cit. pp. 127–8.
[4] Sisson, op. cit. p. 48.

develop sound and efficient working methods'.[1] This professional training is imparted by means of *conférences* and *séminaires* rather than by formal lectures, and by part-time staff, usually serving Civil Servants and, to a lesser extent, university teachers, rather than by full-time staff. A *conférence* is a discussion group of about a dozen cadets which is conducted by a *maître de conférence*, and which examines in depth practical problems dealing with his particular specialism or with the particular branch of the public sector in which he is serving. Cadets attend several of these conferences during their period of studies, and their attendance involves searching for information from original sources, studying it, analysing it, discussing it with his fellow-students, drawing conclusions and presenting the results in the form of an official memorandum. The students' written work during the *conférences* is carefully examined by the *maîtres de conférence*. A *séminaire*, like a *conférence*, is carried out by a group of about a dozen students under the direction of a *chef de travaux*, but it entails the study over a period of several months of a more complex and a more far-reaching administrative problem and terminates in the preparation of a collective report proposing specific solutions. Each student participates in at least one *séminaire*. In effect this seems to be training in committee work and in the reconstruction of divergent views in a general report.[2] Subjects that figure prominently in the second year curriculum include economic, financial and social policy, statistics, accountancy, administrative law and international relations. In addition, there are a certain number, or even a series, of lectures given to the cadets by *quelques personalités marquantes* about important topical subjects. There is also instruction in foreign languages, and cadets are expected to acquire 'des bases aussi solides que possible' in a second modern language. There are exercises in physical culture and in the practice of various sports, which are compulsory unless the cadets are exempted on medical grounds. The performance of the students during this exacting régime of activities is rated and taken into account for the final examination classification.[3] The cycle of studies just described is

[1] Bertrand, op. cit. p. 181.   [2] Gaffney, op. cit. pp. 128–9.
[3] Ibid. p. 129.

interrupted towards the end of the year to enable a new *stage* to be undertaken, the *stage d'enterprise*, a period of up to three months during which the students are sent to work in large organisations in either the private or public sector of industry. The student is, if possible, placed directly under the head of the company or, where the company is a very large one, under the head of one of its main divisions. The cadet is expected to do a real day's work in this situation and he has every incentive to give of his best because, again, his performance is formally assessed and its rating will count in the final School examination.[1] Back again for a second time to the E.N.A. after the termination of the *stage d'enterprise*, the student has about five more months to go before the completion of his training. In this period of studies special prominence is given to social subjects and the method of tuition used is largely by way of *séminaire*. The techniques of organisation and methods in public administration are also studied. In this way 'the School intends this final period of studies to be more orientated than the earlier similar period towards work immediately related to administrative activity because this period of training immediately precedes the effective entry of the students on the discharge of their official duties. The study of languages is continued as also are the sporting activities.' Spread out over the latter portion of the training period, the cadets are subjected to a series of six tests, which may be oral, minimum duration thirty minutes, or written, duration four to six hours; and to oral tests in two modern languages or, except in the case of those aspiring to the diplomatic service, in one modern language with a test in some other subject. The marks scored in these tests are added to the marks awarded for performance during the *stages*, for the memorandum of the *stage d'administration* and for performances in the exercises, mainly at *conférences* and *séminaires*, during the periods spent at the School; and the total aggregate marking, with a sixty per cent weighting being given to the tests, determines the order

[1] Ibid. It is interesting to note that writing in the mid-1950s, a former Director of the Treasury Training and Education Division said that he was 'much impressed' by the practice of seconding E.N.A. cadets to industry (Hubback, op. cit. p. 104).

E

of merit of the cadets. The students can then select their preferred careers on the basis of their place in the order of merit. Naturally, the higher-placed cadets choose the careers which seem to offer them the best prospects, which means entry to one of the *Grands Corps de l'État*, such as the *Conseil d'État*, *Inspection Générale des Finances*, *Cour des Comptes*, or Ministries like External Affairs, Interior and Finance. The result is that 'certain corps or Ministries always get the cream of the talent, leaving other Ministries and more specialised careers with the tail-end of the list'. This is what the reforms of 1945 were partly supposed to avoid, but the reason that this situation persists does not really lie in the passing-out system of the E.N.A., 'but rather in the failure to fuse administrative careers and to achieve a levelling out in prospects of promotion'.[1] Although it has not been able to fulfil all the ambitions of its founders, the E.N.A. still 'constitutes a great experiment in the recruitment of and training of higher civil servants'; while it is also fair to say: 'Rarely if ever have young administrators been given the opportunity of acquiring such a wide range of practical knowledge.'[2]

[1] Gaffney, op. cit. pp. 129–30.
[2] This was the verdict of F. Ridley and J. Blondel, *Public Administration in France* (1964) p. 40. The ambitions of the founders of the E.N.A. were fully described by T. Feyzioglu, 'The Reforms of the French Higher Civil Service', in *Public Administration* (1955), being largely what he termed 'measures taken to democratise and to provincialise recruitment' (pp. 78–9). Feyzioglu concluded from his researches that there had not been much progress towards the democratisation of the Higher Civil Service 'so far as the social origins of Higher Civil Servants are concerned' (p. 181), while the Paris region also continued to provide a more than proportional share of entrants (pp. 173–4). Writing a decade later, Dr Parris found much the same picture, drew attention to the continued dominance of the Parisian *Sciences Po*, and observed: 'only far reaching reforms in the French educational system could redress the inequalities imposed by social class, and by place of birth, residence, and education' (Parris, op. cit. p. 407). Dr Parris did believe, however, that more success had been achieved regarding the aim of unifying the Higher Civil Service, stressing the value of the informal ties built up by administrators having had a common education at the E.N.A. (ibid. pp. 407–8). Dr Parris made very clear, however, the continued prestige of the *Grand Corps* which, as is noted in the text, continued to offer the most attractive careers (ibid. pp. 398–9 and 402). Reforms proposed by the French Government in 1964 aimed at increasing the unity of the Civil

It is not difficult to understand Professor Robson's admiration for the French approach to the post-entry training of administrative cadets, remembering his belief that 'the social sciences can be of unique value in assisting a Civil Servant to understand the social, economic and political background to his working environment'. He had advocated in 1956 that members of the Administrative Class 'should in their early years be given an opportunity, or even be required, to take courses for the Diploma of Public Administration at one of the Universities, if their previous education has left them completely ignorant of economics, political science, social history, sociology, social psychology, and so forth'. But what Professor Robson wanted above all to see established was a Civil Service Staff College, an idea that had been rejected by the Assheton Committee, which would provide courses comparable with those of the E.N.A. and the Indian Administrative Training School at Delhi which he also admired.[1] Writing in 1961, Robson condemned brief training courses such as the Junior Administrative Course as being 'unlikely to get below the surface of any problem', and his verdict on Civil Service training policy was: 'Superficiality is more than a danger: it has become almost a doctrine.'[2]

A serving Permanent Secretary, Sir Maurice Dean, made it clear in 1961 that opinion in the Administrative Class at that time was very much against a staff college. An alternative, which had also been rejected by the Assheton Committee, but which Sir Maurice Dean personally favoured, was for an appropriate university course to serve as post-entry training for the young administrator.[3] Harold Laski had advocated a similar idea in 1943,

Service 'and to allow for better use of senior staff'. The Government intended, among other reforms, to give the corps of civil administrators the formal status of a *Grand Corps*: a change which they hoped might 'foster unity and make careers more attractive at a time when recruitment is becoming more difficult because of the competition from private enterprise' (Ridley and Blondel, op. cit. p. 43).

[1] William A. Robson, op. cit. p. 58.

[2] William A. Robson, 'The Present State of Teaching and Research in Public Administration', in *Public Administration* (1961) p. 220.

[3] Sir Maurice Dean, 'The Public Servant and the Study of Public Administration', in *Public Administration* (1962) pp. 22–3.

believing: 'What gives its salt to University life is the width of the horizons it has to span, the variety in the outlook of its teachers, the need, in its students, to test the values at which they have provisionally arrived against other values born of contact with a different experience or a different discipline.'[1] Dean's views were less colourful, and indeed his proposed scheme was far too modest in scope to be a worthwhile advance. He had wanted to send Assistant Principals 'to a University for (say) a term to learn something about the academic side of public administration before they become too immersed in the detailed work of the Civil Service'.[2] Dean said: 'Looking at the balance of advantage and disadvantage, I see in one scale the possible lifelong effect of a postgraduate University term, not for what is learnt but for ideas acquired and doors opened. In the other scale there is the cost, in a lifetime of official duties, of a term away from Whitehall, say eight weeks in all. To my way of thinking, the balance is in favour of the University term.'[3] The careful weighing of the balance in this context seemed superfluous, remembering that until comparatively recently the Assistant Principals would normally have done two years in the Armed Forces, during which they would have been fortunate indeed to have acquired any useful administrative experience. This was not, admittedly, an argument for 'wasting' still more time; but quibbling over two months, in any case far too short a period for a worthwhile course, seemed unnecessary. Fortunately, in the post-Plowden atmosphere of a greater emphasis on the need for more professionalism, there was, as a Treasury Under-Secretary later put it, 'a growing feeling' that the Junior Administrative Course 'did not go far enough'. A small inter-departmental committee under Treasury chairmanship examined the question in the course of 1962, and from its report evolved the idea which led to the setting up of the Centre for Administrative Studies in October 1963.[4] The centre aimed to give what the Head of the Civil Service described as 'a highly

---

[1] Harold J. Laski, 'The Education of the Civil Servant', in *Public Administration* (1943) p. 19.   [2] Dean, op. cit. p. 23.   [3] Ibid. pp. 23–4.
[4] *Fifth Report from the Select Committee on Estimates* (1963–4) *Evidence*, question 542.

intensive training to young members of the Administrative Class in public administration, statistics, economics, and various specialities within these broad headings'. The early courses lasted for fourteen weeks for all Assistant Principals, with an additional seven weeks – twenty-one in all – for those who were 'operating in economic departments where specialised skill in economics, statistics and so forth may be especially valuable'.[1] The increase in the length of the period of training was officially described as 'a fundamental change and was consciously made as such'.[2]

The Centre for Administrative Studies was, indeed, as Sir Laurence Helsby said, 'an extremely important and significant experiment'.[3] In 1966, in addition to ten morning sessions, including lectures, demonstrations and syndicate study, at the Royal Institution designed to give Assistant Principals in their second year an introduction to 'some basic concepts of science',[4] the centre's training programme included a three-week structure of government course intended for Assistant Principals after about six months' service; and a twenty-week course on economics, statistics, new management techniques, Government and industry and the operation of business companies, for Assistant Principals in their third year of service. The centre ran two three-week and two twenty-week courses in each course year. Each course was planned for thirty members, and this capacity enabled the centre to take the whole of the annual intake of Assistant Principals through the courses, and to make available a number of places for the equivalent grade in the Diplomatic Service: in the 1965–6 course year that Service was taking a total of sixteen places on the two twenty-week courses that were held. As was evident, the original distinction between the studies undertaken by Assistant Principals in 'economic' as opposed to 'non-economic' departments had not been retained: it had, in fact, been abandoned as early as October 1964. The initial three-week course had been partly constructed from elements that in the original course had been found too elementary for Assistant Principals in their third,

---

[1] Ibid. 103. [2] Ibid. 560. [3] Ibid. 103.
[4] H.M. Treasury, *Management Training in the Civil Service. Report of a Working Party* (1967) para. 14.

but which were thought to be of value in an introductory year, course.[1]

The initial structure of government course included an introduction to the structure and problems of local Government, parliamentary procedure, financial control, the preparation and progress of legislation, and a few 'legal' sessions, such as 'the administrator and legal problems', and 'tribunals and enquiries'. There were also a few sessions on 'techniques', such as speaking in public and at committee meetings.[2]

The emphasis in the twenty-week course was on economics and statistical and mathematical techniques for administration. More than half of the total time was spent on economics, the study of which was divided into two parts. The concepts of micro- and macro-economics were taught in the first part, while the second part was based on the study of a series of economic problems and provided members with an opportunity to revise the concepts they had studied and to apply them to current questions such as the balance of payments, pricing and investment policy in the public sector and the problems of developing countries. About fifteen per cent of the time was spent on statistics, techniques in aid of administration and an experimental short preliminary course on mathematical concepts to introduce members to linear algebra, functions and elementary calculus. The section of the course on Government and industry, for example, relations with the private sector of industry, the nationalised industries and industrial relations, and the section on the operation of business enterprise, together occupied a further fifteen per cent of the time. The balance of the time was given to project evaluation and control, which meant techniques such as discounted cash flow, cost benefit analysis, network analysis and P.E.R.T., ending with a detailed study of financial control problems in certain fields of Government expenditure, and to a short section on the international setting.[3]

Regarding training methods, a distinction can be drawn between the first part of the course, which covered the study of the

---

[1] C. D. E. Keeling, 'The Treasury Centre for Administrative Studies', in *Public Administration* (1965) pp. 191 and 193–4.
   [2] Ibid. p. 192.   [3] Ibid.

main concepts of economics, statistics and new management techniques, and the latter part of the course. In the first part, each half-day session devoted to a subject normally included one lecture of an hour. Many of these were informal with questions accepted at any stage. In economics, the lecture was followed by written work or discussion groups on alternate days. The written work was a series of short questions designed to bring out quickly whether the member had understood the economic concepts being taught. Written exercises also followed lectures in statistics and management techniques. Members prepared an elementary programme for a computer, and carried out network analysis exercises, one of which was directed by a firm of business management consultants.[1]

In the second half of the course the methods changed. In the study of economic problems small lecture-classes or seminars for twelve to eighteen members were used whenever possible with members preparing views on questions circulated for discussion. The sections on Government and industry and on business enterprise, were based mainly on reading, on visits to organisations to interview staff and on report sessions. Most of this part of the course was based on either syndicate or group work. Courses operated in three syndicates of ten, or six groups of five, depending on the subjects under study. The directing staff of the centre did not usually do the actual teaching, but arranged for it to be done by the most suitable people from the universities (the major source), government departments and business.[2]

Remembering that it was as late as 1961 that an advocate of more formal post-entry training for the Assistant Principal, Sir Maurice Dean, was so carefully weighing up the balance between a university term spent on such training and eight weeks or so 'lost' to the Service, in a sense the C.A.S. courses almost amount to a revolution. However, as it is still the case that the British Assistant Principal does not receive as wide a post-entry training as his French counterpart one may still doubt if the revolution has gone far enough. That question will be discussed in the fourth part of

[1] Ibid. p. 194.   [2] Ibid. pp. 194–5 and 197.

this chapter after a consideration of the facilities at present available at later points in administrators' careers to train them for higher administration.

III   TRAINING FOR HIGHER ADMINISTRATION

Writing in 1943, one of H. E. Dale's suggestions for curing the faults that he had found in his former Administrative Class colleagues was that its members should be granted two sabbatical years or at least half years during their service: 'The first to be taken at about 30 and to be spent in the country, but in an occupation and environment totally dissimilar to anything they have known before: and the second at the age of about 45 to be spent as a rule abroad.'[1] The Assheton Committee recognised such opinions as Dale's, and they observed that 'there comes a time, normally, we suggest in the early 30s, when either a complete change of environment or an opportunity to stand back from one's job and to shake oneself free from the daily routine is most desirable in order to gain a broader vision and some fresh experience'. To some extent this could be obtained within the Service by transfer from one department to another and by transfer from headquarters to out-station or vice versa.[2] Something more than this was wanted, however, and the committee recommended that selected Civil Servants, in their early thirties, should be granted 'a period of sabbatical leave to pursue an approved course or undertake a task of research, either in this country or abroad. Such leave should be with pay and should count as service for purposes of pension.'[3] The committee strongly approved of schemes whereby selected officials would be

> given an opportunity to travel abroad to study aspects of Government or public administration likely to be of value. If the problems of the business world are different from those of the Civil Service, the problems of other Governments are essentially similar. Study

---

[1] Harold E. Dale, *The Personnel and Problems of the Higher Civil Service* (1943) p. 12. Dale had, of course, expressed similar ideas in the classic work, *The Higher Civil Service of Great Britain* (1941) pp. 220–3.
[2] *Assheton Report*, para. 109.   [3] Ibid. para. 114.

of the ways in which they are tackled abroad would be worthwhile in itself as a safeguard against insularity, as well as providing
a stimulant which would be of great benefit to the Service.

Although the numbers who could take advantage of these arrangements would be small, the committee believed, with justice, that
such experience would be 'of particular value in the training of
those destined for the highest posts'.[1] The Assheton Committee
were less enthusiastic about long-term secondments to industry,
restricting themselves to the belief that there was 'scope for visits
and periods of observation, varying in duration from a week or
so to a maximum of 2 or 3 months'.[2] The committee saw more
promise and less difficulty about secondment to, or indeed interchange on a two-way basis with, a local authority.[3]

The post-war experience was that few attachments to private
industry and to local authorities actually took place; but the official
opinion was that the Assheton Report's proposals for sabbatical
leave and travel abroad have been put into effect 'on quite an
extensive scale'.[4] Although they have changed in detail during the
period since the Assheton Report,[5] the present arrangements are
as follows. Civil Servants of Assistant Secretary or Principal rank,
or corresponding standing in the Professional or Scientific Officer
Classes, have the opportunity of securing Harkness Fellowships of
the Commonwealth Fund, New York, and Nuffield Travelling
Fellowships. Of the Harkness Fellowships thirty are awarded
annually in the United Kingdom for study in the U.S.A., and
Civil Servants compete for these. Since 1961 usually only one,
occasionally two, have been awarded annually to Civil Servants.
Nuffield Fellowships were taken over by the Government from
the Nuffield Foundation in 1961, and three annual awards are
usually made to Civil Servants, one of which is normally given
to a member of the Professional or Scientific Officer Classes, for
study in overseas parts of the Commonwealth or, exceptionally,
in countries outside the Commonwealth other than the U.S.A.

[1] Ibid. para. 115.   [2] Ibid. paras 110–111.   [3] Ibid. para. 112.
[4] David Hubback, 'The Treasury's Role in Civil Service Training', in
Public Administration (1957) p. 104.
[5] The position in the mid-1950s was given in the *Priestley Evidence*,
appendix II, Note by the Treasury on Sabbatical Leave, pp. 74–6.

Administrative and analogous grades can compete with non-Civil Servants for two further types of Fellowship. Firstly, for a Gwilym Gibbon Research Fellowship through which they can study a problem of government at Nuffield College, Oxford, which can include short visits abroad if these are thought necessary and approved by the college. Secondly, for one or more of the Simon Research Fellowships for advanced study or research in the social sciences at the University of Manchester and exceptionally elsewhere, including study abroad. Sabbatical leave is also granted for attendance at certain other institutions. Firstly, twelve Assistant Secretaries or their equivalents attend a one-year course at the Imperial Defence College: eight of them are drawn from either the Ministries of Defence and of Technology or the Diplomatic Service, with the remaining four places being open to general competition among other departments, some of which, but not all, having an overseas complement. Secondly, on each six-month course at the N.A.T.O. Defence College one place is reserved for a Principal or Assistant Secretary, or equivalent ranks, and this place usually goes to a Civil Servant from either the Ministry of Defence or the Diplomatic Service. Thirdly, four Civil Servants, mainly administrators and scientists and, more rarely, professional staff, normally drawn from the defence and economic departments, attend a six-month course at the Joint Services Staff College.[1] Fourthly, 'in

[1] *Priestley Evidence*, appendix II, Note by the Treasury on Sabbatical Leave, pp. 74–6, as amended by the Treasury at the request of the author. The Treasury were kind enough to let me have the following observations about sabbatical leave: 'Sabbatical leave (i.e., leave with pay) is granted to selected Civil Servants holding, or likely to hold, positions of high responsibility. Such leave is not confined to Administrative Staff. It is granted by departments in consultation with the Treasury and the period of such leave does not normally exceed one year. Instructions to departments state that the main purpose of sabbatical leave is to help a promising man to become, in the long run, a better Civil Servant than he otherwise would have been, by giving him an opportunity at a suitable stage in his career to broaden his experience. Two other objects may also be achieved; he may acquire new ideas and knowledge of direct benefit to the work of the department or the Service, and he may perform a useful ambassadorial function. This concept of sabbatical leave derives from the Assheton Report on the Training of Civil Servants (1944, Cmd 6525, paragraphs 108–117). Sabbatical leave in the Civil Service has had a broader definition than is customary in the academic

1966-7 it is expected that four Civil Servants, all Principals, will attend 12-week courses at the London Business School and about seven, including several professional and scientific staff, the courses of similar length at the Manchester Business School';[1] presumably similar arrangements will be made in subsequent years. Fifthly, six Principals or equivalent normally attend each of the four courses annually held at the Administrative Staff College at Henley.[2]

The residential courses given at the Administrative Staff College provide an interesting and important example of the type of training for higher administration that is secured by some of the more fortunate Civil Service administrators. During the year beginning September 1966, the College ran four ten-week courses. Each course was limited to sixty-six members, drawn from industry, commercial and financial organisations (thirty-six to forty-two); from nationalised industry (eight or nine); from the Civil Service (six); and from the trades unions, local authorities and H.M. Forces (up to six). In addition, six vacancies were

---

world. It has included sabbatical leave for advanced study, e.g. in a foreign country or at a University; attendance at the Imperial Defence College or the Administrative Staff College; secondment (primarily for training) to jobs abroad or to a local authority; and attachment to industry. Secondment dictated by the immediate needs of the work and involving a full-time job would not normally rank as sabbatical leave, although some of the advantages of sabbatical leave may be achieved as a by-product. In practice secondment for training purposes has been little used because it has been found difficult to operate successfully. In the past the bulk of sabbatical leave which has been granted has consisted of attendance at a set course, often connected with the broader aspects of the individual officer's normal work. The Treasury is now revising the instructions on sabbatical leave so that attendance at a course will in future normally form part of official duty and not be counted as sabbatical leave.'

[1] H.M. Treasury, *Management Training in the Civil Service. Report of a Working Party* (1967) para. 24.

[2] *Priestley Evidence*, appendix II, Note by the Treasury on Sabbatical Leave, pp. 74-6, as subsequently amended by the Treasury. Until recently eighteen Civil Servants have attended the Administrative Staff Colleges held each year: now the number is twenty-four. This figure 'has been determined by the wish of the Administrative Staff College to have one, but not more than one, Civil Servant in each syndicate' (H.M. Treasury, *Management Training in the Civil Service. Report of a Working Party* (1967) para. 24).

reserved for overseas candidates whose education and experience in any of the above fields had been gained outside this country. Candidates had to be nominated by their employers. Men and women between thirty-three and forty-two were eligible: candidates outside this age range only being considered in exceptional circumstances. The basic qualification was practical experience not academic distinction, although overseas candidates had to have a full command of both spoken and written English. Selection was by competitive interview.[1]

The course was obviously intended for managers and administrators already holding positions of substantial authority who were likely to qualify for still greater responsibilities. The course was designed so that its members learned to see their role in their enterprise in relation to its main objectives and in its total environment; to understand the implications for their enterprise of government policies and of the changing domestic and international situation; to evaluate their own experience and attitudes against those of people of similar standing and ability working in other enterprises and in other countries; to assess new knowledge,

---

[1] *The Administrative Staff College Handbook* (1966–7), p. 6. The Administrative Staff College was founded in 1946, as 'an independent organisation without political, social or economic bias. It is recognised as a Charity by the Board of Inland Revenue. It is financed mainly by fee income and partly by voluntary subscriptions mostly under seven-year covenants. The courses are designed for men and women drawn from industry, commerce, the trade unions and all forms of the public service, who already hold positions of substantial authority and are likely to qualify for still greater responsibilities. It is intended for those who are well grounded in their own careers either by experience alone or by a combination of experience and formal education. The studies at Henley examine the principles and practice of management and administration. They enable the members of each session to assess their past administration. They enable the members of each session to assess their past practices and future responsibilities, to exchange experience with each other, to meet and confer with leading personalities and specialists in different walks of life, to extend their knowledge over a wide field and to consider the impact on their present and future work of advances in thought and techniques. The objective is essentially long term. Most nominators look upon attendance at Henley as the last stage of substantial full-time training in the career of a promising executive or administrator.' (Ibid.)

thought, techniques and methods and their application in management; to develop the skills of obtaining decisions from a group of people of diverse expertise, experience and temperament; to assess wisely and quickly what was important in unfamiliar areas and situations; and to appreciate the particular responsibilities and problems of top management. The course aimed to raise the major issues that faced managers, being framed so that 'it brings together in a systematic and progressive way both the acquisition of new knowledge and the critical examination of experience'. The course demanded 'the active participation of members' and called for 'a substantial amount of individual study'. Members of the course were organised in working groups referred to as syndicates drawn from a wide range of enterprises, and carefully selected in order to secure varied experience within each group.[1]

In terms of design the course at the Administrative Staff College was divided into five parts, with a number of sub-divisions, together with some background subjects. In Part I members described and compared the structure of their enterprise and their own position in it so that each member became acquainted with the experience of his syndicate colleagues. In Part II of the course members examined the internal management of an enterprise, concentrating their attention on employment policies and practices up to the first level of supervision; organisation and structure, coordination and communication, delegation, control and accountability; management information, for forecasting, planning control and decision-taking, its uses and limitations; and the behavioural sciences 'in so far as they throw light on the factors which encourage men and women to work well and with satisfaction at all levels'. Overlapping Parts II and III members studied current problems and developments in specialist functions of which they had experience, such as marketing, overseas trading, production, personnel, finance, banking and management services. For this purpose specialists were grouped together, the studies culminating in a detailed survey of the work in each group by the other members of the course. Part III covered the activities which

[1] *The Administrative Staff College Guide for Prospective Members,* p. 5.

involved relationships with other enterprises and institutions, such as:

> the raising of money from outside sources, alternative methods, timing, shareholder control, relations with the City, risk; the relationships between employers and organised labour, the origins, evolution and characteristics of Trades Unions and Employers' Organisations, negotiation procedures and the role of the Government; the pattern of relationships between Central and Local Government and industry and commerce, Government regulation, control and stimulation – export promotion – advisory and consultative committees – planning machinery.

In Part IV the whole of the preceding material was drawn together and used in studies of the management problems of an enterprise as a whole, in action, in the context of changing conditions. Some of the separate issues studied were: the response to short-term economic fluctuations and long-term growth, rationalisation or contraction; the exploitation of innovation in production, product, distribution or organisation; and the handling and development of managers in all kinds of enterprise, in business and the public service. Concurrently with Part IV, the syndicates studied developments in international commerce and industry and political and economic trends, in particular as they affected Britain's position as an industrial and commercial nation. Part V of the course was 'a consideration of the distinctive role and capacities required of those who carry responsibility at the highest levels': it aimed to provide 'an opportunity to reflect on the course as a whole and to judge how to maintain the unity and continued direction of the enterprise and a vital contact with the environment'. The teaching of management techniques was not one of the objects of the course, but members were expected to appreciate the nature and use of these techniques and the course made provision for such an appreciation. Background studies were also used in support of the main subjects of the course. The biographies of well-known administrators of the past were studied; members were given an opportunity to review their methods of keeping themselves well-informed on current affairs; and a series of talks were given on current economic problems. The whole course was supported by talks and visits to syndicates by some thirty to forty experienced figures in the world of industry, commerce and government, from academic experts and members of the staff. Visits in small groups were made to thirty or more commercial, industrial and government establishments in order to gain information or to see an organisation in action. All these were directly related to sub-divisions of the course of studies.[1]

The work of the college was centred on the syndicate, a group of ten or eleven members representing the varied interests present on the course, who remained in the same syndicates for most of the time. Because of the great importance attached to the work of members in their syndicates particular care was taken in selection both for each session and for each syndicate. The membership of each session was built up so that it had a proportion of each type of enterprise in which members worked and of different functional backgrounds. The proportions varied slightly from session to session but a typical syndicate was composed of six or seven members from industrial, commercial and financial firms of different sizes, one or two from nationalised industry, one Civil Servant, one from a foreign country and one or two from Trades Unions, local authorities or the Armed Forces. The same members represented the following functional backgrounds: two or three production, two or three marketing, one banking, one or two research, one or two accounting and from two to four other functions, such as personnel, education, purchasing, management services and general management. Each of the six syndicates was a microcosm of the whole session of sixty-six members.[2] The staff college's method of teaching was of group work carried out against time.[3] In nearly every major subject dealt with, the syndicates had to embody their views in a report produced by a definite day and hour. These reports were presented to the college as a whole,

---

[1] Ibid. pp. 6–8. The teaching of management techniques is not one of the objects of the course. Because it is regarded as important that members appreciate the nature and use of these techniques, especially where rapid developments are taking place, however, the Course of Studies makes provision for such an appreciation (ibid. p. 9).

[2] Ibid. p. 9.

[3] D. K. Clarke, 'Educating the Administrator', an essay in A. Dunsire (ed.) *The Making of an Administrator* (1956) p. 35.

and issues arising from them were discussed. The syndicates worked under one of their own members as chairman, with another member as secretary. The college appointed the chairmen and secretaries before the session began in such a way that all had opportunities of filling these posts. There was a general rule that the chairman was a layman in the particular subject: he had to use experts without being an expert himself. As chairman he had to get the group through their task against a definite time-table, and he had to defend in public the views of his group. This was not a particularly popular assignment among members, but the college considered that it was 'a very valuable training for the future'.[1] That verdict could, indeed, be extended to cover the whole course which took the members right away from their domestic and work routines, and gave them what would probably be their only chance in their working lives 'to sit back and look at their normal job from the outside'.[2]

As regards management courses for staff in mid-career:

> For staff at Principal and Assistant Secretary level, the Treasury ran for several years a 2-week non-residential Management and Communication course, and a 2-week residential Organisation and Management course respectively. These courses were not confined to members of the Administrative Class but were attended also by staff in equivalent ranks from the Executive, Professional, Scientific and other Classes. They were started before the Centre for Administrative Studies was set up and so were not intended for staff who had at an earlier stage received training at the Centre. Indeed, each of the two versions of the 2-week courses was intended for staff who had received no previous management training, and there was a substantial over-lap between the content of the two courses.[3]

The Treasury introduced experimentally, from the autumn of 1966, a new group of management courses and seminars and decided to abandon both the two-week courses:

> This new group of four short courses is made up of a 6-week course in 'Economics' which was started for Principals in 1965, a 3-week course on 'Decisions and Techniques', a 3-week course

---

[1] Ibid. p. 34.   [2] Ibid. p. 29.
[3] H.M. Treasury, *Management Training in the Civil Service. Report of a Working Party* (1967) para. 21.

on 'Organisation and Staff Management' and a 4-week course in 'Social Administration'. Staff would take three of these courses over a period of several years, adding up in all to ten or twelve weeks' management training. As far as Principals are concerned, the Treasury are concentrating initially on taking through the courses all who joined the Service as Assistant Principals in 1957–60 inclusive, and were thus just too old to attend the long courses which started in 1963 at the Centre for Administrative Studies. But these courses will be attended also by some members of the Executive, Professional, Scientific and other Classes in the age range 30–37. At Assistant Secretary level the 2-week courses have been replaced by residential seminars of length varying from two to five days, each devoted to a single subject, e.g., management techniques or the development of A.D.P.[1]

A recent development has been

a 2-week residential seminar described as the Public Service/ Private Enterprise course, organised jointly by the Treasury and private industry. It has been attended by equal numbers of Civil Servants (at Assistant Secretary or Under-Secretary level, with an age-limit of around 45) and people of similar standing from both private enterprise and nationalised industry. The aim has been to assemble a group of able men in order to consider problems of mutual interest, reach some understanding of the different backgrounds against which they work, and exchange views. These seminars have been most successful in providing a meeting point between Whitehall and the industrial world.[2]

Such developments may have, if only slightly, mitigated the Plowden Committee's criticism made in 1961 that it was doubtful if 'a large enough proportion of the abler Assistant Secretaries and their equivalents in the Professional, Scientific and other Classes was likely in the course of their careers (or early enough) to get the benefit of the training provided and to develop the attitude of mind which actively seeks efficiency and economy'.[3] Even taking into account departmental training arrangements and fellowships, scholarships and other opportunities for sabbatical leave gained on the initiative of the individual, the main concern about training for higher administration is not so much about its quality

---

[1] Ibid. paras 21–2.   [2] Ibid. para. 26.
[3] The Plowden Group, *Control of Public Expenditure* (1961) para. 52.

but about its scope and availability. This concern has been one of the factors behind the continuing advocacy, by certain outside commentators, of the establishment of a Civil Service Staff College.

IV THE STAFF COLLEGE PROPOSAL AND THE TREND TOWARDS PROFESSIONALISM

The Select Committee on National Expenditure in a 1942 report recommended 'the creation of a Staff College to which picked members of the Administrative and Professional Classes, as well as promising members of the Executive and Clerical Classes, could be sent after a few years' service'. The syllabus was to concentrate on courses in public administration and on modern developments in trade and industry, economics and the social services.[1] The proposal was severely criticised, largely because the college was to be limited to Civil Servants. Dale viewed the committee's scheme without enthusiasm, arguing that anything which tended to bring Civil Servants into contact with men of other professions was to be encouraged and anything with the contrary tendency was a mistake.[2] Professor Laski considered that it would be 'a grave error of judgment to segregate officials from the rest of the population'.[3] Sir Gwilym Gibbon saw post-entry training schemes in general as suffering too much 'from the old scholastic spirit': in his opinion, life was 'the true educator' and he remained 'open-minded but unconvinced'[4] about the staff college idea. More important was the fact that the Select Committee's plans did not find favour with the Assheton Committee.

[1] *Sixteenth Report from the Select Committee on National Expenditure* (1941–2) para. 121.

[2] Harold E. Dale, *The Personnel and Problems of the Higher Civil Service* (1943) p. 14.

[3] Harold J. Laski, 'The Education of the Civil Servant', in *Public Administration* (1943) p. 19. In the previous year, Professor Laski had written: 'steps should be taken to create a Staff College for the Administrative Class and for promising recruits from the lower grades'; see his Introduction to J. P. W. Mallalieu, *Passed to You Please* (1942) p. 11.

[4] Sir Gwilym Gibbon, 'The Civil Servant: his Place and Training', in *Public Administration* (1943) pp. 88–9.

It believed that post-entry training should be 'in the main for new entrants and not, primarily, for persons selected as suitable for promotion after some years of experience'.[1] It concluded, therefore, that the Government should not 'associate itself with the establishment of a Staff College as hitherto advocated'.[2] It wanted attention to be concentrated on the needs of the Assistant Principal which, as we have seen, it saw as being best catered for by short courses conducted by the Treasury. At various times in the twenty years following the Assheton Report of 1944, outside commentators such as Professor Robson criticised the adequacy of these courses and, for this reason and because they also wished to see the facilities for training for higher administration extended, they continued to call for the establishment of a Civil Service Staff College that would become 'a centre which would serve as a focus for training in public administration'. But, until at least the early 1960s, the Civil Service could be seen as 'still struggling to overcome its traditional belief that public administration can be learned only by doing',[3] a struggle which tradition comfortably won, so that, just as the Assheton Committee wished, the staff college proposal both remained and remains unimplemented.

Hopes about its eventual establishment were, however, raised once more when the Centre for Administrative Studies was founded in 1963. As representing a more professional approach to the post-entry training of Assistant Principals, the establishment of the C.A.S. was 'a promising beginning',[4] but, compared with his French counterpart, the Assistant Principal was still much undertrained. Although in those departments, notably the Post Office,[5] that have a regional or local office system, there are training schemes under which the Assistant Principal spends time at the circumference of central Government activities, it is fair to say

[1] *Assheton Report*, para. 46.　　　　[2] Ibid. 47.
[3] William A. Robson, 'The Present State of Teaching and Research in Public Administration', in *Public Administration* (1961) p. 220.
[4] William A. Robson, 'The Reform of Government', in *Political Quarterly* (1964) p. 209. Professor Robson went on to ask if it was not too much to hope for that the C.A.S. might evolve 'from its present modest scope' to become a Civil Service Staff College.
[5] R. J. S. Baker, 'The Training of Assistant Principals in the Post Office', in *Public Administration* (1963) pp. 71–2.

that the British administrative cadet does not receive the equivalent of *stage d'administration*. We do not, of course, have in this country institutions comparable with French Prefectures. As Dr Parris has observed, however: 'Perhaps the Town Clerk's office in a large county borough would provide experience most nearly comparable in value. It should not be impossible to arrange for such a period of attachment of, say, four months during the first two years in the Administrative Class.'[1] Compared with the wide range of studies given at the E.N.A. in the cadets' second year, the C.A.S. do not at present attempt more than to give a grounding in economics, statistics and elementary management techniques. It is interesting to note that the Heyworth Committee on Social Studies, while welcoming the establishment of the C.A.S., argued that 'in view of the growing appreciation in the departments of the value to them of social science research', the centre's syllabus 'should include all the social sciences that have a contribution to make to administration', including presumably social psychology, political science and sociology as well as economics.[2] Even if the French go too far in describing the modern administrator as being 'a social scientist in action',[3] in an era when the administrator is often confronted with scientific and technological problems about which he cannot challenge the specialised advice of the experts, a training in the social sciences might well enable him not only to look at such problems from the traditional political, financial and organisational standpoints, but also in terms of their economic and social implications. In the time available, the C.A.S. course can hardly measure up to one of the more exacting honours degree

[1] Henry Parris, 'Twenty Years of L'École Nationale d'Administration', in *Public Administration* (1965) p. 410.

[2] *Report of the Committee on Social Studies* (chairman: Lord Heyworth) Cmnd 2660 (1965) para. 133, p. 42. The Heyworth Committee had earlier observed that even when it was concerning itself with economic matters – the particular example given being an incomes policy – the problems facing the Government were 'just as likely to involve for their solution the expertise of the social psychologist, political scientist or sociologist as that of the economist' (ibid. para. 125, p. 40).

[3] André Bertrand, 'The Recruitment and Training of Higher Civil Servants in the United Kingdom and France', an essay in William A. Robson (ed.) *The Civil Service in Britain and France* (1956) p. 175.

courses, whereas Professor Chapman has described the E.N.A. studies as being of doctoral standard.[1] The C.A.S. has no equivalent of the *stage d'enterprise*, although with its section on the operation of business enterprise the centre does make an attempt to lessen the British Assistant Principal's ignorance of the private sector. An Assistant Principal who takes the course visits five different firms to study different aspects of business, and the companies concerned make available their senior staff to discuss freely with the cadets the organisation of their firms and business problems generally.[2] The Assistant Principals probably find this of some value, but greater benefits would probably follow if they were called upon to do a real job in industry and commerce; and to do this rather than just watch others work would be likely to take rather longer than the two months assigned to the French cadet, possibly three times as long.

The C.A.S., although an advance, is merely a beginning along the road to having a professional Civil Service. The French have secured benefits from their system of initial post-entry training for administrative cadets, and no one on our side has provided sound argument for failing to go the whole way with them. What is needed is a British E.N.A. and, although this subject is discussed at length in chapter 6, the following observations can be made at this point. One feature of the initial training course should be that it ought to begin as soon as the administrative cadets come into the Service. The Treasury say that they believe:

> Assistant Principals come with more enthusiasm to an intensive and rigorous course of study at the Centre after spending two years working in Government departments, than they would if they came as immediate post-graduate students. We also find that experience in two or three different posts in a Government department during their first two years of service is often relevant to subjects under study at the Centre.[3]

One suspects that a good deal of the Treasury's enthusiasm for timing the major part of the C.A.S. course to take place when the

[1] Brian Chapman, *The Profession of Government* (1959) p. 122.
[2] C. D. E. Keeling, 'Treasury Centre for Administrative Studies', in *Public Administration* (1965) pp. 196–7.
[3] Ibid. p. 191.

Assistant Principals have normally completed their probation is concerned with economy. If this is the case it is a particularly narrow-minded approach, especially when one remembers that wastage at Assistant Principal level is only about seven per cent.[1] All the graduate entrants to the generalist side of the Service should, immediately after entry into the Service, embark upon about two and a half years of post-entry training. As will be seen later, this should take the form of two spells of nine-months' instruction in the social sciences, statistics, and management techniques, with, between these two spells, one year of practical experience, one half of which would be spent doing a real job inside a headquarters office of a central government department, and the other half doing a real job in either a regional or local office of such a department, or a local authority, or a public corporation, or a private industrial or commercial company. Moreover, if an amalgamated Executive–Administrative Class is created, and if it is to be a true amalgamation and not a mere change of nomenclature, then all of its entrants, graduates or otherwise, should be required to take, or, in the case of later promotees into it, have at least the option of taking, the course of post-entry training. Much has been made of the irrelevant pre-entry university studies undertaken by the majority of direct entrants to the Administrative Class, but even more pressing are the needs for professional training of young men and women who have normally never been to university at all. The needs of the specialist turned administrator – a subject not dealt with in the Assheton Report – will have to be catered for on a more ambitious scale than at present if members of the specialist groups are successfully to transfer into general management, as may tend to happen more often in the future.

The scale of the above described courses would seem to demand the establishment of a Civil Service Staff College, which would also provide at least part of the training for higher administration needed in the Civil Service. The staff college would, therefore, aim to be an institution which combined the roles of the French

[1] *Sixth Report from the Select Committee on Estimates* (1964–5) *Evidence*, appendix 10, p. 260.

École Nationale d'Administration and their *Centre des Hautes Études Administratives*.[1] Particularly as a result of recent developments which have improved its scope, the most urgent need has now become to extend the availability of training for higher administration. Talk in the Service, recorded by Sir Maurice Dean, of the staff college proposal 'returning in full circle to the Administrative Staff College',[2] ignored the fact that at the most only twenty-four Civil Servants a year attend that college's courses, while the opportunities for sabbatical leave are also modest. Even if the training for higher administration courses at the Civil Service Staff College were limited to the members of the classes which compose the Higher Civil Service, it would contain 'a cross-section of the professional life of the nation wide enough to offer an outstanding and challenging opportunity for courses on general administration with groups of students so interesting and diverse that each would find participation a stimulating and worthwhile experience'.[3] However, the needs of the Positive State

---

[1] The *Centre des Hautes Études Administratives* was described by Brian Chapman, *The Profession of Government* (1959) pp. 128–30. Professor Chapman observed: 'The French Centre des Hautes Études Administratives has not established itself as firmly in the French administrative structure as it might have done. It remains an adjunct to the E.N.A., partly because it is dependent on the E.N.A. for accommodation, but mainly because the E.N.A. is taken seriously whereas the C.H.E.A. is not' (p. 128). Professor Chapman showed that the effectiveness of the C.H.E.A.'s four-month courses had been lessened by the fact that, because of financial difficulties and the reluctance of the central administrations to release their officials for a long period, the courses are part-time. Members attend for two or three days a week, spending the rest of their time on their own job (p. 129). The principal object of the C.H.E.A. course is 'to rejuvenate and re-humanise the officials who attend the course, and to prepare them while still in early middle age for the mental adjustments which will be necessary when they are called on to fill the highest posts'. Chapman concluded that the C.H.E.A. 'has not even begun to achieve this objective. In comparison with the E.N.A., the experiment of the *Centre des Hautes Études Administratives* has not been a success' (p. 130).

[2] Sir Maurice Dean, 'The Public Servant and the Study of Public Administration', in *Public Administration* (1962) p. 22.

[3] F. J. Tickner, 'Public Service Training in the Past Decade', in *Public Administration* (1956) p. 38. Professor Chapman, drawing upon his wide knowledge of European public administration, has made clear the

would seem to dictate that those attending the higher administration courses should also include some administrators drawn
from the local authorities, the public corporations and private
industry and commerce: the experience of the Administrative
Staff College has shown that the Assheton Committee was mistaken in believing that a course useful both to those working in the
public and the private sectors could not be drawn up. The Civil
Service Staff College need not set out to be the exclusive source
of training for higher administration for Civil Servants, but to
extend the scope available: Civil Servants would still attend
courses at such institutions as the Imperial Defence College and
receive similar and preferably extended opportunities for sabbatical leave. The Civil Service Staff College idea was, unfortunately,
shelved once again when the Osmond Committee, reviewing
Civil Service Training in 1964, spoilt an otherwise valuable and
constructive report by suggesting that the whole question should
be reconsidered when there was more experience of the Centre
for Administrative Studies.[1] This was a very cautious approach

---

need for more and better training for higher administration: 'Most
countries are beginning to realise that if senior officials are not to arrive
at the highest posts jaded, harassed and narrow, they must be given a
breather in the middle of their career when they can benefit from intellectual stimulation and a rest from current business. Also, even when
different groups have mixed together in the course of their training, there
is a great need for people from different branches of the public service
and private industry to associate together consistently over a period
after they have had experience of the burdens of authority. Mutual
comprehension and mutual instruction is extremely valuable, and is
perhaps the best way to ensure that senior administrators grow in stature
as they assume greater responsibilities.' (Brian Chapman, *The Profession
of Government*, 1959, p. 130.)

[1] *Osmond Report* (1964) paras 96–103. The Osmond Committee
recommended: 'further and more detailed consideration should be given
to the possibility of a central institution for the higher training of – but
not exclusively of – Civil Servants. Such an examination should be
undertaken as soon as a review of the Centre for Administrative Studies
is possible. It then ought to produce a more definite assessment of the
need for, and the cost of, such a new establishment' (para. 102). This
consideration 'should be given by a committee drawn from a wider
field than that of the National Whitley Council, including non-Civil
Servants, but including both Official and Staff Side members of the
Council' (para. 103).

and, fortunately, shortly afterwards, in November 1965, a Treasury Working Party was appointed and asked to consider the training needs for middle and higher management in the Civil Service and to submit recommendations on the length, content and organisation of such training, taking account of the long-term future of the Centre for Administrative Studies and the desirability or otherwise of setting up a Civil Service Staff College. The Working Party was 'expected to report by the end of 1966', and its findings were to be made available to the Fulton Committee.[1] The Working Party, in fact, achieved its target and its findings are discussed in Chapter 6. As the result of this latest investigation into training in the Civil Service, there is a distinct possibility that a Civil Service Staff College will at long last be established.

A question that the Fulton Committee will also have to consider is that concerning exchanges of staff between the Civil Service and private industry and commerce. When asked about such exchanges, the Head of the Civil Service, Sir Laurence Helsby, said in 1964 that while he saw 'a place for some exchanges', he was inclined to doubt whether those who had experienced them would be 'better men for this particular experience – better than they would have been if they had enlarged their experience within the Service'.[2] The Treasury Establishments Officer believed that exchanges would not be particularly valuable, saying that in the comparatively short career of the Civil Servant 'there are limits to what, I might say, are the sort of fancy things you can do'.[3] More recently, official policy has been to encourage short secondments to industry and commerce,[4] but the above sentiments while, at first sight, appearing to be mere conservatism, have their validity. There is no point in Civil Servants being seconded to industry or commerce or indeed anywhere else except

[1] H.M. Treasury, *General Note on Training in the Civil Service* (1966) p. 8.

[2] *Fifth Report from the Select Committee on Estimates* (1963–4) *Evidence*, questions 1088–9.

[3] Ibid. question 1014.

[4] *Sixth Report from the Select Committee on Estimates* (1964–5) *Evidence*, question 757. Sir William Armstrong, who gave this information, added that staff shortages have made it difficult to implement this policy fully.

to do a real job. At least as regards industry and commerce, unless one already possesses the relevant specialisms, the training for such a job seems bound to take about two years. It also has to be done successfully and experience has to be acquired. This could mean two, probably four more years. This would mean six years out of the Civil Servants' careers at a job outside public administration acquiring experience that will still not amount to a wide knowledge of industry or commerce. Certainly, some administrators with such knowledge are needed in the Civil Service, but they would be best secured by late-entry recruitment. Generally, one would agree with Sir Laurence Helsby in doubting the value of secondments to industry or commerce compared with broadening experience of management within the Service.

Recent changes in the post-entry training arrangements of the Administrative Class have meant that no longer does training for the administrative cadet consist of an almost exclusive reliance on 'the moral and intellectual discipline of apprenticeship in an office where the affairs of Government are transacted'.[1] The establishment of the Centre for Administrative Studies has breached the old position, and the Fulton Committee may recommend that the centre should be developed into a Civil Service Staff College. As for the Administrative Class itself, its separate existence may not survive the Fulton Committee's examination of the structure of the Service: a possibility being that it will be merged with the Executive Class, its working relationship with which will now be examined.

[1] C. H. Sisson, *The Spirit of British Administration* (1959) p. 34.

CHAPTER FOUR

The Relationship between the Executive and Administrative Classes

I THE DISTINCTION BETWEEN POLICY AND EXECUTIVE WORK

ACCORDING to the Reorganisation Committee of 1920–1, the duties appropriate to the Administrative Class were those concerned with 'the formation of policy, with the co-ordination and improvement of Government machinery, and with the general administration and control of the departments of the Public Service'.[1] In their initial analysis the committee bracketed the Administrative Class together with an Executive Class,[2] but the structure that they eventually outlined consisted of separate hierarchies, with the Executive Class being assigned 'the higher work of supply and accounting departments, and of other executive or specialised branches of the Service'. This work was to cover

> a wide field, and requires in different degrees the qualities of judgment, initiative and resource. In the junior ranks it comprises the critical examination of particular cases of lesser importance not clearly within the scope of approved regulations, or general decisions, initial investigations into matters of higher importance, and the immediate direction of small blocks of business. In its upper ranges it is concerned with matters of internal organisation and control with the settlement of broad questions arising out of business in hand or in contemplation, and with the responsible conduct of important operations.[3]

Like the remainder of the generalist side of the Service, the direct-entry recruitment arrangements of the two classes were related to 'well-defined stages in the educational system of the country':

---

[1] *Interim Report of the Reorganisation Committee* (1921) para. 43.
[2] Ibid. paras 16 and 17.   [3] Ibid. para. 32.

the Executive Class, like its predecessors the Second Division and the Intermediate Class, was to secure its direct entrants from the ranks of eighteen-plus school leavers, while the Administrative Class continued to aim to secure its from the cream of the university honours graduates.[1]

The Executive Class's spheres of activity were firmly restricted during the inter-war period, but the changing and expanding role of the State made distinctions such as those which were maintained between the Executive and Administrative Classes increasingly unreal. Looking back on his wartime experiences in the Ministry of Supply, Sir Oliver Franks later commented: 'I was impressed by the closeness of the link between policy and execution. One sometimes hears it said that Administrative Civil Servants are concerned with policy but leave execution to others: at best this is a dangerous half truth.'[2] Yet, in 1947, the very year in which Franks wrote those words, when the generalist side of the Service was reorganised, the Administrative and Executive Classes were still kept separate. As even the Treasury had to admit in 1953 that in practice, 'It is not always possible to draw a clear-cut distinction between policy work and executive work',[3] it is not very surprising that, by the time that the structure of the Civil Service came to be reviewed by the Fulton Committee, appointed in February 1966, the more progressive members of the Executive Class had come to advocate a merger between the Executive and Administrative Classes, or that this proposal had come to attract outside attention and support. What follows is

[1] *Written Statement submitted to the Tomlin Commission by the Civil Service Commissioners* (1929) para. 3. To be precise the pre-1914 age limits for candidates for the Second Division were 17–20, and for the Intermediate Class 18–19½ (*MacDonnell Evidence*, questions 309–10). The Reorganisation Committee recommended that recruitment to the Executive Class should be 'by open, competitive, written examination between the ages of 18 and 19': the syllabus of the examination being framed 'with reference to the standard of development reached at the end of a secondary school course' (para. 33).

[2] Sir Oliver Franks, *The Experience of a University Teacher in the Civil Service* (1947) p. 11.

[3] *Factual Memorandum submitted by the Treasury to the Priestley Commission* (1953) para. 268.

some discussion of the relationship between the work of the Executive and Administrative Classes and a consideration of the pre-Fulton proposals for the amalgamation of these classes, prefaced by an examination of the current opportunities available to the Executive Class for advancement to the Administrative Class, as seen in their historical context.

II PROMOTION FROM BELOW INTO THE ADMINISTRATIVE CLASS

The Trevelyan–Northcote Report had not dealt with promotion from below into the highest class of the Service, and when the Service came to be gradually reconstructed after 1870 the question of provision for such promotions naturally came to be one of the major subjects that faced the various official investigations into the Service that were made from time to time. The Treasury's official attitude was expressed in a letter that it wrote to the Colonial Office in 1884:

> Although the number of Lower Division clerks promoted to the Higher Division must always bear a small proportion to the number not so promoted, it is not necessary that they should be an insignificant proportion of the Upper Division. On the contrary, My Lords look forward to that Division being largely replenished, in certain departments from the best members of the Lower Division. It will probably always be necessary to reserve a power of direct appointment to the Upper Division, but there are many departments in which this power need not – so far as My Lords can foresee – be exercised habitually or even frequently. Promotion from the Lower to the Higher Division may, therefore, fairly be considered as a legitimate aspiration for the superior members of the former.[1]

The Treasury, however, did not have the power to ensure that the various departments followed such policies, and the Home

[1] The Treasury's letter to the Colonial Office, dated 19 June 1884, was reproduced in a memorial submitted by the Lower Division clerks of the Home Office to the Ridley Commission (appendix to their *Second Report*, p. 528).

Office and the Colonial Office itself maintained 'an absolute bar' to such promotions, which caused the Lower Division clerks at the Home Office to complain bitterly about 'the division of the clerical class into severely defined classes with a practically insuperable barrier between them'.[1] The architect of open competition, Robert Lowe, was one of those 'entirely against promoting people from one class to another'. He wanted the Lower or Second Division clerks to look for opportunities within their own career hierarchy because 'when a man gets an office, his duty is to learn his business in it, and not to be taking up his time in trying to get higher; I should not at all encourage the notion of clerks going from the second class into the first class'. Although he believed that the Lower Division clerks 'ought to be allowed to compete' in the open competition for the Higher Division, he was against giving them an age concession.[2] The Playfair Commission took a more liberal attitude on that particular question, but their general feeling was that promotion from below into the Higher Division 'should be a matter of rare occurrence'. This was thought to be necessary 'if there is to be any educational test for the Higher Division; and it is reasonable, not only because the original qualifications are lower, but also because the character of the work in the inferior grades will be rarely calculated to develop superior capacities'. Promotions from below needed a certificate from the Civil Service Commissioners, granted upon a special recommendation of the head of the department concerned and with the assent of the Treasury, and with the details published in *The London Gazette*;[3] and the Lower Division clerks were made eligible for such promotions after ten years' service. The Treasury reduced this minimum qualifying period from ten years to eight and improved the Second Division hierarchy after the Ridley

---

[1] *Ridley Evidence*, questions 11,140, 12,449 and 12,450; the Lower Division clerks made their remarks in their memorial, p. 528.

[2] *Playfair Evidence*, question 3124; and *Childers Evidence*, question 4436. As Benjamin Jowett later wrote of Lowe: 'It was really an aristocracy of education and intelligence, not a democracy, with which he was in sympathy.' (A. Patchett Martin, *The Life and Letters of the Right Honourable Robert Lowe, Viscount Sherbrooke*, 1893, vol. II, p. 491.)

[3] *First Playfair Report* (1875), p. 18.

Report, which had called for 'all prizes of the Service to be open to exceptional fitness'.[1]

Naturally enough, the representatives of the Second Division clerks maintained in their evidence to the MacDonnell Commission that its predecessor's aims had not been realised. They complained about the continuing barrier between the Divisions, and they drew up a scheme which proposed the abolition of the First Division as a separate class. They believed that the most obvious argument against the barrier was that 'practically no attempt is made to utilise the ability which cannot but be present in any large body of men recruited in the manner of the Second Division'. They pointed to:

> The attainment of high qualifications by Second Division clerks; for example, it is not an uncommon thing for a Second Division clerk to become a barrister, or for him to take a degree at London University. High honours in the B.Sc. (Economics) at London University have been taken by Second Division clerks, and there are not included in this number many others who take courses in special subjects, but who do not feel able to spare the time necessary for taking the full degree course.

They quoted the opinion of Professor Edwin Cannan at the L.S.E., whose views were all the more interesting because he was no social democrat. Talking about his evening students, Cannan said that he had been 'rather struck' with the quality of the Second Division Civil Servants: 'I dare say, as an average, their ability is not very high, but the ability of the people who come to us, who are, of course, a picked lot, is very considerable.' Cannan emphasised that he had known 'a good many of these Second Division Civil Servants, who are really very capable, so much so that it makes

---

[1] The ten-year qualifying period was established by the Order in Council of 12 February 1876 which created the Lower Division. The Ridley Commission (*Second Report*, para. 47) made it clear that the Lower Division clerks had no right to promotion after the elapse of that period, but they wanted provision to be made to reward 'exceptional fitness' (para. 48). The Treasury later announced that it had reduced the qualifying period. (*Paper showing the manner in which the recommendations of the Royal Commission with respect to the Civil Service have been dealt with*, 1894, p. 10, para. 7.)

me doubt whether the present chasm between the two Divisions is expedient'.[1]

The MacDonnell Commission, quite rightly, was in favour of a university entry into the Service, and it saw this as being best achieved by maintaining a separate Administrative Class, rather than abolishing it as the Second Division clerks had wanted.[2] The commission had taken to heart the lessons of an unfortunate experiment along those lines that had taken place in the customs department.[3] They quite fairly drew attention to the considerable career opportunities for the Second Division clerks to secure promotion 'in ordinary course' within their own hierarchy.[4] Regarding promotions 'not in ordinary course' to the First Division, the MacDonnell Commission, to its credit, condemned, and forced the Treasury to reform, the existing rules which often financially penalised the Second Division man who was promoted in late career.[5] The commission believed that, in any case, such promotions should preferably take place in early career because there was 'no more training for the real duties of administration, which requires freshness of mind, individuality and judgment, than a long period of routine work, however faithfully performed;

---

[1] Statement of the Association of Clerks of the Second Division (pp. 483–93) contained in appendix v to the *Second Report of the Mac-Donnell Commission* (1912). Cannan talked in his evidence to the Royal Commission on University Education in London (1911, questions 7112 ff.) about the superiority of the 'social environment' of Oxford, which led that university's products, although apparently less intelligent than his evening students, not to 'violate' his feelings as much as his own students' manner.

[2] *MacDonnell Majority Report* (1914), ch. III, para. 42: the commission's conclusion being that 'the best education taken in conjunction with the training and formative influence of University life produces the best type of Public Servant'.

[3] *MacDonnell Majority Report*, ch. III, para. 43.

[4] Ibid. ch. VIII, paras 19–21. The Second Division which numbered 4000 clerks had about 800 posts above it which it could regard as legitimate promotion outlets (para. 21).

[5] *MacDonnell Majority Report*, ch. VIII, para. 22. The working of the Treasury Circular of 11 December 1899, which governed such promotions, was criticised by the former Secretary to the Office of Works (question 17,520). The commission itself made inquiries, and the Treasury revised the relevant provisions (questions 35,790 and 36,078).

if, therefore, a man has sufficient capacity to fit him for administrative work, his fitness should be ascertained as early as possible in his career'. The commission recommended that 'the period of service qualifying for promotion from the existing Second Division to the Administrative Class should be reduced from eight to six years'.[1]

The procedure for promotion to the First Division examined by the MacDonnell Commission was largely that recommended by their Playfair predecessors. The first stage was that the departmental head had to make a special recommendation certifying that the Second Division clerk had 'so distinguished himself among the members of his class by exceptional ability and merit and has shown such special qualifications for the duties of the post in question that it would be for the interest of the Public Service that he should be specially promoted'. Then the Treasury had to grant their approval and the Civil Service Commissioners had to issue a certificate of qualification. The action of the Commissioners was little more than a formality because they did not insist upon 'requiring a clerk so presented to them for promotion to undergo an examination even of a qualifying standard because in most cases an educational test at all approaching the severity of the Class I examination would prove prohibitive'. But the MacDonnell Commission approved the requirement of recertification because it gave occasion 'for the exercise by the Treasury of that central control to which we attach importance'. Without such control 'there would be a danger of different standards of efficiency being adopted in different departments as qualifying for promotion, and of unduly frequent promotion from a lower to a higher class depressing the standard of the higher class and thereby decreasing its efficiency'. The Commission did not suggest that the classes below the First Division would not 'produce able men fit to take their places side by side with the best products of the Class I examination'. But they did believe that 'such men are exceptional, and it is in order to limit promotion to the men who are really exceptional that the restriction has been imposed and should, in our opinion, be maintained'.[2]

[1] *MacDonnell Majority Report*, ch. VIII, para. 23.   [2] Ibid. paras 6 and 13.

The MacDonnell Commission's inquiries into the extent to which Second Division clerks had been promoted to situations normally filled by the Class I examinations showed that over the period 1892–1911 inclusive, the total number of such promotions was seventy-three, which meant an annual average of 3·65. Over the same period the total number of situations filled from the open competition was 467, giving an annual average of 23·35, which meant that the number of officers promoted from the Second Division stood to the number recruited by the Class I examination in the ratio of 13·5 to 86·5.[1]

The MacDonnell Commission drew attention to the fact that the promotions from below had 'not been very evenly distributed either over the whole Service or over those departments in which officers of the Administrative Class are employed'. That class was actually to be found in only sixteen of the sixty departments in which the Second Division clerks served, which meant that for over 36 per cent of those clerks there was no possibility of class-to-class promotion apart from transfer.[2] Even in the departments which employed both classes the numbers had been very uneven. In the case of the Admiralty, the Board of Trade and the Board of Inland Revenue promotions had been very numerous but there were other departments in which no such promotion had ever taken place. The MacDonnell Commission believed that 'it would be unreasonable to expect that an even ratio of promotion from the Second Division to situations ordinarily recruited by the Class I examination should be preserved throughout the Service'. Nevertheless, they considered that the extremes of disparity which they had noticed were 'prima facie indications that the policy of different departments had not been adequately controlled and coordinated at least in this respect'. The commission believed that 'such control and co-ordination ought to be more effectively exercised by the Treasury'.[3]

In dealing with the representations made to them by the Second Division clerks, the MacDonnell Commission said that their evidence had shown 'a tendency to regard these promotions rather with reference to the total strength of the Second Division than to

[1] Ibid. para. 14.   [2] Ibid. para. 16.   [3] Ibid. para. 17.

that of the Administrative Class'. The commission pointed out that, as the Second Division numbered about 4000 and the Administrative Class only about 450, it was obvious that the percentage of Second Division clerks who did secure promotion to the Administrative Class was bound to be very much lower than the percentage of those who did not. The commission had found that about one-sixth of the Administrative Class had been promoted from below, a figure which they said could not be regarded as inconsiderable.[1] Given the social climate of the time, this was a fair comment.

The MacDonnell Commission's views about the value of a direct entry into the Administrative Class from the universities were also shared by the Reorganisation Committee, who also wanted to see a central authority established which would handle promotions from below into the class. They wanted Assistant Principal vacancies to be open to those 'already in the Service who show early proof of real ability and promise of being able to discharge in the course of time, higher administrative functions'. The committee also favoured direct promotions from below to the Principal and Assistant Secretary grades for those who showed administrative potential later in their careers. Advancement to the Administrative Class was made a 'straight line' promotion in 1922, which meant that not only the procedure described by the MacDonnell Commission was dispensed with, but also the minimum service requirement.[2]

The Administrative Class's attitude towards promotion from below was more important than the formal procedures, and this was displayed in the evidence given by leading administrators to the Tomlin Commission. Sir Arthur Robinson summed up the general view when he said that men promoted to the Administrative Class did well, but from the standpoint of rising to the top the examination entrants were better because they were more

---

[1] Ibid. para. 15.

[2] *Interim Report of the Reorganisation Committee* (1921) paras 45, 51 and 52. That 'straight line' promotions no longer needed recertification by the Civil Service Commissioners was announced in *The London Gazette* of 7 Mar 1922.

adaptable.[1] Sir John Anderson had similar opinions, but he did say that when he had a vacancy for an Assistant Principal in the Home Office, the first thing he did was to look around for possible promotees from below, and only if he was unsuccessful in this review did he ask the Civil Service Commission to assign him someone from the examination. Sir John said that it was important that the Administrative Class should contain both the university entrant and the promoted man, although he did not believe that the Home Office, where promotions from below had been very rare before 1914, had yet had enough experience to enable him to say what were the right proportions of the two types. Sir John did consider, however, that direct entrants had qualities that made them more mobile. He said that it very often happened that one could find a man who was admirably suited to administrative work within a limited sphere, and one might be glad to promote an officer from below to such a post; but he added that there would be a loss of elasticity if too many posts of that kind were carried in a department.[2]

There seems little doubt that there was a great deal of talent going to waste in the general classes below the Administrative Class. The Director of the L.S.E. told the Tomlin Commission that the college had always had a very large body of such Civil Servants studying for a degree there in the evenings, and he said that some of them were among the college's best students.[3] Professor Laski wrote in 1931: 'I have myself taught able young officials of this kind; and neither their attainment of a brilliant degree in subjects relevant to their departmental work, nor even the publication of researches of importance in that field, has led to their being given special opportunity to be seconded for better work.'[4]

Of those who were fortunate enough to secure promotion, Sir Albert Flynn, a leading Civil Servant, wrote in 1928 that they

[1] *Tomlin Evidence*, question 12,598: Robinson being Permanent Secretary to the Ministry of Health.

[2] Ibid. questions 2153 and 2320.

[3] Ibid. question 11,423: the Director being Sir William Beveridge.

[4] Harold J. Laski, 'The Tomlin Report on the Civil Service', in *Political Quarterly* (1931) p. 509.

were as good as the best of the Administrative Class in force of character, power of command and width of outlook; and they generally knew 'the office and its real business better than the higher class man, who usually spends much of his junior time private secretarying – the likeliest road to preferment but a one-sided training'. Flynn thought that half of the administrative posts could be satisfactorily filled from the ranks, but that proportion 'could not be exceeded without the risk of finding too few men equal to the topmost posts'.[1] Rather less faith in the virtues of the promotee was shown by Lord Chorley, who wrote in 1944 that the average promoted man was disappointing:

> One would expect to find those who have worked their way up filled with exceptional energy and initiative, whereas they are filled only with exceptional industry and regard for precedent. They are invariably men of personal charm, so much so that one wonders whether selection boards place this quality as the first desideratum, exceptionally helpful, and, indeed, full of human qualities. But they are apt to shy at accepting personal responsibility for any step at all away from the recognised paths, are peculiarly susceptible to any possible criticism, and, in short, represent the Service in its more static, rather than its more dynamic aspects.[2]

As for the extent of promotion from below during the inter-war period, the readily available statistics give an unclear picture. The Treasury told the Tomlin Commission that, during the years 1921–8 inclusive, appointments to the Administrative Class by competition and promotion respectively numbered eighty-four and forty-seven. Such figures did not take account of the 200 or so who had entered the Administrative Class by means of the post-First World War Reconstruction competition.[3] The Tomlin

---

[1] Sir Albert Flynn, *The Problems of the Civil Service* (1928) pp. 32–3.
[2] R. S. T. Chorley, 'Some Thoughts on the Civil Service', *Agenda*, vol. III, no. 4, 1944, p. 120.
[3] Sir Russell Scott gave the commission the Treasury's figures (*Tomlin Evidence*, question 80). Although Scott's evidence should have been definitive as he was Controller of Establishments at the Treasury, the Society of Civil Servants certainly called their accuracy into question (*Tomlin Evidence*, appendix IX, paras 327, 332 and 336). The precise number of appointments to the Administrative Class under the Reconstruction regulations after the First World War was 203, 198 of whom were

Report of 1931 stated that 'about one-quarter of the officers now serving in the Administrative Class had been promoted to that Class from other Classes'.[1] But it was probable that this percentage included transfers from the specialist groups, and it seemed doubtful whether in 1939 more than one-fifth of the Administrative Class had been promoted from below. Taking into account the relative size of the Administrative and Executive Classes, promotion from below was better described by Sir Russell Scott's phrase as 'the process of exceptional promotion', than as being 'very rare' as Flynn had said. Flynn had seen the Service as being divided into castes, with the Administrative Class not admitting 'the caste of the plains', and with the Permanent Secretaries seeing the ruling class of the Service as the peculiar property of the residential universities.[2] The leading positions in the Administrative Class were normally filled by men drawn from such backgrounds, but even in 1914 about sixteen per cent of the class as a whole had been promoted from 'the caste of the plains', and that percentage had been very probably increased during the inter-war period. The failure to establish a central authority to supervise promotions from below until 1936 may well have indicated a lack of enthusiasm for such advancement,[3] but there was no need to see this entirely as a conspiracy based on social prejudice. The distribution of posts within the Administrative Class appeared to lead to a promotion blockage within the class, at least in the

---

ex-servicemen (*Third Interim Report of the Lytton Committee on the Appointment of Ex-Servicemen to posts in the Civil Service,* June 1921, para. 23).

[1] *Tomlin Report* (1931) para. 103. The commission's statistics may well also have contained transferees across from the Foreign Service, who would be more accurately classified as direct entrants.

[2] *Tomlin Evidence,* question 80; Flynn, op. cit. p. 30.

[3] When machinery was set up in 1936 for promotions from Executive Officer to Assistant Principal, it was established on the assumption that 'in view of the relatively small numbers of vacancies which arise annually in the Assistant Principal grade, it will be necessary that the number of officers nominated by departments should be kept low'. The official side refused to contemplate service-wide promotions from Higher Executive Officer to Principal (*Whitley Bulletin,* May 1935, p. 15).

1920s;[1] while, in any case, direct-entry recruitment to the Administrative Class was such an easy business during the inter-war period that there was little incentive to search the other classes for undiscovered talent. The pressures of the Second World War and its aftermath were to provide that incentive.

In contrast with the Reconstruction competitions that had been held after 1918, those held after the Second World War included limited competitions whereby established Civil Servants could compete among themselves for a quota of Assistant Principal vacancies. These competitions represented an important break with the inter-war practice by which the main means of advancing to the Administrative Class had either been by departmental promotion, or by taking the academically exacting open competition, handicapped by the lack of time for preparation, and with the sole advantage of an age allowance of two years. The Limited Administrative Competition became part of the normal Administrative Class recruitment pattern in 1948, having assigned to it one-fifth of the annual total of Assistant Principal vacancies. Candidates had to be between twenty-one and thirty years of age, with at least two years' established service, and they had to be nominated by their departments. The upper age-limit was later reduced to twenty-eight, while the requirement of departmental nomination was finally abolished in 1956. Originally the selection process was restricted to a competition along the lines of Method II of the open competition, but in 1956 it also became possible to compete by a Method I style of examination.[2]

[1] This was certainly the picture painted by the First Division Association in their evidence to the Tomlin Commission (*Tomlin Evidence*, appendix VIII, paras 41–59). Although one tends to distrust evidence given by a vested interest, there was no doubt that early promises to regulate the number of Assistant Principal and Principal posts, so that the former would normally secure promotion to the latter grade after 'about 7 to 8 years', were not fulfilled. The F.D.A. estimated (para. 55) that on current (i.e. 1930) complements one-third of the Assistant Principals could not hope to go beyond Principal. The inter-war practice was to treat the Assistant Principal grade not as a training grade, but as a substantive rank (see Sir John Anderson's evidence, questions 2147 and 2193).

[2] *National Whitley Council Report*, 'Recruitment to Established Posts in the Civil Service during the Reconstruction Period' (chairman:

The record of the Limited Administrative Competition over the period 1948–66 was disappointing. After its first three years, the competition failed to fill its vacancies in any year, and over the whole period it only managed to fill about fifty-two per cent of the Assistant Principal vacancies assigned to it. An analysis of the published details about successful candidates showed that between 1952 and 1966 the Executive Class provided fifty-two and the Special Departmental Classes accounted for thirteen of the seventy successes; the total being made up by three Customs and Excise Officers, a Telecommunications Traffic Superintendent and a departmental professional officer. Thirty-three of the seventy had university degrees, and three had secured first class honours. One welcome feature was that one-third of the graduate successes had degrees in economics and related subjects: all but one of the remainder had arts degrees. Nine of the successful graduates had been educated at either Oxford or Cambridge, and sixteen had been educated at the University of London, several of them having taken advantage of that university's facilities for part-time study for degrees.[1]

The unsatisfactory general record of the Limited Administrative Competition led to an experimental scheme being introduced in 1963, which aimed at finding young Executive Officers who were of Administrative Class quality, but who were not brought forward under the existing arrangements. Establishments Officers in departments with Administrative Class cadres were asked to review the Executive Officers in their department who had served at least four years in that grade, and to select two per department to be given an eighteen-months' trial on Administrative Class work.

J. A. Barlow), Nov 1944, paras 45–50. The actual working of the system was described in the *Reports of the Civil Service Commissioners*: notably their *84th Report*, section XIII, paras 2–3; *86th Report*, paras 55–6; *87th Report*, para. 12; *91st Report*, para. 14; *92nd Report*, para. 18.

[1] Appendix III, Table 5 of this book makes very clear that the record of the limited administrative competition had been rather depressing. The statistics given in the text have been derived from the personal details given about successful candidates in this competition in the *Reports of the Civil Service Commissioners* for the years 1952–66 inclusive.

At the end of the trial period, the Executive Officers considered suitable were nominated to the Civil Service Commissioners, who put them through appropriate but abbreviated C.S.S.B. procedures. This was followed by an appearance before a departmental board, with Civil Service Commission representation, after which successful candidates would be promoted to Assistant Principal in their own departments. While this experimental scheme was in operation there was to be no change in the arrangements for the Limited Assistant Principal examination.[1] This pilot scheme in fact produced eight Assistant Principals, and the Treasury said that it would be repeated.[2] The introduction of this scheme can be seen as a partial reversal of the trend of post-war policy, because it represents a return to a system of departmental promotion to Assistant Principal.

Direct promotions from below to Principal posts are open to members of the Executive Class aged thirty and above, most of the candidates usually being of at least Higher Executive Officer rank. Such promotions have until relatively recently normally been made departmentally, with selection being made by 'a departmental board with which the Civil Service Commission is usually associated'. There are now, however, in addition, provisions for centralised class-to-class promotion to Principal 'mainly intended to provide opportunities for people in departments with little or no Administrative cadre': candidates for such advancement are nominated by their departments, and selection is by the C.S.S.B. and Final Selection Board machinery.[3] The first of such centralised competitions for promotion to Principal was held by the Civil Service Commissioners in 1955 for candidates nominated by departments with no administrative staff; and in 1960, the Commissioners helped the Post Office to choose its promotees, candidates having to attend the C.S.S.B. and take tests similar to those employed in Method II, and they were then interviewed by a departmental board on which the Commissioners were represented.

---

[1] *Civil Service Opinion*, Oct 1963, pp. 266 and 275.
[2] *Treasury Factual Memorandum to the Fulton Committee* (1966) para. 99.
[3] Ibid. para. 101.

Following this experiment, the Treasury agreed to a centralised promotion procedure in 1961 for which as many departments as wished could nominate candidates. In this particular operation, for example, 175 candidates from forty-two departments attended the C.S.S.B. tests, of whom 124 were invited to appear before a Final Selection Board. Thirteen candidates were recommended to their departments as suitable for immediate promotion to Principal, of whom three belonged to departments without an administrative cadre. Several of the runners-up were subsequently promoted, or transferred to duties where their administrative potentialities could be given a further trial. The official view was that this method of centralised selection ensured the application to candidates from all departments of a common standard of promotion: it enabled departments to test their own standards and, in the case of large departments, to have an impartial assessment of candidates working away from headquarters; and it brought into the field a number of candidates from departments which offered no careers in the Administrative Class.[1] When service-wide class-to-class reviews for promotion to Principal were held in 1964 and 1965, the same procedure was followed.[2]

[1] Civil Service Commissioners, *87th Report* (para. 34), *90th Report* (paras 46–7) and *95th Report* (p. 4).

[2] About the 1964 competition, the Civil Service Commissioners observed that the shortage of Principals in the Service had been accentuated by the increased demands made upon the Service: 'It was therefore necessary to make every effort to ensure that those in other grades and classes within the Service were given the opportunity for promotion or transfer into the Administrative Class if they possessed the necessary qualities of mind and personality. Such opportunities are always present but it was decided to supplement them by repeating the Service-wide review which was held in 1961 with centralised selection through the Commission. This form of review has the particular advantage that it facilitates promotion opportunities for suitable officers serving in departments with few Administrative Class posts. 106 candidates were nominated by 47 departments, and 31 were found suitable for promotion to the Administrative Class as Principals. Of these 20 were promoted in their own departments, and the remainder were transferred elsewhere.' (*98th Report*, pp. 1–2.) About the 1965 competition the Commissioners wrote: 'Departments were again asked to nominate suitable officers from other grades and classes to take part in a centralised promotion exercise for Principal posts. On this occasion the departments concerned were mainly those

There are thus three routes by which a member of the Executive Class can advance to the Administrative Class. Promotion to Assistant Principal is open to the class's younger members either by success in the limited competition, or by temporary direct promotion needing subsequent confirmation. Direct promotion to Principal or, more rarely, above is open to the class's members who are aged at least thirty. As the Executive Class is about thirty times as big as the Administrative Class, class-to-class advancement is necessarily exceptional rather than normal for its members. Nevertheless, the Treasury estimated in 1965 that 40 per cent of the Administrative Class was drawn from the Executive Class,[1] and it is with this in mind that an examination follows of the relationship between, and the pre-Fulton proposals for the merger of, the two classes.

III THE RELATIONSHIP BETWEEN, AND THE PRE-FULTON PROPOSALS FOR THE FUSION OF, THE EXECUTIVE AND ADMINISTRATIVE CLASSES

In 1965, the Select Committee on Estimates conducted an important investigation into direct-entry recruitment to the Civil Service, which naturally led them to survey the structure of that Service and particularly the role of its governing class, the Administrative Class. The committee asked Sir Laurence Helsby, the Head of the Civil Service, if he saw the divisions of responsibility between the different classes remaining much the same. Sir Laurence replied that, while it was difficult to say that things could remain just as they were, he still favoured the retention of a separate Administrative Class. It was interesting to see that he

---

which had little or no administrative cadre of their own. The selection process was on the same lines as in the exercise held in 1964 and 9 candidates were successful.' (*99th Report*, p. 5.)

[1] *Sixth Report from the Select Committee on Estimates* (1964–5) *Evidence*, p. 23.

did not follow the same line that the Treasury witnesses had taken
before the Priestley Commission, in resisting claims for pay
equality from the Society of Civil Servants, the Executive Class's
'trade union', and from the specialists' representatives, of reserving
the description of 'administration' for the duties of the Administrative Class.[1] On the contrary, Sir Laurence said that, as the size
of the Administrative Class was only about one half per cent of
the total Civil Service, it would be 'quite wrong to assume that
any large proportion of all administrative work in the general
sense could possibly be done by such a small group'. He added:
'The great weight of the day-to-day administration in the Service
is carried by the Executive Class, by the Scientific Officer Class and
by the senior grades of the number of other Classes who provide
the aggregate of probably something around ten per cent of staff
engaged in administration in the broad sense, which is necessary
in this kind of organisation.' As to the relationship between the
duties of the Executive and Administrative Classes, Sir Laurence
argued that there should continue to be 'a small Administrative
Class remaining separate from the general service Class responsible
for the day-to-day run of administration'. The Administrative
Class was responsible, not for administration but 'for somewhat
specialised functions which seldom had any precise counterpart in
outside organisations, particularly in the industrial and commercial
sphere, until you get right up to board level'. He accounted for
these specialised functions by pointing to 'the sheer size and complexity of the Government machine. It has ramifications and a
complex system of inter-relationships between organisations
which have no counterpart in less sophisticated machines.' The

---

[1] For example, *Priestley Evidence*, questions 4114–15. The Treasury
maintained: 'The case put by the Society depended very largely on the
proposition that the Executive Class is engaged in administrative divisions
in departments and that is only true of a small minority of the Class,
and one gets perhaps a little misled if one only looks at that minority.'
It was difficult to give an accurate figure, but the Treasury estimated that
'more likely under rather than over 10 per cent of the Executive Class
are employed in administrative divisions' (*Priestley Evidence*, question
3263). An 'administrative division' being one in which the Administrative
Class was employed: the implication was that 'administration' was not
performed elsewhere.

accountability of the Civil Service to Ministers and through them to Parliament also introduced a factor of public accountability 'which does not arise in the same form in other organisations in this country'.[1]

The Administrative Class was, therefore, seen by Sir Laurence Helsby as being engaged in something more than 'the top layer of direction in any organisation', which had been Lord Bridges's definition of administration[2] and, indeed, this task had been seen as being shared with the other leading classes of the Higher Civil Service. But the picture drawn by Sir Laurence was the traditional one of the special nature of ministerial responsibility being seen as dominating the careers of the leading administrators, who were mainly concerned with consultation and co-ordination. The direct needs of the Minister might well dominate the official lives of Under-Secretaries and above in the administrative hierarchies of the more politically-sensitive departments. But, as has already been argued, although the situation varied between departments, it was doubtful if this was true of the Assistant Secretary grade and those Principals and Assistant Principals who were not private secretaries. Their attentions were as much concerned – if not, in the case at least of the two lower grades, more concerned – with the actual subject matter of their divisions. With the Assistant Secretary grade representing the ceiling of the average direct-entrant's career, not to mention that of the transferee and promotee, the idea that the Principal, for example, should remain free from specialisms so that he could one day be the Minister's non-specialist personal adviser, was not only an attitude of doubtful value, but also one concerned with a not particularly likely possibility. Although seventeen out of every twenty members of the Administrative Class were to be found in the lower three grades, naturally enough those in such grades, particularly the direct entrants, looked to the higher grades and copied their 'style' and

---

[1] *Sixth Report from the Select Committee on Estimates* (1964–5) *Evidence,* questions 807–8.

[2] Sir Edward (later Lord) Bridges, 'Administration: What is it? and how can it be learnt?', an essay in A. Dunsire (ed.) *The Making of an Administrator* (1956) p. 3.

order of priorities. As Sir Norman Brook once observed,[1] managerial responsibilities were not high in that order of priorities, and one of the explanations for this was probably that management tends to be looked on as the sphere of the separate Executive Class.

The demarcations that are still maintained between certain grades of the Executive and Administrative Classes are not very convincing. To take the most obvious example, the Treasury admitted in evidence to the Priestley Commission: 'It is not always possible to draw a clear-cut distinction between policy work and executive work, so that in many cases jobs are done by Chief and Senior Executive Officers which are of the same broad level of responsibility as that of Principals.'[2] The Treasury later qualified this view by saying that the work done by Chief and Senior Executive Officers, in what they called 'administrative divisions', even when they worked directly to an Assistant Secretary, did not mean that

---

[1] As will be noted again later, Brook wrote in a Management Efficiency Circular of June 1957: 'What we need in the Service is a better concept of leadership. . . . I am sure that members of the Administrative Class are not sufficiently alive to the great responsibility which they should carry in management duties.' (*Whitley Bulletin*, Nov 1964, p. 158.)

[2] *Treasury Factual Memorandum to the Priestley Commission* (1953) para. 268. It is interesting to note that the Society of Civil Servants reminded the Priestley Commission that in 1946 the official side of the National Whitley Council had proposed: 'The upper structure of the Executive Class will remain as at present but My Lords consider that in future there should be free interchangeability between members of the Chief Executive Officer grade and members of the Principal grade, where such interchangeability is convenient from the point of view of departmental organisation. They consider also that it may be appropriate in some cases that Senior Executive Officers should in future be used in the larger administrative divisions where they are not already so used on the type of work which has been described during the War as "near Principal".' The official proposals were subsequently dropped in favour of the arrangements announced in Treasury Circular 5/47 (Extended Use of the Executive Class). The Society understandably pointed out: 'Nevertheless, there is interchangeability between the Chief Executive and Principal grades in a number of departments and Senior Executives are employed on administrative work which would otherwise be done by Principals. The official proposal in 1946 recognised the relationship between the Executive and Administrative grades which the Society suggested in their evidence but which the Treasury now attempt to deny.' (*Priestley Evidence*, appendix II (6) para. 16.)

they were performing the duties of a Principal.[1] A Treasury witness elaborated this view in saying that in most departments there were

> particular seats where it is not wrong to employ a Principal but where, at a particular time with a particular man available, it is also not wrong to employ a Chief Executive. There may be a very difficult seat working up perhaps to major legislation with all that that involves – papers for the Cabinet, briefs to Ministers, instructions to draftsmen, Parliamentary requirements, and all that – where you need a Principal and a good one at that. Perhaps after a few years when the legislation has settled down, you could have that job carried along quite satisfactorily by a Chief Executive whose strength lies rather in the length of his experience and his complete familiarity with the work than, shall I say, in his ability to deal with the constructive, or what we think of as policy considerations. The difference between the Principal grade and the Chief Executive – and more so the Senior Executive – is largely a difference of versatility. The Principal is expected to be able to switch from one job to another with a different content, quite apart from being able to cope more adequately with the policy side of the work. I think there is no doubt at all that the Principal is a much more valuable agent than the Chief Executive Officer, even the Chief Executive Officer employed in an administrative division. What I have said for the Chief Executive goes too for the Senior Executive, only more so![2]

Although the highest grade of the General Executive Class, the Heads of Major Executive Establishments, included the holders of such posts as the Director of Savings in the Post Office Savings Bank, and directors of accounts and accountants general and directors of contracts in certain other departments, in the Treasury's view it was still not supposed to face the same broad levels of responsibility as an Under-Secretary.[3] The next two highest grades, those of Principal and Senior Chief Executive Officer, were also thought to be distinct from that of Assistant

---

[1] *Priestley Evidence*, question 3623.

[2] Ibid. In answering question 3264, the Treasury made it clear that, in framing paragraph 268 of their Factual Memorandum, they had consulted 'representative Establishments Officers' and had been advised that the sentences about the working relationships between Principals, S.E.Os and C.E.Os 'would not lay us open to the Society's unjustified arguments'. In the event, this proved poor advice.

[3] *Priestley Report*, paras 429 and 444–9.

Secretary, although a small number of what were known as 'Executive Assistant Secretaries', on the Principal Executive Officer scale, were found, particularly in the regional organisations. They were employed when the Treasury thought that there was 'insufficient policy content in the job to warrant Administrative Class grading'.[1] Sir Henry Hancock told the Priestley Commission that the work of a regional controller in a Ministry like that of Pensions and National Insurance was 'a big managerial job'. Such Principal Executive Officers had to control large staffs; they had a big machine to keep running; they had to see that payments were made to thousands of people; and they had to meet local committees of an advisory nature. But, drawing on his experiences at the Ministry of Food, Sir Henry argued that they were distinct

> from the Assistant Secretary proper in as much as they are not asked to work out a new policy on any subject from the start. They are frequently consulted, and properly consulted, in fact consulted with great profit and value, on adjustments of policy which appear to be justified by the turn of events on a particular line of administration, but they are not asked to create a new policy, and, generally speaking, those people would not be in their element. In fact they might well be completely lost if you set them down in Whitehall and said 'Now we have got to legislate on food and drugs, what shall we do about it?' That is not their job. It would not be fair to say that to them, but they have a very responsible job in administering and managing a big block of staff and work.[2]

The rather patronising tone in which these leading Civil Servants spoke of the Executive Class probably betrayed their attitude towards management in general. It might be all very well for the unimaginative product of a routine executive career to concern himself with such mundane matters, but for the 'real challenges' – what better than the happy versatility of the all-rounder? Perhaps the creation of a merged Executive–Administrative Class,

---

[1] *Treasury Factual Memorandum* (1953) paras 267–8.

[2] *Priestley Evidence*, question 3623. Sir Henry's description of the S.C.E.O. as 'a rare animal', in a later part of his answer, presumably referred to his own experience, because the *Priestley Report* (para. 428) showed that there were well over twice as many S.C.E.O.s as P.E.O.s in the Executive Class as a whole. The current structure of the General Executive Class is shown in appendix III, table 1.

which would attach a greater importance than at present to management, would eventually lead to the emergence of leading administrators with a broader, and more appropriate, type of experience. Although the Society of Civil Servants did not propose the amalgamation of the Executive and Administrative Classes in their evidence to the Priestley Commission, some of their arguments, notably about pay relativities and promotions between those classes, pointed in that direction.[1] In 1956, a then member of the Executive Class, Dr Gladden, called for 'the abolition of a distinct Administrative Class' and the substitution for it of

[1] *The Society of Civil Servants' Statement of Evidence to the Priestley Commission* (1954) set out proposals that pay relativities should be established between certain administrative and executive grades, notably between Under-Secretaries and Heads of Major Executive Establishments (ibid. paras 129–30), Assistant Secretaries and Principal Executive Officers and Senior Chief Executive Officers (ibid. paras 122 and 124–5). In answering the Treasury's objections, the Society later argued that the duties of Principal Executive Officers and Senior Chief Executive Officers did not deserve to be rated below those of an Assistant Secretary: 'Theirs are administrative and top management jobs which should not be under-graded because of an outmoded distinction between two Classes which at this level are carrying the same measure of responsibility.' The Society added: 'Similarly, the managerial and specialised duties of the Chief Executive Officer and Senior Executive Officer grades, are worth as much to the State as the "policy" functions of the Principal. The versatility required of these grades on the management, supply and accounting, and specialised duties of the Service and in their relations with members of the public and representatives of industry is greater than that required of most Principals employed exclusively in an administrative division. Although the duties may be different the responsibilities are of the same level and justify the pay relationship suggested by the Society.' The Treasury's suggestion that Chief Executive Officers were 'less valuable agents than Principals' was disputed by the Society: 'If they are employed less freely on administrative work than Principals it is because of the equally responsible work for which they are required elsewhere in the Service and because the Treasury continue to pursue a policy of segregation of the two Classes in an area of the Service where interchangeability could be greatly extended.' The Society proposed that the two classes 'would continue to be employed separately and in collaboration where the duties can be clearly distinguished as Executive and Administrative'. They complained, however: 'The grading distinction in the Civil Service between executive and administrative work has had the effect that the managerial work is regarded as of lower quality than administrative work.' The Society asserted: 'The administration of the social services and of ex-headquarters officers involving control,

'one Civil Service Class concerned broadly with Public Service management',[1] and a practising administrator, Frank Dunnill, also wrote that 'it would probably be no bad thing' if 'the present, rather forced distinction between the Executive and Administrative Classes were to disappear'.[2] Certainly, the existing segregation of the two classes does deny 'practical organisational and managerial experience to direct entrants to the Administrative Class', as Mr Leslie Williams, the Society's present General Secretary, has argued.[3] In any case, as Dr Gladden has recently suggested, while it may have been realistic at the time of the Reorganisation Report 'to assign policy making to the senior Class, and executive work, defined in terms that pointed to management, to the middle Class (which was to be mainly involved in finance, audit and supply duties)', that might well not be so now, because:

> Since then the vast expansion of management with the increase in local offices services in a number of departments, the recent recognition in the Plowden Report of the increasing importance of managerial skills in the central administration, and the considerable extension of Executive work to cover new activities like programming for A.D.P. and pay research, have combined to render the division between the Executive and Administrative Classes even more difficult to define.

Dr Gladden rightly believed that the time had surely come to recognise that members of both classes were concerned with

---

organisation, and management, is laid upon Executive grades who are responsible for the conduct of Government business in the regional and local offices. This work of social administration and management is of no less importance than the work carried out traditionally by members of the Administrative Class and makes a far greater impact upon the average citizen. A revaluation of functions and responsibilities in relation to those of the Administrative Class is overdue and would be reasonably met by the relativities suggested by the Society.' (*Priestley Evidence*, appendix 2 (6) paras 13, 14, 15 and 19.) When one adds in the Society's views that promotion to the Administrative Class from below should be 'normal' rather than 'exceptional' (*Priestley Evidence*, questions 1086–7), one can see the beginnings of the call for the creation of a fused Executive-Administrative Class.

[1] E. N. Gladden, *Civil Service or Bureaucracy?* (1956) pp. 169 and 171.
[2] Frank Dunnill, *The Civil Service. Some Human Aspects* (1956) p. 205.
[3] Leslie Williams, 'Structure of the Civil Service', in *Civil Service Opinion*, Nov 1963, p. 303.

administration in its broadest and most responsible sense, and to amalgamate the classes.[1] It would be unfortunate, however, if a merged Executive–Administrative Class was to be created on the basis of 'the extended use of the Executive Class': in some ways that extension has already gone too far and, in a sense, what is needed is the extended use of the Administrative Class. The Executive Class does 'constitute the steel framework of the Civil Service',[2] but any temptation to think of it as being 'professional' in supposed contrast with the 'amateurism' of the Administrative Class should be avoided. It is surprising that even the harshest critics of the Administrative Class, such as Dr Bray, usually find little wrong with the Executive Class. Indeed, that observer has written of 'the excellent Executive Class',[3] which is surely to overstate the quality of its personnel. The reliance of the Executive Class on direct promotion from below is all too often forgotten by writers about the Service, and there are reasons to believe that the direct-entry recruitment arrangements for the generalist side of the Service have got out of touch with the educational structure to which they were so closely linked in 1920.

Remembering the convincing evidence that was given to the MacDonnell and Tomlin Commissions about the high intellectual quality of the Executive Class and its forerunners (in what after all were times of restricted alternative opportunities), and looking at the Robbins Committee's statistics, one wonders if the Society would find it so easy to paint a similar picture now. The Society's task would, however, be enviable compared with that which would face the Civil Service Clerical Association, the Clerical Class's 'trade union', if it attempted to convince the Fulton Committee that the Clerical Class had a considerable proportion

---

[1] E. N. Gladden, 'Abolish the Executive Class!', in *Civil Service Opinion*, Jan 1964, p. 6. Dr Gladden expanded on these ideas in an article called 'Time for Reform' in the following issue of that journal (pp. 38–40).

[2] *Sixth Report from the Select Committee on Estimates* (1964–5) *Evidence*, p. 132: the phrase was that of Professor W. J. M. Mackenzie, being contained in his stimulating Memorandum to that committee about 'Recruitment to the Civil Service'.

[3] Jeremy Bray, 'Britain's Administrators', in *The Sunday Times*, 5 Sep 1965.

of potentially outstanding administrators. For not only has the range of alternative careers improved, but the fact is that in, say, 1962 it was about three and a half times as likely, compared with 1938, that a talented young person would still be receiving full-time education at the age of nineteen.[1] In terms of direct-entry recruitment to the Civil Service such changes have meant that at Clerical Class level, where before the war in recruiting from sixteen-plus school leavers they had been almost embarrassed by the severity of the competition,[2] the Civil Service Commissioners' post-war experience, in contrast, was one of considerable difficulty in securing sufficient entrants of the right quality from that age group. What young people of ability are still attracted to the Clerical Class, unlike before the war, have every chance of swift advancement into the Executive Class by either the open or limited competition routes. But as the Clerical Class can now be entered at any age from sixteen to fifty-nine, it does not just consist of such career entrants, or even these plus girl clerks with ambitions almost wholly matrimonial: it consists of the inevitable ex-Armed Forces entry, the equally inevitable promotees from below, married women and a medley of middle-aged entrants presumably attracted by routine, security and a generally slow pace of work.[3]

[1] *Report of the Committee on Higher Education* (chairman: Lord Robbins) 1963, ch. III, table 1, p. 11.

[2] In their 1929 statement to the Tomlin Commission, the Civil Service Commissioners said (para. 20) that there was 'a danger that the number of competitors in the Clerical and Writing Assistant examinations may become embarrassingly large'. It did not, however, follow that the inter-war Clerical Class, apart from its direct entrants, was full of untested talent: on the contrary, indiscriminate ex-Armed Forces recruitment into its ranks after the First World War gravely weakened its quality (*Barlow Reconstruction Report*, 1944, para. 21).

[3] In 1962 the Civil Service Commissioners observed about Clerical Class recruitment since the war: 'A comparison between the pre-War and post-War periods shows the great changes that have come about in supply and demand. In 1938 nearly 4000 candidates were certificated for appointment but there were 5000 more who could have been accepted if there had been vacancies. In 1953 we offered posts to all candidates of acceptable standard, but the number certificated was only 3000 odd and a large number of vacancies remained.' The Commissioners said that in more recent years recruitment had increased 'very substantially', and shortages in many areas had been made good. Even so 'about 4000

(*footnote 3, page 180, continued*)
vacancies remained at the end of 1962, most of these being in London and the Home Counties'. The Commissioners observed: 'The increase in recruitment has been achieved by greatly widening the field of candidates and by introducing new forms of competition. Before the War, posts in the Clerical Class were filled by open competitive written examination among boys and girls of school-leaving age and by promotion of people from the lower grades of the Service. Now we have open competitions for candidates of all ages up to 59, as well as limited competitions for people already in the Civil Service and special competitions among ex-members of Your Majesty's Forces.' The Commissioners said: 'The main source of Clerical Class recruits,' – by which they presumably meant direct entrants – 'however, still lies in the competitions for candidates under 20. The two written examinations which are held each year, in January and September, have continued to attract substantial numbers of candidates; but the major method of recruitment among school leavers has for some years been the competition based on qualifications gained in the G.C.E. and corresponding Scottish and Northern Ireland certificates. (6000 vacancies were filled from this competition in 1962, as compared with 1500 from the two written examinations.) This form of recruitment, introduced at first on a small scale in 1953, enables boys and girls to obtain a Clerical Class post without written examination if they have passes in five subjects (including English language) at Ordinary level. Candidates may, if they wish, apply to be considered before they take their G.C.E. examinations, so that, if successful, they can take up appointment without delay when they know their results. Up to 1961 all G.C.E. candidates were interviewed, but the entry is now so large that it is no longer possible to continue this practice. Applications in 1962 rose to 14,000, and interviews were dispensed with where the circumstances made this appropriate.' (*96th Report*, p. 2.) By 1965: 'The main feature of recruitment to the Clerical Class was an increasing use of delegation arrangements which enabled employing departments to recruit boys and girls with appropriate qualifications in G.C.E. (or corresponding) examinations and to nominate them to the Commission for permanent appointment. In 1965 this method was used only to supplement recruitment, by country-wide written examinations, conducted by the Commission. In 1966 it will become the main method of entry to Clerical posts and will be extended to adult candidates also. The Commission will continue to hold open competitions by written examination, but only for posts in London and certain other areas where the number coming forward with the prescribed G.C.E. etc. qualifications is well short of demand. The Commission will also, as before, hold competitions throughout the country restricted to people already in Government Service and to those leaving the Armed Forces and Overseas Civil Service.' (*99th Report*, p. 7) The Civil Service Commissioners have, therefore, faced, at times, considerable difficulties in Clerical Class recruitment which they have attempted to solve with some ingenuity. The statement in the text that talented members of the Clerical Class have better chances

Yet, it is from this class that about sixty per cent of the Executive Class is drawn by direct promotion.[1]

The direct entrants do not even form one-fifth of the Executive Class. Fortunately, although it has obviously been slacker than in the inter-war period, competition to secure direct entry at this level has remained reasonably difficult until relatively recently.[2]

(*footnote 3, page 180, continued*)
of swift promotion to the Executive Class compared with their pre-war counterparts follows from the definite slackening in the competition for direct entry to the Executive Class, and from the establishment of the limited executive competition in 1949 – a competition that failed to fill all its vacancies in any year between 1952 and 1964. Appendix III, Table 3 of this book shows the structure of the General Clerical Class as at 1 January 1966: the natural promotion outlet of the Clerical Officer is to Executive Officer, the Higher Clerical Officer grade being retained for jobs which are purely routine supervision.

[1] Since 1959, official policy has been to preserve the level of direct promotions to Executive Officer at about that experienced between 1953 and 1957, namely 62·1 per cent of all annual vacancies and, in fact, the average promotion rate attained between 1959 and 1963 was 62·5 per cent (*Red Tape*, Aug 1964, p. 383). The relevant figure for 1963 was 60·2 per cent (*Civil Service Opinion*, Aug 1964, pp. 228–9), and the Society of Civil Servants have informed me that the figure for 1964 was 62·4 per cent, for 1965 it was 59·7 per cent, and for 1966 it was 54·8 per cent. The source of entrants to the Executive Officer grade for 1965 is shown in Appendix III, Table 2 of this book.

[2] The full post-war picture is given in Appendix III, Table 4. As late as 1963, the Civil Service Commissioners could observe: 'The number of Executive Class vacancies has again been very large, but there has been no difficulty in filling them, apart from posts in certain of the Departmental Executive Classes, notably Audit Examiners in the Ministry of Housing and Local Government, Examiners in the Board of Trade Insolvency Service, Actuarial Assistants in the Government Actuary's Department and Assistant Examiners in the Estate Duty Office of the Board of Inland Revenue.' (*97th Report*, p. 2.) In 1964, however, the Commissioners commented: 'In Executive Class recruitment there has been a shortfall in 1964 not only in some of the Departmental Executive Classes, where it had been found difficult to fill vacancies in recent years, but also in the General Executive Class. The deterioration is the result of increasing vacancies; the number of posts filled rose from about 1500 in 1963 to 1800 in 1964 but the number of vacancies rose from about 1600 to more than 2200.' (*98th Report*, p. 3.) The next year saw a similar story with the Commissioners recording: 'The rapid expansion of work in Government departments led to a further large increase in 1965 in Executive Class vacancies. Additional competitions were held and steps

Nevertheless, it is perhaps as well that in this group of direct entrants is what Professor Mackenzie has called 'a small stream of rather moderate graduates',[1] for university expansion has been

taken to make existing competitions more effective. About 2500 candidates accepted appointment as Executive Officers, against about 1800 in 1964 and 1500 in 1963. Even so some 500 vacancies were unfilled.' (*99th Report*, p. 6.) In their next report, the Commissioners observed: 'In our Report for 1965 we said that the rapid expansion of work in Government departments had led to a further large increase in Executive Class vacancies. This increase continued during 1966, when some 3400 candidates were appointed, an increase of about 900 over the previous year. There was some increase in the number of school-leavers coming forward for the Executive Class. In 1966 for the first time we interviewed candidates before we knew their G.C.E. Advanced Level results provided that they were willing to accept appointment in London. Those considered suitable were declared successful subject to their obtaining the required academic qualification. 341 candidates were seen under this arrangement and of these 289 obtained the necessary 'A' level passes – a significant contribution to recruitment in London where the main shortage in the General Executive Class has always centred. Where there were recruitment problems outside London we undertook extensive local advertising, particularly in order to help staff the offices set up by the Board of Trade to deal with the new scheme for investment grants.' Two changes were made in the regulations for Executive Class recruitment during 1966: 'The upper age limit was raised from 24 to 28 and we announced the acceptance of qualifications other than University degrees or those based on the General Certificate of Education and the Scottish Certificate of Education, provided that they were of an equivalent or higher standard. The first competition with the revised upper age limit was held in October and attracted a record number of applications. For the Departmental Executive Classes, supplementary recruitment to certain grades continued throughout the year. In addition, a special effort was made to interest candidates in computer programming and during 1966 we were asked to fill some 200 Executive posts providing opportunities for work with computers. These openings were featured prominently in the Commission's advertising and successful Executive Class candidates were given a short aptitude test designed to assess their suitability for work of this nature.' The Commissioners concluded: 'Despite additional competitions and widespread advertising, the record number of candidates recruited to the Executive Class still fell short of the number of vacancies. Nevertheless with large numbers of candidates still coming forward we see some prospect that during 1967 Executive Class recruitment will once again meet the needs of departments.' (*100th Report*, pp. 11–12.)

[1] Mackenzie, op. cit. para. 27 (b) p. 133. The Civil Service has never found it difficult to attract some graduates into the Executive Class ever since it began the practice in July 1949 (*84th Report of the Civil Service*

considerable compared with when the MacDonnell and Tomlin
Commissions looked at the Service. The Robbins Report's statistics showed that the percentage of the most relevant age group
entering the universities as full-time students in 1962 was four

---

Commissioners, section v, para. 17). Five per cent of the Executive Class
vacancies to be filled from outside the Service were allocated to a special
competition by which graduates could enter that class, and subsequent
Reports of the Civil Service Commissioners indicated that the fourteen
Method I competitions held under this scheme, until it was discontinued
after 1962, succeeded in filling 83 per cent of the vacancies assigned to it.
In 1962 the Commissioners remarked upon: 'A striking new development
is the growth in popularity of the Executive Class among University
students since it became possible for them to compete, by interview only,
in the G.C.E. competitions. In 1961, of the 1612 candidates declared
successful in open competitions, 153 were graduates – 29 by Method I,
and 124 in the G.C.E. examinations.' (*95th Report,* p. 17.) A year later the
Commissioners said: 'In our last Report we commented on the growing
popularity of the Executive Class among those at the Universities. This
trend continues. In 1962, of the 1581 candidates declared successful in
open competitions 149 were graduates, 34 by Method I and 115 in the
G.C.E. competitions.' (*96th Report,* p. 10.) No Method I examination
was held after 1962 because the Commissioners felt that it had been
rendered unnecessary by 'the raising of the upper age-limit' and 'the
admission of graduates to two of the three annual Executive Class competitions based on G.C.E. qualifications'. In 1963 the Commissioners
estimated: 'About a hundred graduates now enter the Executive Class
each year through the G.C.E. competitions.' (*97th Report,* p. 2.) In 1964
the Commissioners observed: 'The age limits and qualifications prescribed
provide for the entry of graduates to the Executive Class, and over 100
graduates or final year students were successful in 1964. As the Universities expand and an increasing proportion of able sixth formers,
the traditional source of Executive Class open competition recruitment,
goes on to higher education we would hope that more graduates will be
attracted to the General and Departmental Executive Classes which,
apart from providing good opportunities for promotion to the Administrative Class, offer in themselves careers as satisfactory and worthwhile
as are likely to be had in the middle ranks of industry and in other outside
employment.' (*98th Report,* p. 3.) Sir Laurence Helsby, the Head of
the Civil Service, later told the Select Committee on Estimates (*Sixth
Report,* 1964–5, *Evidence,* question 804) that he estimated that in 1964
'we recruited 120-plus University graduates to the Executive Class'.
The Executive Council of the Society of Civil Servants told the Society's
1966 Conference that about 150 graduates had entered the Executive
Class in 1965, observing that the present graduate entrants to the Executive Class were, for the most part, of Pass degree or Third Class Honours
standard.

per cent compared with only 0·8 per cent in 1900, 1·5 per cent in 1924, 1·7 per cent in 1938, and 3·4 per cent in 1955.[1] It was, therefore, five times as likely that a talented young person would have the opportunity of receiving a university education in 1962 compared with 1900, and well over twice as likely as in 1938. Without pretending that the educational system has attained perfection, a contention that, not least, would ignore the influence of environment on academic performance, such statistics tend to lend support to Professor Mackenzie's view, about the traditional source of direct entrants to the Executive Class, that 'the A level entrants include a diminishing proportion of potentially outstanding people'. Certainly, the chances of finding such people among the ranks of the non-graduate entrants to the Executive Class has declined dramatically compared with 1900 and considerably compared with 1938. While, as Professor Mackenzie revealed, there is in addition a leakage from the Executive Class from among the more ambitious of its G.C.E. Advanced Level entry. He said that 'one finds in a civic University that there is a steady stream of young Executives who decide after two or three years in the Service to go to a University after all, if their academic standard is good enough'. He was told by such students that life in the Service 'soon becomes unbearably dull', that they had not felt 'stretched intellectually' by their duties and they had not seen 'anything ahead but rather slow advancement to a decent but moderate income'.[2]

[1] *Robbins Report*, ch. III, table 4, p. 16.

[2] Mackenzie, op. cit. para. 28 (a) p. 33. Since 1963 the only method of entry into the Executive Class for young people from outside the Civil Service has become a series of annual competitions based on G.C.E. qualifications and their Scottish and Northern Irish equivalents: a method of entry originally introduced in 1956. To be eligible for these competitions, candidates have to have as a minimum G.C.E. or equivalent passes in English language at Ordinary Level and four other acceptable subjects including at least two at Advanced Level obtained at the same examination. There is no written examination and selection is by interview, competitions being held in January, April, June, September and October. The age limits for the September competition are at least $17\frac{1}{2}$ and under $19\frac{1}{2}$; while the limits for the other competitions are at least $17\frac{1}{2}$ and under twenty-eight – the upper limit having been twenty-four until 1966; no candidate being allowed to compete in more than one

This is not altogether a surprising picture, for such direct entrants come young into the lower part of the generalist side of the Service, the tone of which is set by the Executive and Clerical Classes. They come in at the bottom of a hierarchy where the seniors above seem all too often to have attained their status only by time-serving, and who see their role simply as being no more than keeping the existing machine ticking over. A practising administrator, Frank Dunnill, writing in 1964, talked about the Executive Class in terms recognisable to any who have served in its ranks when he described the 'worthy stolidity' of its members, with their 'implicit assumption that Man is made to suit the needs of the Service and not the reverse' and their capacity 'for making new questions fit old answers'. He gave as an example the actual conduct of Organisation and Methods work in the Service, and his views contrasted with the type of glowing job descriptions that the Society presented to the Priestley Commission. Dunnill said that under predominantly Executive direction it has become 'far more concerned with detailed methods than with broad organisations'. He believed: 'As it is, the calling in of O. & M. to look at a genuine administration problem is very often a frustrating and time-consuming process.' As with many other spheres

---

competition in the same year. These latter competitions, as noted above, have attracted substantial numbers of university graduates. The various G.C.E. competitions do not have a monopoly in providing direct entrants from outside the Civil Service, but since 1963 the only other sources of direct entrants have been ex-members of the Armed Forces and the Overseas Civil Service (Civil Service Commission, *The Executive Class of the Home Civil Service*, 1966, p. 56; Civil Service Commission, *Civil Service Posts for Graduates*, 1967, p. 84; *Reports of the Civil Service Commissioners*, 1945–66). As noted earlier, in 1966 the Civil Service Commissioners changed the regulations for Executive Class recruitment when they announced 'the acceptance of qualifications other than University degrees or those based on the General Certificate of Education and the Scottish Certificate of Education, provided they were of an equivalent or higher standard' (*100th Report*, p. 11): presumably the Commissioners were referring to C.N.A.A. degrees and to the Certificate of Secondary Education. It is worth noting that the traditional Executive Class written examination, modified in 1946 by the introduction of an interview, declined sharply in effectiveness after 1954 and was discarded in 1963. The post-war recruitment record of the Executive Class is given in appendix III, table 4.

of Executive activity, Dunnill thought that the conduct of O. & M. would have 'much more breadth, imagination and drive, if it had been found possible to get more administrators involved in it'.[1]

Dunnill shared the opinion of Dr Gladden and the Society's General Secretary, Mr Leslie Williams, that the Service's performance in the field of management would probably be improved by merging the Executive and Administrative Classes but, without denying that class's need for greater professionalism, he rightly placed more emphasis than they do upon the advantages that would come from an extended use of the Administrative Class. Dunnill believed that there is a need for a larger university entry into the generalist side of the Service, saying that a deliberate infusion of run-of-the-mill graduates might give the Service 'new blood which would in itself be useful in the management context'.[2] To some extent this is already happening, but presumably Dunnill has in mind something along the lines of the present Special Departmental Classes. They provide careers which Professor Mackenzie has described as 'distinctly attractive to general graduates who are competent and efficient but not notably ambitious'. Although the entrants to the cadet grade of the Ministry of Labour, despite the grandeur of their initial title, simply face a routine Executive Class career, those who join the Tax Inspectorate of the Inland Revenue, certainly, and the Assistant Postal Controllers, possibly, do as Mackenzie said, 'meet a serious challenge to their intellect and sense of responsibility', while members of the Tax Inspectorate do 'acquire skills potentially valuable outside the Service'.[3] If it were practicable, one marked advantage of extending the Special Departmental Classes arrangement across the whole generalist side of the Service would be that it would raise the intellectual quality of the generalist grades outside the present Administrative Class; but, as will be argued later, one doubts if the Service can be made attractive enough to sufficient numbers of graduates of the right quality unless all graduates enter that Service on similar terms.

[1] Frank Dunnill, 'External Relations of the Administrative Class', in *Civil Service Opinion*, Apr 1964, p. 106.
[2] Dunnill, op. cit. p. 107. [3] Mackenzie, op. cit. para. 28 (c) p. 133.

By whatever means, a considerably increased graduate entry must be an essential pre-condition of an amalgamated Executive–Administrative Class, and should such a class be created one would hope that, while it would not be 'departmentalised' as was the pre-war Executive Class, it would attempt to combine the flexibility of a generalist structure with the greater specialisation demanded by the complexity of the range of duties now assigned to the Executive and Administrative Classes. It would be more realistic too, without wishing to impose a completely uniform grading system on the Service, if the sort of ideas that the Society advanced before the Tomlin Commission about the creation of an 'Executive Corps' were revived. This 'Corps' embraced the present General and Departmental Executive Classes[1] as well as the Special Departmental Classes, and it might be better to see the creation of a merged Executive–Administrative Class in terms of amalgamating the present ruling class of the Service with an 'Executive Corps'. The resulting structure would be a series of specialised

---

[1] *Tomlin Evidence*, appendix IX, paras 142–3. As the Society then said one feature that all these groups had in common was 'the executive or directory or managerial function'. The Departmental Executive Classes numbered 27,620 in 1966 (that is about thirty-eight per cent of the total strength of the Executive Class). The various departments and branches they are employed in are: the Exchequer and Audit Department, the Government Actuary's Department, the Home Office Immigration Service, the District Audit Staff of the Ministry of Housing and Local Government, the Ministry of Labour, the Board of Trade Bankruptcy Service; and in the Estate Duty Office, and the Chief Inspector of Taxes Branch of the Department of Inland Revenue (Civil Service Commission, *The Executive Class of the Home Civil Service*, 1960, part II, pp. 36–45). The Departmental Executive Classes, which deal with accounting, auditing, actuarial work and the wide field of tax law, represent a numerous and specialised fringe to the General Executive Class. That class itself can be seen as being employed on accounting and auditing duties among the wide range of functions that include contracts and supply work, statistical work, Organisation and Methods, staff inspection duties, and major responsibilities in the field of automatic data processing. The Executive Class as a whole has a very varied range of responsibilities running from the supervision of Clerical and sub-Clerical staff to the management of regional and local offices; and from the holding of major posts in branches, divisions, and departments of lesser political importance, to assisting the Administrative Class with what it sees as its special role.

hierarchies of two broad types. The first type would be those concerned with duties peculiar to a particular department or group of departments, and the second type would be concerned with specialisms of wider application. Each of these hierarchies would have its own promotion outlets, and planned postings would take place between them so that an entrant was not sentenced to, say, town and country planning, or accounting work, or programming for A.D.P. or establishments work for the rest of his career, although he would have every incentive to tackle them professionally before being transferred to other duties. This sort of approach, and indeed any sort of merger, would, as Leslie Williams has pointed out, underline the existing need for a more vigorous training programme,[1] aiming not only to give instruction in the relevant specialisms, but also to provide a general background to increasingly specialised duties.

The grade structure of the merged class need not be totally uniform, but there seems no reason why the general pattern should vary greatly. As Leslie Williams has written, it would be relatively easy to amalgamate the now separate Executive and Administrative grades at Assistant Secretary level and above: the Heads of Major Executive Establishments becoming Under-Secretaries, and the Principal Executive Officers and Senior Chief Executive Officers entering the Assistant Secretary grade. The real problems start at Principal level where, although it would be straightforward to absorb all the Chief Executive Officers into a merged Principal grade, there is the question of what happens to the Senior Executive Officer grade. Williams's suggestion was that some of that grade should be made Principals, and the remainder should be assigned, with a special salary allowance, to the Higher Executive Officer grade which would then become the main support grade. Turning to the direct-entry recruitment grades, the General Secretary's view was that recruitment would still continue at the different educational levels, and he pointed to the increase in the amount of graduate recruitment to the Executive Class as a trend that would probably continue. He wanted to see the Assistant Principal grade abolished, with such recruits entering

Williams, op. cit. p. 303.

the Executive Officer grade 'at the age 25 point' on that salary scale, and then they would 'perhaps proceed automatically to the H.E.O. scale pending promotion to Principal'.[1] It can be objected that the graduate entrants, although they would have to receive a market-orientated initial salary, should not 'proceed automatically' anywhere. They should enter the Executive Officer grade and, after having received a common and extended and much more professionalised course of training than at present, they should compete not only among themselves but also with the other members of that grade for future advancement. But whatever the merits or faults of Leslie Williams's draft scheme, at least initially he found it easier to propose changes in the *status quo* than to secure his members' support for them. As he himself recognised, the implementation of his proposed scheme would not be easy, with a notable problem being that in the local office field it would be difficult to employ the new combined Principal grade, while the routine career expectations of direct-entrant Clerical and Executive Officers would be affected by changes in structure at Higher and Senior Executive Officer level. Probably feeling that their promotion prospects would be harmed, in 1965 the rank and file membership of the Society rejected, by a substantial majority, the idea of making the creation of an amalgamated Executive–Administrative Class official Society policy.[2]

[1] Ibid. Dr Gladden suggested that the sort of entrants who now come in as Assistant Principals should be given H.E.O. status, if not pay, when they joined the Executive–Administrative Class ('Abolish the Executive Class', in *Civil Service Opinion*, Jan 1964, p. 7). If this was done, it would be difficult to present the Executive–Administrative Class to potential entrants, particularly graduates not now attracted by the Service, as being different from the existing arrangements, and it is therefore hard to see how the creation of a merged class on this basis could help to meet the recruitment problems that exist under the current arrangements.

[2] The defeat of the merger proposal was reported in *The Daily Telegraph*, 4 May 1965. A paper submitted by the Executive Council of the Society of Civil Servants to the 1965 Annual Conference summarised the views of the Society's sections and branches. It was clear from this paper that the substitution of two grades for the three grades of Higher Executive Officer, Senior Executive Officer and Chief Executive Officer was unacceptable to a large number of branches, representing a substantial majority of the membership. The 1965 Annual Conference agreed that

However, the structure of the generalist side of the Service would be best left alone if 'routine expectations' are to govern its reconstruction: only radical reforms are worthwhile. The first of these should be that direct entry, particularly from the universities, should be encouraged at the expense of promotion from below from the Clerical Class despite the internal difficulties that this might well cause in the Service. According to the C.S.C.A. 'a good leavening of Clerical promotees – people with years of practical experience on the job – will counter any tendency towards dilettante amateurism among direct entrants whose only qualifications are academic'. The C.S.C.A. wanted all entry into the Service to be 'at ground level':[1] but others can convincingly

---

the question of the merger of the Administrative and Executive Classes should be kept under review and a further report made to the Conference by the Executive Council in due course.

[1] *Red Tape*, Apr 1964, p. 197. The idea that all entrants to the generalist side of the Civil Service should start 'at ground level', is, of course, not new. A notable advocate of such a policy was W. J. Brown, a famous General Secretary of the C.S.C.A. who, when an Independent M.P., told the House of Commons on one occasion that the structure of the Civil Service was 'the antithesis of democracy'. He said that 'you cannot have a democratic community without having a democratic Public Service', and he asserted: 'We shall not get the dynamic Civil Service we need while educational classification and not character or capacity, determines the place a man shall occupy throughout his life.' (House of Commons, *Official Report*, 1942–3, vol. 386, cols 679–80.) Like all advocates of universal entry 'at ground level', Mr Brown insisted that the university graduate would not be debarred from entering the Civil Service, which was nothing if not 'democratic'. He wanted to make the graduate entrant 'start level with the others', being granted promotion 'if he is the better man' presumably at clerical work, but this was not likely because non-graduates had 'a vastly greater aptitude for handling men and affairs' (ibid. col. 679). The attraction of such a career to the graduates is never made clear. Similar arguments to those advanced by W. J. Brown were expressed by his successor, as General Secretary of the C.S.C.A., L. C. White in an article about 'The Civil Service', in *Political Quarterly* (1944); and more recently the leading officials of the association have talked once more about the 'initiative and ambition' to be found in the Clerical Class being frustrated by the effects of 'the outmoded Class structure which still exists in the Civil Service'. This is maintained 'by imposing different educational levels of entry which divide the Service into three distinct Classes', thus segregating the staff 'into first-, second- and third-class compartments', which 'makes for inflexibility and

(*footnote 1, page 191, continued*)

rigidity' and raises 'unnecessary barriers between the Classes'. The association believes that increased efficiency cannot be achieved until this 'old-fashioned, outworn relic of social class distinction' has been abolished. The association says: 'Other comparable organisations including the police, the banks and some large corporations have got away from a caste system based on entry at different levels, determined by educational and social background. Practically all intake is at ground level. All have the right and opportunity to progress up the ladder. Educational qualifications can help swifter movement up the ladder, but they are not used to create water-tight divisions and artificial barriers.' The association, however, was under no illusions about the difficulties of securing the changes that it desired. Its President, Mr J. Bryce, told the 1965 Annual Conference that 'our fight to modernise the Civil Service is not going to be easy. There is still too much of the "horse and buggy" mentality at top level at the Treasury.' (*Red Tape*, Apr 1964, p. 197, and July–Aug 1965, pp. 297–8.) Perhaps there is, but scepticism can be expressed about the likelihood of the Clerical Class leading nothing less than a fight to modernise the Service. It can also be seriously doubted that making all entrants to the generalist side of the Service come in as clerks, whether in the name of an abstract principle like 'democracy' or simply to improve the promotion prospects of the members of the present Clerical Class, will lead to better senior administrators emerging than under the current arrangements. As Australian experience suggests, a lengthy apprenticeship on routine work would be hardly calculated to make them 'dynamic'. In many ways, it is the arguments of the C.S.C.A. which are 'outmoded' and which savour of a 'horse and buggy mentality'. For the association takes too little account either of the social and educational revolution that has taken place over the last twenty years, or of the implications of the full employment society that in many ways has made that possible. From the very beginning of the implementation of the Trevelyan–Northcote reforms right up to 1939, one gains a picture of a Service having closely related its structure to the educational system and, in a period of restricted alternative opportunities, securing far more talent than it needed for its duties, particularly at executive and clerical level. Since the war, without either overstating the improvement in the educational system or pretending that it has attained perfection or suggesting that social origins no longer matter, there can be no questioning the proposition that opportunities to secure, for example, a university education have increased considerably for those drawn from ordinary backgrounds, and the same is true of career openings generally. It is not clear why anyone with 'initiative and ambition' now joins the Clerical Class or, if they do, why, given the limited competition machinery and the fact that the executive open competition is now a milder hurdle than in the past, they stay in its ranks for very long. Even as regards direct promotion it is no longer the case since the 1947 reforms that there is what W. J. Brown, *The Civil Service: Retrospect and Prospect* (1943) p. 18, once described as only 'a small stream of promotions' into the Executive Class: with about 60 per cent

argue that there is no worse preparation for the more creative types of Executive Class work, let alone Administrative Class duties, than a dozen or more years on simple routine work, and they can point to Australian experience to support their case.[1]

(*footnote 1, page 191, continued*)
of that class drawn from this source it is more like a river in full flood. As to the general structural reforms advocated by the C.S.C.A., one does not need to look much further than the outside instances it quoted. The police – now making some attempt to attract graduate entrants – and the banks one would have thought that they were awful warnings rather than examples to be followed, while the C.S.C.A. might perhaps care to name the private corporations where all entry is 'at ground level': in these days of graduate development schemes it would seem that the more progressive companies are moving or have moved in the direction of differential recruitment and away from that favoured by the C.S.C.A.

[1] The higher posts of the Public Service of the Commonwealth of Australia have traditionally been filled by promotees from the ranks, as was noted with approval by R. K. Kelsall, *Higher Civil Servants in Great Britain* (1955) p. 42. This was because 'the legislation which established the permanent Public Services of the States and Commonwealth in the period close to the turn of the century was framed in the dominant spirit of Australian egalitarianism' (Solomon Encel, 'The Recruitment of University Graduates in the Commonwealth Public Service', in *Public Administration*, 1954, p. 217). British observers should perhaps remember: 'Anyone who criticises the Australian Public Service for not modelling its recruitment policy on the British should remember that no section of Australian commerce or industry accepted the Northcote–Trevelyan assumptions about the Arts graduate.' (J. D. B. Miller, *Australian Government and Politics*, 1966, p. 168.) However, in 1933 the traditional policy was modified slightly when, after continued representations by the universities, the Government amended the appropriate legislation so as to allow up to 10 per cent of normal clerical appointments in a year to be filled by graduates, although their starting salaries had to be within 'the lowest clerical scale in the Service' (P. W. E. Curtin, 'Recruitment', an essay in R. N. Spann, *Public Administration in Australia*, 1960, p. 340). Small numbers of graduates did enter the Service between 1934 and 1939, but the Service overwhelmingly relied upon 'ground level' entry, coupled with a massive amount of recruitment from the ranks of the ex-First World War veterans. Not surprisingly, the Commonwealth Public Service found after 1939 that there was 'a virtual absence in the Service of officers who, by natural endowment, educational background, and experience were equipped to deal with the new types of functions which the Service was called upon to perform' (Howard A. Scarrow, *The Higher Public Service of the Commonwealth of Australia*, 1957, p. 110). When the war came 'the Civil Service had broken down and outside help had to be called in', meaning that graduates were 'drafted

Like all staff associations, the C.S.C.A. has to contend that its membership consists of massed ranks of untried talent; but there is no need for the Fulton Committee to take such views very

---

wholesale into Commonwealth departments' (Encel, op. cit. p. 223, quoting Professors Giblin and Ashby respectively). Some of these wartime entrants were retained in the Service, and like the pre-war graduate entrants, they have done far better than their 'clerical' rivals in securing senior positions (Curtin, op. cit. p. 341; Scarrow, op. cit. pp. 111–14). After the war also greater recourse was had to 'exceptional methods' of increasing graduate recruitment, so that by 1954 it was possible to observe that the most important development in post-war recruitment policy 'has been the great intake of University graduates from the non-technical faculties' (Encel, op. cit. pp. 223–4). Encel drew attention to the effects of university expansion upon the likelihood of securing the required higher talents by relying mainly on 'ground level' entry, commenting: 'Though the staff associations may persist in their refusal to admit the fact, differential recruitment is inevitable in a large and complex bureaucratic machine.' Encel, however, recognised that 'the whole matter is not merely one of administrative readjustment', and he concluded: 'Fundamental changes in the nature both of society and government are taking place in Australia, and without action at the political level it is unlikely that the needed reforms will ever be achieved.' (Ibid. p. 227.) The Boyer Committee of Inquiry into Public Service Recruitment, reporting in 1958, urged that the normal principle of open competitive recruitment to the equivalent of our Clerical Class should be modified in three important respects. Firstly, 'the limit of ten per cent to the annual recruitment of graduates should be abolished so that as many as possible could be brought in – and at a more attractive commencing salary'. Secondly, the next level of the Service 'should be transformed into something more nearly approaching a flexible version of the Administrative Class of the British Civil Service to which men of proven qualifications and abilities from inside or outside the Service might be "graduated", to form, in effect, several levels of a *corps d'élite*'. Thirdly, 'subject to certain safeguards, all necessary provisions be consolidated and, if necessary, widened for recruiting experienced talent from outside the Service'. The amending Public Service Act of 1960 did not, however, adopt the more novel elements of these recommendations. Nevertheless, 'within the forms of the existing legislation, departments are of necessity sifting out an *élite* of the highly educated and talented and accelerating their advancement to those levels where their trained abilities are available to cope with the mounting complexities and technicalities of public policy and administration'. (L. F. Crisp, *Australian National Government*, 1965, p. 405.) The political action called for by Encel took about a decade to materialise, but there are now arrangements, normal rather than exceptional, whereby general graduates can enter the Service with an initial salary about the clerical maximum.

seriously. The youngsters of ability in the Clerical Class have every opportunity of securing early promotion to the Executive Class just as they would have to a merged class. The level of later direct promotion ought to be drastically reduced: the emphasis should be on improving standards and greater professionalism, not the fulfilment of 'routine expectations'.

Therefore, if a merged Executive–Administrative Class is created on the above lines, the early years spent by entrants into the Executive Officer grade – which would include all graduate recruits to the generalist side of the Service as well as G.C.E. Advanced Level entrants and Clerical promotees – should be treated as a training period. The timing of this training period would vary with the type of entrant, but not the length or general content of the training. If further advancement is to be open to all, then all must receive a thorough grounding in what will be their profession. This means a course of training lasting about two and a half years, which should be a combination of practical experience and instruction not only in such subjects as the social sciences, statistics and management techniques, but also in the various specialisms to which entrants have been assigned. However much against the British tradition, appropriate tests or written examinations should be held to evaluate the trainees' knowledge, and the failure satisfactorily to complete the training period should, of course, call into question the tenure of the individuals concerned.

Despite the disappointing results of the Limited Administrative Competition, a more active policy of searching out young talent from within the Service should be pursued. Improvements in the educational system may well have lessened the chances of finding outstanding material in the ordinary executive entry, but have hardly ruled them out completely. The desire of some young men to 'earn their living' almost at once after leaving school at eighteen and the probably irreversible trend towards young marriage, provide two factors that may lead to the Executive Class continuing to attract youngsters of considerable ability into its ranks. It ought to be possible for the Service to introduce, if only initially, on a small scale, some kind of Civil Service Scholarship scheme, perhaps on a 'sandwich' basis, whereby serving Civil

Servants of talent would have the opportunity of a university education on full salary. They might have to take rather longer over their studies than the normal honours course – and such studies would have to be associated with the sort of training programme outlined above – but one can see them perhaps spending about six months at the university and, allowing for annual leave, dividing the remainder of the year between practical work in their departments and private study on their books. There would have to be a restriction on the choice of subjects read at the university in favour of degrees offering either the most relevant background to a Civil Service career, particularly the social sciences, or those that include management skills, for example, statistics. The scholarships could be held at any university: the appropriateness of the course offered should be the criterion. The Civil Service scholars would not necessarily later secure swifter promotion than their contemporaries, but they would be able to compete with the graduate direct entrants on less unfavourable terms. In any case, the sort of merged Executive–Administrative Class outlined above would offer as little as possible to the time-server and would instil a much needed competitive atmosphere into the Executive part of the fused hierarchy.

In 1955, the Priestley Commission expressed 'great sympathy' with the views advanced by the Society of Civil Servants in their evidence about 'the interlocking of managerial and policy work'.[1] Nevertheless, as we have seen, ten years later, the rank and file membership of the Society had been unwilling to make the creation of an amalgamated Executive–Administrative Class official Society policy. With the spur behind them of having to present evidence to the Fulton Committee which had been appointed three months earlier, the Executive Council successfully secured, at the Annual Conference of the Society in May 1966, the reversal of the decision of a year earlier, and the establishment of a merged Executive–Administrative Class became Society policy.[2] More surprisingly,

[1] *Priestley Report* (1955) para. 459.

[2] Although the 1965 Annual Conference had rejected making the creation of an amalgamated Executive–Administrative Class the official policy of the Society of Civil Servants, the Executive Council considered that the appointment of the Fulton Committee had led to a new situation

in what, at least at first sight, seemed to be complete contrast with their evidence to the Priestley Commission and to the Select Committee on Estimates only a year before, the Treasury, in their submission of evidence to the Fulton Committee, advocated that a form of amalgamated Executive–Administrative Class should be created.[1] Therefore, with wide agreement about its desirability, it seems likely that the Fulton Committee will recommend that some type of fused Executive–Administrative Class should be formed. This subject and the relevant evidence will be discussed in chapter 6, but it should be said at this point that an amalgamated Executive–Administrative Class will have to be an open hierarchy in two senses. Firstly, the trend towards a measure of later outside recruitment will have to continue. Secondly, the recently-increased level of transfers from the specialist hierarchies, to which a more specialised Executive–Administrative Class would be closer in any case, will have to be sustained. A merged Executive–Administrative Class, orientated towards professionalism, would provide, in its lower grades, valuable support to, and, in its higher ranks, it would be an essential element in, a Higher Civil Service which, to give higher status to the specialist, will have to be integrated.

---

which required urgent consideration of Society policy about the structure of the Civil Service. Taking care this time to recognise the need to retain the Senior Executive Officer grade where this grade was specifically necessary, for example in local offices, the Executive Council of the Society outlined a new Management Grades Structure – to be formed from a merger between the Executive and Administrative Classes – in a paper submitted to the 1966 Annual Conference, and secured its approval of making the creation of such a structure official Society policy.

[1] H.M. Treasury, 'The Future Structure of the Civil Service', a note submitted to the *Fulton Committee on the Civil Service* (1966) paras 6–8.

CHAPTER FIVE

The Professionals, the Scientists and the Generalists

I THE PLACE OF THE SPECIALIST

AT one of the first dinner parties that he attended at Oxford, the newly appointed Professor Lindemann, later Lord Cherwell, expressed his misgivings about the status of science in Oxford to the wife of the Warden of All Souls. 'You need not worry,' she assured him, 'a man who has got a First in Greats could get up science in a fortnight.' Lindemann credited himself with replying: 'What a pity your husband has never had a fortnight to spare.'[1] This conversation, although set in the early 1920s, in an exaggerated form does give a sense of the greater esteem given to arts studies in this country as opposed to those in science, and the differential would be even more marked if technology was brought into the picture and probably as much if the social sciences were considered too. It would be surprising if the structure of the Civil Service did not reflect this respect for the non-vocational as opposed to vocational education.

As has already been said, the Regulatory State did not need either large numbers or several varieties of specialists in its Civil Service. Many of those who were employed were either lawyers or inspectors, and this picture did not change very much before 1906, so that Sir Warren Fisher was to some extent justified in telling the Tomlin Commission in 1930 that the experts, which the central Government had by then come to employ, could be seen as 'relative innovations' compared with the traditional administrators and clerks. He did not suppose that 'they got a great welcome anywhere, any more than the women got a great

---

[1] R. F. Harrod, *The Prof. A Personal Memoir of Lord Cherwell* (1959) pp. 52–3. Harrod was convinced that Lindemann's brilliant reply was a subsequent gloss.

welcome'. His belief that 'all that has now passed'[1] was not shared by the specialists' representatives in their evidence to the Tomlin Commission. For example, the Institution of Professional Civil Servants told the Commission in 1930: 'Viewed in relation to the structure of the older non-technical Civil Service, the medley of grades comprising the structures of the Professional, Scientific and Technical Classes of the Civil Service resembles an accumulation of outbuildings about an historic edifice. Those outbuildings do not conform to the period or style of the main structure, nor are they themselves of one period or style.' Evidence of the medley of styles of structure was afforded by the fact that within these classes, comprising less than four per cent of the non-industrial Civil Service, there were more than 500 distinct grades, differing not merely in their technical nomenclature but also in their standard of remuneration. Among these classes none of the existing forms of structure or organisation could be recognised as 'typically' professional, scientific or technical. The forms of structure differed 'between sub-departments of the same department, and they differ even between small groups within the same sub-department. Each of these different structures is a "watertight compartment" with its own standard and methods of recruitment and its own conditions of service, grades and salary scales.' The I.P.C.S. also complained about the inadequacy of the career hierarchies of, and the general opportunities open to, the specialist.[2]

The Association of Scientific Workers told the Tomlin Commission: 'To an increasing degree the work of the administrator is that of co-ordination. In some cases these functions may consist of correlating the recommendations of experts in different branches. In other cases the work of administration may consist in devising compromises between the conditions recommended by the impartial specialist and the limitations dictated by political expediency.'[3] The I.P.C.S. did not question the importance of these

[1] *Tomlin Evidence*, question 18,780.

[2] *Tomlin Evidence*, appendix XI (statement submitted by the I.P.C.S. 1930) part II, 'Structure and Organisation of the Civil Service including Methods of Recruitment', paras 15–18.

[3] *Statement submitted to the Tomlin Commission by the Association of Scientific Workers* (1930) para. 29.

or any other functions of the Administrative Class, but it did question the soundness of the assumption that these functions were inherently superior; and it considered that this assumption was based on an erroneous conception of relative functions and a false standard of relative values.[1]

The I.P.C.S. complained about the specialists' exclusion from direct access to the Minister, which they said illustrated the belief that the expert was innately inferior to the administrator. In almost all departments the specialist groups were 'generally found to be overlaid by an administrative secretariat, the technical head of a particular group being held responsible to the Permanent Secretary or to some lower member of the non-technical staff'. In the normal course of events, and unless the expert had the privilege of direct access to the Minister by virtue of special circumstances such as personal acquaintance: 'All his plans and ideas in connection with matters coming within his purview are subject to filtration and interpretation by an officer or officers who must, in the nature of things, be less competent to appreciate their significance.'[2] Sir Arthur Newsholme, a former Principal Medical Officer of the Local Government Board, had written: 'The Minister not infrequently knows of his skilled technical advisers' views only through a summarised minute written by the Minister's private secretary or departmental secretary, or through a verbal statement of these views by his Secretary.'[3] The I.P.C.S. commented: 'In comparison with the grave risk of distortion and misunderstanding which must accompany such pretensions of omniscience on the part of the intervener, the offence to the status and dignity of the expert implied by the procedure may be regarded as of secondary importance.'[4] The essentially inferior position assigned to the specialist might, however, lead to his being ignored altogether. A former Permanent Secretary to the Ministry of Agriculture, Sir Francis Floud, said in 1923: 'I have known cases in which Administrative Officers have come to

[1] *Tomlin Evidence*, appendix XI, part II, para. 23.
[2] Ibid. paras 24–5.
[3] Sir Arthur Newsholme, *The Ministry of Health* (1925) p. 92.
[4] *Tomlin Evidence*, appendix XI, part II, para. 26.

decisions on technical questions without ever consulting the technical advisers of the department.' Floud said that this was 'clearly indefensible'.[1] In the opinion of the I.P.C.S. the limitations upon the specialists constituted 'an unwarranted disparagement of their rightful functions and responsibilities, and are at variance with the position and prestige accorded to the expert both in the Local Government Service and in the community generally'.[2] This last statement was not very fair. The preference for the amateur over the professional, both in 1930 and possibly even now, is a characteristic of 'the community generally' in this country, not just the Civil Service. The comparative supremacy of the specialist in local Government was not altogether surprising as the local authorities were actually carrying out functions: the role of the central Government was rather different in that it had also to consider the merits and demerits of alternative proposals, a process in which technical expertise was not the only factor involved.

The I.P.C.S. also told the Tomlin Commission that 'the system of filtration of technical projects through administrative channels is open to criticism in that it leads not infrequently to duplication of effort'. The Permanent Secretary or the other senior administrators could not always give personal consideration to the reports or suggestions of specialist officers, and in practice that duty was 'delegated to officers whose status is even lower than that of the specialist officers directly concerned, with the result that attempts may be made by junior lay officers to criticise technical details any adequate knowledge of which is beyond their competence'. In the sphere of financial control, the I.P.C.S. realised that 'the enthusiasm of the expert for the completion of projects peculiar to his province may warrant some extraneous control'. But they were, understandably, not satisfied that 'these controlling duties should be monopolised by non-technical officers'; and they maintained that 'a system under which officers responsible for technical services of primary importance are unable to expend

---

[1] Sir Francis Floud, 'The Sphere of the Specialist in Public Administration', in *Public Administration* (1923) p. 122.

[2] *Tomlin Evidence*, appendix XI, part II, para. 28.

even the most trifling sums without administrative sanction leads not to economy, but to waste of time and energy and therefore of public money'. Among the examples the I.P.C.S. cited was the 'rigid control' of the Post Office Engineering Department by the administrative secretariat.[1]

The I.P.C.S. also pointed to the exclusion of specialists from administrative posts, commenting: 'Although it is stated officially that no barrier exists to prevent the promotion of the technical expert to high controlling positions in the Service, the I.P.C.S. maintains that the door to administrative preferment is in fact almost as effectively closed to Professional, Scientific and Technical officers possessing administrative talent as if they were excluded by statutory enactments.'[2] The I.P.C.S. disputed the general thesis that 'a professional, scientific or technical training *ipso facto* disqualifies its possessor from performing the duties of the highest administrative posts'. Still less did it justify the exclusion of the technical expert from posts of immediate administrative control of his division: 'Yet this particular method of maintaining the established theory of the essential inferiority of the technical expert is not confined to a refusal to consider his claims to preferment to an administrative post situated outside his immediate sphere of activity; it also takes the more serious form of stifling his aspirations to a position of control in his own sphere'[3] and the I.P.C.S. gave some disturbing examples. The institution was even prepared to concede that a random sample of specialist officers 'might perhaps yield a smaller number of persons possessing an innate faculty for administration than would a similar sample of non-technical personnel'. But, the I.P.C.S. added, to assume that 'the field of specialist employment is absolutely barren of fruit of this character is to impose upon the search for administrative talent limitations which are inimical to the best interests of the Civil Service and therefore of the country'.[4] They considered that the specialist had a particularly strong case to be considered for leading administrative posts in departments 'in which questions of administration and policy are largely determined by considerations

---

[1] Ibid. paras 29–31.   [2] Ibid. para. 36.
[3] Ibid. paras 37–40.   [4] Ibid. para. 42.

of a technical character', and one example the I.P.C.S. gave was that the Chief Engineer would be 'peculiarly well fitted' for the Permanent Secretaryship of the Post Office.[1]

This was not the sort of view that Sir Evelyn Murray, the current Permanent Secretary of the Post Office, put to the Commission. He said that there was 'nothing to prevent a member of the engineering staff being transferred to the secretariat', but it was 'perfectly true that no engineering officer had been so appointed'. By the time such an officer of outstanding capacity 'had demonstrated exceptional ability for administration and organisation, he would necessarily possess fairly long service and would probably have shown marked technical qualifications. His technical experience and training would be sacrificed on transfer while his success as an administrator would be problematical and it would very rarely be the case that the man's value to the Service would be enhanced'. Murray did not believe that technical questions would be more effectively handled if the administrative staff were recruited in part from the technical side. This was 'an entire misapprehension', for 'if the recommendations of the technicians are overruled it is not on technical grounds but for reasons of policy or finance'. If the administrative staff were recruited in part from technicians 'a body of quasi-experts would grow up in the secretariat who would tend to press their views on technical matters possibly in opposition to those of the technical departments'. Murray felt that concentrating expert engineering advice in the proper division was the best means 'of giving it the weight it deserves'.[2]

Even the Tomlin Commission, during what Menzler described as 'their cruise through the specialist classes',[3] observed about the Post Office: 'We should have expected that, over a period of years, some technical officers would have been found to possess qualities rendering desirable their transfer to the Administrative

[1] Ibid. para. 43.
[2] *Tomlin Evidence*, appendix XVIII (Selections from Supplementary Statements submitted to the Commission) part II (29): 'Transfer of Engineering Staff at the Post Office to the Administrative Staff'.
[3] F. A. A. Menzler, 'The Expert in the Civil Service', an essay in W. A. Robson (ed.) *The British Civil Servant* (1937) p. 173.

side. We were told, however, that no officers from the technical side had ever been promoted to an Administrative post in the department.'¹ As to the general question of specialists having opportunities to fill leading positions in the administrative hierarchy, the Tomlin Commission was convinced that their claims were usually considered, but that it was 'inevitable that most Administrative posts should be filled by officers with Administrative rather than specialist experience'.² Sir Warren Fisher had assured them that in filling the highest posts, it would be 'ridiculous' to suggest that he would say: 'Here is a lawyer or scientist, and therefore he shall not be considered for any job at all.' He told the commission that despite 'this prejudice which is supposed to exist against the professional and scientific men', two Permanent Heads of Departments had begun their careers as specialists, and the commission faithfully recorded this in the report.³ The Tomlin Commission also said: 'Whatever may have been the position in the past, we heard no evidence to justify the view that at the present time specialists are ignored. There is no real danger that their advice will not be placed before the Minister or official on whom falls the final decision on the issue under consideration'.⁴ Fisher had told them that although the Service was 'a whispering gallery' he had heard of no instances of professional advice being ignored, and he dismissed the I.P.C.S.'s complaint as 'an amiable grievance that has no foundation of fact'.⁵ The Tomlin Commission also considered, and rejected, an I.P.C.S. proposal to ensure that specialists had access to Ministers by putting the Permanent Headships of Departments in commission, and having boards at the top of Ministries on which 'the responsible technical experts take their share on equal terms with the Administrative heads in discussion with the Parliamentary heads of the department.'⁶ The Tomlin Commission, moreover, saw no value in the I.P.C.S.'s scheme to construct a 'Graded

¹ *Tomlin Report*, para. 233.   ² Ibid. 181.
³ *Tomlin Evidence*, questions 18,781–2; *Tomlin Report*, para. 181.
⁴ *Tomlin Report*, para. 178.
⁵ *Tomlin Evidence*, questions 18,835 and 18,778.
⁶ *Tomlin Evidence*, appendix XI, part II, para. 48. *Tomlin Report*, para. 177.

Technical Service' of two tiers which would replace the existing multiplicity of grades. This 'Service' was to be divided into 'General Grades', closely related to grades in other Civil Service classes, and a comparatively small number of 'Special Grades'. The I.P.C.S. wanted the principle of interchangeability of specialist staffs in different departments to be adopted so far as considerations of technique permitted.[1] The Tomlin Commission rejected all these ideas and contented themselves with advocating a greater measure of common recruitment to the same chaotic structure.[2]

The commission had not been so complacent about the state of the Post Office, and they had recommended an inquiry into its organisation.[3] The result was the Bridgeman Committee, whose 1932 report was, in Menzler's opinion, the first to devote 'any serious attention to the place of the specialist'.[4] The committee advocated the reorganisation of the Post Office to reduce the previously autocratic powers of the secretariat,[5] and one of their most important conclusions was that engineering experience was 'insufficiently brought into the consideration and formulation of general policy'.[6] They believed:

> In an organisation such as the Post Office, which depends so much upon scientific discoveries and developments and their practical application, we consider it essential to bring engineering and research into more intimate touch with the general problems of administration. The object of this closer relationship is two-fold; the engineer, on the one hand, will be in a position to visualise the picture as a whole, and thus to direct his activities into those

[1] *Tomlin Evidence*, appendix XI, part II, paras 62–86.

[2] *Tomlin Report*, paras 184–91.   [3] Ibid. para. 234.

[4] F. A. A. Menzler, op. cit. pp. 168–9, referring to the *Report of the Committee of Enquiry into the Post Office* (chairman: Viscount Bridgeman) 1932.

[5] The Bridgeman Committee's actual words were: 'The autocratic isolation of the Secretariat in relation to the Engineering and Accountant General's departments and the narrow and specialised meaning attached to the word "Administrative" in respect to staff generally, in our opinion, prevent these two departments from taking an adequate part in the general scheme of control.' (*Report*, para. 100.) The committee also condemned 'over-centralisation' in para. 128.

[6] *Bridgeman Report*, para. 101.

channels where the need for progress and development is greatest; while, on the other hand, those who are charged with the day-to-day running of the administrative machine will be able to avail themselves of the scientific point of view to the fullest extent.[1]

The Bridgeman Committee also made the valuable suggestion:

> As regards access to Administrative posts, we consider that there should be no bar to a technical officer holding such posts, provided he has shown himself to possess administrative ability. Generally speaking, we think it to be true that the specialist in any walk of life tends to remain a specialist; but there are of course well-known exceptions to the contrary, and we consider that where a member of the technical staff has shown that he possesses administrative talent, he should be eligible for other appointments.[2]

As a result of the Bridgeman Report, the Post Office was reorganised and the traditional structure was replaced by a functional board presided over by the Postmaster-General, coupled with regional decentralisation.[3] In place of the Permanent Secretary there was to be a Director-General, whose duty, 'under the chairmanship of successive Postmasters-General', would be 'to ensure that Board decisions are made effective, that continuity and unity of policy are maintained, and that the general machine of administration works smoothly and effectively. His position relative to that of other members of the Board would be that of "primus inter pares".'[4] Naturally, Menzler, who had been a leading figure in the I.P.C.S., was convinced that the new Post Office structure represented 'a simple panacea of general application'.[5]

Menzler also commented that there was 'no suggestion that there is a deliberate policy of keeping the expert in subjection',[6] although one would have thought that the I.P.C.S. had as good as made such a suggestion. Menzler shrewdly observed, writing in 1937, that the status of the specialist in the Civil Service 'which to the casual observer may seem no more than one of the peculiarities of the Service, is profoundly symptomatic of society's attitude towards

[1] Ibid. para. 131.   [2] Ibid. para. 122.
[3] Ibid. paras 108, 113–25 and 128.   [4] Ibid. para. 111.
[5] Menzler, op. cit. p. 181.   [6] Ibid. p. 185.

those who are reshaping, with ever-increasing velocity, their social environment'.[1] No doubt many in the Civil Service did regard the specialist as 'an inconvenient intruder', and even reasonably sympathetic outside observers seemed unable to properly make up their minds about the place of the expert. In 1938, Laski wrote that 'as between two able men, the specialist is less likely to become a successful administrator in the modern State than, say, one who has been trained in the Honours school of Literae Humaniores at Oxford'. The administrator's art was 'of relevant selection and significant emphasis', and thus was produced 'by the best kind of humanistic training'.[2] In 1931, Laski had written that 'the administrator must predominate over the technician', and that 'as a general rule, it is the former, and not the latter, who should attain the highest Administrative posts'. The 'unanswerable defence of this standpoint' was that 'it safeguards the attainment of proportion in administration'.[3] Yet in 1926, the same writer had said: 'The one big innovation for which I am above all anxious is that the technical expert shall be deliberately considered for the highest Administrative posts.'[4]

The Second World War and its aftermath did bring considerable changes, notably in the regrouping of the specialist hierarchies and in their improvement, but one of Laski's former colleagues could still complain in 1964 about the Service's reluctance to promote members of the specialist classes to leading administrative posts, even where they possessed 'outstanding administrative

[1] Ibid.

[2] Harold J. Laski, *Parliamentary Government in England* (1938) p. 323.

[3] Harold J. Laski, 'The Tomlin Report on the Civil Service', in *Political Quarterly* (1931) p. 517.

[4] Harold J. Laski, 'The Place of the Professional Civil Servant in Public Administration', in *State Service* (1926) p. 190.

[5] William A. Robson, 'The Reform of Government', in *Political Quarterly* (1964) p. 209. Before leaving the inter-war period entirely it is worth noting the opinion of Sir Henry Tizard: 'Before the year 1936, the academic scientists lived in a little world of their own, with their own hierarchy, their own levels and even their own honours list, which took the form of elections to the Royal Society, Medals and special lectures, and as a closed community the system worked pretty smoothly. The

ability'.[5] This, and the other aspects of the role of the expert in the Positive State, will be returned to after a survey of the major groups of specialists in the present Service.

II   THE MAJOR GROUPS OF SPECIALISTS

The Scientific Officer Class

In 1946, the scientific side of the Civil Service was reconstructed, with a three-tier structure replacing the two-tier division of Scientific Officer Class and Assistant Class that had been established as the result of the Carpenter Report of 1931. The highest tier of the new structure was still called the Scientific Officer Class and had assigned to it 'the main responsibility for scientific advice, research, design and developments in the Civil Service', and it was recruited primarily from first and second class honours graduates. Its major support was provided by the Experimental Officer Class, which was a reorganised and strengthened version of the old style Assistant Class. Upon the Experimental Officer Class was devolved a good deal of the work which in the pre-war years had been done by Scientific Officers, but which did not demand the highest academic qualifications. The direct entrants to the new class were mainly drawn from the G.C.E. 'A' level educational stream, but it also came to attract graduates. It was underpinned by a new Scientific Assistant Class, recruited from the G.C.E. 'O' level stream. The overall effect of the post-war reorganisation was therefore to set up three well-defined classes

---

scientists who were in the Government service were, with rare exceptions, second rate. The state of national emergency which culminated in the War had brought practically every scientist who was any good into the Government Service in one way or another.' (Ronald W. Clark, *Tizard*, 1965, pp. 369–70.) Tizard wrote these words in 1945, and they act as a corrective to the I.P.C.S.'s and A.S.W.'s glowing descriptions of their members, although it does not, of course, justify the inter-war status of the specialist nor does it justify the maintenance of the attitudes of that period today.

on the scientific side, with permanent recruitment being conducted by means of centralised competition in place of the former system of departmental recruitment, and with a measure of inter-class promotion.[1]

The recasting of the Scientific Civil Service in 1946 had followed the investigations of the Barlow Committee on Scientific Staff who, in their 1943 report, had asserted that 'the Government had

[1] Reference was made to the *Carpenter Report* (1931) which established the pre-war structure, and to the *Treasury Factual Memorandum to the Priestley Commission* (1953) paras 207, 208 and 211: the definition of the duties of the Scientific Officer Class was given in the *Treasury Factual Memorandum to the Fulton Committee* (1966) para. 466. The present structure of the Scientific Officer, Experimental Officer and Scientific Assistant Classes is given in Appendix IV, Tables I and IA of this book. The Treasury told the Fulton Committee that permanent recruitment to the Scientific Officer Class was 'by continuous competition for the Scientific and Senior Scientific Officer grades. The age limits are: under 29 for Scientific Officers and between the ages of 26 and 31 for Senior Scientific Officers. The qualifications normally required are a University degree, or a Diploma in Technology, or an equivalent qualification with First and Second Class Honours in a scientific subject (including engineering) or candidates are required, in addition, to have had at least three years' appropriate postgraduate or other approved experience. Many of the entrants to the Class, particularly those in research establishments, came in initially as temporaries. Many of these later obtain establishment through open competitions. Generally about two-thirds of the successful candidates in the S.S.O. and S.O. competitions are already temporary Civil Servants. The normal method of filling posts above the recruitment grades is by promotion, but recruitment by special open competition for particular posts is also employed.' In making recommendations for appointment, the selection board predictably 'gives weight to the candidates' capacity for original research or development'. There are also opportunities for members of the Experimental Officer Class aged at least 31 to enter the Scientific Officer Class by promotion. In addition, there is the Scientific Research Fellowship scheme: 'Research Fellows are recruited at Principal Scientific Officer, Senior Scientific Officer and Scientific Officer levels. Fellowships are tenable for three years (with the possibility of extension to five years for Principal Scientific Officers) at scientific establishments. The Fellowships are offered by way of open competition, which takes the form of an interview; there are no age limits. Principal Research Fellows must have been engaged for a considerable time in productive research and enjoy a high reputation in their fields; for Senior Fellowships at least three years postgraduate research experience is required; and at least two years for a Junior Fellowship.' (Ibid. paras 471–7.)

failed in peace-time to attract into and retain in its Service a proper proportion of the best scientists produced by the Universities'. The fault seemed to them to lie partly in the standards of remuneration and the prospects of promotion offered, but at least as much in general conditions of service and the relations between government research and the scientific world outside.[1] By this remark, the committee was referring to the tendency of government science to be isolated which not merely had an effect upon its quality, but acted as a hindrance to recruitment because: 'Young scientists, ambitious to obtain recognition for their work and to keep abreast of new developments, are discouraged from embarking upon a career which appears to remove them from contact with the Universities with learned societies and the research side of industry.[2] The Priestley Commission were told: 'Before the War, Government scientific establishments were considered rather indecent places to work in' but that 'the War did a lot to break that down.'[3] So had the implementation of some of the Barlow Committee's recommendations, for the government scientist was 'now encouraged to attend meetings of learned societies and similar bodies when papers are being read which have a connection with his official duties. Similarly on suitable occasions he is encouraged to undertake short courses of lectures at Universities, and to give talks at the request of undergraduate societies.' Many government scientists now have opportunities to travel abroad, and

> not a few have established international reputations as a result of their contributions to overseas conferences. Apart from attendance at general and specialised conferences, members of the Scientific Civil Service are often required to make short visits or considerable tours to overseas laboratories to extend their knowledge of work on their own specialities. Some may also represent their departments at technical policy meetings in various parts of the world.[4]

[1] *The Report of the Barlow Committee on Scientific Staff* (1943) para. 5. This was printed as an annexe to *The Scientific Civil Service. Reorganisation and Recruitment during the Reconstruction Period*, Cmd 6679 (1945).

[2] *Barlow Report on Scientific Staff*, para. 15.

[3] *Priestley Evidence*, question 3411.

[4] Civil Service Commission, *The Scientific Civil Service* (1965) p. 6.

Nevertheless, in general, it is still probably true that the scientist of the highest quality still makes his career in fundamental research at the universities, despite the improved quality of the facilities available in government establishments. The fact that a large proportion of government scientific work is military, and accordingly is cloaked in secrecy, is a major obstacle to recruitment. This has not been such a deterrent since the war as it had been in the 1930s, since a generation has grown up to whom the conditions of military science are taken for granted, and the position has been eased by such measures as facilities for submitting secret work for university doctorates; but there is always the fact that some of the best men will be deterred by secret work. Industry has the handicap of needing to retain trade secrets, but it can outbid the Government for the exceptional candidates.[1]

The Civil Service has been flexible in its recruitment procedures bearing in mind:

> In an era of full employment, the young science graduate of high quality has no difficulty at all in finding employment when he leaves the University. Indeed, he often has a choice of several posts, and as a result he is generally unwilling to look for a permanent appointment immediately. Often his aim is to gain experience in more than one kind of work, perhaps to travel abroad, and to defer his final choice of a career until he can make it in the light of personal knowledge of different types of employment. Consequently, if he is attracted to the Scientific Civil Service, he frequently prefers to enter it initially in a temporary capacity and he usually has ideas on the kind of work he would like to do.[2]

Young scientists prefer to become members of a particular team or establishment, rather than to join the Scientific Civil Service as such. Posts in that Service are usually offered in the first instance as unestablished posts, with recruitment handled by the departments, followed by 'subsequent confirmation by the Commission

---

[1] Civil Service Commissioners, *Memorandum to the Priestley Commission*, para. 7; *Priestley Evidence*, questions 528–34 and 569. The Civil Service Commissioners admitted in 1965 that 'we still fail to attract enough of the really outstanding men to the Scientific Class' (*99th Report*, p. 2).

[2] *95th Report of the Civil Service Commissioners*, p. 5.

when both sides have made up their minds'.[1] For example, it was
estimated in 1965 that about seventy-five per cent of the Scientific
Officer Class vacancies in the then Ministry of Aviation are
filled directly, while the remainder were recruited in an established capacity, initially through the Civil Service Commission;
almost all those who originally enter on a temporary basis apply
for establishment within four years. Liaison with the universities
is handled by such bodies as the Royal Radar Establishment at
Malvern and the Royal Aircraft Establishment at Farnborough,
rather than by the Ministry's headquarters, because they are 'far
more vital and attractive than the Ministry of Aviation as such'
to the young scientists.[2]

Nevertheless, the overall recruiting position for scientists is
unsatisfactory. Of the scientists just below the highest class, the
Service attracts its fair share and it has openings for a whole range
of ability: the individual research worker, the person who has some
capacity for research but who is better at administering a small
group, or even someone who is not in the strictest sense a scientist
at all, but has a gift for making the wheels go round in technical
administration.[3] But, as the Civil Service Commission said in
1965, the Service does not attract as many of the really outstanding
young scientists as they would like, and it commented that it was
possible that 'our system of pay on entry, which does not permit
any recognition of the really top-class men, may have some
bearing'.[4] This is despite the fact that the Service offered Research
Fellowships to such candidates and guaranteed them advancement
to Principal Scientific Officer, the equivalent of an Administrative
Principal, by their early thirties.[5]

The extent of the range of activities undertaken by the Scientific
Officer Class can be shown by brief descriptions of the type of

[1] Civil Service Commissioners' Memorandum to the Select Committee
on Estimates (*Sixth Report*, 1964–5) para. 26.
[2] Select Committee on Estimates (*Sixth Report*, 1964–5) 'Recruitment
to the Civil Service'; *Evidence*, questions 404–14.
[3] *Civil Service Commissioners' Memorandum to the Priestley Commission*, para. 7; *Priestley Evidence*, question 503.
[4] Memorandum to the Select Committee on Estimates, op. cit. para. 27.
[5] Civil Service Commission, *The Scientific Civil Service* (1965) pp. 4
and 9.

work done in four of the hundred or more research establishments in which members of that class are employed. The work of the Ministry of Technology's National Physical Laboratory at Teddington, Middlesex, includes basic and applied research into the fields of physics, engineering physics, metallurgy, autonomics and mathematics. Research into physics includes such subjects as 'nuclear and electron-spin resonance, radiology, acoustics, atomic frequency standards, optics, ultra-high pressures, spectroscopy, polymer physics and high-pressure physics'. Research into engineering physics deals with such subjects as 'aerodynamics up to hypersonic speeds, aerodynamic behaviour of industrial structures, ship hydrodynamics (model testing, propeller design and performance etc.)'. Research into the field of metallurgy includes such subjects as 'dislocation theory, chemical thermo-dynamics, physics of metals, high-purity metals'. In the field of autonomics, research is conducted into 'computer design, mech-anical translation, character recognition and adaptive control', while in the field of mathematics among the subjects dealt with are 'differential equations, theoretical physics, high-speed computing, and numerical analysis'. The laboratory also has the responsi-bility for establishing and maintaining the primary British stan-dards of fundamental physical quantities, which is work that involves the application of modern techniques to methods of measurement of very high precision'.[1] In almost complete contrast to the type of research conducted at the National Physical Laboratory is that conducted at the Ministry of Defence's Chemical Defence Experimental Establishment at Porton near Salisbury in Wiltshire. This Establishment conducts

> research and development work on the defensive aspects of chemical warfare, and on protection against dust and toxic hazards in industry, agriculture and national undertakings. There is collaboration with other organisations in research on pest and weed control. Specific fields of research include: synthesis of toxic compounds involving extensive research in hitherto little explored fields of organic chemistry; detailed studies (physio-logical, physio-chemical, biophysical or pharmacological) of toxic compounds to determine their precise mode of action, with a

---

[1] Ibid. p. 40.

view to the development of adequate therapeutic measures; formation and properties of dispersions of solid and liquid particles of controlled particle size and concentration. Studies of the precise factors involved in the filtration of aerosols by fibrous media, with a view to the development of high-efficiency filters for incorporation in respirator containers and filtration plant for various purposes.[1]

In almost complete contrast again is the work of the Freshwater Fisheries Laboratory of the Department of Agriculture and Fisheries for Scotland at Pitlochry in Perthshire. The laboratory is primarily concerned with research into the activities of

salmon, sea trout, and brown trout, as well as other freshwater fish such as pike and perch. Present work on salmon includes studies of the freshwater phases in the life cycle of this fish, work on the effects of hydro-electric developments on salmon fisheries and stocks, and census work. Present work on brown trout includes studies of their behaviour, observations on growth and maturity, and investigations of trout populations. Studies of other parts of the freshwater community, particularly work on the bottom fauna, and the chemical and physical aspects of the environment are linked with the work on fish.[2]

Finally, and once more in complete contrast with the preceding example, one can consider the Forensic Science work which is carried on in the Home Office Laboratories at Birmingham, Bristol, Cardiff, Harrogate, Nottingham, Preston and Newcastle, and in the Metropolitan Police Laboratory at New Scotland Yard. These establishments work in close liaison with police forces on the scientific detection and prevention of crime. The work involves 'the examination of exhibits in the laboratories and visits to scenes of crimes in order to secure material for submission in the event of Court proceedings'. The laboratory work in particular covers

a wide field of scientific enquiry and research (mainly chemistry and biology) and includes chemical analyses; examination of materials by ultra-violet, infra-red and X-radiation; identification of traces of material by emission, absorption and X-ray spectroscopy; work on documents, inks, etc.; comparison work applied to fine details on tools, toolmarks and fragments of various kinds; identification of marks on weapons, bullets, cartridge cases, etc.;

[1] Ibid. p. 26.   [2] Ibid. p. 45.

comparison microscope work of various other kinds; the identification of seeds and of fragments of plant and animal tissues;
tests for semen and identification of spermatozoa; tests for blood,
including identification of blood groups, parasites, etc.; patho-
logical work of many kinds; photographic work, in connection
with most of the above for demonstration purposes; toxicological
investigations; examination of explosives, motor accidents and
suspicious fires.[1]

It can, therefore, be safely concluded that it is difficult to
generalise about the work of the Scientific Officer Class, except to
say that its work requires people trained in almost every scientific
discipline, although most of the class can be classified as mathe-
maticians, physicists, chemists or engineers.[2] For the most part
the class is stationed in research establishments throughout the
country, although some members are employed in the central
direction and administration of research in the headquarters
divisions of such departments as the Ministry of Technology.[3]
It is not possible to define with precision the duties of the various
grades of this class but, broadly speaking, members of grades
up to and including Principal Scientific Officer are engaged in
carrying out the scientific work itself; those in higher grades are
responsible for the direction and administration of scientific work.
Below Principal Scientific Officer level it is accepted that the
precise grading of a post at any particular time is largely dependent
on the qualities and experience of the man who fills it. For this
reason flexible complementing operates, no distinction being
drawn for complementing purposes between staff in the Scientific
Officer and Senior Scientific Officer grades. In the grades above
Principal Scientific Officer there is provision for 'special merit
appointments' to enable officers to be freed from administrative
and managerial responsibilities in order to concentrate on their
individual scientific work, where this is judged to be of outstanding
quality and importance. The appointments commonly involve
promotion for the scientists concerned. Also engaged in research

---

[1] Ibid. p. 30.
[2] Civil Service Commissioners' Memorandum to the Select Committee
on Estimates, op. cit. para. 25.
[3] *Treasury Factual Memorandum to the Fulton Committee* (1966) para. 470.

work, often of a specialised nature or on an individual as distinct from a team basis, are, as was noted earlier, a number of Research Fellows who hold posts tenable for a few years.[1] Taken as a whole, however, the Scientific Officer Class career hierarchy does not compare very favourably with the prospects open to the Assistant Principal. In 1966, although about forty-six per cent of the Administrative Class posts were of Assistant Secretary rank or above, only about twenty-three per cent of the Scientific Officer Class posts were of comparable status.[2]

The Works Group of Professional Classes

Just as the scientific side of the Service was reorganised in 1946, so a Works Group of Professional Classes was constructed in the same year to cover a variety of professions mainly concerned with engineering in its various forms, building and estate management and surveying, which had before the war been recruited and organised on a departmental basis. A review of these classes had shown that the qualifications required of their entrants were much of the same type: namely, membership of an appropriate professional institution and/or a university degree appropriate to the particular profession, coupled with several years' professional experience; that age limits for recruitment were broadly similar; and that duties and responsibilities were broadly comparable, despite distinctions of profession and some departmental variations of function within a profession. A reorganisation then followed in which a series of general service classes was created with standardised rates of pay and conditions of service, and with permanent recruitment conducted on a centralised basis by the Civil Service Commission.[3]

[1] Ibid. paras 468–9.

[2] Appendix I, Table 1, and Appendix IV, Table 1 refers.

[3] *Treasury Factual Memorandum to the Priestley Commission* (1955) paras 232, 241–3 and 250. Although in 1937 common scales for some grades in a number of professional classes in a few departments were introduced, it was not until 1946 that a series of general service professional classes concerned with works were introduced (*Treasury Factual Memorandum to the Fulton Committee*, 1966, para. 19).

The Works Group is not therefore one class, but a group of professional classes.[1] It includes engineers of all specialisms, architects, maintenance surveyors, quantity surveyors, estate surveyors and lands officers, valuers, planning officers and inspectors of many kinds. Their duties include advisory and consultant work; decisions on the professional aspects of statutory requirements; the original design and preparation of complete schemes; the managerial control and direction of the processes which translated paper schemes into production; and the operation, maintenance and inspection of systems which have been set up. In some departments professional staff are directly responsible for the design, planning, erection and maintenance of building and engineering works; in others, they act as consultants or they are employed in vetting schemes prepared by other bodies such as local authorities. Some engineers are directly responsible for the design and manufacture of equipment for the Forces; others exercise a supervisory function over production contracts with

[1] The Treasury told the Fulton Committee: 'The present organisation of the professional classes is complex and has come about over a long period. The centre core is called the Works Group. This is a Group of general service classes with common structures and pay scales and comparable entry requirements. The classes are architects, maintenance surveyors, quantity surveyors, estate surveyors, lands officers, civil engineers, mechanical and electrical engineers and sanitary engineers. The Works Group proper, however, includes only about a third (4250) of the 11,400 professional staff in the Service. The others are members either of departmental variants or related Classes. Some of these are practically indistinguishable from Works Group Classes (e.g. the departmental class of mechanical and electrical engineers in the Ministry of Aviation); other diverge from the Works Group norm to varying degrees in structure, pay and entry standards. Members of the Works Group are found in a number of departments but architects, maintenance, quantity and estate surveyors are mostly employed by the Ministry of Public Building and Works, lands officers by the Ministry of Agriculture, Fisheries and Food, the Department of Agriculture and Fisheries for Scotland and the Defence departments, and mechanical and civil engineers by the Ministry of Public Building and Works and the Ministry of Transport. The main departmental variants and related classes are engineers in the Ministry of Aviation and Army Department, the Royal Naval Engineering Service, Post Office engineers, planning officers and housing and planning inspectors in the Ministry of Housing and Scottish Development Department and valuers in the Inland Revenue.' (*Treasury Factual Memorandum to the Fulton Committee*, 1966, paras 559–51.)

private industry, and others again are engaged on research and development work. Estate surveyors, land commissioners and land officers are responsible, in an advisory or executive capacity, for the purchase, sale, lease and management of real property, urban and rural. Typical statutory inspection functions, carried out by professional staff, are the inspection of public service vehicles, the investigation of accidents on railways and those involving aircraft, the survey of construction, equipment and crew standards of ships.[1]

The Works Group Classes are divided into several tiers: the Basic, Main, Senior, Superintending and Directing Grades, while there are in addition several top posts which are individually graded.[2] The recruitment point was originally supposed to be the Basic Grade, but a perennial failure to attract suitable entrants has led to posts being offered in the Main and higher Grades as well with the Civil Service Commission having the power to exercise discretion about starting salaries. There is a general shortage of professional engineers, with the Service being handicapped because many young engineering graduates are committed to return to the firms which have sponsored them at university.[3]

[1] Ibid. paras 556–8.

[2] The structure of the Works Group Classes and the variant and related Classes is shown in Appendix iv, Table 2.

[3] The Treasury recently described recruitment to the Works Group and related Classes in the following terms: 'The normal qualification requirements (which, for engineers, are under review) are corporate membership of the appropriate professional institution, plus professional ability and experience. Selection is by interview. In some departments, however, Basic Grade engineers can be appointed without corporate membership. Normally entry is by continuous open competition and, as occasion demands, by *ad hoc* competition to the Basic Grades, for qualified candidates between the ages of 25 and 34. Candidates over the age of 34 who are temporary Civil Servants and who have served in Government departments as temporary officers in the appropriate Class for at least nine months continuously up to the date of their application can also compete. Exceptionally but to an increasing extent, where the Main Grade posts cannot be filled by promotion there has been direct recruitment to posts at Main Grade level. This has notably been done for architects, quantity surveyors, civil engineers and mechanical and electrical engineers. There were no rigid age limits but the main field of recruitment has been from candidates aged 35 and over. There has also been recruitment to the Senior Grade especially where the Main Grade is the recruitment grade (e.g. with planning officers). A large proportion of the entrants to the

(*footnote 3, page 218, continued*)
Basic Grade, particularly to the Engineering Classes, are people who have qualified for entry while working in sub-professional grades in the Service. If they are within the age limits they enter through the normal competition. If over 34 they enter by departmental promotion. In addition is the recruitment of Engineering Cadets. Cadets must be under 26 and must have an Honours degree or Diploma in Technology in a relevant subject. They are trained in departments, usually for two years, on programmes designed to satisfy the training requirements for corporate membership of a professional institution. After training they are appointed as Basic Grade engineers.' (*Treasury Factual Memorandum to the Fulton Committee*, 1966, paras 565–8.) It is interesting to note the observations made by the Civil Service Commissioners in 1964 on this general subject: 'The recruitment of engineers into the Basic Grade of the Professional Works Group continues to be difficult. Many of the undergraduates in the engineering schools of the Universities, the Colleges of Advanced Technology and the Technical Colleges are supported by industrial firms and after graduating they tend to return to their sponsors. Competition for the remainder is keen. Recruitment to Engineering Cadetship is still disappointing. The Basic Grade in the Works Group is unattractive to young architects and surveyors.' The Commissioners also commented: 'The response to offers of posts above the Basic Grade in the Works Group has been much greater and the results more satisfactory' (*98th Report*, pp. 2–3). In 1965, the Commissioners wrote: 'In the Works Group of Professional Classes a feature of the year has been the expansion of the demand for architects and planners, of whom there is a national shortage. We are fairly successful in filling posts in this field in the Senior Grade, but in the highly competitive national situation, and in a period when a major review of the pay of the Works Group was being undertaken, the number of Main Grade applicants was inadequate in relation to the number of posts to be filled, and successful candidates were frequently unable to accept the starting salary we could offer, even where we were prepared to offer increased starting salary in recognition of useful experience acquired outside the Service. We have also been making greater use of our discretion to consider for Main Grade appointments well-qualified candidates below the age of 35. Recruitment to the Basic Grade, however, virtually ceased last year. On the engineering side the picture is slightly better in that in the Basic Grade there has been a steady, though inadequate, flow of entrants who have acquired professional qualifications in sub-professional grades, including an increasing number who have benefited by departmental training schemes. The success of some of these training schemes suggests that the Service can compete with other employers for school leavers more successfully than for professionally qualified staff.' (*99th Report*, p. 6.) The Treasury were, therefore, justified in telling the Select Committee on Estimates in 1965 that the shortfall in the recruitment of engineers was a 'major concern to them (*Sixth Report*, 1964–5, *Evidence*, question 210), and the generally gloomy picture of professional recruitment to the Service presented to

The role of the professional engineer in the Service provides an interesting example of how the Service's role has itself changed, for until comparatively recently the Government's need for engineers was confined almost entirely to the civilian services connected with the armed forces – the manufacture of guns and ammunition, for example, and the repair and construction of ships and equipment for the Royal Navy. But the increasingly important part which technical developments have come to play in society in the last few decades has meant that more of the matters with which the Government has to concern itself are of technical aspects, and on these it is essential for the Ministers to have available in their departments the advice and assistance of professional engineers. In addition, many government departments are directly responsible for the execution of engineering work, both for civil and for military purposes. As a result, the modern Civil Service includes representatives of practically every branch of the engineering profession, and with 5500 in its ranks it is the largest single employer of engineers in the country. Of these, some 1800 are engaged in the design, production and supply of equipment of all kinds to the Armed Forces and to certain civilian services. About 1700 are concerned with the design, construction and maintenance of roads, dockyards, airfields and buildings of all kinds, including Government Research Stations, offices and other establishments. This group includes about 1000 civil engineers, the remainder being mechanical and electrical engineers who design and install the wide range of plant and services required. Some 1600 work on the design, installation and postal and communications services and on navigational aids. The remainder are responsible for the many technical aspects of the work of inspection, licensing and control, which a number of government departments are required to do by statute. The professional engineers are assisted by about 25,000 technical staff and about 10,000 drawing

---

(*footnote 3, page 218, continued*)
the Select Committee by the I.P.C.S. has been shown to be accurate (ibid. appendix 5 to the Minutes of Evidence, para. 7). About 1966, the Civil Service Commissioners wrote: 'recruitment to the Works Group of Professional Classes has again been difficult' (*100th Report*, p. 11).

office staff, while the industrial labour force, directly employed by the Government on production, construction and maintenance, numbers about 250,000.[1]

A feature of the Works Group and its variant and related classes is that the career hierarchy, with only about eight per cent of its posts of Assistant Secretary status or above, compares very poorly with the Administrative Class hierarchy which has about forty-six per cent of its members in such grades.[2]

The Legal Class

Although in the 1930s vacancies for lawyers in the Civil Service had attracted as many as a hundred or more candidates for a single post,[3] the Barlow Committee had, nevertheless, found in 1944 that 'the deficiency of capable men in the Legal Civil Service is at present so great as to create a very serious situation, and that it is urgently necessary to take action now in order that the Public Service may obtain the lawyers it will require'.[4] As a result, the Legal Class was reconstructed in 1946, the position improved, and in 1967 the strength of the class was about 700 barristers, advocates and solicitors.[5]

[1] Civil Service Commission, *Engineers in the Government Service* (1964) pp. 1–2.
[2] Appendix I, Table 1 and Appendix IV, table 2 refers.
[3] *Priestley Evidence*, question 2339.
[4] *The Report of the Committee on Legal Departments of the Civil Service* (chairman: Sir Alan Barlow) 1944, para. 9.
[5] *Supplement to the Treasury Factual Memorandum (Medical and Legal Staffs) submitted to the Priestley Commission* (1954) para. 8; Civil Service Commission, *Lawyers in the Government Service* (1967) p. 1. The size and structure of the Legal Class is given in Appendix IV, Table 3. The Treasury told the Fulton Committee: 'The work of the Legal Class includes advice on the legal implications of questions of major policy, the preparation of Government Bills and the drafting of subordinate legislation, litigation, conveyancing and advice on the legal aspect of day to day administration.' (*Factual Memorandum*, 1966, para. 349.) Although in almost all the main government departments legal branches are headed by a lawyer with Head of a Legal Branch grading, the numbers and structure of the Legal Class in each department vary greatly. The

The work of the Legal Class can be divided into five categories. Firstly, its most important duties lie in the sphere of the creation

---

grade of Deputy Head is found only in a few departments. In most others there is a deputy at Principal Assistant Solicitor level, but sometimes a number of Assistant Solicitors nevertheless report direct to the head of the branch. Assistant Solicitors roughly corresponding in status to Assistant Secretaries in the Administrative Class are heads of sections. In addition to dealing with the more difficult and complex day-to-day work and to assisting with and advising on the higher grade work, they are normally responsible for supervision, and allocation of work between both Senior Legal Assistants and Legal Assistants. (Legal Assistant is not a training grade, since staff have already had working experience before entering.) The grading of legal posts presents unusual difficulties, particularly at the lower levels, since much depends upon an officer's knowledge and experience of a particular type of work rather than on his general experience. Largely for this reason, a system of 'flexible complementing' is operated between Legal Assistant and Senior Legal Assistant. The effect is that after a certain time in the basic grade, normally about six years, and subject to a minimum age limit, at present thirty-two, a man's increased capacity may be recognised by promotion to Senior Legal Assistant, his job being upgraded with him if necessary. In exceptional cases there is also the possibility of more rapid advancement to the Senior Legal Assistant grade for 'those of exceptional ability'. There is thus no clear-cut change in responsibility between the two grades, which are normally used in parallel (ibid. paras 351–2; Civil Service Commission, *Lawyers in Government Service*, 1967, p. 29). Recruitment to the Legal Class is by open competitive interview normally to the grade of Legal Assistant. Candidates must be between twenty-four and thirty-nine years of age. For posts in England and Wales recruits are required to be either Barristers called to the English Bar or Solicitors admitted in England and Wales; for posts in Scotland they must be either Advocates or qualified Solicitors in Scotland. Recent legal experience in England is essential for posts in England; similar experience in Scotland is desirable but not essential for all posts in Scotland. Experience of work similar to that carried out in the legal branches of departments in which the posts occur is an advantage (*Treasury Factual Memorandum to the Fulton Committee*, 1966, para. 354). The recent recruiting record of the Legal Class has not been very good as the Civil Service Commissioners made clear in 1965 when they wrote that although they had been able 'to recruit enough Legal Assistants to prevent the shortage of lawyers from getting worse,' there were[6] still a large number of unfilled posts. It seems that changes in the age limits, an improved salary scale, and the provision for more rapid promotion to Senior Legal Assistant, have had little effect.' (*99th Report*, p. 5) Fortunately, however, as regards 1966, the Commissioners were able to record 'a significant improvement in the recruitment of Legal Assistants' (*100th Report*, p. 10).

of the law, namely, in preparing the material which goes to Parliamentary Counsel to be embodied in statutes, advising the administrators on that material before it was sent up and drafting statutory instruments. Since the war, Acts of Parliament are much shorter, giving powers to Ministers to amplify them by statutory instruments, which are almost entirely prepared by government lawyers. The work involves discussing with the administrators what policy they want, what policy is feasible and then producing the instrument in terms which are intelligible. Secondly, after the law has come into existence, comes the next most important duty of the class which is to advise the administrators on how to put the statutory requirements into practice. Thirdly, beyond the purely advisory work, there is civil litigation with the class having responsibility for the conduct of proceedings at levels ranging from departmental tribunals to the High Court. Fourthly, comes criminal prosecution. Some departments have to conduct a large number of comparatively small prosecutions for breaches of regulations; others have to conduct a large number of prosecutions which, on the face of them, appear to be small but each of which is a case of fraud depending on a different pattern of fact; while, above that level, in some departments it is necessary to conduct from time to time very substantial prosecutions for fraud and conspiracy, where proceedings in the Magistrate's Court may last for several days. In both civil litigation and criminal prosecution the government lawyer acts in the capacity of solicitor, briefing counsel. Fifthly, comes conveyancing work, most of which is concentrated in the Treasury Solicitor's office. The Treasury Solicitor has to convey factories and aerodromes and estates which are handed over when their owner dies, in settlement of death duties, which are very large individual jobs which do not compare with the ordinary run of conveyancing in private practice.[1]

In some respects, therefore, the duties of the Legal Class involve professional activities similar to those found in private practice, such as giving legal opinions and instructing counsel; in others, the duties of the class are peculiar to the government

[1] *Priestley Evidence*, question 2301.

Service, such as the drafting of statutory instruments. A peculiar
feature of the work of the class is the extent to which much of it,
on the general departmental side, is concentrated in the office of
the Treasury Solicitor, who is the legal adviser and solicitor for all
government departments and establishments who do not have
their own. For some years before the war it was the practice to
discourage the formation of new legal departments, and to provide
for the needs of new government departments by increasing the
scope and staff of the existing legal departments, usually that of the
Treasury Solicitor, although detached branches were set up where
necessary.[1] At present, the Treasury Solicitor has a qualified
staff of over 100; the Ministry of Agriculture, Fisheries and
Food, H.M. Customs and Excise, the Ministry of Housing and
Local Government (with the Ministry of Health), the Board of
Inland Revenue, the Land Registry, the Post Office, the Director
of Public Prosecutions, the Public Trustee, the Ministry of Social
Security and the Board of Trade have thirty to fifty each, while the
legal staffs of other departments range from a score to half a
dozen.[2] Another feature of the Legal Class is that twenty-four
per cent of its members are of Higher Civil Service status, while
the class also has, with the sole exception of the recently formed
Government Economic Service, the most favourable percentage
of posts of Under-Secretary grading and above of the leading
specialist groups.[3]

The Medical Officer Class

Although, like most other leading specialist groups, the Medical
Officer Class was reorganised in 1946,[4] it did not take its present

---

[1] *Supplement to the Treasury Factual Memorandum (Medical and Legal
Staffs) submitted to the Priestley Commission* (1954) paras 3 and 6.

[2] Civil Service Commission, *Lawyers in the Government Service* (1967)
pp. 2–3.

[3] Appendix IV, Table 3.

[4] *Supplement to the Treasury Factual Memorandum (Medical and Legal
Staffs) submitted to the Priestley Commission* (1954) para. 24.

form until after the Howitt Report of 1951.[1] The Howitt Committee merged the pay scales of the General Service Class, which was employed in about half of the departments and said to be engaged on clinical work, and a departmental class known as the 'Health' group consisting of Medical Officers employed in the Ministry of Health and the remaining departments, who were said to be engaged on medical administrative work, and who had previously received higher pay.[2] The Howitt Committee also considered the desirability of a completely unified Medical Service, under the central control of the Chief Medical Officer of the Ministry of Health, but they concluded that the advantages of greater flexibility and better regulated career prospects, which might be expected to result, would be outweighed by the interference with departmental control and responsibility which it might involve.[3]

Medical Officers in the Civil Service have a range of duties almost as wide as the theory and practice of medicine itself. Firstly, in a number of departments, they examine difficult and intractable cases occurring in general practice; for example, in the work of the regional medical service of the Ministry of Health. Secondly, they are responsible for the general supervision of the whole of the medical aspects of the National Health Service. Thirdly, they are responsible for advising Ministers on legislation, regulations or on general public advice needed in the prevention, control or treatment of many diseases such as industrial and infectious diseases. Fourthly, they are responsible for advising public authorities and industrial and commercial organisations on major health issues. Fifthly, they are responsible for the health organisation of establishments such as those of the Ministry of Aviation, which partly reproduce the medical organisation of large industries but more importantly involve work of an entirely novel and exploratory character arising from the nature of the work of these establishments. Sixthly, in the Prisons department

[1] *Report of the Committee on the Pay and Organisation of the Civil Service Medical Staffs* (chairman: Sir Harold Howitt) Aug 1951.

[2] *Howitt Report*, op. cit. paras 3 and 5; together with paras 6, 7 and 8 of their *Interim Report* (Apr 1951).

[3] *Howitt Report*, paras 26–9.

H

of the Home Office, Medical Officers are responsible not only for the normal medical treatment of prisoners and medical administration for prison staffs, but for the psychiatric treatment now a feature of prison work; and as well as special work in this field, they assist the Courts in certain cases.[1]

One unusual feature of the Medical Officer Class is that, although only three per cent of its members are of Under-Secretary status or above, all Medical Officers receive salaries

[1] *Memorandum of Evidence submitted by the Civil Service Medical Officers Joint Committee to the Priestley Commission* (1954) para. 25. The Treasury told the Fulton Committee: 'Medical Officers are employed on a wide range of duties. These include the general supervision of the medical aspects of the National Health Service; advising on the control and treatment of industrial and infectious diseases and other major health issues; the clinical examination of cases similar to those found in medical practice generally, particularly in connection with employment in the Civil Service and with claims for pensions and disablement benefits; managing health services in industrial organisations, such as those of the Ministry of Aviation; and the medical treatment of prisoners.' (*Treasury Factual Memorandum,* 1966, para. 375.) The structure of the Medical Officer Class is shown in Appendix IV, Table 4, and the Treasury recently described it in the following terms: 'The Medical Officer grade is responsible for carrying out most of the day-to-day work falling to members of the Medical Officer Class. Indeed some two-thirds of the Class is in this grade. A Medical Officer is required to have outside experience before appointment. Medical Officers may be attached to the headquarters of departments where they are likely to be concerned with the giving of advice on medical matters to regional organisations of the Ministry of Health, or the Ministry of Pensions and National Insurance, to H.M. Prisons (Home Office) or to the Factory Inspectorate (Ministry of Labour). Posts above Medical Officer level are to be found in the headquarters of these Ministries and a few others which employ smaller medical staffs. In a headquarters establishment a Senior Medical Officer is normally responsible for a specific block of work with a subordinate staff of Medical Officers, or is engaged on specialised work. The officer in charge of the medical staff in the regional offices of the Ministry of Health and the Ministry of Pensions and National Insurance is normally graded Senior Medical Officer. A Principal Medical Officer has a wider responsibility or may be concerned with work requiring specialist qualifications.' (Ibid. para. 377.) The Treasury added: 'Recruitment is normally to the basic grade with selection by interview. Candidates must be fully qualified and registered medical practitioners, and should have the particular qualifications or experience appropriate to the posts for which they wish to be considered. While the minimum age of recruitment is in general 28, more experienced candidates are required for some posts.' (Ibid. para. 378.)

that at least equal the Principal's minimum.[1] Another feature, in contrast to the other major specialist groups discussed already, is the extent to which outside recruitment is resorted to in order to fill the highest posts in the class.[2]

The Professional Accountant Class

Before 1936, the Civil Service only employed about fifty professional accountants, and most of them had been engaged on cost accounting and allied processes in relation to admiralty contracts, and the majority of the remainder had been concerned with the investigation of the more complex cases of suspected income tax evasion. Cost accounting and other financial investigations necessitated by the rearmament programme of 1936–9, and the rapid increase in armaments production after the outbreak of the war, multiplied the demand by the Service and supply departments for professional accountants. The undertaking by civil departments of fresh responsibilities which brought them into close and difficult relationships with business and industry, such as the institution of price controls and subsidy schemes and the related enforcement machinery and the development of State trading and allied activities, resulted in a further increase in that demand and at the end of the war there were over 1100 professional accountants in the Service. The peacetime reduction in the number and scope of the various civil controls and in armaments production had led to a lessened demand for professional accountants: by 1952

---

[1] *Treasury Factual Memorandum to the Fulton Committee* (1966) para. 376.

[2] The representatives of the Medical Officer Class had complained about this situation in their evidence to the Priestley Commission in 1954 (Civil Service Medical Officers' Joint Committee's Memorandum, op. cit. para. 70). That it persisted a decade later was made clear by the Treasury in their evidence to the Fulton Committee for, although they said that recruitment to the Medical Officer Class is 'normally to the basic grade', the statistics they presented of the recruitment position of that class in the preceding six years showed that in 1962 and 1965 respectively, outside recruitment took place at Deputy Chief Medical Officer and Senior Principal Medical Officer level, that is to posts of Under-Secretary status. (*Treasury Factual Memorandum*, 1966, paras 378–9.)

about 500 were employed, only about half of whom were established,[1] while in 1966 334 were employed, with all but fifty-nine of them established Civil Servants.[2]

Before the war, the accountants were organised in a series of unrelated departmental classes, but in 1946 they were grouped together in a single general Professional Accountant Class recruited centrally by the Civil Service Commission, with a common structure and common conditions of service.[3] Compared with

[1] *Report of the Committee on the Organisation, Structure, and Remuneration of the Professional Accountant Class of the Civil Service* (chairman: Sir Thomas Gardiner) 1952, para. 8.

[2] Appendix IV, Table 5.

[3] *Gardiner Report* (1952) para. 9. The Treasury told the Fulton Committee about the duties of the Professional Accountant Class: 'Most Government accounting work is carried out by the Executive Class, with assistance from the Clerical Class, but in a few departments there is work which calls for the services of professionally qualified accountants with wide practical experience of accounting practice in industry and commerce. Where it is necessary to obtain high level professional advice on accounting matters it is the practice to obtain the services of outside consultants.' (*Treasury Factual Memorandum*, 1966, para. 80.) The Treasury said that the main grade of the Professional Accountant Class is that of Senior Accountant, Accountant being largely a recruiting grade. The normal hierarchy ends with the grade of Chief Accountant, but there are a small number of directing posts above that level. A few departments employ accountants in an advisory capacity. The grading of these posts depends very much on the job in question rather than the presence of more junior accountants in the same department. The Ministry of Technology and the Board of Trade are the departments which employ most professional accountants (ibid. para. 82). Recruitment to the Professional Accountant Class is by open competitive interview to the grades of either Accountant or Senior Accountant. Candidates for the Accountant grade must be at least twenty-three years of age on the date of their application: there is no upper age limit, but in appointing persons in a permanent capacity, departments expect 'regular and effective service for a reasonable period', and the Commissioners take this requirement into account. Candidates for the Senior Accountant Grade should normally be at least thirty and under forty-five years of age on the date of application, although there are special arrangements for those with at least two years' temporary service in the grade and for former members of either the Armed Forces or the Overseas Civil Service. In all cases 'membership of the Institute of Chartered Accountants in England and Wales (or its Scottish or Irish equivalent) or the Association of Certified and Corporate Accountants is essential'. Candidates are also required 'to have had professional experience, including

private business and industry, the role of the professional accountants in the Service is a restricted one, for the great bulk of government finance, accounting and auditing, which involve no contact with outside business and industry, is assigned to the Executive Class, whose members tend to hold many of the higher financial and accounting posts. The Professional Accountant Class is employed in those departments which have close relations with business and industry where their training in, and practical experience of, commercial accountancy is of special value, and particularly those departments which are large buyers and which operate their own production factories.[1] Where it is necessary to obtain high-level professional advice on accounting matters, it is the practice to obtain the services of outside consultants.[2] As a result, the Professional Accountant Class has no posts at all of Under-Secretary status and above, and only seven of its 334 posts are definitely of Assistant Secretary status.[3] Like most committees reporting about specialist groups in the Service, the Gardiner Committee examining the role of the Professional Accountant Class in 1952 wanted to see more opportunities made

---

experience in a professional office either before or after qualification' (ibid. paras 83–4; Civil Service Commission, *Home Civil Service Accountants and Senior Accountants*, 1967, pp. 1–2).

[1] *Gardiner Report* (1952) paras 7, 10 and 39; Civil Service Commission, *Home Civil Service Accountants and Senior Accountants* (1967) p. 1. The Gardiner Committee said in 1952 that the class's functions were ill-balanced and lacking in variety, being largely concerned with cost accounting and auditing, and they commented upon the failure to use professional accountants on the negotiating side of contracts work (*Report*, paras 38–9). The most recently available descriptions of the duties of the Professional Accountant Class suggest that, at least as far as the Ministries of Defence and Technology are concerned, this situation has been remedied to some extent. (Civil Service Commission, *Accountants in the Government Service*, 1966, pp. 4–6; Civil Service Commission, *Home Civil Service Accountants and Senior Accountants*, 1967, pp. 4–5.)

[2] *Treasury Factual Memorandum to the Fulton Committee* (1966) para. 80.

[3] Ibid. para. 81. The criterion used for determining Assistant Secretary status was salary and therefore only the seven Director posts in the class definitely qualify although the highest part of the Assistant Director salary scale does exceed the Assistant Secretary salary minimum.

available for professional accountants to transfer across into the Administrative Class.[1]

The Statistician Class

In 1946, a Statistician Class was created parallel to the Administrative Class, and members of the Statistician Class, though recruited separately, were intended to be interchangeable with the Administrative Class, so that the Civil Service Commission had to look for graduates not only with a special knowledge of statistics, but suitable in general for administrative work. In 1966, the Statistician Class numbered 165, with its grades of Assistant Statistician, Statistician and Chief Statistician corresponding to the grades of Assistant Principal, Principal and Assistant Secretary in the Administrative Class: there were also twelve higher posts.[2]

[1] *Gardiner Report* (1952) para. 39.

[2] Civil Service Commission, *Statisticians in the Government Service* (1960) para. 1 and (1965) p. 1: *Treasury Factual Memorandum to the Fulton Committee* (1966) para. 483. The structure of the Statistician Class is given in Appendix IV, Table 6. The Treasury told the Fulton Committee: 'Members of the Statistician Class organise, direct and supervise the statistical work carried out by Government departments and also form the senior staff of the Central Statistical Office, which acts as a central advisory, consultative and co-ordinating office for Government statistical services. There is a close relationship between much of the statistician work and policy matters and members of the Class should generally be sufficiently adaptable to cover both aspects.' (*Treasury Factual Memorandum*, 1966, para. 482.) The Treasury said about the structure of the Statistician Class: 'There are grades in the Class corresponding to each of the grades up to Under Secretary in the Administrative Class. There are also a number of higher posts. The number of posts varies very considerably between departments, some having one or two only. More usually the number will be between six and twelve, and there may also be some specialist Executive staff (usually at C.E.O. or S.E.O. level) who, although having no professional qualifications, are capable of applying some statistical techniques. The division will be headed by a Chief Statistician or a more senior member of the Class according to size. Policy responsibilities above Under-Secretary level do not normally arise in the statistical divisions and the higher posts are to be found only in the Central Statistical Office and the Board of Trade, where the weight of statistical work and the number of staff is much larger than in other departments.' (Ibid. paras 484–6.) In describing recruitment to the Statistician Class, the Treasury said: 'There are annual open and limited competitions for Assistant Statistician

(*footnote 2, page 230, continued*)
posts. For the open competition, candidates must be between 20–27 years of age. They must normally possess, or obtain by the summer in which the competition is held, a University Honours degree in statistics or a first or second class honours degree in which statistics is a principal subject, or a first or second class honours degree together with certain acceptable qualifications in statistics, or a higher degree involving work of at least second class honours degree standard, or a postgraduate University certificate or diploma in statistics, or a Diploma in Technology with first or second class honours in statistics or in mathematics with statistics as a principal subject. Selection is by interview. There is no departmental promotion to the grade of Assistant Statistician, but a limited competition for recruitment to this grade is held annually for candidates from within the Service who are between 24–34 years of age with at least two years' established service before the governing date of the competition. Likely candidates for advancement to Assistant Statistician are given as wide a range of relevant experience as possible. No formal entry qualifications are required but the competition is of a high standard and consists of a written examination in general subjects followed, for those who qualify, by a second written examination in statistical subjects. Those who qualify in both parts of the examination proceed to an interview before a selection board. Candidates who have the academic qualifications required for the open competition may be exempted from the whole of the written examination and others with suitable qualifications in statistics may be exempted from the statistics examination.' (Ibid. paras 486–7.) Open competitions are also held for recruitment to the grade of Statistician. Candidates must be at least twenty-eight years of age, and hold a university degree or a diploma of technology in statistics, or in mathematics or economics or other appropriate main subjects combined with statistics; they are expected to have a wide statistical experience. Normally they should have been awarded first or second class honours in their degree or diploma, or held a higher degree, but if they are not so qualified, they may be considered if their experience of statistical work makes them specially suitable for the Statistician Class. Selection is by interview (ibid. para. 488). There is also annual recruitment to the grade of Cadet Statistician. Candidates must be between twenty and twenty-six years of age, with the same age extensions as for Assistant Statistician, and must possess, or obtain in the summer of the year in which the competition is held, a university degree or a diploma in technology, preferably with first or second class honours (upper second where the second class is divided), in mathematics, economics, or other appropriate subjects. Selection is by interview. Successful candidates are required to undertake a one-year university course leading to a higher degree in statistics or to a post-graduate certificate or diploma in statistics. Cadets who satisfactorily complete the course are promoted to the grade of Assistant Statistician (ibid. para. 489). There are also arrangements to enable officers serving in other classes to acquire the qualifications required for entry to the Statistician Class (ibid. para. 490).

The statistical reports issued by departments range from the full
Census of Population, usually taken every ten years, to regular
weekly, and sometimes even daily, statements. The Annual
Abstract of Statistics, produced by the Central Statistical Office,
contains tables prepared by about fifty departments and official
bodies. Members of the Statistician Class organise, direct and
supervise the statistical work carried out by government departments, and they are directly involved in the formulation of
government policy and advise Ministers and senior officials on
statistical problems of all kinds.[1] Broadly, the work of the Government Statistical Service is to bring statistical techniques to bear
on the analysis of information, the solution of administrative
problems and the estimation of future trends, so that the Government may be provided with statistical and other information
needed for the efficient conduct of its business; and to collect,
analyse and publish information which will be of interest to
businessmen and manufacturers, to research workers and to the
public.[2] Ideally, the government statistician needs not only his
specialised knowledge, but also the ability to understand administrative problems so that he can properly use that knowledge.[3]
Not surprisingly, the Civil Service has found it very difficult
indeed to recruit such people and, from its inception, the
Statistician Class has had a perennial recruitment problem.[4]

The Government Economic Service

The State's commitment, specifically recognised in 1944, to manage
the economy meant that the post-war Civil Service would need

[1] Civil Service Commission, *Statisticians in the Government Service*
(1965) p. 1.   [2] Ibid. pp. 1–2.   [3] Ibid. p. 2.

[4] The various statistics in the *Annual Reports of the Civil Service
Commissioners* for the period since 1945 demonstrate this clearly: for
example, the Commissioners observed in 1965: 'Recruitment to the
Statistician Class continues to reflect the national shortage and the Class
is much under strength' (*99th Report*, p. 5). The Treasury told the
Select Committee on Estimates in 1965 that the continuing failure to
recruit statisticians was 'a major concern' to them on the recruitment
front (*Sixth Report*, 1964–5, *Evidence*, p. 42 and question 210). In 1966,
the Civil Service Commissioners recorded that 'the shortage of statisticians remains acute' (*100th Report*, p. 10).

to have more professional economists in its ranks than previously because, as Sir Robert Hall, then the Government's Economic Adviser, wrote in 1955: 'The special province of the economist is the economic system as a whole, and the relation between the workings of its different parts. This is a difficult subject and requires special study.'[1] Sir Robert Hall's appointment, which he held from 1947 to 1961, when he was succeeded by Professor Alexander Cairncross, was an indication of the increased importance attached to professional economic advice. However, as successive critics pointed out during that period, the actual numbers and gradings of the economists who were recruited into the Service remained modest in comparison with the Administrative Class, who still, outsiders feared, provided the most influential advice that Ministers received on economic matters.[2] One particularly severe critic, Dr Balogh, in his evidence to the Radcliffe Committee on the Working of the Monetary System, called for the reform of the departments dealing with economic policy as an essential condition of all progress, saying: 'Such reform ought to encourage the employment in the formulation of economic policies of men who are aware of elementary economic considerations.' Balogh asserted: 'In present conditions the predominance of the non-professional is likely to destroy the material basis of survival.'[3] This was rather a melodramatic statement, but

[1] Sir Robert Hall, 'The Place of the Economist in Government', *Oxford Economic Papers* (1955) p. 125.

[2] The more important critics who complained about the inferior status of economists in the British central government machine were Robin Marris, 'The Position of Economics and Economists in the Government Machine. A Comparative Critique of the United Kingdom and the Netherlands', in *Economic Journal* (1954) pp. 759–83; I. M. D. Little, 'The Economist in Whitehall', in *Lloyds Bank Review* (1957) pp. 29–40; and P. D. Henderson, 'The Use of Economists in British Administration', in *Oxford Economic Papers* (1961) pp. 5–26. Ely Devons, 'The Role of the Economist in Public Affairs', in *Lloyds Bank Review* (1959) pp. 26–38, in contrast argued that this role ought to be very modest in any case. The role of the Economic Adviser to H.M. Government was described, and an evaluation of Hall and Cairncross was given, by Samuel Brittan, *The Treasury under the Tories 1951–1964* (1964) pp. 66–71.

[3] Committee on the Working of the Monetary System (chairman: Lord Radcliffe) *Principal Memoranda of Evidence*, vol. III, Memorandum submitted by Dr Thomas Balogh, para. 18: the Memoranda were pub-

since the late 1950s, when Balogh wrote, both the Conservative Government, with the National Economic Development Council, and its Labour successor, with the Department of Economic Affairs, have tried to bring more professional economic advice to bear on policy formation.

Several of the new Ministries, established by the Labour Government, elected in 1964, recruited economists, partly by taking over staff from the N.E.D.C., and partly from the universities; the D.E.A. obtained all its economists in this way.[1] Being almost exclusively on short-term contracts, they were not recruited through the Civil Service commission, but joined the D.E.A. 'because they were personally known to members of the department and identified as specialists in their field'.[2] One result of this sudden influx of economists was the decision to establish a Government Economic Service in 1965 and to provide a career structure for economists who subsequently become established. The existing Treasury class of Economic Advisers has been extended to include the economists in other departments. It is intended that the Service should foster the balanced use of economists by different departments, and make possible greater mobility between departments. It is not envisaged that all economists will become established: a provisional figure of one-half had been decided upon.[3] In the Treasury's opinion, the setting

---

lished in 1960 although the committee, of course, reported in 1959. Dr Balogh also made a bitter attack upon the quality of the Administrative Class in his essay, 'The Apothesis of the Dilettante', which was published in Hugh Thomas (ed.) *The Establishment* (1959).

[1] *Sixth Report from the Select Committee on Estimates* (1964–5) *Evidence*, question 711.

[2] Ibid. question 713.

[3] Ibid. question 716. The Treasury told the Fulton Committee that until the creation of the Department of Economic Affairs and the Ministry of Overseas Development, the Treasury itself had employed most of the economists in the Civil Service and they had been organised as a Treasury departmental class. The Treasury said that each of these three departments now employed substantial numbers of economists; and, with economists being employed increasingly in other departments, a general service class of Economists was established in 1965 (*Treasury Factual Memorandum*, 1966, para. 292). The structure of the Government

up of the Government Economic Service will aid recruitment
as well as increasing flexibility in the use of economists.[1]

Economic Service is shown in Appendix IV, Table 7. The Treasury
described it in the following terms to the Fulton Committee: 'The grades
up to and including Senior Economic Adviser correspond with the
Administrative Class grades up to Assistant Secretary. Gradings at the
higher levels are *ad hoc* in many cases, and even in the lower ranges a high
proportion of the staff at present employed are on short-term contracts
within the pay range of their grade. Also, considerable use is made of part-
time staff, particularly at the higher levels.' (Ibid. para. 293.) At the
beginning of 1966 about one-fifth of the Government Economic Service
consisted of permanent staff (ibid. para. 292).

[1] The Treasury told the Fulton Committee: 'Since the Government
Economic Service was set up, the recruitment of established staff has
been at the three levels of Senior Economic Adviser, Economic Adviser,
and Economic Assistant. But a high proportion of the class continue to
serve on a temporary basis, many on contracts for periods varying from
two to five years. This meets the wishes of potential recruits. Appointments on five year contract are made with the sanction of the Civil
Service Commission and in the 1966 competition applicants for posts
at the three levels mentioned will be able to choose between established
appointment or appointment on a five year contract with superannuation
under the Federated Superannuation System for Universities.' (Ibid.
para. 294.) The qualifications required are a first or second class honours
degree (or postgraduate degree) in economics or a closely related subject.
For the two higher grades, candidates must also have had experience in
teaching economics, or in research, or in an economic advisory capacity.
Candidates for Senior Economic Adviser posts must be economists of
standing, with published work to their credit. Senior Economic Advisers
must be over thirty-five; Economic Advisers must be over twenty-eight,
and candidates for Economic Assistant appointments must be between
twenty and thirty (ibid. para. 295). In 1966, recruitment of Cadet
Economists was introduced. Candidates must be between twenty and
twenty-seven years of age and must have, or obtain in 1966, a degree in
economics or in any other subject. Successful candidates will undertake
a one or two-year university course in economics according to their
qualifications. The courses must be approved by the Treasury. The
conditions of service and pay scales are the same as those for Cadet
Statisticians. Cadet Economists who obtain a satisfactory qualification
at the end of their postgraduate course will be promoted to the grade of
Economic Assistant, either in an established capacity or on a five-year
contract according to their own wishes (ibid. para. 296). The Civil
Service Commissioners wrote of 1966: 'Recruitment to posts of Senior
Economic Adviser, Economic Adviser, and Economic Assistant in the
Government Economic Service fell well short of the needs of departments.
Recruitment to a new grade of Cadet Economist began during the year
and made a promising start.' (*100th Report*, p. 10.)

III   THE ROLE OF THE EXPERT IN THE POSITIVE STATE

The Administrative Class's traditional view of the place of the specialist in the Civil Service was well summarised by Sir Francis Floud, then Permanent Secretary to the Ministry of Agriculture, writing in 1923. In his view, the first essential quality of a good administrator was adaptability, and he believed that this quality was 'more likely to be found in men who have had a good general education and have been initiated at an early stage into the daily routine of civil administration than in men who have become specialists in one particular branch of knowledge'. What Floud called 'the ordinary non-technical Civil Servant' soon acquired 'a great capacity for seeing both sides of a question'.[1] On the other hand, adaptability was 'not usually a distinguishing feature of the specialist. He may be described as seeking for absolute truth, whereas the lay Civil Servant looks for something which will work'.[2] It followed that 'the sphere of the specialist should be mainly advisory rather than executive', for Floud felt that, as a general rule: 'The specialist is rightly so enthusiastic about his own particular work that he is in danger of lacking that sense of proportion and that recognition of political, financial, and practical limitations which every administrator must learn to possess.'[3]

Floud's remarks raised several points; a major one being that he did not distinguish enough between the various types of experts. It could hardly be reasonably said that the engineer does not 'look for something which will work'. As a current Permanent Secretary, Sir James Dunnett, has said, the administrator and the engineer need not have much difficulty in working together:

> The engineer is after all a man who throughout his professional training and in his early professional years has been responsible for doing things rather than, though not excluding, advancing the bounds of knowledge. He has been brought up in a strictly practical field and he realises the place and importance of money, and it follows that he should have little difficulty in understanding and accepting the role of the administrator.

---

[1] Floud, op. cit. pp. 124–5.   [2] Ibid. p. 125.   [3] Ibid. p. 126.

Dunnett believed that in dealings between engineers and administrators: 'Neither side should be troubled by any philosophic doubts about the proper role or *raison d'être* of each other.'[1] It was a different matter, however, with scientists who, at least in the creative part of their careers, literally were 'seeking for absolute truth'. Drawing on his experience in the Ministry of Supply, Dunnett said: 'in departments responsible for large scientific programmes there is occasionally a tendency for the scientist to look at the administrator as a necessary appendage, but not as somebody who is going to have or is capable of having any great effect on policy.' He said that the scientist might well feel that 'the mantle of intellectual superiority has passed to him', and Dunnett complained about scientists who regarded administration 'as a trade that anybody with reasonable intelligence can pick up, if not overnight, at least in a short time'.[2]

There was certainly little appreciation of the role of the administrator in the I.P.C.S.'s evidence to the Priestley Commission, for they insisted that the leading specialists had to be

> in direct line of responsibility to the Minister and there should not be any interpolation of another officer purporting to hold responsibility and to give advice when in fact he can become only a transmitter of the advice of others. Transmission of professional advice is full of danger when it is done by a non-professional person. It is also, and this is the primary point, a means of lowering the value and status of the professional person and thereby demeaning the whole profession and structure.[3]

This was similar to the evidence that the I.P.C.S. had put before the Tomlin Commission. But in the intervening period the relative position of the major groups of specialists in the Higher Civil Service had advanced considerably, and their leading posts were usually of Deputy Secretary status or better.

In reply, the Treasury had felt able to argue that the specialist's point of view was given sufficient weight in the formulation of

[1] Sir James Dunnett, 'The Civil Service Administrator and the Expert', in *Public Administration* (1961) pp. 228–9.

[2] Dunnett, op. cit. p. 224.

[3] *Memorandum of Evidence submitted to the Priestley Commission by the Institution of Professional Civil Servants* (1954) para. 87.

policy and in the higher management of departments, and that there was close and continuous contact at all levels between the administrative and specialist staff. They gave the example of the Post Office, where the Engineer-in-Chief was a member of the Post Office Board, and he was closely concerned with 'the settlement of the high policy and management of the department': and so, similarly, was the Chief Regional Engineer at Regional Board level. The Treasury said that in the Ministry of Health the medical staff played a continuous part in the formulation of policy: they were 'in the picture' at all stages. In the then Ministry of Supply also, the senior professional men played a large part in the general administration and frequently initiated policy matters. The heads of the two major professional groups, the Chief Scientist and the Director-General of Ordnance Factories, were members of the Boards which dealt, respectively, with policy on research and development and the organisation and operation of the Royal Ordnance Factories. More general questions of policy were considered at weekly meetings under the chairmanship of the Permanent Secretary, which were attended by Controllers and the Chief Scientist. The top professional men had access to the Minister on matters within their fields of responsibility. The Treasury concluded that as regards access to the Minister and the formulation of policy, senior professional men were in much the same position as members of the Administrative Class of equivalent status.[1] They believed that although there might perhaps havei been grounds twenty years before for a feeling among the specialists that 'their advice is not always sufficiently sought or considered', there seemed little ground for such a feeling today.[2]

Nevertheless, when one looked at the structure of the Higher Civil Service, it was still the case that the Administrative Class dominated its ranks above Under-Secretary level, and that class held the overwhelming majority of posts of Permanent Secretary status. Just as in the days of the Tomlin Commission, the I.P.C.S.

[1] *Priestley Evidence,* appendix 1: Note by the Treasury (no. 6) called 'Access of Professional Staff to Administrative Posts', para. 14.
[2] Ibid. para. 15.

still looked enviously at the administrative hierarchy, claiming careers of similar opportunities for its members, and advocated more frequent transfers across of specialists into the Administrative Class.[1] This latter policy had found favour with the Barlow Committee on Scientific Staff which said in 1943 that although there had been no bar to such transfers, very few had taken place, and they believed that if transfers of this kind were more frequent 'the business of Government might well benefit from the introduction of a different outlook, particularly in departments whose work is concerned with scientific and technical processes'. The Barlow Committee thought that 'more should be done than at present to open this avenue of advancement to scientists who have shown capacity for a wider field of administration'.[2] The Gardiner Committee on the Works Group said in 1951 that it would be an advantage to the departments in which the Group were employed

> if professional officers who have shown a flair for administrative work were transferred to Administrative posts to a greater extent than is at present the case. The evidence which we received shows that in theory at any rate, the claims of professional officers are kept in mind when the vacancies in the Administrative staff occur, but no great enterprise seems to have been displayed in seeking out likely men and the number of transfers which actually takes place strikes us as disappointing. This is particularly so in the case of the Ministry of Works – a department which is primarily engaged on professional work and which employs a large professional staff.[3]

This last criticism drew a reply from the Permanent Secretary to that Ministry, Sir Harold Emmerson, who denied any prejudice against transferring across professionals and gave examples of such transfers. He said: 'In the case of architects and engineers we found no enthusiasm for transfer to Administrative jobs. I think it was partly that the men themselves did not want to lose the

---

[1] This theme runs through the *Memorandum of Evidence submitted to the Priestley Commission by the Institution of Professional Civil Servants* (1954) being discussed at length in paras 90–117 (pp. 18–25).

[2] Barlow Report on Scientific Staff, op. cit. para. 13.

[3] *Report of the Committee on the Organisation, Structure and Remuneration of the Works Group of Professional Civil Servants* (chairman: Sir Thomas Gardiner) 1952, para. 47.

position that they wanted in the profession, and they did not feel
that a period of secondment would stand them in good stead in
spite of assurances given to them.'[1] Emmerson believed that such
transfers had to take place relatively early in a specialist's career,
but he did not consider that the men in the Works Group had
much opportunity to show 'a flair for administrative work' until
they reached a directing job and 'by that time it may be too late'.
With transfers in early career: 'It is very much a case of the man
himself being willing to be transferred and the management being
willing to give him a trial.'[2]

Some of Emmerson's points also made their appearance in the
Treasury's evidence about this question given before the Priestley
Commission. The Treasury gave some statistics which showed that
outside the Post Office, where 'since the 1930s it has been the
policy to make appointments to the Administrative Class from
the professional staff', the number of specialists transferred across
was modest.[3] In commenting on the figures, the Treasury said
that what the administrator really required was 'common sense
working on long experience of actual administration'. Administration was 'not a science which can be studied from textbooks but an
art which has to be learned from experience and its successful
exercise usually calls for long training on the job'. As Floud and
Emmerson had said, the administrator was best caught young,
and the Treasury argued that, generally speaking:

> It is desirable that professional staff who are to be transferred to
> the Administrative Class should be so transferred in their early
> years and usually to the Principal grade. They then have to take
> their chance with other Principals for Assistant Secretary posts
> and similarly for the higher posts. Meanwhile, should they take
> this chance, they are losing touch with the professional side,
> which frequently finds it difficult to take them back on promotion
> should they not make headway on the Administrative side. This
> means that the good professional man (among whom are likely to
> be found the potential Administratives) is often reluctant to

---

[1] *Priestley Evidence*, questions 2899–2900.
[2] Ibid. question 2907.
[3] 'Access of Professional Staff to Administrative Posts', op. cit. paras
4–8.

sacrifice the profession of his choice and his career in that sphere
for the unknown prospects on the uncharted seas of the Administrative side. This means that, not infrequently, the ablest of the
professional men do not desire to transfer.[1]

The Treasury also said that not only did it usually take time 'to
acquire the experience essential to a successful member of the
Administrative Class', but in general 'the longer the time spent on
purely professional work the more difficult is the professional
specialist likely to find it to adapt himself to the rather different
attitude of mind required of the administrator.[2]

Sir Richard Way, Permanent Secretary to the Ministry of
Aviation, told the Select Committee on Estimates in 1965 that
engineers tended to be more interested in administration than
scientists, and he added that he had 'always felt strongly that the
desire of scientists to serve in the Administrative Class has been
greatly exaggerated'.[3] The biennial reviews of Scientific Officers
for transfer to Principal posts which had taken place in the
Ministry of Aviation, and its predecessor, over the previous ten
years, had shown a poor response, and Sir Richard had found no
evidence of a large number of scientists 'raring' to get into the
Administrative Class. Scientists had told him: 'We are perfectly
happy where we are. We should like to go on doing our science.
We see that eventually when we reach higher grades in the
Scientific Class we shall be integrated into the administration of
the department, anyhow.'[4] The Permanent Secretary said that the
abolition of the distinction between administrators and scientists
would deter 'a lot of young men who join us to do a scientific job
of work'. His Principal Establishments Officer added: 'If we were
to make it clear to a young scientist when he joined us that he
might work for two or three years at Farnborough and then be
appointed to the finance branch of the Ministry of Aviation he
would not join us. They want to be scientists.'[5]

[1] Ibid. para. 11.   [2] Ibid. para. 12.
[3] *Sixth Report from the Select Committee on Estimates* (1964–5) *Evidence*,
question 474.
[4] Ibid. question 475.
[5] Ibid. question 472. However, an exercise undertaken in 1964 by the
Civil Service Commissioners 'designed to facilitate the transfer of

To those who shared Sir Henry Tizard's view that, 'Administration is a job for people who have been trained to administrate, but if they have to administrate scientific activities they must have had a broad general scientific education',[1] the state of affairs described by Sir Richard Way was, at first sight, disturbing. Assuming the retention of the existing structure of the Civil Service, and given the normal sources of direct entrants and promotees to the Administrative Class, the only way to approach Tizard's aim was for there to be a generous number of transfers across from the scientific side. What was interesting was that the Ministry of Aviation's experience contrasted with that of private industry, which found that, in general, far from scientists wanting to remain indefinitely within the wholly scientific sphere, the majority wished to broaden their experience and go into general management. Shell had found among their specialist staff that: 'There are relatively few who want promotion within their own rather narrow function.'[2] I.C.I., for whom 'the boundary line between the specialist job and an administrative job is a very thin one', had found that they had no problem in translating specialists into administrators.[3] In commenting on the Ministry of Aviation's views, the I.P.C.S. pointed out that 'the experience of firms like I.C.I. shows that transfers to broaden experience are not unpopular or a disincentive to recruitment'. They said that the

---

members of the Scientific Officer Class into the Administrative Class' was reasonably successful. Thirty-five candidates nominated by departments under the scheme appeared before the Final Selection Board. Fifteen of them were judged likely to make a successful career in the Administrative Class but two candidates subsequently declined transfer. The remainder were posted to other departments for a six-months trial period on administrative work. The Commissioners recorded: 'Of these 11 have already been found suitable for permanent transfer to the Administrative Class as Principals' (*98th Report*, p. 2) and the Treasury later told the Fulton Committee that the competition had realised thirteen successful candidates (*Treasury Factual Memorandum*, 1966, para. 99).

[1] Ronald W. Clark, op. cit. p. 372.

[2] *Sixth Report from the Select Committee on Estimates* (1964–5) *Evidence*, question 605.

[3] *Fifth Report from the Select Committee on Estimates* (1963–4) *Evidence*, questions 908–9.

evidence of the reviews to which the Ministry of Aviation referred was no indication whatever of either the scientist's or the technologist's attitude to administrative work. The reviews were conducted at Principal level, and the successful scientist had to give up his scientific work, not just for a short period, but for the rest of his career. To add to the disincentive of giving up science, which was his basic interest, there was no immediate incentive from a career point of view. The young scientist in the earlier years of his career had prospects which broadly matched those in the early years for the Assistant Principal: the prospects of reaching Principal Scientific Officer were roughly similar to those of the young administrator reaching the Principal grade, and the two grades had the same salary scale. The I.P.C.S. maintained: 'If posts at Assistant Secretary level were offered to scientists later in their careers the story would be very different.' The I.P.C.S. asserted that posts at that level had 'never been on offer to other Classes', and they thought that it was significant that 'the Ministry of Aviation did not mention the number of Scientific Class members (or those from other specialist Classes) appointed to Assistant Secretary or Under-Secretary posts': the I.P.C.S. knew of no such case.[1]

Although more recently they have broadened their interpretation of the term, the Administrative Class have traditionally reserved the description 'administration' for what they see as their special role concerned with the working of the convention of ministerial responsibility.[2] Others prefer the view expressed in the Treasury's evidence to the Priestley Commission that 'many holders of senior professional posts are largely engaged in administration in the sense that they are running their own professional units and discharge managerial functions'.[3] In departments such as the former Ministry of Supply, as Sir James Helmore made clear in 1954, at the highest level, the specialist was performing

[1] *Sixth Report from the Select Committee on Estimates* (1964–5) *Evidence*, appendix 5, para. 34, p. 248.
[2] The definition of the role of the Administrative Class given by Sir Richard Way (*Sixth Report from the Select Committee on Estimates* (1964–5) *Evidence*, question 480) was particularly eloquent.
[3] 'Access of Professional Staff to Administrative Posts', op. cit. para. 3.

substantially an administrative function different in its content from that of the administrator, but of equal significance in determining policy. Both the leading specialists and the leading administrators were contributing 'to the totality of managing the operations of a department'. In framing a policy, Helmore said:

> You can expect the administrator, so to speak, to write the paragraph about the financial and Parliamentary side of this, and the scientist or the engineer, or the soldier or airman in our case to write the paragraph about the engineering application of this, or the users' point of view of it, but those finish, not as separate paragraphs contributed by obviously different authors, but as contributions to a policy.[1]

Speaking in 1965, Sir Richard Way described the Chief Scientist of the then Ministry of Aviation and the two Chief Scientific Officers of Deputy Secretary status below him, including the Director of the Royal Aircraft Establishment at Farnborough, as 'doing enormous administrative jobs'. The Director, however, was 'not an administrator', although Sir Richard maintained that 'at the higher ranks' the distinction between specialists and administrators 'just does not exist'.[2] It could well be asked what useful purpose was therefore served by maintaining a formal distinction.

Indeed, in addition to the improvements in the specialist hierarchies that have been a general feature of the post-war period, and particularly of the years since the Priestley Report of 1955,[3] there have been at least six cases within the last twenty

[1] *Priestley Evidence*, questions 2475, 2478 and 2480.

[2] *Sixth Report from the Select Committee on Estimates* (1964–5) *Evidence*, questions 471–2.

[3] The I.P.C.S. recently wrote: 'Anticipating the development of science and technology, the Priestley Commission saw no objection in principle to an increase in the number of posts in the Scientific Officer and Works Group Classes with the same salaries as Permanent Secretaries. In 1965 the Treasury advised the Institution that the number of posts in those Classes graded at above Under-Secretary level had increased by some 40 per cent over the period since the Priestley Commission, while the total number of Scientific Officers and Works Group Classes had increased by 12 per cent.' (*Evidence presented by the Institution of Professional Civil Servants to the Fulton Committee*, 1967, para. 40.) Nevertheless, thirty-three of the thirty-six posts of Permanent Secretary status are filled by members of the Administrative Class (ibid. para. 27).

years of 'notable departures' from the tradition of 'the separation of professional and non-professional staff into distinct organisational units, and the placing of the primary responsibility for each department's work on the general administrative divisions'.[1] Firstly, as early as 1949, the Ministry of Education established

> an Architects and Building Branch headed jointly by a Chief Architect and an Assistant Secretary. Within the Branch, however, the organisation is fairly conventional; there are no sections which are professional and non-professional combined. Nevertheless, the development work of the Branch (as opposed to the day-to-day administration of school building programmes) is nearly always done by small, mixed professional and administrative teams set up *ad hoc* to deal with a particular project.

Secondly, in 1958, following the report of a committee under General Lord Weeks, the War Office set up a Works Directorate. In accordance with the recommendations of the Weeks Committee, the Works Directorate was headed jointly by the Chief Architect (known as the Director General of Works) and an Under-Secretary. Below them, instead of professional and non-professional staff being grouped, on traditional lines, in separate branches, there was a mixed organisation. Thus, of the six branches, three were headed jointly by professional and non-professional staff and of the nineteen sections seven had a joint professional and non-professional head. This reorganisation marked a substantial departure from tradition; it was notable not only in its own right but because of the influence which it subsequently had on reorganisation in other departments, especially the Ministry of Transport and the Ministry of Public Building and Works. Thirdly, in 1962, the Ministry of Public Building and Works was given

> greatly increased responsibilities, which included the absorption of the War Office Works Directorate. To accommodate these the Ministry underwent, a year later, a major reorganisation; this involved an extensive redeployment of administrative and professional staff. Administrative (and to some extent executive) Civil Servants were linked with equivalent ranking professional

---

[1] D. E. Regan, 'The Expert and the Administrator: Recent Changes at the Ministry of Transport', in *Public Administration* (1966) p. 150.

Civil Servants and given joint responsibility for particular areas of the Ministry's work.[1]

Although it was stressed that they were 'equal partners' and that it was 'essential to the Ministry's success that administrative and professional staff should regard themselves as engaged in a common enterprise',[2] it was fair to observe that the administrators and the professionals had 'carefully assigned separate functions within their joint sphere of responsibility'.[3] Fourthly, in 1963, under the auspices of the Ministry of Housing and Local Government, the Joint Urban Planning Group was created to serve that Ministry, the Ministry of Transport and the Scottish Development Department. The Group had responsibility for

[1] Ibid. p. 151.

[2] When the Ministry of Public Building and Works was reorganised in 1963, the relationship between administrative and professional staff was described in the following terms: 'It is essential to the Ministry's success that administrative and professional staff should regard themselves as engaged in a common enterprise. They are equal partners, and neither can carry out his duties alone. But with the growth of group working a clear definition of basic responsibilities is needed, so that no doubt may develop about where responsibility for a particular duty or decision lies. The administrator will be responsible, if necessary in consultation with the Treasury, for ascertaining and agreeing the requirements of the user departments and for deciding whether they should be met by building or leasing, and when, where and at what cost they should be provided, as well as for any matters of general policy affecting these issues. The professional officer will be responsible for supplying the administrator with estimates of cost, for the placing and execution of the programme authorised by the administrator, for the designs adopted and for ensuring that the requirements are adhered to and the cost not exceeded, as well as for any matters of professional policy affecting the methods of planning and execution. In carrying out these basic responsibilities each will require the close collaboration of the other. For example, the task of clarifying the requirement of the user department will often call for extensive consultation between the administrator and the professional officer before the project as a whole can be passed to the professional staff for execution. The professional officer, on the other hand, will need to refer back to the administrator if the client seeks to make a significant change in his requirement or if there is difficulty about timing or the expected cost exceeds that already authorised.' (*The Reorganisation of the Ministry of Public Building and Works*, Cmnd 2233, 1963, paras 18–20 and appendices B and C.)

[3] D. E. Regan, 'The Expert and the Administrator: Recent Changes at the Ministry of Transport', in *Public Administration* (1966) p. 151.

developing the techniques required for implementing the concepts embodied in the Buchanan Report on 'Traffic in Towns' (which stressed the need to integrate land use and transport planning) and for other aspects of urban planning, particularly town centre redevelopment and the renewal of the older residential areas. The Group included administrative and professional staff from the Ministry of Housing and Local Government, and was under the joint headship of an Assistant Secretary and a Deputy Chief Planner. Although organised on traditional lines with administrative, engineering, planning and architectural 'wings', the work was carried out by mixed teams so that the widest multi-disciplinary approach could be adopted. Since 1965, the Group has been headed jointly by an Under-Secretary and a Deputy Chief Architect/Planner and other organisational changes are being introduced or considered. In particular, it is proposed to merge the Group into an Urban Planning Directorate. This would involve an increase of staff and an extension of the ambit of the work on new and expanded towns and housing research and development. The Directorate would continue to be composed of professional and administrative staff and to include some Ministry of Transport personnel.[1]

Fifthly, according to its first Permanent Secretary, Sir Maurice Dean, from the inception of the Ministry of Technology in 1964 it was

always intended to form a mixed organisation – that is to say, one in which administrators, engineers and scientists were mixed appropriately throughout the organisation. In the early days this was not possible as we had to use our inadequate staff to do a vast majority of jobs. But we managed to form a mixed Computer Division on 1 October 1965, and we are now turning the whole organisation over to the new pattern. We have now about a dozen divisions dealing with our various activities, mostly containing a mixture of scientists, engineers and administrators – reporting to a mixed hierarchy. Everyone seems to like the organisation though I cannot yet say how successful it will prove. If it succeeds, it will be something of an advance in the history of organisation technique.[2]

However, the best informed outside commentator, D. E. Regan, considered the new headquarters organisation of the Ministry of

[1] Ibid. pp. 151–2.
[2] Sir Maurice Dean, 'The Machinery for Economic Planning: IV. The Ministry of Technology', in *Public Administration* (1966) p. 58.

Transport to be 'the most important development of all'. Those parts of the Ministry's duties which were not overwhelmingly specialised or administrative were integrated during reorganisations which took place in early 1964 and in the autumn of 1965. No uniform structure was established because much depended on the nature and volume of work, but the structure that tended to emerge after the second and most important reorganisation was of joint professional and non-professional heads at division and branch level with a single person drawn from either side in charge at group level. Mr Regan said that there had occurred the hoped-for improvement in the morale of the Ministry's engineering staff, partly because of 'the generally greater involvement of the engineers in major decision making'. It was too soon to know if either the recruitment of engineers or the efficiency of the Ministry would be improved by integration.[1] Mr Regan predicted that all departments 'which contain a large body of professional Civil Servants are likely to find it difficult to resist pressure to introduce some form of integrated structure', and he concluded: 'It will be interesting to see what recommendations the Fulton Committee make on this subject.'[2]

It certainly will. No doubt the Fulton Committee will consider the desirability or otherwise of forming an integrated Higher Civil Service. The improvement in the specialist hierarchies in recent years, which have given the leading posts Deputy Secretary and Permanent Secretary status in some cases,[3] has ensured that the

[1] D. E. Regan, 'The Expert and the Administrator: Recent Changes at the Ministry of Transport', in *Public Administration* (1966) pp. 153–63.

[2] Ibid. p. 164.

[3] As will be seen, it is sometimes difficult to be precise because in some Classes 'the top posts are individually graded', but the following general picture emerges when one looks at the statistics for 1 January 1966. The Scientific Officer Class had sixteen permanent and $5\frac{1}{2}$ temporary members who occupied posts above Chief Scientific Officer or Under-Secretary level. The Works Group of Professional Classes seemed to have fewer posts at that sort of level, although twenty-four of its members received salaries ranging from between the Assistant Secretary maximum and the Under-Secretary salary to between the salaries of a Deputy Secretary and a Permanent Secretary, although no member of the Works Group had Permanent Secretary status. Together with seven posts definitely above Under-Secretary level, the Legal Class had fifteen

expert has secured his essential right to be consulted about policies that fall within his specialism. But, apart from the Statistician Class, the specialist hierarchies have remained entirely separate from that of the Administrative Class. Certainly, any reorganisation would have to make available such schemes as that of individual merit promotion in the Scientific Officer Class, whereby the scientist can continue doing the work at which he is a specialist, does not need to assume hierarchical responsibility and yet can gain promotion right up to the rank of Chief Scientific Officer.[1] But the recent changes in the organisation of the Ministries of Transport and of Technology point in the direction of a greater degree of unity being introduced into the Higher Civil Service by the fusion of the various hierarchies with, as at I.C.I., virtually no boundary or 'a permeable membrane' between the administrative and specialist jobs.[2] By a policy of wider interchange the tendency of the specialist to underrate or simply not to understand political pressures may well be modified, as may that of the generalist to mistrust the expert.[3] There would be no need for an

---

posts of Deputy Secretary status and two posts of Permanent Secretary status. The Medical Officer Class had seventeen posts of Under-Secretary status and better. Eight members of the Statistician Class were on a salary scale ranging from Under-Secretary level to Deputy Secretary. The Economist Class had seven permanent and $6\frac{1}{2}$ temporary members earning salaries that in some cases ranged to points between Deputy and Permanent Secretary level. In contrast, the highest post in the Professional Accountant Class had a salary equivalent to the Assistant Secretary maximum. (*Treasury Factual Memorandum to the Fulton Committee*, 1966, paras 81, 291, 350, 376, 467, 483 and 564.)

[1] *Sixth Report from the Select Committee on Estimates* (1964–5) *Evidence*, question 466.

[2] *Fifth Report from the Select Committee on Estimates* (1963–4) *Evidence*, question 908.

[3] There are, of course, specialists who know 'more and more about less and less', but Sir Henry Tizard was justified in complaining about all specialists being so labelled (Clark, op. cit. p. 370). The well-worn pre-war gibe that 'Where there are five economists there will be six opinions and two of them will be Keynes's' (Sir James Grigg, 'The British Civil Service', an essay in Joseph E. McLean (ed.) *The Public Service and University Education*, 1949, p. 156) was to some extent misguided, because the reason why 'Where there are two economists, there will be three opinions' (Devons, op. cit. p. 26) lies in the fact that economics is not yet an exact science. While this means that economists'

Administrative Class specialising in the workings of the doctrine of ministerial responsibility: members of an integrated Higher Civil Service would develop the appropriate skills as a part of their job. Possibly most Permanent Secretaries would still be drawn from the traditional source, but there would be more chance of administrative talent in the specialist ranks being utilised if relations were closer, and of more promotions like that of Sir Gordon Radley, an engineer, to be Director-General of the Post Office.[1] The creation of a unified Higher Civil Service would not merely continue the post-war trend of the improvement in the status of the specialist. It would widen the backgrounds and types of experience of the field from which the leading administrators were drawn: a development very much in accord with the role of the Civil Service in the Positive State.

---

opinions should be treated as such and not as faultless pronouncements – a rule that may well only apply to other specialists' advice when other factors outside their specialism are involved – it does not follow that the decisions on such matters should be left to generalists, often without previous knowledge of the subject matter concerned, but thought, in Sir Francis Floud's phrase, to possess 'a great capacity for seeing both sides of the question'.

[1] *Sixth Report from the Select Committee on Estimates* (1964–5) *Evidence,* question 590.

CHAPTER SIX

Conclusion

I CONSTITUTIONAL MACHINERY AND THE NATIONAL REAPPRAISAL

THE centenary of the Trevelyan–Northcote Report was celebrated during one of our periods of national complacency. In what was a coronation year there was a great deal of talk about a new Elizabethan age in which Britain would recapture the glories she once knew. It would have been more realistic to have thought in terms of a reappraisal of Britain's role in the modern post-war world rather than of past glories. But in more ways than one, the country's attitudes remained rooted in the 1930s when Britain had indisputedly been a great power, and when she had possessed the financial strength to act as the world's banker. Britain was not now equipped for either role, but she still attempted to police a large part of the world and continued to invest abroad in developed countries on a vast scale sums that would have been better used in helping to modernise her own manufacturing and service industries. Moreover, the pound sterling remained one of the world's two major reserve currencies, perennially open to speculation and based on what had become a very shaky economy. Indeed, part of its shakiness followed from the rigidities imposed by maintaining the pound at a fixed exchange rate after the devaluation of 1949. The unwillingness to face up to changes in our external circumstances was accompanied by a marked slowness to appreciate how the nature of our internal affairs had altered. The nationalisation measures, the Beveridge social welfare schemes and the Keynesian economic doctrines had largely been designed with reference to the mass unemployment society of the 1930s. Partly through the very adoption of Keynesian methods of managing the economy, however, full employment was consistently attained in post-war Britain. The overriding economic problem became not mass unemployment, but inflation. This was partly because the Government's commitment to full employment was interpreted in the spirit that every man should have a job irrespective of whether or not he was fully employed doing it. The artificially created shortage of labour, that necessarily accompanied widespread under-employment, led to persistent cost inflation. The failure to pursue a policy of the redeployment of labour made all the harder the country's attempts to keep within reasonable bounds the visible trade gap which had been laid bare by the diminution of our invisible export earnings compared with the pre-war period. Private industry, having sheltered behind protective tariffs since 1932, and having been subjected to unimaginative State planning under the Attlee Government, not surprisingly proved to be an indifferent competitor in world markets. The greatly expanded public sector of industry, working in an atmosphere of full employment and inflation that was the very opposite of the milieu it had originally been devised to operate in, also had a disappointing record. The Labour creators of the nationalised industries had not given them the appropriate economic criteria for such a situation, while the Conservatives took fully ten years to work out more realistic financial aims for those industries. Of course, the whole picture was not bleak: a social revolution of sizeable proportions had taken place based on the wider educational opportunities that had followed the Butler Act of 1944, and the comparative economic prosperity that resulted from full employment once the post-war austerity period had passed. But by the early 1960s it was beginning to be widely felt about our post-war record that although we had done well, we should have done better: our failure to secure entry into the European Economic Community in 1963 opened the flood gates of criticism.

Professor Brian Chapman voiced the views of a school of thought when he contended in 1963 that 'the source of our present ills is institutional, and lies in a mistaken veneration for old ideas, and a refusal to examine them coolly and objectively. We have failed in recent years to achieve a reasonable proportion of right and wise decisions in matters of major policy. Others have done better.'[1]

[1] Brian Chapman, *British Government Observed* (1963) p. 7.

Chapman believed that Britain's decline as a great power 'has probably been accelerated by her failure to provide herself with policy-making institutions adequate for the needs of the complex modern State. In political and administrative reform, as in economic reform, she has missed several opportunities which her European neighbours have grasped.' Chapman heaped much of the blame for our national malaise upon the Administrative Class of the Home Civil Service, whose quality he considered 'does not compare very favourably with its European counterparts'.[1] Certainly the Administrative Class, which has described itself as 'the chief source of advice to Ministers',[2] cannot be absolved from sharing some of the responsibility for the poorer aspects of our recent record. Equally, few observers would now either deny that our institutional framework needs reforming or that the failure to recast it has obviously promoted poor decision making. But, without suggesting that the two can be entirely divorced, our main trouble has surely been over ends rather than means. The 'others' who 'have done better' in the European context that Chapman uses are presumably Germany and France. But their 'economic miracles' could not have taken place had they shouldered burdens on the British scale. Moreover, their 'miracles' may well have owed more to the spur provided by national catastrophes such as Germany's overwhelming defeat in the Second World War, and France's humiliation in Algeria, than to any superiority in institutional arrangements. One economist, perhaps under-rating its achievements in remodelling the structure of the French economy before 1958, has even written of the widely praised French economic planning machinery that while it 'contributed something' to France's much envied recent rate of economic growth, 'readiness to devalue contributed a great deal more'[3]. Whatever the reasons for her neighbours' economic successes, the great task now facing Britain, having successfully avoided national catastrophes comparable with those suffered by France and

[1] Ibid. p. 33.
[2] Civil Service Commission, *Administrative Group of Appointments* (1967) p. 9.
[3] Samuel Brittan, *The Treasury under the Tories 1951–1964* (1964) pp. 338–9.

Germany, and therefore without a similar goad behind her, is to recast her national attitudes so as to achieve her own 'economic miracle.' Perhaps the reform of the Civil Service, which is our main concern here, together with any concomitant reconstruction of our political institutions, are essential pre-conditions for the attainment of this goal, as the Chapman school maintains, but without more realistic national aims with regard to our commitments as a holder of a world reserve currency, as a world banker and as a military power, the beneficial results to be expected from such reforms are bound to be limited.

To take a recent example, the establishment of the Department of Economic Affairs in 1964 can be seen as a potentially valuable institutional reform. It can be argued that there has long been a need for a central department which 'stands for the interest of the economy as a whole', which has 'no major executive functions', which has 'no sectional departmental interest to defend', and which for these reasons is therefore well placed 'to ensure that the overall interests of the long-term development of the economy are allowed full weight in inter-departmental discussions leading to economic policy making'.[1] To those who believe that the City and the Bank of England have too much influence over the Treasury, the transfer of the responsibility for long-term economic policy from the Treasury to the D.E.A., whose contacts are mainly with both sides of industry, is a welcome development. However, given the undertaking by the Government to maintain the fixed exchange rate of sterling, and the pressure on the balance of payments caused by speculation against the pound, the great cost of our overseas defence commitments, and the only recently modified policy of investing widely abroad, not surprisingly short-term considerations – the sphere of the Treasury – have continued to dominate economic policy making during the brief history of the D.E.A. Without a change in the order of priorities pursued by successful Governments, a change which possibly eventually the D.E.A. may succeed in helping to bring about, it

[1] Sir Eric Roll, 'The Machinery for Economic Planning: 1. The Department of Economic Affairs', in *Public Administration* (1966) pp. 5 and 11.

would be unwise to expect too much from either this or other institutional developments.

This is not, of course, to urge the maintenance of the *status quo*, for there is a distinctly Victorian air about far too many of our political institutions. Some form of representative regional government, for example, may well now be more relevant than the present local government system, which was largely devised before the advent of the motor car, the widespread use of which alone has made nonsense of its divisions between counties and county boroughs and urban and rural districts, and which has meant that environmental planning, at the very least, must be treated on a wider scale than is possible under the present arrangements. There is a need to revise parliamentary procedure which still savours of the period when Parliament really did make and unmake Governments, and to equip it for its principal modern role, which is to inform the general public on matters relevant to the electoral decision in the normally lengthy formative period between the official election campaigns. There is no very good reason for leaving the central government machinery as it is. The Labour Government's changes in 1964 were grafted on to the existing structure rather than effecting a rationalisation of it. Indeed, the 1964 changes in the Civil Service also had the appearance of being grafted on to the present structure, despite the importing into the machine of some political appointees. There was no attempt to cut out dead wood at the same time so that the size of the Service, perhaps already excessive in some of the lower grades, has been increased still more. It is still possible to say that 'much of the character of the Civil Service of today derives to no inconsiderable extent from the Trevelyan–Northcote Report',[1] and although Lord Bridges meant that remark as a compliment to the effectiveness of the Report, others may legitimately wonder if it is also a compliment to the Service. As the Civil Service is perennially an Aunt Sally for outside critics, and as Dale observed, 'when things go badly' there occurs 'the minor metamorphosis of Aunt Sally into

[1] Sir Edward (later Lord) Bridges, 'The Reforms of 1854 in Retrospect', an essay in W. A. Robson (ed.) *The Civil Service in Britain and France* (1956) p. 25.

scapegoat',[1] one hesitates before joining the chorus calling for its reform. The real need is for a reconstruction of machinery of Government: to concentrate upon improving the quality of the men who help to work that machinery, like recasting institutions without changing the ends pursued, is only a partial answer. Yet, in this conservative country, the prospect of even partial reform must be welcomed, and the present Prime Minister held out that prospect when on 8 February 1966 he announced the appointment of what he called 'a strong committee' under the chairmanship of the Vice-Chancellor of the University of Sussex, Lord Fulton, to examine 'the structure, recruitment and management, including training, of the Home Civil Service.' These 'very broad terms of reference' do make possible 'a fundamental and wide ranging inquiry' into the Service 'in the tradition of the great inquiries of the past',[2] and in conclusion to this book an examination will be made of the lines along which the reform of the Civil Service might take place, with particular regard to the Administrative Class, and including a discussion of the main relevant written evidence submitted to the Fulton Committee during the first year of its inquiries.[3]

[1] H. E. Dale, *The Personnel and Problems of the Higher Civil Service* (1943) p. 2.

[2] House of Commons, *Official Report* (1965–6), vol. 724, cols 209–10. It is interesting to note that in the ranks of 'the great inquiries of the past', the Prime Minister included 'the Tomlin Commission of 1931'. Despite the wide terms of reference given to the Tomlin Commission of 1929–31, it is difficult to see in what way its report was 'great'. The commission worked during a period of severe economic crisis which handicapped it in making any sensible recommendations about pay and conditions, while it was reviewing a Service structure that had only recently been reconstructed, and the workings of which had been obscured by massive ex-Armed Forces recruitment. Mr Wilson has, however, ensured that the Fulton Committee will not be so dependent on official sources of information as was the Tomlin Commission by guaranteeing that it will be given the staff, statistical help and research assistance that it needs for its formidable task (col. 211).

[3] That is, the written evidence that was submitted to the Fulton Committee in the period between its appointment and 31 March 1967, and which either the individuals or the organisations or the government departments concerned were willing to make available to the author.

II THE ADMINISTRATIVE CLASS, THE HIGHER CIVIL SERVICE AND THE POSITIVE STATE

If the Fulton Committee is to discharge its brief to design a Civil Service 'which will meet the country's needs for many years to come',[1] one of its first tasks should be to examine the present relationship between Ministers and Civil Servants. The special role of the Administrative Class, the governing class of the Civil Service, has been built around the convention of ministerial responsibility, and it seems to this observer that the nature of this convention has been changing over the last fifteen years in a manner which has important implications for the Civil Service. In addition to the questions raised in the evidence submitted to it by the First Division Association about the political anonymity of Civil Servants, and the proposals made to it by the Labour Party, aimed at increasing the extent of political control over the policies pursued by government departments, the Fulton Committee could well examine all the evidence bearing on the question of the Minister–Civil Servant relationship including, for example, such notable cases as the Crichel Down affair, the debate about whether or not to have an Ombudsman, the Ferranti affair, and the activities of the Select Committee on Nationalised Industries.

Three relevant aspects of the working of the doctrine of ministerial responsibility were exhibited by the Crichel Down affair, which was concerned with the actions of the Ministry of Agriculture, and five of its Civil Servants, and one non-Civil Servant who was acting as a Crown Receiver for the Commissioners of Crown Lands, in particular, in disposing of an area of '725 acres of chalk downland' in North Dorset compulsorily purchased in 1937; the affair culminated in the resignation of the Minister, Sir Thomas Dugdale, on 20 July 1954.[2] The first aspect exposed

[1] House of Commons, *Official Report* (1965–6) vol. 724, col. 210.

[2] The Crichel Down debate took place on 20 July 1954 upon the motion 'that this House do now adjourn', and it is recorded in House of Commons, *Official Report* (1953–4) col. 530, cols 1178–1294. In the speeches of Sir David Maxwell Fyfe (particularly cols 1285–7) and Herbert Morrison (notably col. 1274) there were important statements about the application

I

(*footnote 2, page 257, continued*)

of the doctrine of ministerial responsibility. Sir Thomas Dugdale's speech is naturally of interest (cols 1178–94), especially when he chose to reply to accusations that his officials had wilfully misled him: 'Although there were certain inaccuracies and deficiencies in the information given me, when I took my decision, I had the main facts before me, and my advisers were certainly not guilty of wilfully misleading me. I underline the word 'wilfully'. (Cols 1186–7.) Sir Thomas made it clear that he thought that 'it would be deplorable if there were to be any departure from the recognised constitutional position. I, as Minister, must accept full responsibility to Parliament for any mistakes and inefficiency of officials in my department, just as when my officials bring off any successes on my behalf, I take full credit for them.' (Col. 1186.) Sir Thomas ended his speech dramatically: 'Having now had this opportunity of rendering account to Parliament of the actions which I had thought fit to take I have, as the Minister responsible during this period, tendered my resignation to the Prime Minister, who is submitting it to the Queen.' (Col. 1194.) One can observe that the conviction that his ministerial culpability was such as to entail resignation was slow in entering Sir Thomas Dugdale's mind. His first statement on 15 June 1954 (House of Commons, *Official Report*, 1953–4, vol. 528, cols 1745–6) – upon receipt of the *Report of the Public Inquiry ordered by the Minister of Agriculture into the disposal of land at Crichel Down* (Cmd 9176, B.P.P. 1953–4, XI) – far from indicating that he took such a serious view of the position, gave the impression that the public obloquy of the Civil Servants concerned relieved him of obligation. The Public Inquiry was conducted by Sir Andrew Clark, and the factual narrative of his report provides the best available guide to the complexities of the Crichel Down affair. As a result of the report's strictures, a committee was appointed under Sir John Woods 'to consider whether certain Civil Servants should be transferred to other duties', and it reported in July 1954 (Cmd 9220, B.P.P. 1953–4, vol. x). The Civil Servants concerned either were, or had been, transferred to other duties, although the committee chose to record their 'strong impression' that 'some part of the deficiencies disclosed in the handling of this case may have been due as much to the organisational relationship between the headquarters of the Ministry of Agriculture and Fisheries, the Agricultural Land Commission and the Agricultural Land Service as to the faults of individuals' (para. 9). Possibly, but even if one agrees that the Clark Report was generally too lenient towards the politicians and too harsh towards at least one of the Civil Servants, nevertheless, much of the behaviour of those Civil Servants was deplorable, and one doubts if the 'organisational relationship' referred to, although perhaps clumsy, was a major cause of that. One 'organisational relationship' that the Crichel Down case did call into question as to its desirability was the 'system of employing local firms of estate agents and surveyors as Crown Receivers on a part time basis'. Sir Andrew Clark doubted whether this system was satisfactory, feeling that there was 'a lack of adequate control' over their activities (*Clark Report*, Conclusions 16 and 23).

was concerned with Dugdale's actual resignation, which was seen by one observer as meaning that there was a constitutional convention that if Ministers 'fail to take early and effective action to counter potential miscarriages of justice or policy within their departments, they must expect to step down from office'.[1] This view ignored the fact that five weeks earlier in presenting the report of the relevant public enquiry, Dugdale had thought it sufficient to merely acknowledge his personal responsibility for the actions of the Civil Servants concerned:[2] there was no indication that he expected to 'step down from office'. Indeed, his actual resignation came as 'a surprise to the whole House', including 'those members of his own party who had been most

[1] *The Economist*, 24 July 1954, p. 263.

[2] On 15 June 1954, Sir Thomas Dugdale made a statement after questions in response to a question from Mr Robert Crouch (North Dorset): the whole exchange is contained in House of Commons, *Official Report* (1953–4) vol. 528, cols 1745–7. Because Sir Andrew Clark had made it clear in conclusion 25 of his report that 'there was no trace in this case of anything in the nature of bribery, corruption or personal dishonesty', the Minister said: 'The Inquiry has thus achieved my main purpose, which was to deal with any rumours and suggestions of this kind.' He continued: 'The Report contains criticisms of the actions and conduct of the Agricultural Land Commission and of a number of individuals. So far as those criticised are persons – and most of them are – for whose conduct I am answerable as a Minister of the Crown, the responsibility rests with me. That responsibility I wholly accept. I have naturally given to those who are criticised an opportunity of making to me such observations as they wished on those parts of the Report which referred to them. Having considered the observations and explanations I have received, I must in fairness say that I have formed a less unfavourable view of many of the actions taken by those concerned than appears in the Report. Mistakes and errors of judgment were made which those concerned regret as much as I do: and steps are being taken, so far as possible, to see that these do not happen again. In view of the nature of the errors themselves and of the public way in which they have been exposed, I am satisfied that no further action by me in relation to them is necessary.' Sir Thomas Dugdale concluded by thanking Sir Andrew Clark for his report, asserting that the Agricultural Land Commission was 'fulfilling a useful function', announcing that 'the Government have decided to reimburse Commander Marten for reasonable costs incurred in being represented at the Inquiry', and promising to make a statement about 'The general policy relating to the disposal of land purchased compulsorily for public purposes as soon as a debate can be arranged' (cols 1745–6). There was no mention of a ministerial resignation.

critical of the Minister's handling of the Crichel Down affair':
their main object had been to secure sterner disciplinary measures
against the Civil Servants concerned than the Minister seemed
prepared to take, and one observer said that they 'were not happy
when they realised that he had been driven to resignation'.[1]

[1] *The Times*, 21 July 1954, p. 6. In the Crichel Down debate, Mr
Herbert Morrison alleged that Sir Thomas Dugdale's resignation was 'a
victory for the 1922 Committee' which had secured 'the scalp of the
Minister' (House of Commons, *Official Report*, 1953–4, vol. 530, col.
1283). Certainly in the end the Cabinet felt a scapegoat to be necessary
in order to help to appease those Conservative backbenchers who were
outraged by the Ministry of Agriculture's handling of the Crichel Down
case. 'The scalp of the Minister' was not perhaps what those backbenchers
were really after but what they had to be satisfied with. One recalls that the
reaction of Mr Robert Crouch – the Conservative M.P. most intimately
connected with the case on the back benches – to the statement made by
Sir Thomas Dugdale on 15 June 1954, was not to call for the Minister's
resignation but to ask him: 'Do I hear my right hon. Friend aright that no
steps are being taken against those Civil Servants who were so foolish
during the transfer of this land from one department to another? Is he
going to let them hold their appointments – men who wrote letters which
in the Inquiry were proved to be incorrect and untrue?' (House of
Commons, *Official Report*, 1953–4, vol. 528, col. 1746). However, in a half-
hour speech about the Clark Report which he gave to the Conservative
Members' Food and Agriculture Committee on 17 June 1954, Sir
Thomas Dugdale insisted: 'if they wanted a head on a charger, it would
have to be his, for he must carry the responsibility for all that occurred.
That, he explained, was the constitutional practice. He implied that,
within the Ministry, action would be taken against those who had been
criticised, but he made it clear that he did not consider that to be a matter
for the committee.' The debate that followed was 'tense and angry'.
What was the good of an inquiry, asked some, if the Minister was going
to daub whitewash over the facts it had disclosed? An account of the
Food and Agriculture Committee's view was sent to Sir Winston
Churchill, and the Prime Minister decided to appoint the Woods Committee to review the position of the Civil Servants criticised by Sir
Andrew Clark. 'While this investigation went on and before the debate
in the Commons finally took place on July 20, there was time for the 1922
Committee – the powerful committee which embraces every Conservative M.P. who is not a member of the Government – to hold three
meetings. At the first, the feeling against the Civil Servants in the Crichel
Down affair had developed almost to fever pitch. Many desired not only
that these men should be disciplined. Many voiced their suspicions that
this was no isolated case and inveighed against bureaucracy in Government
departments as a whole. A clear statement of Government policy on the
general problem was felt to be desirable and it was resolved to invite two

(footnote 1, page 260, continued)

Ministers to attend a further meeting.' One was Mr R. A. Butler and the other was Sir David Maxwell Fyfe. They faced the committee separately. Mr Butler's meeting seems to have passed off quietly; but that addressed by Sir David on 15 July 1954 was stormy. 'Sir David Maxwell Fyfe gave the meeting a carefully reasoned statement of the constitutional relationship between Civil Servants, Ministers and Parliament. He offered an assurance that a closer check would be kept in future on the departments involved in the Crichel case. But many of his listeners were irritated because he gave no clue to the Government's intentions or future policy. Had he been able to disclose the recommendations of the Prime Minister's Committee on the Civil Servants and the Government's readiness to accept them he might have been able to turn the tide, even then. But that he could not do.' When he sat down, Mr Crouch stood up and led the critics. About a score of other M.P.s supported him, *one* of whom 'snapped out a clear demand that Sir Thomas Dugdale should resign'. Four days after this meeting, Sir Winston Churchill discussed the situation with Dugdale: 'At that meeting the scapegoat was selected.' (R. Douglas Brown, *The Battle of Crichel Down*, 1955, pp. 115–17, and 119–20.) On 20 July 1954 – his 57th birthday – Sir Thomas Dugdale resigned. The reaction to Sir Thomas's resignation among some of the Conservative backbenchers, as shown in the Crichel Down debate, tends to bear out the belief that they had really been hunting for the scalp of the Civil Servants, not that of the Minister. The first speaker, from the Government backbenches, Mr Anthony Hurd, the M.P. for Newbury, said that when Sir Thomas had received the Clark Report he had been 'unwise to allow himself to be persuaded that the Civil Servants implicated deserved no further censure than the Report contained. That worried us a great deal when we heard the statement of the Minister in the House on 15 June. I wonder who persuaded the Minister that discipline should not be exercised on the Civil Servants who had been found at fault? The Minister is a kind-hearted man, but I think this was carrying his Ministerial responsibility too far. I think we should be told whether the Minister was over-persuaded and, if so, on what grounds that pressure was exerted on him. We have heard of the offer of the Minister's resignation this afternoon. If there are to be resignations we want to be quite sure where the cap fits.' Noting Sir Thomas Dugdale's announcement of changes in land transaction procedure, Mr Hurd concluded: 'I am sorry, having reached these decisions in policy – particularly those affecting the administration of his department – that he has felt that he must offer his resignation to the Prime Minister. I am sorry that the Prime Minister has felt bound to submit the resignation to Her Majesty the Queen. I should like to have seen – dearly liked to have seen – my right hon. Friend finish his job at the Ministry of Agriculture. Is it too late for that decision to be reconsidered? I know that my right hon. Friend carries the personal good will of all of us in the House. I believe that the best interests of the country will be served, now that these major decisions of policy have been taken by the Cabinet, if my right hon. Friend remains

Professor S. E. Finer's researches later showed that Dugdale's slowness in offering his resignation was not unconstitutional, for he found that there was no 'rule' which stated that a Minister must 'be punished through loss of office for all the misdeeds and neglects of his Civil Servants which he cannot prove to have been outside all possibility of his cognisance and control'. Finer believed that 'whether a Minister should resign is simply the (necessarily) haphazard consequence of a fortuitous concomitance of personal, party and political temper'. Finer placed Dugdale, along with fifteen other Ministers of the previous hundred years, in the 'plain unlucky' category: 'Not for these sixteen the honourable exchange of offices, or the silent and not dishonourable exit. Their lot is public penance in the white sheet of a resignation speech or letter.' The Professor also concluded that in the sense

---

(*footnote 1, page 260, continued*)

at the Ministry of Agriculture for some time, to complete the task which he started, and which he has carried out so well hitherto.' (House of Commons, *Official Report*, 1953–4, vol. 530, cols 1214 and 1217.) Mr Crouch was still concerned with the problem of the Civil Servants' behaviour in his speech: 'Why should the Civil Service be a class by itself? Why should not Civil Servants be subject to disciplinary measures in the same way as other sections of the community? Members of Her Majesty's Armed Forces are subject to court-martial and, if found guilty, are fired. Members of the legal, medical and other professional bodies are subject to disciplinary measures and in the case of misconduct are dealt with in the proper way. Why should not the Civil Service form a disciplinary body to deal with the type of person who has been mentioned in this report?' (Ibid. cols 1234–5.) It is also interesting to note that the Conservative M.P. for Berwick upon Tweed, Viscount Lambton, although concluding that 'taking all in all' Dugdale's resignation was 'the best course he could take', deplored the fact that the Civil Servants concerned were 'to remain in the Civil Service although they deliberately deceived the Minister' (cols 1272–3). Viscount Lambton pointed to the large size of the Civil Service, that it was 'scattered throughout the whole length and breadth of the Country', and he talked of 'the extraordinary difficulty of the Minister, particularly when he is held to be responsible for the action of any Civil Servant' (cols 1271–2). Viscount Lambton's conclusion was: 'Now that the Minister has resigned, we must review the whole scheme of Ministerial responsibility, and consider whether or not it is possible for a Minister to be fully responsible for all the people under him. Above all, we must see that the Civil Service does not in any way believe that it can make mistakes like this, and, as it were, get away with it.' (Col. 1273.)

that 'the Minister alone speaks for his Civil Servants to the House and to his Civil Servants for the House, the convention of Ministerial responsibility has both the proleptic and compulsive features of a "rule" '.[1] That observation is of particular interest when one considers the second aspect of the working of the doctrine of ministerial responsibility revealed by the Crichel Down affair, for the manner in which the disposal of land was handled in the Ministry showed the extent to which the Ministers concerned relied on the advice of the officials who were dealing with the case. As D. N. Chester wrote: 'for sixteen or so months this particular case was under the nose of the Minister or his Parliamentary Secretaries and senior officials'.[2] At some stage of the case, both the Minister and Mr Nugent, one of his Parliamentary Secretaries, corresponded with and personally interviewed Lieutenant-Commander Marten, whose determined efforts eventually led to the public inquiry. The other Parliamentary Secretary, Lord Carrington, even visited Crichel Down and produced a report for the Minister. Yet, neither Dugdale, Nugent, nor Carrington, despite certain obvious financial disadvantages in the scheme, seriously questioned the idea of establishing 'a new model farm' with which certain of their official advisers were undoubtedly 'infatuated'.[3] A large part of the blame for the deliberate failure to implement a promise about placing the tenancy of the land open to public tender, the gist of Marten's grievances, must be assigned to the Commissioners of Crown Lands of whom the Minister was the

[1] Samuel E. Finer, 'The Individual Responsibility of Ministers', in *Public Administration* (1956) pp. 393–4.

[2] D. N. Chester, 'The Crichel Down Case', in *Public Administration* (1954) p. 394.

[3] The factual narrative of the *Report of the Public Inquiry ordered by The Minister of Agriculture into the disposal of land at Crichel Down* (1954) gives full details about the manner in which the case was handled: paras 22–3, 40–2, 70–1, 90 and 97–9 deal with ministerial actions, the direct quotes in the text are taken from Sir Andrew Clark's conclusions, in this instance no. 2 (p. 27). While Sir Thomas Dugdale can be considered to be 'plain unlucky' at having to be forced to resign, one should not perhaps feel too sorry for him. He did fail to think out what the Conservative government's policy was to be in respect to state agricultural holdings, and this was one of his major responsibilities: see Peter Self and Herbert Storing, *The State and the Farmer* (1962) pp. 118–19.

one with responsibility for 'matters of major policy': the policy
pursued, however, of granting the tenancy to a particular favoured
farmer, was that preferred by the Permanent Commissioner, a
Civil Servant. Traditionalists can, of course, argue that the
Minister was still 'responsible' in some way for the Permanent
Commissioner's actions; but it is at least interesting to reflect as
to who was supposed to be responsible for the Crown Receiver, a
non-Civil Servant, who initiated and rigidly adhered to the policy
of granting the tenancy to one particular farmer, whom in fact he
selected.[1] The third aspect exposed was that, far from showing the
effectiveness of the traditional means of remedying maladministration, the Crichel Down affair revealed their limitations. As
Professor Birch commented: 'The mismanagement in this affair
was not exposed as a result of questions put by the landowner's
M.P. to the Minister, which is the traditional method of approach.
This method was tried, but it met with no success.'[2] As Professor
Hamson argued: 'It required the initiative and energy, and the
wealth and position, of Commander Marten so as to insist with the
Minister – so to badger the Minister, if you will – that the Minister
should even consider the possibility of holding an inquiry. An
inquiry of the Crichel Down kind is not held except by the especial
grace and favour of the Minister.' Moreover, when an inquiry is
held 'the report is simply a private and confidential report to the
Minister. It is a matter to be decided by him in consultation no
doubt with his advisers, what, if anything, is to be done with the
report when he has received it.' Sir Thomas Dugdale decided to
publish the report of the Crichel Down Inquiry, although there
was no legal obligation upon him to do so.[3] When one recalls also
that Marten secured the backing of the National Farmers' Union,

[1] The role of the Commissioners for Crown Lands was described in the
factual narrative of the *Report of the Public Inquiry ordered by the Minister
of Agriculture into the disposal of land at Crichel Down* (1954) para. 45;
the part played in the Crichel Down affair by the Crown Receiver is
inextricably interwoven with the remainder of the story as unfolded in
the factual narrative, paras 45–102 and conclusions 12–13, 15–16 and
23–4 of the Clark Report.

[2] A. H. Birch, *Representative and Responsible Government* (1964) p. 146.

[3] C. J. Hamson, 'The Real Lesson of Crichel Down', in *Public Administration* (1954) pp. 385–6.

probably the pressure group with most influence in Whitehall, there is a great deal to be said for Professor Birch's view: 'The fact that the redress of an undoubted grievance required such a combination of factors should properly be disturbing rather than reassuring to those who believe that the British system offers an adequate protection to citizens against the misuse of governmental power'.[1]

The disquiet aroused by the Crichel Down affair about the traditional means of exposing 'bias, neglect, inattention, delay, incompetence, ineptitude, perversity, turpitude and arbitrariness'[2] in the actions of Civil Servants has never really died down since. For some years it found expression in the campaign for a British 'Ombudsman' or Parliamentary Commissioner, and it is interesting to note that in the debate about the Bill to establish that office, which took place in the autumn of 1966, the government spokesmen were very eager to cast doubt upon 'the efficacy of our present methods of dealing with complaints about maladministration'.[3] Introducing the Bill, Mr Richard Crossman said:

> when it comes to investigating maladministration, our Parliamentary system of Questions, followed by letters where the answer is unsatisfactory, an Adjournment Debate and, very occasionally, in the last resort, a departmental inquiry or tribunal, is often deficient in one particular, and in this respect makes things far too easy for the Executive. What it lacks is the cutting edge of a really impartial and really searching investigation into the workings of Whitehall.[4]

Mr Crossman described the Parliamentary Question and Members' correspondence with departments as only being able to elicit from the Minister 'an investigation which is usually far from complete'. He asserted that the investigations of the Parliamentary Commissioner 'will provide the back bench Member, once he knows it aright, with a new and powerful weapon which, up to now, neither he individually nor we collectively as a House has

---

[1] A. H. Birch, op. cit. p. 146.

[2] This was Mr Richard Crossman's tentative definition of 'all of the qualities which make up maladministration', which he advanced in introducing the second reading of the Bill to create the office of Parliamentary Commissioner (House of Commons, *Official Report* (1965–6), vol. 734, col. 51).

[3] Ibid. col. 43.   [4] Ibid. col. 44.

ever possessed – the possibility of impartial investigation into alleged maladministration'.[1] Mr Niall MacDermot, in replying to the debate, was even franker than the Leader of the House about the failings of the existing redress of grievance machinery. He recalled a recent case, brought to his attention by a Member, which was concerned with allegations that a Civil Servant had shown personal bias in conducting certain affairs:

> I could not investigate it personally. All I could do was to call upon a senior official of the department to investigate and prepare a report which I read very carefully with the evidence. I was satisfied by the report. I had not had the advantage of seeing any of the witnesses or persons, and all I could do was to assure the hon. Member that I was satisfied, and he had to take that assurance. That is the kind of case where I would have felt happier – as probably would the hon. Gentleman and his constituent – to have had an officer such as the Parliamentary Commissioner to whom that complaint could have been referred.[2]

The subsequent appointment of a Parliamentary Commissioner, who, in dealing with the cases assigned to him, will be able 'to go wider and further than anyone except the Comptroller and Auditor General',[3] seems bound to have implications for the working of the doctrine of ministerial responsibility. The doctrine will no longer be a screen behind which acts of maladministration will be hidden. When the Parliamentary Commissioner, having conducted 'a really searching and really impartial investigation' into a case, presents his report, the Minister 'responsible' will surely be placed in much the same position as he is when he receives a report from the Public Accounts Committee. He will have to accept it and, should it be critical, take the appropriate remedial action. Therefore, not only will a department's financial accounts

[1] Ibid. col. 43. Mr Crossman added: 'The knowledge that the Parliamentary Commissioner is there, eager to get to work; the knowledge that he can act only in response to complaints from Members and is, therefore, in the strictest sense a servant of the House; the knowledge that when he acts he will be able to go wider and further than anyone except the Comptroller and Auditor General – this knowledge would surely put heart into those backbenchers who feel they count for much more than Lobby fodder.'

[2] Ibid. cols 168–9. Mr MacDermot was Financial Secretary to the Treasury.   [3] Ibid. col. 43.

be liable to thorough extraneous review, so will almost all its area
of administration.[1]

[1] Under the Parliamentary Commissioner Act, 1967 – as is made clear in
schedule 3 to that act – the following matters are not subject to investigation. Firstly: 'Action taken in matters certified by a Secretary of State
or other Minister of the Crown to affect relations or dealings between the
Government of the United Kingdom and any other Government or any
international organisation of States or Governments.' Secondly: 'Actions
taken, in any country or territory outside the United Kingdom, by or on
behalf of any officer representing or acting under the authority of Her
Majesty in respect of the United Kingdom, or any other officer of the
Government of the United Kingdom.' Thirdly: 'Action taken in connection with the administration of the government of any country or
territory outside the United Kingdom which forms part of Her Majesty's
dominions or in which Her Majesty has jurisdiction.' Fourthly: 'Action
taken by the Secretary of State under the Extradition Act 1870 or the
Fugitive Offenders Act 1881.' Fifthly: 'Action taken by or with the
authority of the Secretary of State for the purposes of investigating
crime or of protecting the security of the State, including action so taken
with respect to passports.' Sixthly: 'The commencement or conduct of
civil or criminal proceedings before any court of law in the United
Kingdom, of proceedings at any place under the Naval Discipline Act
1957, the Army Act 1955 or the Air Force Act 1955 or of proceedings
before any international court or tribunal.' Seventhly: 'Any exercise of
the prerogative of mercy or of the power of a Secretary of State to make a
reference in respect of any person to the Court of Appeal, the High Court
of Judiciary or the Courts-Martial Appeal Court.' Eighthly: 'Action taken
on behalf of the Minister of Health or the Secretary of State by a Regional
Hospital Board, Board of Governors of a Teaching Hospital, Hospital
Management Committee or Board of Management, or by the Public
Health Laboratory Service Board.' Ninthly, action taken in matters
relating to contractual or other commercial transactions, whether within
the United Kingdom or elsewhere, being transactions of a government
department or authority to which this act applies – that is all the major
government departments – and not being transactions for or relating to
the acquisition of land compulsorily or in circumstances in which it
could be acquired compulsorily or the disposal as surplus of land acquired
compulsorily or in such circumstances as aforesaid. Tenthly, action taken
in respect of appointments or removals, pay, discipline, superannuation
or other personnel matters, in relation to service in any of the Armed
Forces of the Crown or in government departments or indeed 'service
in any office or employment, or under any contract for services, in respect
of which power to take action, or to determine or approve the action to
be taken, in such matters is vested in Her Majesty, any Minister of the
Crown or any such authority as aforesaid'. Eleventh: 'The grant of
honours, awards or privileges within the gift of the Crown, including the
grant of Royal Charters.'

In the 1964 House of Commons debate about the high level of profit secured by Ferrantis in fulfilling a guided weapons contract for the then Ministry of Aviation, M.P.s on both sides of the House expressed considerable misgivings about the nature of ministerial responsibility. A Labour Member, Mr George Wigg, envious of the powers accorded to American Congressional Committees, believed that the Ferranti case showed that the House of Commons 'ought to have a Defence Committee with more powers than the Estimates Committee has, perhaps something |akin to the Public Accounts Committee, to look at the Estimates as a whole, with the power to take evidence on oath and to send for papers and persons and to ascertain the facts'.[1] This proposal attracted the support of a Conservative Member, Sir Arthur Vere Harvey, who asserted rightly that M.P.s are 'frequently inhibited in defence debates'.[2] A Liberal Member, Mr Eric Lubbock, spoke of 'the incompetence of the technical cost officers' in the department concerned, which had led to the over-generous terms of the Ferranti contract.[3] Sir Arthur Vere Harvey suggested that the quality of these officers compared unfavourably with their counterparts in industry as did the width of their experience. He considered that the Minister 'should have got some outside help', and employed 'hired teams of highly skilled cost accountants with great experience in this type of work'.[4] Another Conservative, Sir William Robson Brown, deplored the small proportion of leading Civil Servants in the technological departments with the appropriate specialist training.[5] Sir William went on to suggest that 'every spending department should have a Minister of State responsible solely and entirely for the placing of contracts and the accountancy that goes with it. That man should be appointed for his experience in the field and should have behind him a complete and well-equipped branch to deal with these matters.' Sir William believed that such arrangements, by which a Minister of State would 'stand at the Dispatch Box and answer questions and explain the way in which the matters are controlled', would lead

---

[1] House of Commons, *Official Report* (1963–4) vol. 694, col. 493.
[2] Ibid. col. 504.   [3] Ibid. col. 523.
[4] Ibid. cols 509–10.   [5] Ibid. col. 521.

to a state of affairs in which 'I do not think that we would ever again have a debate of this kind'.[1] Others were less sanguine. A fellow Conservative, Mr Costain, while recognising that 'it is the tradition of this House, and it may have to remain so, that ultimately a Minister is responsible for everything that goes on in his department', expressed his dissatisfaction with the present working of the constitutional convention of ministerial responsibility when he compared the position of a Minister with that of the owner of a large motor car: 'The Minister sits in the back of the car and the accounting officer is his chauffeur. That gives a simple idea of how the policy and administration of a Ministry works. The Minister tells the chauffeur where to go and if the chauffeur has an accident, regardless of the circumstances, it is the fault of the Minister.' In view of 'the growth in the size of the projects which Ministers now have to deal with', Mr Costain proposed that 'perhaps, in the future, we shall have two Ministers, a political Minister and a commercial Minister':[2] it was not clear from his speech whether or not the latter Minister would be directly responsible to the House or not. Another Conservative Member, Sir John Barlow, was even able to point out about ministerial responsibility for the Ferranti contract: 'The present Minister was not in the department at the time that this went through.'[3] Thus, in a debate on what was clearly a fault in a government department, a number of M.P.s on both sides of the House implied that they found the doctrine of ministerial responsibility unworkable and unreasonable.

Some idea of how the type of specialised investigatory committee that Mr George Wigg had said in the Ferranti debate was needed in the defence sphere might work can be secured from the record of the Select Committee on Nationalised Industries which, since 1956, has made 'a vital contribution to the public accountability of the nationalised industries.'[4] As David Coombes has written:

Perhaps the most notable features of the Select Committee on Nationalised Industries have been its preparedness to deal with

---

[1] Ibid. cols 520 and 522.   [2] Ibid. cols 488–9.   [3] Ibid. col. 473.
[4] David Coombes, *The Member of Parliament and the Administration* (1966) p. 204.

questions of policy, for which some Minister was responsible, its habit of criticising Ministerial action, and its readiness to recommend changes in Government policy toward the nationalised industries. Although the Committee has been exhibiting these features for the past eight years the British Constitution is still (supposedly) intact, at least, no one has complained that those Ministers who are concerned with nationalised industries are less responsible or less answerable as a result of the Committee's work. Indeed, the Ministers concerned have been far more answerable than they might have been otherwise – for essential information, which was inaccessible by Parliamentary Question, has been unearthed by the Committee. The general lesson to be learned from the Committee's experience is that Select Committees of the House of Commons can and do deal with Government departments on questions of policy. The Select Committee on Nationalised Industries has become an integral part of the life of the Ministry of Power, the Ministry of Transport, the Ministry of Aviation, and certain divisions of the Treasury.[1]

Such a close relationship has inevitably led to intimate working contacts with leading Civil Servants and in presenting their evidence to the Select Committee, they have not behaved in the classical manner described by H. E. Dale. He had seen the Civil Servant placed in that position as being 'a mouthpiece of his Minister' who could answer questions about 'facts and figures,' give the reasons why 'such and such things were done or not done' and who could 'explain the grounds of the Minister's policy'. But if he was asked, directly or by implication: ' "What do you think yourself of the policy?", and the question is not disallowed by the Chairman, he must either decline to answer, or say he has no opinion other than his Minister's'.[2] Coombes successfully showed that this description was misleading, and observed: 'Civil Servants, at least in the Ministries mentioned above, do far more than this, and have had their own expressions of opinion published in the Select Committee's minutes of evidence.'[3]

That Civil Servants are already to a limited extent identified publicly with their responsibilities has also been made clear by

[1] Coombes, op. cit. pp. 210–11.
[2] H. E. Dale, 'Parliament in relation to the Civil Service', an article in Sir Gilbert Campion (ed.) *Parliament. A Survey* (1952) p. 123.
[3] Coombes, op. cit. p. 211.

the representatives of the Administrative Class, the First Division Association, in their evidence to the Fulton Committee about the political anonymity of Civil Servants.[1] The F.D.A. said: 'senior Civil Servants give oral evidence to the Public Accounts Committee, the Estimates Committee and the Select Committee on Nationalised Industries; they are excused from answering questions on matters of policy, but this does not, in practice, exclude very much'. The Association pointed out:

> some Civil Servants – and especially members of the professional grades – read papers, make speeches, or otherwise take part in public discussion, on such occasions as formal inquiries, Local Government committee meetings, or professional gatherings; their views appear in professional publications, and (in a limited way because the issues are seldom of sufficiently general interest) in the national press, on the radio or even on television.

The F.D.A. added:

> as a matter of everyday routine, Civil Servants consult particular sections of outside opinion about the evolution and application of policy. For this purpose a number of departments have consultative committees on particular subjects. These consultations are usually confidential. Informal contacts with interested individuals (including academics) are quite common. The machinery of the Economic Development Committees and the Regional Development Committees was set up to provide opportunities for exchanges of this kind.

In the Association's view

> these contacts are insufficient and can give an impression outside the Service that Civil Servants are not fully in touch with public opinion. But in practice the 'public' is different for each subject and for most matters it does not mean the electorate as a whole but quite a small section of it. The people to whom the Civil Servant may profitably address himself are those who want to know more about the subject in general or want to know in some detail how particular aspects of a policy affect them. They may also want the opportunity to feed back to the Government machine some of the

---

[1] *Evidence presented by the Association of First Division Civil Servants to the Fulton Committee on the Civil Service* (1967) part II, paras 1–9. It is interesting to note that the Fulton Committee specifically asked the F.D.A. for 'its views on the problems thrown up by the imposition of anonymity on Civil Servants' (ibid. para. 2).

problems that policies raise for them. It is entirely right that there should be greater communication of this sort. We think that public policy would be better conceived and better understood if Civil Servants were prepared and encouraged to participate in discussions of this kind.

The F.D.A. recognised that a policy of greater openness had its risks. Firstly, there was 'the risk of starting rumour; if Civil Servants take part in discussions on a particular proposal then it may be taken to indicate future Government intentions'. Secondly, there was 'the risk that individual Civil Servants will be regarded as supporting or opposing particular policies, or measures, and their views may be thought to be at variance with those of their Minister (or a successor Minister)'. Thirdly, the Civil Servant 'may imply that he dissents from settled policy, whereas in no public exchange would it be permissible for this to happen'. The F.D.A. conceded that all these situations 'could be embarassing to Ministers as well as to officials', but they thought that these risks were acceptable. They did not envisage their members

> participating in the more artificial confrontations of television journalism, or in any exchange where objectivity is at a discount. Moreover, a Civil Servant who participates in open exchanges would be foolish to commit himself to outright support of a proposed policy and the rejection of all its alternatives; it is usually possible to discuss policies and their implications intelligently and informedly without plumping for one course to the exclusion of all others. We think that, for the rest, the more generally that open participation in these exchanges is accepted and practised, then the less significance will be read into this participation in itself and the less importance will be attached to the occasional embarrassment. In some areas of policy there may even now be little room for development in these directions, and in a few there are special problems of security. But in most areas we think the emphasis should be on taking and creating opportunities for informed discussion, rather than on avoiding it, and that this change of attitude would make a valuable and substantial difference to the quality of the work of the Service.

The Association concluded by saying:

> We see open exchanges as being particularly valuable in the exploration of long term policy options, in the explanation of

settled policy, and in discussion of its application. The risks of embarrassment are greatest when policy is in the later stages of formation at or near Ministerial level. At this stage it would rarely be opportune for officials to take part in the more open type of discussion. But the more professional or academic the forum in which the discussion is held, the smaller the risk of subsequent embarrassment, and, in general, the greater the value of the discussion to all participants. As a rather obvious working rule it could be said that the less appropriate the occasion is for officials to speak then the more appropriate it may be for Ministers to do so.[1]

The most interesting part of the evidence submitted to the Fulton Committee by the Labour Party was their examination of the problem of maintaining political control over departments that have become larger and have acquired more complex duties as a result of the expansion in the business of government. The Labour Party still considered that, once he had established himself, a strong Minister who had 'a clear idea of what he wants done', and who could 'convince his Civil Servants that it is both possible and desirable', could rely on the loyal support of those Civil Servants.[2] More generally, however, the Labour Party believed that the authority of Ministers had been undermined by such developments as inter-departmental committees of officials: 'The Minister may not be consulted until the officials have arrived at an agreed compromise; and if he then wants to disagree, he can only do so at the cost of telling the officials to go back and put forward a different view from the one they have been arguing for against the other departments.'[3] Without either making clear that they understood the practical necessity in modern conditions of

[1] Ibid. paras 4–5 and 7–9. The F.D.A. also argued: 'There are two other advantages that would stem from Civil Servants participating more openly in discussions on questions of policy. The first is the effect on recruitment: there is some evidence that the anonymity of the Civil Service is a deterrent to some recruits. The second advantage comes from the fact that Civil Servants constitute a significantly large section of informed opinion in this country; they have a useful contribution to make to informed debate.' (Para. 6.)

[2] *Evidence presented by the Labour Party to the Fulton Committee on the Civil Service* (1967) para. 21.

[3] Ibid. para. 20.

some decision by leading Civil Servants about what material
should or should not be submitted to Ministers,[1] or substantiating
what were, understandably, interpreted by the First Division
Association as being grave accusations about the professional
integrity of certain of those Civil Servants – accusations from
which the Prime Minister firmly disassociated himself[2] – the

[1] Sir Charles Cunningham has written that a government department
'should have an understanding of the Minister's general attitude and
habit of mind'. He said that it was 'up to the department to present to its
Minister its assessment of the factors he must take into account in a
way which ensures that they are fully understood. So it must form a
judgment of his background of knowledge of a matter submitted for his
decision as well as of his general approach to policy-making. Some
Ministers are not content unless a case presented to them sets out not
only the facts which have to be taken into account but every step in
the argument leading to the conclusion reached. Others prefer a concise
and cogent statement of the grounds which lead the department to make a
particular recommendation. With the press of business which a Minister
has to deal with in these days of intense Government activity, the latter
course is usually preferred; and the Civil Servant who fears that by
adopting it some relevant consideration may be overlooked can comfortably salve his conscience by putting the detail into an appendix.' ('Policy
and Practice', in *Public Administration*, 1963, pp. 231–2.)

[2] In a television interview shown on 20 January 1967, the Prime
Minister, Mr Harold Wilson, firmly repudiated the Labour Party's
allegation when he said: 'This idea that Ministers don't know what
is going on, and that Civil Servants keep facts away from them – if I
could be told the name of any Minister who is subject to that situation,
I don't think he would be a Minister for very long. It rests with the
Minister to control his department. I find the Civil Servants do what is
required once they get a clear lead. I think you could get that situation
if a Minister failed to give a clear lead, but then he shouldn't be a
Minister.' The Prime Minister was then asked to confirm that he did not
subscribe to the view expressed in the Labour Party evidence to the
Fulton Committee that some Ministers become tools of their leading
officials because they do not get information. Mr Wilson's reply was: 'As
I say, name one and I'll know what to do with him.' ('Where Power
Lies. The Prime Minister interviewed by Ian Trethowan', in *The
Listener*, 9 Feb 1967, p. 184.) Correspondence released on 20 January
showed that on 12 January Mr W. A. Wood, Chairman of the First
Division Association, wrote to Mr Wilson on behalf of the Administrative,
Statistician and Economist Classes of the Civil Service 'who carry the
main responsibility for advising Ministers on policy'. Mr Wood wrote
that one passage in the Labour Party's evidence to the Fulton Committee
which had received wide publicity had roused deep resentment among the
association's members as it amounted to an attack on the integrity of the

Labour Party went on to talk about 'the amount of information which in some departments at least, is kept from the Minister', and observed:

> Of course, it is possible for the Minister to find out what is going on in his department if he asks the right questions and asks to see the right files. But an enormous amount of work goes on in a department which the Minister knows nothing of; some of it research work which produces important results which are never shown to the Minister (with the result that he may in good faith reply to a Parliamentary Question that the information is not available when in fact it is available but not to him); some of it planning work which may be deliberately concealed from him, either because it might lead him to support policies which the department does not (or does not yet) approve of, or even because it is being done in preparation for a future Government of a different political colour. It is this secrecy that makes some Ministers tools of their departments a good deal of the time. It is impossible for a Minister to have an adequate grasp of an issue if he plays no part in the long process of discussion which precedes the formation of policy but merely gets a bowdlerised version of it from his Permanent Secretary when the final choice has to be made between the policies which the department finds acceptable.[1]

The Labour Party, therefore, believed that there was 'a need to strengthen the Minister; the "temporary politician" in his department in relation to the "permanent politicians", his Civil

---

Service: 'This is the allegation that information is deliberately withheld from Ministers and that replies are consequently given in Parliament which wrongly deny the availability of information. As a portrayal of the general approach of the service to Ministers and to Ministers' relations with Parliament, this is a travesty of the true situation. Newspaper reports have associated the names of particular Ministers, including your own, with the Labour Party's evidence. We think our members are entitled to an assurance from you that Ministers do not in fact hold the opinions attributed to them or, if no such assurance can be given, to be furnished with the evidence on which the assertions are based.' The reply that Mr Wood received indicated that the Prime Minister's views would be made clear in his television interview on 20 January in which, as we have seen, he specifically rejected the Labour Party's allegation (*The Times*, 21 Jan 1967, p. 8).

[1] *Evidence presented by the Labour Party to the Fulton Committee on the Civil Service* (1967) para. 19.

Servants',[1] and, as a means of achieving such strengthening, they urged the Fulton Committee to give explicit recognition to the right of Ministers to make two kinds of temporary appointment to the Service.

First of all, the Labour Party envisaged 'the recognition of a limited number of "posts of confidence" ' to which 'experts who are called in to help to implement the particular policies of the Government of the day' would be appointed. These appointments would be 'at a fairly high level or special provision must be made for access to the Minister', because 'it would be quite pointless to bring an expert into the Service to do a specific job and then allow him to get lost in the internal machinery of the Ministry, denied access to the Minister and without the means of making good use of the committee structure'. The Labour Party did not expect that there would be very many of these appointments:

> But a new Government coming into office often has a number of policy proposals that are particularly controversial or mark a very radical change from what has gone before. A considerable amount of work may have been done while in Opposition. It seems entirely sensible that someone who has done that essential work and is completely committed to the policy should have a hand in seeing it implemented. It is not that permanent officials are likely to obstruct it, nor would we want to prevent them from giving it a rigorous critical examination and pointing out to the Minister the difficulties in the way of the course of action proposed. Equally their help would be needed to draft legislation and to guide it through Parliament. But in present circumstances the official is not an expert and if he is not fully convinced by a particular policy the temptation will always be there to try to achieve the general aims of the policy within the existing framework with which he is familiar. Alternatively, if the policy cannot be recast in this way his whole training and normal method of working will not fit him for the job of driving it through the various departmental and inter-departmental committees. His urge must always be to conciliate and to compromise.

The Labour Party conceded that 'the relationship between the "temporary expert" and the permanent Civil Servant might prove a difficult one', but they thought that 'with good will on both sides,

[1] Ibid. para. 22.

the resulting "creative tension" could make the collaboration a highly valuable one'. They emphasised that such temporary appointments would normally be 'fairly short term – for as long as it took to get a particular item of legislation on the statute book – but would in any case terminate with the life of the Government'.[1]

The Labour Party also proposed that a second kind of temporary appointment to the Civil Service should be explicitly recognised when they argued that a Minister on assuming office

> should have the power to appoint a limited number of personal assistants (perhaps up to four) with direct access to him and to all the information in his department. These would form his personal *cabinet*. They would take no administrative decisions themselves. They would have neither the size nor the power of, for instance, their counterparts in France. Indeed, the pronunciation alone is French, the *cabinet* we propose is a British response to British needs. Its function would be to act as an extra pair of eyes and ears, to stimulate him.

The basic reason that the Labour Party had for recommending such a step was that

> as departments have grown in size and in complexity, the load on the political head has grown greater. The result is that a Minister can be a lonely man. He may be supported by one or two junior Ministers, but often he will not have chosen them himself, and they too will in any case be busy men. We believe a Minister can profit greatly from having a number of close personal advisers with him in his department.

The exact use made of the *cabinet*, or indeed its use at all, would depend on the Minister, but the Labour Party saw it as having 'three chief functions'. [Firstly]

> a research function: they would help him with the work of policy formulation within his department, keep in touch with what was going on in the department, and thus enable a meaningful political intervention in the early stages of the evolution of policy and assist the Minister in marrying his own ideas with those of the official machine. They might also help to brief the Minister on items on the Cabinet agenda.

---

[1] Ibid. paras 60–2.

[Secondly]

> a liaison function: to perform such briefing adequately, they
> would need to be in close touch with other Ministers through
> members of their 'cabinets'. This sort of network would parallel
> the informal links which exist at present between officials in the
> different departments and again act to restore the balance between
> the politician and the official.

The third function was less easy to define, but the Labour Party
saw it as being that of 'transmitting the political impulse from the
Minister to officials working in the department who may rarely or
never see him. They must provide a point of contact.' The Labour
Party concluded:

> Though the *cabinet* is a fairly radical departure from traditional
> practice, we feel that it should not be too difficult to accommodate
> in the sort of Civil Service we envisage. It will be performing a
> 'political' function which, though it parallels the function of the
> private office at some points, is essentially different. Once the
> private office becomes accustomed to the loss of its exclusive right
> of guardianship there should be little reason for friction.[1]

The Labour Party's evidence as a whole, although of considerable interest, does not amount to a related set of proposals for the
reform of the Civil Service, so that when the Labour Party talks of
'the sort of Civil Service we envisage' what that means in practical
terms is not always clear. For example, the Party is in favour of

> a move towards the practice in the United States whereby depart-
> ments are typically composed of bureaux which have an identity
> of their own and considerable permanence in their heads and
> staff. This gives to members of the staff far more scope for
> pursuing a particular line of policy than the rather anonymous
> subdivisions of British Ministries. There is an identity between
> staff and policy which does not now exist.

It is possible that a recognition of the need to treat departmental
functions as needing specialisation might lead to the development
of 'something like this form of organisation', and that 'a natural
result of this might be the emergence in each department of a
small body of men with equal access to the Minister and an end of
the existing concentration of power in the hands of one man, the

[1] Ibid. paras 63–9.

Permanent Secretary'. As part of 'its initial examination of the structure of Government', the Fulton Committee 'should look very closely at the possibility of dividing Ministries in this way',[1] but what the committee ought to ask the Labour Party is how this proposal ties in with their other suggestions about the creation of ministerial *cabinets* and 'posts of confidence'. Are these latter suggestions dependent upon Ministries being subdivided into bureaux, or are they seen – as seems to be implied in the relevant passages of the Labour Party's evidence – as being able to be introduced into the existing system? This question is important because as regards ministerial *cabinets*, it is not merely insular to say that 'it is significant that one wants to use the French pronunciation' when discussing them, for they are 'an idea foreign to us'.[2] They are features of parliamentary systems such as those of Belgium, Italy and France which either do not have, or assign a negligible role to, Junior Ministers, Parliamentary Private Secretaries and Permanent Secretaries.[3] In such countries there is, moreover, a tendency for government departments to be organised as a range of executive directorates with the ministerial *cabinet* providing the link between them and the Minister. It may or may not be preferable that British government departments should be organised similarly, but they do at present have what can be described as a pyramidal structure with the Minister at, and his Junior Ministers and Permanent Secretary and other leading Civil Servants near, the top. There would, therefore, be difficulties in introducing ministerial *cabinets* into British government departments, not least that, indicated by the present Prime Minister in 1964, of 'a sort of false division' between the *cabinet* and the Civil Servants,[4] which might well mean a duplication of functions

---

[1] Ibid. paras 54–5.

[2] Ministerial *cabinets* were described in such terms by Lord Bridges, 'Whitehall and Beyond', in *The Listener*, 25 June 1964, p. 1017; Robert Neild, 'New Functions: new Men?', in *The Listener*, 27 Aug 1964, p. 304, saw Lord Bridges's remarks as 'a revealing glimpse' of insularity.

[3] A. Dutheillet de Lamothe, 'Ministerial Cabinets in France', in *Public Administration* (1965) p. 366.

[4] In 1964, when asked in a television interview by Dr Norman Hunt whether or not there was a strong case for any Minister who is taking over a new department bringing in his own little private *cabinet*, that is,

at some points. Apart from a possible loss of dramatic effect,
it is difficult to see why the Labour Party did not describe this
particular proposal in terms of strengthening Ministers' private
offices. Professor Robson has argued, for example: 'it would be a
great advantage to a Minister if he could bring two or three trusted
advisers into his private office on a salaried basis to help in the
formation of departmental policy. They would not be established
Civil Servants and would expect to leave when a change of Government, or even a change of Minister, occurs.'[1] The Labour Party's
proposals about the creation of 'posts of confidence' recall the provisions made in Sweden for such political appointments, one
group of which are made to 'the key administrative posts for putting
into effect the programme of the Government of the day'.[2] The
Swedish governmental system is, however, very different from

---

a few men whom he particularly trusts, who are dedicated to what he
wants to achieve, to help him get his policies through that department,
Mr Harold Wilson, then the Leader of the Opposition, replied: 'I am
rather hesitant about this in the departments, and I say this because of
my own experience in the Cabinet Secretariat and also as a Civil Servant
as well as a Minister. There is a danger that you get a sort of false division
between his political *cabinet*, if you want to use that phrase, and the
Civil Servants. My own experience, having tried as a Minister to bring
in one or two outside experts with the right political approach, was that I
did far better when I relied in my private office on loyal Civil Servants who
knew what I wanted and saw to it that the rest of the department knew
what I wanted.' ('Whitehall and Beyond', in *The Listener*, 5 Mar 1964,
p. 380.) Speaking in a television interview as Prime Minister on 20
January 1967, Mr Harold Wilson, specifically asked about the Labour
Party's proposal in its evidence to the Fulton Committee that each
Minister should have his own 'kitchen Cabinet', said: 'If I thought this
was necessary, I would have done it in Government.' Mr Wilson remarked
that, as he had said two years ago, 'before I came into Government . . .
it would be necessary to recruit outside people, business-men, economists,
economic experts, into the two new growth Ministries I had in mind to
create – the Ministry of Technology and the Department of Economic
Affairs – and this has been done. I do not believe in a large-scale recruitment into the ordinary departments.' ('Where Power Lies. The Prime
Minister interviewed by Ian Trethowan', in *The Listener*, 9 Feb 1967,
p. 184.)
    [1] William A. Robson, 'The Reform of Government', in *Political
Quarterly* (1964) p. 201.
    [2] Brian Chapman, *The Profession of Government* (1959) pp. 276–9.

our own. Their Ministries are 'small groups of immediate advisers to Ministers' having 'no more than a dozen or so officials'.
The bulk of the administration is the responsibility of about
sixty Royal Boards, which are recruited separately from the
Ministries, over which Parliament has 'no direct authority' and
which are subject to 'the minimum control practicable' on the
part of Ministers.[1] The Swedish system, therefore, does not have
a convention of ministerial responsibility comparable with our
own. It may not be any the worse for that, but the introduction
into the British system of arrangements that can be said to be
similar to Swedish 'posts of confidence', like the introduction of
ministerial *cabinets*, may raise problems to which the Labour
Party have not sufficiently addressed themselves. As well as asking
them to spell out the precise roles of the political appointees to
the Service in relation to the permanent Civil Servants and within
the present framework of British government departments, the
Fulton Committee can also ask the Labour Party how they would
hope to fill the large number of political appointees' posts that
they propose. However, for all the lack of cohesiveness in their
evidence, the Labour Party deserve credit for attempting to think
of solutions for the very real problems of maintaining political
control over government departments in modern conditions.
Although they looked at European governmental systems in
borrowing such institutions as ministerial *cabinets* to include
among their proposals, the Labour Party seem to envisage the
eventual development of an American-style Civil Service in which,
although the overwhelming majority of positions would be filled by
career Civil Servants, certain major posts would be filled by the
politically committed, and responsibility for administration would
be openly acknowledged by those conducting it.[2] This is perhaps
a direction in which the British Civil Service may eventually move.

[1] Ibid. pp. 49–51.
[2] Among the works consulted about the American Civil Service were
the following: Paul P. Van Riper, *History of the United States Civil Service*
(1959); Wallace S. Sayre (ed.) *The Federal Government Service* (1965);
David T. Stanley, *Changing Administrations. The 1961 and 1964 Transitions in Six Departments* (1965); David T. Stanley, *The Higher Civil
Service. An Evaluation of Federal Personnel Practices* (1965).

Whatever the Fulton Committee's conclusions either about the evidence submitted to it by the First Division Association and the Labour Party or about the current working of the doctrine of ministerial responsibility, the committee has been told by the Prime Minister:

> The Government's willingness to consider changes in the Civil Service does not imply any intention on its part to alter the basic relationship between Ministers and Civil Servants. Civil Servants, however eminent, remain the confidential advisers of Ministers, who alone are answerable to Parliament for policy; and we do not envisage any change in this fundamental feature of our Parliamentary system of democracy.[1]

The committee need not interpret this rider to its terms of reference too restrictively. It can observe that, in much the same way as Parliament is experiencing difficulty in exercising its traditional functions of reviewing the activities of the Executive, not least because of the complexity of these activities, the widening of the Civil Service caused by the extended role assigned to the central Government has involved difficulties for ministerial control. In this context, the Fulton Committee can examine the Labour Party's proposals about temporary political appointments to the Service, which are aimed at increasing political control over government departments. Although the committee need not, of course, comment favourably about the desirability of such appointments, it might at least give explicit recognition of the right of Governments to make them, because what Governments choose to do is constitutional under an unwritten constitution. The Fulton Committee might next draw attention to the increased dialogues that do now, and may in the future increasingly, take place between Civil Servants and Parliament. The committee may point to the examples quoted by the First Division Association, observing that the experiences of, for example, the Select Committee on Estimates, 'underline the impossibility of preventing a committee which is concerned chiefly with finding out how financial resources are being used, from commenting directly or indirectly on issues of policy which are bound to present themselves during its

[1] House of Commons, *Official Report* (1965–6) vol. 724, col. 210.

enquiries'.[1] The Fulton Committee might also point to the examples
provided by the committees appointed by the House of Commons
in January 1967 to survey government activities in the spheres of
agriculture and of science and technology. It is difficult to see how
reports from these committees can fail to have implications for
policy, and it is noteworthy that more specialist committees are
to be set up in the 1967–8 session.[2] The Fulton Committee may

[1] Nevil Johnson, *Parliament and Administration. The Estimates Committee 1945–1965* (1966) p. 163.

[2] David Wood, 'Turning talking shop into workshops', in *The Times*,
24 July 1967, p. 8. David Wood, writing about Mr Richard Crossman's
achievements as Leader of the House of Commons in the session 1966–7,
said: 'It was his brief from Mr. Wilson a year ago to make a quick start
on modernising Parliament by subtly combining the roles of Leader of
the Commons and principal party manager. He was to bring in reforms
that gave back-benchers the sense of having a larger say, if not a larger
influence on policy, and as a party manager he was to run Labour's
big majority on a much lighter rein. So it has happened that Mr. Crossman
has set a very personal stamp on the session that effectively ends on
Friday, and he has probably changed Parliament in fundamental and
lasting ways not yet understood. It is characteristic of the man that he had
the audacity or the rashness to make some of his reforms experimentally,
well ahead of the consensus, and consequently both the new devices of
specialist committees and morning sittings are having to be tidied up
while the machine is running. But the experiments have shown the way
to some extremely useful procedures. Audacity is rewarded.' David
Wood continued: 'The main problem with the specialist committees
was widely predicted. How far could the committees be allowed to go by
Ministers in probing departmental actions and policies? Clearly Ministers
and senior Civil Servants would not let themselves be questioned on
confidential matters involving non-governmental outside bodies or on
departmental policy studies that might not eventually lead to policy
decisions. Some Ministers kicked like mules against the risks and embar-
rassments Mr. Crossman's reform might let them in for. The answer has
been the formulation of a code, agreed between Mr. Crossman and the
chairman of the agriculture and science specialist committees, and it will
apply to the three or four new committees to be set up next session.
The code safeguards the confidentiality of departmental dealings with
outside bodies and prescribes that investigation of embryonic policies
should be restricted to departmental proposals already sent forward
to the Cabinet – that is, to Cabinet committee. But there has now been a
further interesting development. It was inevitable that Ministers would
begin to adapt specialist committees to their service, just as Governments
adapt procedure to their service. One bright Minister has explained to
me how the specialist committees will help him enormously in over-
coming the caution and inertia of his own departmental advisers. When

also consider that the introduction of a Parliamentary Commissioner will eventually lead to a situation in which, in so far as they can be satisfactorily distinguished, responsibility for administration will be hived off from responsibility for policy. The committee can comment that such developments will increase the likelihood of individual Civil Servants being identified with individual policies, so that responsibility for administration will be less concentrated than at present. The committee may also observe that in some areas of administration, notably the nationalised industries, the head of the industry plays a quasi-ministerial part; while the Chairman of the Prices and Incomes Board may be seen as having a non-political ministerial role of a different sort. The Fulton Committee would have here a case for recommending the implementation of the proposals made by the First Division Association about lessening the anonymity of Civil Servants. The committee may conclude that certain trends raise questions about the nature of parliamentary control, at present

---

they heave on the brakes to slow him up, he can guide the specialist committee to the subject and build up Parliamentary pressure for the policy he wants. He can even make sure his senior Civil Servants are given a thorough roasting to explain why progress is so slow.' David Wood also said: 'Next session there will be another reform to bring back-benchers into play at an earlier stage in the formation of policy and thereby restore their self-respect by giving them at least equal influence with, say, such outside bodies as the C.B.I., the T.U.C., the N.F.U., and the N.S.P.C.C. In the House and in committee they will be given a chance to use their voices on policy long before they are asked to rubber stamp the policy with their votes. Through the years I have sometimes given chapter and verse of policy decisions agreed between departments and outside bodies that could not be amended in the House without involving a Minister in something near to a breach of faith. Policies have been accomplished facts before Parliament knew they existed.' David Wood's conclusion was: 'The logic of the reforms, both those accomplished and those in prospect, is certainly, I believe, to diminish or extinguish the supreme role of the Chamber. Politicians are being gently weaned away from their historic attachment to the Commons as a talking shop to a new conception of Parliament as a collection of smaller workshops co-ordinated with Whitehall. I suspect that, once the full implications of the Crossman reforms dawn upon them, that is what politicians and the electorate will regard as making far better contemporary sense. Newspapers, broadcasters, and audiences will sooner or later have to readjust to the change – if they are not already weary of the talking shop.'

existing in an idealised form, and one with which M.P.s seem increasingly dissatisfied, and that it will take account of this in fulfilling its task of reforming an apolitical Civil Service subject to political control.

The major part of that task is to review the structure of the Home Civil Service. The written evidence submitted to the Fulton Committee in its first year of working was largely shaped by the nature of the proposals advanced by the Treasury in their evidence suggesting 'some possible lines of reconstruction of some of the central parts of the Civil Service'. Although their proposals as a whole had 'wider implications at the senior levels', the Treasury mainly concerned themselves with the Administrative and Executive Classes, whose work they said ranged 'from the formulation of policy proposals to the management of the machine, both at headquarters and in local and regional offices'.[1] The Treasury said that there were two reasons why 'some reconstruction' of the service was needed:

> First, considerable changes in the country's educational system have been made since the present Administrative/Executive structure was settled, and in consequence our pattern of recruitment is no longer matched to this system. Secondly, the character of the work in the Civil Service has changed in the last 20–30 years by reason of the increasing concern of Government with the economic and social life of the community; and the existing division of the Service into Classes imposes a certain rigidity and lack of flexibility which hinder the deployment of staff in the most advantageous way.[2]

In marked contrast with the evidence which they submitted not only to the Priestley Commission of 1953–5, but also to the Select Committee on Estimates in 1965, the Treasury then went on to recommend that the Administrative and Executive Classes should 'lose their separate identities' and become 'wholly merged in a general management group'.[3] This new management structure, which would 'comprehend the present Administrative and Executive Classes', was to consist of eight numbered grades. Grades I and

---

[1] H.M. Treasury, 'The Future Structure of the Civil Service', a note submitted to the *Fulton Committee on the Civil Service* (1966) para. 1.
[2] Ibid. para. 2.   [3] Ibid. para. 6.

II corresponded to the present Administrative Class grades of Permanent Secretary and Deputy Secretary. Grade III was described as being equivalent to Under-Secretary and, presumably, it would include also those posts at present filled by Heads of Major Executive Establishments. Grade IV was an amalgamation of the Assistant Secretary and Principal Executive Officer grades, although the Treasury recognised that 'the Senior Chief Executive Officer and similar departmental grades might have to be retained' because 'they fill an essential and specific role, particularly in regional organisations'. Grade V was a merger of the Principal and Chief Executive Officer grades, the Treasury commenting that many posts at this level have become 'virtually indistinguishable'. Grade VI was equivalent to Senior Executive Officer, and it was to be 'a senior managerial level, with specific use in certain fields of office management and control'. Below this, Grade VII, the equivalent of Higher Executive Officer, was to represent 'the middle level of office management'; while Grade VIII, formerly that of Executive Officer, was to be 'the basic working grade in the management field'.[1] In addition, the Treasury have proposed that the present Clerical Officer grade should be renamed as Grade IX and the Clerical Assistant grade as Grade X, together forming 'the clerical infrastructure for the management grades above them'.[2] As to recruitment and career development, the Treasury envisaged that 'entrants to this new structure would come in the main from four sources'. The first would be the promoted Clerical Officer, who would 'come into the basic grade, (VIII) normally in the top half of the scale'.[3] The Treasury, however, made it clear that, although the abler members of what is now called the Clerical Class, particularly the young direct entrants, would probably have favourable promotion prospects, Clerical Officers as a whole would have to accept greater competition for promotion because of increased recruitment at higher

[1] Ibid. paras 5, 7 and 18.

[2] H.M. Treasury, 'The Clerical Classes', a note submitted to the *Fulton Committee on the Civil Service* (1966) para. 4.

[3] H.M. Treasury, 'The Future Structure of the Civil Service', a note submitted to the *Fulton Committee on the Civil Service* (1966) para. 8.

levels in the new proposed single-class structure.[1] The second main type of entrant would be the eighteen-year-old 'A' level entrant, who would 'come in on a short scale designed specifically for this type of officer but would proceed on to the main Grade VIII scale after, say, three years. His normal career expectation would be Grade VI – but facilities and opportunities would be there for him to go higher.' The other two sources would be drawn from the graduate entry, which the Treasury recognised 'would need to be much larger than the existing Assistant Principal entry, building up possibly to several hundred a year'. Graduates would enter the Grade VIII scale at an appropriate point, and 'their training and development would be specifically watched': the majority could expect promotion to Grade VII after about five years, and their normal career expectation would be Grade V. The Treasury suggested: 'Within this large graduate entry, a proportion roughly equivalent in size to the present Assistant Principal entry might be "starred" or otherwise designated on the strength of their academic records and their performance at the selection stage. They would enter one or two increments higher up the scale and would have a career in their first years close to that of the present Assistant Principal.' Between these two levels of graduates, however, the Treasury said that 'there could be movement in both directions, both during and after the probationary period'. Those unstarred graduate entrants 'who maintained their performance at, or turned out to be outstanding enough to break into, the higher, or "starred" level, would normally have a period in a private office, which could probably best be covered by promotion to Grade VI, and would then be promoted to Grade V'.[2] However, although the Treasury said that 'training for middle and higher management posts would be an important feature of this new organisation', only the 'starred' graduate entrants were to enjoy arrangements similar to those now provided at the Centre for Administrative Studies. What the Treasury called 'the

[1] H.M. Treasury 'The Clerical Classes', a note submitted to the *Fulton Committee on the Civil Service* (1966) paras 5–6.

[2] H.M. Treasury, 'The Future Structure of the Civil Service', a note submitted to the *Fulton Committee on the Civil Service* (1966) para. 8.

others' were to have 'a shorter course at about the same stage; and subsequently the most promising would have a Middle Management Course at around age 30 to groom them for Grade V. A Senior Management Course in the middle 30s for those going on to higher responsibilities would probably be introduced.'[1] Despite the differences in post-entry training arrangements and, for that matter, their advocacy of a 'starred 'entry to their version of a fused Executive–Administrative Class, the Treasury felt able to emphasise that 'all entrants' to their proposed 'new management structure' would be 'eligible on their merits for promotion to the higher posts'.[2]

Although, in advancing their reasons for 'some reconstruction' of the Civil Service, the Treasury had conceded that the Service had not adjusted itself sufficiently to the emergence of the Positive State, all they subsequently recommended was 'a slightly differently dressed continuance of the present system'.[3] The Treasury's scheme looks like a mildly modified version of that which the Plowden Committee on Representational Services Overseas, reporting in 1964, successfully recommended should be the structure of the new Diplomatic Service. It will be recalled that the Plowden Committee did not favour a proposal put before it for that Service to have a 'one branch' structure with 'different points of entry corresponding to different educational standards and levels of ability' and with 'a single ladder of promotion'. Among the reasons that the Plowden Committee advanced for rejecting such a structure was that it would not take 'sufficient account of genuine and valid distinctions between different types of work and the different qualities needed for these'. The committee instead designed a structure of ten numbered grades ranging from Clerical Officer to Permanent Secretary which maintained 'separate Administrative, Executive and Clerical pay scales, entry points and promotion streams'. The committee said that the members of the new Diplomatic Service 'would be known primarily by their new grade, but there would be no secret about their

---

[1] Ibid. para. 10.   [2] Ibid. para. 9.
[3] *Evidence presented by the Civil Service Clerical Association to the Fulton Committee on the Civil Service* (1966) para. 51.

membership of the Administrative, Executive or Clerical Classes'.[1] The Treasury's proposals for the Home Civil Service do attempt to make a secret of such membership. Their only important

[1] *Report of the Committee on Representational Services Overseas appointed by the Prime Minister under the Chairmanship of Lord Plowden 1962–63*, Cmnd 2276 (1964) paras 100–4. The most important recommendation of the committee was that a unified Service should be created to take in the duties, personnel and posts of the Foreign Service, Commonwealth Service and Trade Commission Service, separate Foreign and Commonwealth Relations Offices in Whitehall being retained (paras 44–5), the unified Service was to be called 'H.M. Diplomatic Service' (para. 51): the committee's recommendations were implemented with effect from 1 January 1965. The Plowden Committee examined the idea of amalgamating branches A and B of the then Foreign Service 'with a single ladder of promotion'. They rejected 'so radical a change', although it was 'at first sight attractive', and devised a scheme which maintained 'separate Administrative, Executive and Clerical pay scales, entry points and promotion streams' (paras 100 and 102). The committee's ten-tier structure – outlined in para. 101 and introduced in 1965 – was as follows:

Grade 1: Permanent Secretary
Grade 2: Deputy Secretary
Grade 3: Under-Secretary
Grade 4: Assistant Secretary
            Principal Executive Officer
Grade 5: Principal
            Chief Executive Officer
Grade 6: Senior Executive Officer
Grade 7: Assistant Principal
            Higher Executive Officer
Grade 8: Assistant Principal
Grade 9: Executive Officer
Grade 10: Clerical Officer.

Grades 8, 9 and 10 were the entry points for the Administrative, Executive and Administrative Classes. Normal promotion for an Executive Class Officer in Grade 7 would be to Grade 6. 'Bridging' from the Executive Class to the Administrative Class would normally take place within Grades 4, 5 and 7. Accelerated promotion from Grade 7 to Grade 5 would be possible for outstanding Executive Officers 'bridging' to the Administrative Class. The Plowden Committee saw their scheme as acknowledging 'true differences of function and ability' (para. 101). It is interesting to note that a delegate to the 1966 Annual Conference of the Society of Civil Servants, representing its membership in the Diplomatic Service, said that in reconstructing the generalist side of the Home Civil Service it was important to have a real breakdown in barriers and not just a paper change as the Diplomatic Service had had. What the Treasury is proposing for the Home Civil Service is just a paper change.

difference from the Plowden scheme is the formal omission of a separate Assistant Principal entry grade; but, in practice, this would be maintained because the 'starred' entrants to Grade VIII in effect would be Assistant Principals and would follow much the same career pattern as at present. Indeed, in attempting to justify having a 'starred' entry, the Treasury argued that 'departments can operate on only a limited scale the arrangements whereby the Assistant Principal is given special training and experience in the early years of his career'. That the nature of at least part of that 'special training' would remain very much the same as at present was made clear when the Treasury said that 'unstarred' graduate entrants, who were singled out for advancement, would make their transition to the 'starred group' following 'a period in a private office'. The 'starred' entrants were also to be offered the same prospects as the present Assistant Principal.[1] Except to list them as numbered grades, the Treasury unfortunately said very little about the higher posts in their proposed 'general management group'. However, there was an indication that the Treasury intended little to change when they said that, at the higher level of general policy posts, 'a high degree of expertise in Government administrative processes and the working of a very complex machine is essential', and added that Civil Servants possessing this 'have acquired a knowledge in depth of public administration which, as a profession, is as exacting in its demands as any other'.[2] These phrases recall the arguments which the Treasury used in favour of retaining a separate Administrative Class in their evidence to the Select Committee on Estimates in 1965, as well as the writings of H. E. Dale.[3] It seems clear that, if the Treasury's proposals for 'a new management structure' were to be implemented, what would be achieved would not be a genuine reconstruction of the generalist side of the Service, but the

[1] H.M. Treasury, 'The Future Structure of the Civil Service', a note submitted to the *Fulton Committee on the Civil Service* (1966) para. 8.

[2] Ibid. para. 13.

[3] For example, *Sixth Report from the Select Committee on Estimates* (1964–5) *Evidence*, questions 807–8; and H. E. Dale, *The Higher Civil Service of Great Britain* (1941) p. 220.

maintenance of 'the Administrative Class in its present form in everything but name'.[1]

This is undesirable because the Administrative Class draws many of its traditions from the period when the State's functions were passive and, despite priding itself on the breadth of outlook of its members, it tends to interpret its role in a narrow manner. The Administrative Class sees itself as specialising in 'the awareness of Ministerial responsibility', as the eyes and ears of Ministers translating their ideas to the remainder of the staff in their departments, and, together with other advice, conveying upwards the collective wisdom of the various 'departmental traditions'. As to the qualities needed by leading administrators many would still agree with what H. E. Dale wrote in 1941: namely, that these depended 'both in constitutional theory and fact' upon what was wanted and expected 'by Ministers'. The 'positive requirements' of Ministers were that their principal subordinates possessed certain personal qualities', namely 'a wide intellectual horizon, the power of selecting the one crucial point from a multitude of relevant facts and arguments, prudence, resolution, invincible common sense' united with 'certain expert knowledge' – not, one hastens to add, of the subjects he deals with, because these can be mastered 'in a relatively short time by an able man who can command the knowledge of trained subordinates', but the 'special art' of the leading official who 'takes with him everywhere the expert knowledge and skill which are one specific excellence of the Civil Servant and are equally valuable in every department – the ability to work the machine of British Government'. The leading administrator

> knows the construction of the whole machine, the position of his own and other departments as wheels of the machine and their relations to other wheels, and the general principles of operation which must be observed if the machine is to work smoothly. Finally, and perhaps most important of all, the machine of Government is constructed of human beings: it is the business

---

[1] *Evidence presented by the Institution of Professional Civil Servants to the Fulton Committee on the Civil Service* (1966) 'Comment on H.M. Treasury's note on "The Future Structure of the Civil Service" ', para. 6

of the high official to know the men who for the time being are, like himself, important parts of the central and controlling mechanism.

The ability to get on well with colleagues and Ministers and to know one's way around 'the stone corridors' and 'the carpeted rooms' of Whitehall and to face, armed with a lengthy apprentice-ship in 'the working of the machine of Government in a Parlia-mentary democracy', tasks largely composed of consultation and co-ordination, was Dale's picture of the ideal administrator.[1]

That the role of the Administrative Class was still seen similarly nearly a quarter of a century later was recently made clear by Sir Richard Way who told a sceptical Select Committee in 1965: 'If the Administrative Class means anything, and I think it does, it is essentially the link between the Minister and the Government machine; this is true of the Permanent Secretary in particular. It seems to me the Minister must look to it to act as a bridge between himself and the department.'[2] Just as Dale rejected the charge of amateurism, arguing that the high official was 'an expert in a difficult art, the detailed working of the Central Government in British Parliamentary democracy',[3] so Sir Richard dismissed it also saying that leading administrators were 'not amateurs in any sense' because: 'They do a job which in itself is a job of expertise in taking the broadest possible view of the problems of Govern-ment'.[4] To attain this 'broadest possible view', the members of the Administrative Class, recruited on the basis of 'general ability' rather than the possession of 'any special acquirements',[5] have traditionally maintained a career pattern and an attitude towards formal post-entry training biased towards retaining this initial emphasis. According to one writer who favours this approach it is not fortuitous because: 'It is connected with a certain

---

[1] H. E. Dale, *The Higher Civil Service of Great Britain* (1941) pp. 212–215.

[2] *Sixth Report from the Select Committee on Estimates* (1964–5) *Evidence*, question 480.

[3] H. E. Dale, *The Higher Civil Service of Great Britain* (1941) p. 220.

[4] *Sixth Report from the Select Committee on Estimates* (1964–5) *Evidence*, question 474.

[5] *Trevelyan–Northcote Report* (1853) p. 14.

reading of the nature of public administration, one which has come naturally in a country where, until at any rate the end of the eighteenth century, the bulk of the administration was in the hands of magistrates, whose great qualification was to have no special qualification but to be reputable, unlearned and in every way ordinary.'[1]

According to the writer of those words, C. H. Sisson, the ideal administrator is still the intelligent layman, recruited on the basis of 'a good general education'[2] and 'best trained by apprenticeship',[3] who bears in mind that he has no pretensions to play a positive role. 'He merely serves his Minister, and since he lives by satisfying the House of the reasonableness and common sense of what he does, the administrator who serves him is the man whose characteristic interest is in the intelligibility of what is done, or rather its explicability in terms Parliament will accept.'[4] In Sisson's eyes, the most serious responsibility of the administrator is to 'lay aside his preferences in favour of an objective assessment of the situation, not in terms of anything he may hold to be good but in terms of the game as it is played in Whitehall': this game is 'the only notion of the good he has a right to'.[5] To Sisson, the administrator was 'an instrument of wills other than his own',[6] and it followed: 'There is no need for an administrator to be a man of ideas. His distinguishing quality should be rather a certain freedom from ideas. The idealisms and the most vicious appetites are equal before him. He should be prepared to bow before any wisdom whose mouth is loud enough.' Such an administrator steers 'what may appear to be a craven course among the various pressures of public and still more of semi-public opinion and the opinion of groups, and his concern is not to come off with victory, in the sense that his opinion prevails, for he has no right to one, but in the sense that in the end he is still upright and the forces around him have achieved a momentary balance'.[7]

Those observers who have taken the opposing view to that of

[1] C. H. Sisson, *The Spirit of British Administration* (1959) p. 33.
[2] Ibid. p. 137.   [3] Ibid. p. 28.
[4] Ibid. p. 38.   [5] Ibid. p. 152.
[6] Ibid. p. 133.   [7] Ibid. p. 23.

Sisson, and who have argued that the leading Civil Servant has a
positive role to play, have been roundly taken to task by Professor
S. E. Finer. In his opinion, such commentators look for qualities
in administrators which are

> far more appropriate to the Ministers than to their minions. The
> Civil Servant makes policy only to the extent that he influences his
> Minister, and the Minister only to the extent that he influences
> Parliament. Of course it is true that our great administrators
> have been *impiger, iracundus, inexorabilis, acer*. Such were the
> Chadwicks, the Trevelyans, the Stephens and the Morants. They
> nagged and drove and beat this country along the road of social
> progress, and everybody remembers them with *reminiscent*
> gratitude after they are dead – but what Cabinet would want a
> Service alive and bursting with them?[1]

Ideally, of course, Ministers should provide the positive element
in British central Government. Armed with a firm grasp of the
complex duties of their departments, Ministers should be using
their powers of leadership to harness the resources of their departments, if needs be supplementing them from outside the Service,
in order to drive through their policies. In modern conditions,
this demands of Ministers not only considerable personal, notably
intellectual, qualities, but also, increasingly, some specialised
knowledge of the general fields in which their departments operate.
In practice, however, in making ministerial appointments – even
allowing for the other limitations on their freedom of choice in
this respect – Prime Ministers must obviously have difficulty in
finding Ministers of such calibre: and, in any case, they tend to
see Ministers in much the same way as the Administrative Class
sees its members: namely, as all-rounders who can change between
not necessarily related jobs without supposedly losing efficiency.
Not surprisingly, therefore, Ministers relatively rarely come to
departments equipped to impose upon them a real measure of
positive political control. It may well still be the case, as Nevil
Johnson recently argued, that Ministers do 'take the vast majority
of policy decisions' in the sense of deciding between the different
approaches suggested by their Civil Servants to carrying out

[1] Samuel E. Finer, *A Primer of Public Administration* (1950) p. 121.

policies:[1] but, is it not rather important from whom the initiative comes? The leading administrator may be 'constitutionally a nonentity'[2] as Sisson maintains, but, as the same writer states, he is also 'undoubtedly a powerful person in the sense that he occupies an influential place in the system and that his advice is always listened to and generally taken'.[3] Therefore, whereas in constitutional theory the leading Civil Servant is assigned a relatively modest role, in practice he wields considerable power. While such an administrator does make policy 'only to the extent that he influences his Minister', the extent of that influence, as Lord Bridges has made clear, may well be very considerable, and there is as little realism in talking of leading Civil Servants as 'minions' as there is, in an era of party discipline, in describing a Minister as only making policy 'to the extent that he influences Parliament'. However, when one looks at the Administrative Class, whose members tend to occupy most of the highest posts of the Service, it seems evident that, as Professor W. J. M. Mackenzie has observed, the class is not intended 'to be a policy-making organisation; or at least it is badly organised as such'.[4] Partly because of the Administrative Class's determination to remain a tiny *élite* despite the pressure of work at the top of the Service, the leading administrators become 'immersed in the day-to-day work of administration'.[5] The Administrative Class's emphasis on having a special role built around the working of the convention of ministerial responsibility has led it to give a low valuation to management, to adopt an order of priorities in which the technical is subordinated to the political and to have a 'crisis mentality' in dealing with problems, scorning preliminary research into their general fields. The Haldane Committee's famous observation that 'in the sphere of Civil Government the duty of investigation

[1] Nevil Johnson, 'Who are the Policy Makers? Conclusion', in *Public Administration* (1965) p. 283.
[2] C. H. Sisson, *The Spirit of British Administration* (1959) p. 104.
[3] Ibid. p. 129.
[4] *Sixth Report from the Select Committee on Estimates* (1964–5) *Evidence*, p. 135, para. 34.
[5] Sir Charles Cunningham, 'Policy and Practice', in *Public Administration* (1963) p. 233.

and thought as preliminary to action, might with great advantage be more definitely realised'[1] still rings true. The Administrative Class, as Professor Mackenzie has commented, has conventionally seen the job of the administrator as being

> to consult and combine rather than to originate. These are intricate functions reflecting our intricate political and administrative structure. A change in the character of the Class would reflect and promote change in the structure as a whole. This would not necessarily be a bad thing; the smoothness of operation secured by such great men as Lord Hankey, Lord Bridges, and Lord Normanbrook has perhaps served to plaster over cracks in an obsolete and crumbling structure.

Professor Mackenzie concluded, however: 'the present "style" of administrators is part of our whole system, and will not change without wider changes'.[2] These changes should now be made for, at present, with the system resting on the assumption of positive ministerial control that is not usually forthcoming, British central Government seems organised only to produce near inertia.

The reform of the Home Civil Service, while not providing more than a partial answer to the problems of British central Government, would still be an important contribution; and the Fulton Committee should go further than the Treasury did in their evidence to it and make one of its leading recommendations that, given certain safeguards, the Executive and Administrative Classes of that Service ought to be genuinely merged. Proposals that would achieve this have been made by the Society of Civil Servants in their evidence to the Fulton Committee.[3] There are

[1] *Report of the Haldane Committee on the Machinery of Government* (1918) p. 6, para. 12.

[2] *Sixth Report from the Select Committee on Estimates* (1964–5) *Evidence*, p. 135, para. 35.

[3] The Society have advocated 'the merger of the Administrative and Executive Classes into a new management grades structure. This would facilitate the more flexible use of staff, enable academic achievements to be backed with practical experience and make it possible for those who have not been to University, to supplement their acquired practical experience with further study and training. In the view of the Society the new structure would produce in the course of time a more diversified higher Civil Service which would be equipped not only to perform the traditional role of tendering advice to Ministers but also to deal more expertly with management functions and ensure that the best possible

(*footnote 3, page 296, continued*)

value is obtained for the public expenditure incurred.' The Society
suggested the creation of a new management grades structure consisting
of eight grades. For 'top management and administration', they proposed
a Grade 1 to correspond with Permanent Secretary, a Grade 2 comparable with Deputy Secretary, and a Grade 3 equivalent to Under-
Secretary and Heads of Major Executive Establishments. For 'higher
management', they proposed a Grade 4 which would comprehend the
existing Assistant Secretary, Principal Executive Officer and Senior
Chief Executive Officer. For 'middle management', they suggested a
Grade 5 embracing Principal, Chief Executive Officer and certain
Senior Executive posts (i.e. where a separate S.E.O. level is not required),
and a Grade 6 consisting of the remaining Senior Executive Officer
posts (i.e. where this grade is specifically necessary, e.g. in Local Offices).
For Management and Management Trainees, the Society proposed a
Grade 7 equivalent to Higher Executive Officer, and a Grade 8 covering
Assistant Principal and Executive Officer. About their structure the
Society observed: 'The retention of the Senior Executive Officer in the
new structure for use in certain fields of office management should not
obstruct the assimilation of this grade to the new Grade 5 wherever this is
practicable. The omission of this grade in areas where it is not specifically required would remove unnecessary tiers in the hierarchy which
might otherwise impede prompt decision making. It is also desirable
that the career pyramid should be so constructed as to make the new
management structure attractive to graduate entrants. From this standpoint it will be necessary to offer a normal career expectation to the new
Grade 5 for the most able entrants from all sources to go beyond.' The
Society also commented: 'The Senior Chief Executive Officer grade lies
between the Principal and Assistant Secretary grades in the Administrative Class. This grade is used almost exclusively in higher management
posts in the Executive Class and quite frequently for a deputy post; for
example, Deputy Regional Controllers. The grade is also used at Assistant
Director level in Contracts, Accounts and Supplies Branches. The
elimination of this grade would create organisational problems in certain
departments but it is very important that unnecessary distinctions should
not be perpetuated between the Administrative and Executive Classes
in the new unified structure. The Society is of the opinion that in
principle this grade should be assimilated together with the Principal
Executive Officer grade at Assistant Secretary level into the new Grade 4.
Consideration might be given to the possibility of the new Grade 4 being
range paid instead of being remunerated on a rather long scale as at
present. Such an arrangement would enable differences of responsibility
within the broad range covered by the grade to be suitably remunerated.'
(*Evidence presented by the Society of Civil Servants to the Fulton Committee on the Civil Service*, 1966, para. 10.) The Society viewed the
Treasury's proposals for a 'starred' entry to their version of the new
management structure with disfavour, saying that they had 'no objection
to starting pay being related to age and qualifications', but that they

very good reasons for carrying through the unification of the
generalist side of the Service beyond the amalgamation of the
executive and higher clerical hierarchies achieved in 1947. The
present structure gives far too low a valuation to management
for, although the traditional definition of the duties of the Administrative Class gives it a potential managerial role in charging
it with 'the coordination and improvement of Government
machinery' and with 'the general administration and control of
the departments of the Public Service', management is normally
seen as the sphere of the Executive Class, and the Administrative
Class tends to place most emphasis upon what it interprets to be
'the formation of policy', together with the various trappings of
ministerial responsibility. Shortly after he became Head of the
Civil Service, Sir Norman Brook complained that members of
the Administrative Class 'are not sufficiently alive to the great
responsibility which they should carry in management duties'.[1]
But, under the present régime they have little incentive to do so,
for although, apart from private secretaries, only those at the very
top, of Under-Secretary rank or better, have frequent contacts
with the Minister, those below understandably take their style of
administration and order of priorities from them for the natural
enough reason that advancement lies in that direction. If the ideal
leading administrator is supposed to be the 'all-rounder' or 'intelligent layman' and the manner in which to achieve that status
is to avoid specialisms, to demonstrate 'versatility' and to concentrate on the acquisition of specially valued skills described in

---

(footnote 3, page 296, continued)
believed: 'it would be wrong to pre-select a particular group of entrants for
further advancement by reference to an academic record alone. It is important that those with an academic achievement should also demonstrate in
their departmental work their suitability for advancement to a higher position before being selected.' The Society, therefore, proposed that 'all University entrants to the management grades structure should enter through
a common channel and be given hard practical experience alongside 'A'
level school leaver entrants and promotees from the Clerical Class before
reaching the selection stage for advancement along the route for which they
would have to prove themselves under test to be suited' (ibid. para. 19).
  [1] Sir Norman Brook wrote these words in a 1957 Management Efficiency Circular (quoted in the *Whitley Bulletin*, Nov 1964, p. 158).

Dale's phrase as 'the ability to work the machine of British Government', then the ambitious administrator of Assistant Secretary status and below will do just that. An attitude tends to develop, as one member of the Fulton Committee once put it, that 'quasi-diplomatic work is at the top of the scale':[1] but when this means, to use his example, that vastly important tasks such as 'formulating and carrying out a road programme' are treated as being mundane, then the Administrative Class's priorities have become out of touch with the needs of the Positive State.

For the government departments are not simply ministerial private offices writ large: they are doing very much more than advising Ministers about policy. Collectively, they exercise, either directly or indirectly, a measure of control over a public sector which employs about a quarter of the national labour force and spends rather over forty per cent of the Gross National Product.[2] In this context, for the Plowden Committee on Public Expenditure to have to 'emphasise the importance of the management responsibility' and the need for Permanent Secretaries to appreciate it, and to have to say of the Permanent Secretary that, 'His responsibilities to ensure that approved policies are carried out economically and that his department is staffed as efficiently as possible for this purpose seems to us no less important than his responsibility for advising his Minister on major issues of policy',[3] is surely evidence of the need for a different type of administrator from that normally produced by the typical Administrative Class career. One of the ways of securing such an administrator and to end the state of affairs in which members of the Administrative Class 'do not typically think of themselves as managers',[4] would be to end the separate existence of the Administrative Class, which is to some extent based on an unreal distinction between policy and execution, and to merge it with the managerial Executive Class. The future administrator would thereby face a much

---

[1] Sir James Dunnett, 'The Civil Service Administrator and the Expert', *in Public Administration* (1961) p. 227.

[2] Plowden Group, *Control of Public Expenditure* (1961) para. 10.

[3] Ibid. para. 47.

[4] Frank Dunnill, 'External Relations of the Administrative Class', in *Civil Service Opinion*, Apr 1964, p. 105.

more widely based, and in many ways more relevant, early career
than at present, and one in which, at the outset, managerial
responsibilities would be acknowledged.

But if the merger of the Executive and the Administrative
Classes takes place it must not do so on the basis of 'the extended
use of the Executive Class':[1] what in a sense is needed is the
extended use of the Administrative Class. Some of the Administrative Class's more hostile critics may like to describe the Executive Class in glowing terms,[2] but others will consider Dunnill's
picture of the 'dogged quietism' and the 'worthy stolidity'[3] of
members of the Executive Class as being very much nearer the
truth. For the career development of its members has been as
stunted by the division between policy and execution in the Service
as that of the administrators has been unnecessarily narrowed.
Any field of work that comes to be considered as mundane by the
Administrative Class, such as Organisation and Methods or staff
inspection, tends to become an executive preserve, and duties in
such spheres are all too often carried out in an unimaginative
manner. For the average Executive Class career, which in most
cases is usually prefaced by a lengthy apprenticeship performing

[1] This is, of course, the title of the famous Treasury Circular 5/47
under which the Executive and higher clerical hierarchies were merged
and the Executive Class was assigned certain former administrative
territory. The circular is reprinted in the *Whitley Bulletin*, Mar 1947,
pp. 36–8.

[2] One notes that Professor Brian Chapman has written: 'While the
quality of the British Administrative Class does not compare very
favourably with its European counterparts, that of the British Executive
Class does.' *British Government Observed* (1963) p. 33. It does not, of
course, follow that the quality of the Executive Class can be sensibly
said to be comparable with that of the Administrative Class.

[3] Frank Dunnill, 'External Relations of the Administrative Class', in
Civil Service Opinion, Apr 1964, p. 106; and his book, *The Civil Service.
Some Human Aspects* (1956) p. 118. It is only fair to add that Dunnill
describes the state of mind of the younger Executives as being of 'restless
self-confidence' (at the latter reference). As Dunnill himself adds, any
brief generalisation would be unfair, but I must say, with less experience
than this excellent writer, that, while I have sensed the restlessness of the
younger Executives, their 'self-confidence' is rarely so evident. I also
disagree with Mr Dunnill that the inertia of the Clericals is largely
'involuntary'.

dismal routine duties in the Clerical Class, is not normally designed to encourage drive or organising ability or breadth of vision. In their review of this area of the Service, the Fulton Committee should not rely on the evidence of the Society of Civil Servants, but ought itself to get the 'feel' of the Executive Class, by sounding out rank and file opinion. It should not take them too long to find that the distaste for 'paper qualifications' is almost as deep as that for departures from well-tried routine, and that 'common sense', rarely defined but always the highest virtue, is supposed to be the monopoly of the non-graduate. The Fulton Committee should thereby gain some idea of the magnitude of its task, and it should also be left with fewer illusions about the quality, and a clearer picture of the limitations, of the Executive Class than some outside observers.

If the Fulton Committee decides to recommend such a merger, it would be best if it saw the fused Executive–Administrative Class in terms of amalgamating the present ruling class of the Service with an 'Executive Corps' consisting of the former Special Department Classes and the present General and Departmental Executive Classes.[1] The new class ought to attempt to combine the flexibility of a generalist structure with the greater specialisation demanded by the complexity of the range of duties now assigned to the Executive and Administrative Classes. Although 'for operational purposes it exists as a number of really small, separate, departmental cadres',[2] the underlying assumption upon which the

[1] The Treasury has submitted evidence to the Fulton Committee about Departmental Classes, the conclusion of which was: 'There is little doubt that the flexibility of the Civil Service, and its abilities to move quickly to meet the changing demands of different administrations, would be seriously at risk if a pattern of Departmental Classes emerged on any more widespread scale than exists at present. It is suggested that the main criterion against which both existing Departmental Classes and any new proposals for the creation of new Departmental Classes should be judged is the necessity to train their members in skills specific to the Department usually with the requirement of a definite qualification, either externally or internally acquired.' (H.M. Treasury, 'Departmental Classes', a note submitted to the *Fulton Committee on the Civil Service*, 1967, para. 8).

[2] W. W. Morton, 'The Plowden Report: III. The Management Functions of the Treasury', in *Public Administration* (1963) p. 33.

Administrative Class rests is that 'the tasks facing the administrator in all departments or indeed in all parts of the same department are broadly similar'.[1] At present, like the politicians with whom some of its leading members closely work, the Administrative Class – as Professor Peter Self said in his evidence to the Fulton Committee – places 'a premium upon breadth of experience, flexibility of attitudes, ease of relationships, and smoothness of decision making: but it does not place the same value upon close knowledge and experience of some particular field of Governmental activity'.[2] Professor Self argued that because 'departmental work is becoming more complex and specialised' it follows that 'a proper mastery of each department's tasks and problems' has become 'more necessary for the effective discharge of departmental work at higher levels'.[3] In modern conditions, as the Acton Society Trust observed in their evidence, the administrator 'must acquire a good working knowledge of, and a developed analytical insight into, the subject matter of the problems with which he has to deal'.[4] It would be undesirable, therefore, if, as the Labour Party has suggested, 'expertise in making use of the Government machinery and the political underpinning of the Minister',[5] the generality of the Administrative Class, became a major specialism in the new Executive–Administrative Class because this would, as now, deter members of that class from acquiring relevant specialised knowledge of their departments' functions. As a rationalisation of the duties at present performed by the separate Executive and Administrative Classes – a rationalisation that should also include the shedding of the tail of Executive Class work that would be more appropriately done by Clerical grades[6] –

[1] Sir James Dunnett, 'The Civil Service Administrator and the Expert', in *Public Administration* (1961) p. 227.

[2] *Memorandum of Evidence presented by Professor P. J. O. Self to the Fulton Committee on the Civil Service* (1966) para. 9.

[3] Ibid. paras 5–6.

[4] *Statement of Evidence submitted by the Acton Society Trust to the Fulton Committee on the Civil Service* (1966) para. 19.

[5] *Evidence presented by the Labour Party to the Fulton Committee on the Civil Service* (1967) paras 45–6.

[6] One notes that an amendment was moved at the 1966 Annual Conference of the Society of Civil Servants which urged the Society's

the structure of the amalgamated Executive–Administrative Class should become a series of specialised hierarchies of two broad types, not necessarily mutually exclusive. The first type would be those concerned with duties peculiar to a particular department or group of departments: for example, town and country planning, social insurance, the economics of transport and, as at present, the

---

Executive Council to take any opportunity offered in giving evidence to the Fulton Committee to advance the view that the best interests of the Executive Class as a whole will be served by shedding the lower grade work that has accumulated to all grades. The Executive Council said that they were sympathetic with the aims of the mover of the amendment, and successfully asked for the amendment to be remitted for fuller consideration. The C.S.C.A. in making proposals to the Fulton Committee for the revision of the clerical structure said about the duties on the generalist side of the Service: 'The work itself does not lend itself to sharp segregation – it shades from one level to the next, and, e.g., the question whether a post is – within present grading – Executive Officer or Clerical Officer is often one for finely balanced judgment.' The C.S.C.A. said: 'If the broad outline of the Treasury's proposed plan of Grades I to VIII survives the Committee's scrutiny and study, then we say that this plan should be continued thus: Grade IX – The superior part of the work now falling to the C.O. grade, plus the lesser work now falling to the present Executive Officer grade. Grade X – The remainder of the work now attached to the C.O. grade, plus the better part of the work of the present C.A. which does not get transferred to machines or computers.' The C.S.C.A. thought that Grade IX would be larger than Grade X and that the standard entrance qualifications would be for Grade IX, as for the present C.O. grade; for Grade X, as for the present C.A. grade (*Evidence submitted by the Civil Service Clerical Association to the Fulton Committee,* 1966, paras 53–6). The Treasury's observation was: 'the level at which work is done is subject to continuous scrutiny by Treasury and departmental staff inspectors. Occasionally blocks of E.O. and C.O. work are found where there can be some down-grading, but the evidence of our staff inspections certainly does not suggest that there is scope for a shift of work of anything approaching the proportions implied in the C.S.C.A. evidence.' (H.M. Treasury, 'The Clerical Classes', a note submitted to the *Fulton Committee on the Civil Service,* 1966, para. 7.) The C.S.C.A. proposals are, of course, designed as a prelude to a pay claim, but they do draw attention to the need to examine the definition of duties at executive-clerical level. With a merged Executive–Administrative Class aiming to attract graduates in substantial numbers they will have to be given interesting work, and not just that which would have attracted the description of either Executive or higher Clerical almost fifty years ago. This is certainly an area which the Fulton Committee should use for its research facilities to explore.

various branches of tax law. The second type would be concerned with specialisms of wider application: such as accounting, auditing, actuarial work and personnel management. Each of these hierarchies would have its own promotion outlets, and planned postings would take place between them, so that an entrant would not be limited forever to either a particular department or a special type of work, although he would have every incentive to tackle them professionally. Such changes would only be revolutionary as regards the amount of formal post-entry training given: this should consist not only of general courses at the Civil Service Staff College, but also short, intensive departmental courses as well, for both initial entrants and those changing between specialisms, should they either wish or be required to, in the development of their career. Certain of the Departmental Executive Classes would be largely unaffected, for example those in the Inland Revenue, although they would be less isolated than at present. The greatest changes would be faced in the Administrative Class and the General Executive Class, although in the latter case what might be called government accounting, and what is called Establishments and Organisation work, are already seen as needing a measure of specialisation: the measure should be increased, as should the practice of acknowledging genuine specialisms generally.

A secondary, but obviously important, argument in favour of a merged Executive–Administrative Class is concerned with the direct-entry recruitment arrangements of the generalist side of the Civil Service. The present structure allows for an entry of the best available graduates at administrative level, with the next numerically significant stage at executive level, aiming to attract entrants with university-entrance qualifications. In between, graduates tend to be attracted to what were until recently called the Special Departmental Classes and some graduates go into the Executive Class: but the overall picture is that the generalist side of the Service has failed to adjust itself to university expansion. Despite such reforms as the introduction of Method II, the post-war recruitment record of the Administrative Class, particularly over the last decade, has been disappointing, and the resulting shortage of Principals is now assuming serious proportions. The Administrative Class still tends to rely for its direct entrants upon Oxford and Cambridge liberal arts graduates. There are special reasons for this, notably that, traditionally, many such graduates look to the Administrative Class for their career and they are often successful candidates because the particular strength of the older English universities, both in terms of numbers and of talent, lies in such subjects: but one of the main factors is that, despite reforms in the recruitment process, the ideal remains that of the 'general purpose all-rounder'. Oxford and Cambridge, particularly the former, have made the production of the 'professional amateur' their special contribution to the Government of this country, and much in the Administrative Class, from the carefully balanced minutes of the Assistant Principal to the maze of inter-departmental committees, perennially looking for the workable compromise, bears this hallmark. One even recalls Lord Bridges bewailing the fact that the Service was 'unfortunately lacking' in 'those expressions of a corporate life found in a College' because it had 'neither hall nor chapel neither combination room nor common room'.[1] The Service certainly needs an *élite*, but not necessarily one of this particular orientation and, to the extent that it should be drawn from the generalist side of the Service, the revised structure outlined above may help to provide a more relevant type of administrator. One believes that the prospect of a more specialised type of career will not deter the better Oxford and Cambridge graduates, in much the same way as one believes that it will prove more attractive than the present general career to the leading graduates of the other universities. As to the methods of recruitment, given the eventual considerable increase in the numbers of graduates, Method II would seem destined to become still more important, particularly now that further steps have been taken in the direction of continuous competition. One implication of the remodelled structure for this Method, following from the abandonment of the idea that administration is homogeneous, would be the need for a deeper and wider probing for job aptitudes at the C.S.S.B. tests. As to

[1] Sir Edward Bridges, *Portrait of a Profession* (1950) p. 32.

the future of Method I, the Acton Society Trust, in their evidence
to the Fulton Committee, have advocated its abolition because
this would 'go some way to remove the ingrained impression that
the only way to enter the Administrative Class is to re-sit Finals'.[1]
Merely to abolish Method I would not necessarily correct an
'impression' that is at least twenty years out of date. Professor
Crick and Mr W. Thornhill, of the University of Sheffield, in
their evidence said of Method I: 'this type of competition has
both a deterrent effect on potentially good applicants (there are
so many other rewarding occupations which attract them and
which do not impose such an obstacle) and a class bias of its own'.[2]
Compared with Method II, which Professor Crick and Mr
Thornhill favour, Method I has the advantage that, without
suggesting that the Service is particularly guilty of such bias, it
provides a means of entry in which the opportunities for social
prejudice are severely restricted because success in it is less dependent upon interview marks. However, Method I's existence
can only be justified so long as it still attracts substantial numbers
of entrants and, because the most recently available statistics
suggest that, compared with Method II, the diminution in its
appeal to candidates continues,[3] its eventual retention must be in
doubt. At present, it can be said that the considerable increase in
graduate recruitment which should follow the creation of a merged
Executive–Administrative Class on the above lines would, as the
Treasury observed about its proposed 'new management structure',
probably cause 'problems in evolving a workable selection procedure',[4] and that these will probably be resolved by developing,
and eventually coming to place reliance on, a form of the existing
Method II.

The question of whether or not some of the direct entrants to

---

[1] *Statement of Evidence submitted by the Acton Society Trust to the Fulton Committee on the Civil Service* (1966) para. 30.

[2] *Memorandum on Recruitment and Training from Professor B. R. Crick and Mr W. Thornhill of the University of Sheffield presented to the Fulton Committee on the Civil Service* (1966) para. 23.

[3] *100th Report of the Civil Service Commissioners*, p. 9.

[4] H.M. Treasury, 'The Future Structure of the Civil Service', a note submitted to the *Fulton Committee on the Civil Service* (1966) para. 8.

the amalgamated Executive–Administrative Class should receive some sort of preferential placing must be faced. Although they recognised that, without 'some change' in the structure of its generalist side, the Civil Service would have great difficulty in attracting a 'bigger share of the young people who receive full time higher education',[1] and although they proposed that all graduate recruits to their suggested 'general management group' should enter at Grade VIII level, as we have seen, the Treasury wanted the equivalent of the present Assistant Principal intake to be 'starred' entrants to that grade. The Treasury attempted to justify this by saying: 'It must be made clear to the most able young men and women that the Service wanted them and that they would have a career from the start no less attractive than is offered now.'[2] The First Division Association have, however, said that they did not believe that

> the Treasury's proposals will improve recruitment either for Assistant Principals or other graduates; indeed we think there is a real risk that the suggested variants of Grade VIII entry (to use the Treasury's terminology for the new Management group) would discourage recruitment of both. The Treasury seek to encourage the recruitment of the ablest graduates by offering them 'starred Grade VIII' posts with training and experience comparable with that of today's Assistant Principals and quick promotion up to Grade V. Many of our Assistant Principal members, i.e., those who have most recently joined the Civil Service, assure us that they would not have been interested in joining under these conditions. They saw a real incentive in seeking to join what they regarded as an élite, with prospects of interesting and demanding work at a fairly early age on promotion to Principal, and of further increases in responsibility, for those who proved themselves, through further promotion. In view of the twenty-five per cent shortfall in Assistant Principal recruitment over the 1956–65 period the Civil Service cannot afford to reduce the attraction of the Service to the most able of University graduates. The Treasury proposals purport to offer the substance of the present Assistant Principal career but in a way which it will be difficult to present to these graduates. They will see only a lowering of the graduate entry standards and, in place of membership of an élite, a vague promise of preferential treatment. If the 'starred'

---

[1] Ibid. para. 3.   [2] Ibid. para. 8.

graduates are well chosen, 'non-starred' graduates will soon realise
that, for all the appearance of equality, they are being offered an
inferior career; on the other hand, if 'starred' graduates are badly
selected and consequently diverted into the 'non-starred' stream,
the better graduate will soon get the impression that a star does
not carry the promised guarantee. We believe that it would be
better to retain two distinct methods of graduate entry by
different competitions, thereby avoiding any illwill which might
be caused in the Service by giving certain Grade VIII staff
special treatment. The people at present brought in as Assistant
Principals might, in future, be brought in at Grade VII with
prospects of promotion to Grade V no later than is normal today.
This is similar to what is done in the Diplomatic Service.[1]

The major problem of recruitment on the generalist side of the
Home Civil Service is how to make it more attractive to more
graduates. Under the arrangements favoured by the F.D.A. and
the Treasury, those graduates who are not made Assistant Principals, their equivalent, or 'starred' entrants, still seem 'unlikely to
be willing to begin a career as second class entrants'.[2] As the
Society of Civil Servants has observed, the implementation of
the Treasury's proposals for 'starring' graduates at the selection
stage 'would inevitably result in the new management grades
structure being regarded by the great majority of graduates as
merely a façade behind which the existing system would be perpetuated'; and one agrees with their conclusion that if the Fulton
Committee decides to

> recommend the amalgamation of the Administrative and Executive
> Classes into a single structure, it is essential that this should be
> seen from the outset to be a unified entity within which individuals
> will have an equal opportunity to progress on the basis of their
> merits. The selection of those whose ability justifies the accelerated
> advancement which will be necessary within a combined structure
> if the more senior posts are to be filled at an appropriate age
> should be made on the basis of criteria which go both under and

---

[1] *Evidence presented by the First Division Association to the Fulton
Committee on the Civil Service* (1966) para. 9.

[2] *Evidence presented by Dr Arthur F. Earle, Principal of the London
Graduate School of Business Studies, to the Fulton Committee on the
Civil Service* (1966) para. 10.

deeper than those envisaged by the Treasury based as these are solely upon academic record and performance at initial selection tests.

The society emphasised that it considered it 'essential that this selection process should only take place when all entrants to the management grades structure, graduates and non-graduates alike, have been able to demonstrate their abilities by their actual performance of Civil Service duties'.[1] Despite what the F.D.A. say, it is hard to believe that the sort of graduates who at present come into the Service as Assistant Principals would not still be attracted by a genuine merged Executive–Administrative Class. The range of alternative careers open to such graduates is not all that wide, and in few of the alternative careers would they receive a 'promised guarantee' of preferential treatment for future promotion, while, with Civil Service pay based on 'fair comparisons' with outside salaries in comparable jobs, the entrant to the Service could expect, except at the very top, much the same financial rewards as he would receive outside its ranks. The Home Civil Service will still have many important leading posts to offer, and, as now, a great deal of interesting work to be done. The sort of graduates who now come in as Assistant Principals will have no need to assume that promotion will be slower than at present, but only that they will have more competition to face in seeking it. It is difficult to believe that the right sort of graduate will not have sufficient faith in himself to believe that he will not be successful in the promotion race. In my view the designation of those deserving of accelerated promotion should not be made during the selection process, as the Treasury and the F.D.A. favour, and it ought not to take place, as the Labour Party suggested, after a period of common training for all entrants:[2] it should be a function of personnel management within the Civil Service.

While one agrees with the Liberal Party in approving the widespread recognition of the fact that 'the Universities rather than school leavers must be increasingly looked to to supply what has

---

[1] *Supplementary Evidence presented by the Society of Civil Servants to the Fulton Committee on the Civil Service* (1966–7) paras 3 and 5.

[2] *Evidence presented by the Labour Party to the Fulton Committee on the Civil Service* (1967) para. 82.

hitherto been the Executive Class',[1] however successful the new structure is in attracting more graduate entrants of the right quality, even from previously barren sources, still greater efforts will have to be made to locate talent in early career in what is now the Executive Class. As the Society of Civil Servants stated: 'It should be policy to make a more positive search for talent within the Civil Service and to develop and use it fully.'[2] Promotion from below is almost a virtue in itself in some eyes, while others see it as a means of keeping the Service 'sweet', which it may do,[3] but its real justification is on the grounds of efficiency not sentiment – it is needed because of the lasting imperfection of the educational system, and the fact that formal educational qualifications do not invariably indicate administrative capacity. The depressing results of the Limited Administrative Examination perhaps suggest that the chances of securing potentially outstanding administrators in the Executive Class, as it is now recruited, are considerably less favourable than they would have been at the time of the MacDonnell or Tomlin Commissions. Nevertheless, the desire of some young men to 'earn their living' almost at once after leaving school at eighteen and the probably irreversible trend towards early marriage provide two factors that may lead to the

[1] *Evidence presented by the Liberal Party to the Fulton Committee on the Civil Service* (1966) para. 4.

[2] *Evidence presented by the Society of Civil Servants to the Fulton Committee on the Civil Service* (1966) para. 23.

[3] Sir Stanley Leathes suggested this in his evidence to the Tomlin Commission (question 22,332). It may, of course, keep the Service 'sour' in some respects. The Civil Service Commissioners certainly place more emphasis than their private competitors on 'promotion prospects', which is wise up to a point. But, when it is remembered that the direct entrants to the three leading generalist classes can, on the average, only look forward to two promotions during a career of perhaps forty years (namely, C.O. to H.E.O., E.O. to S.E.O. and A.P. to A.S.), particularly in the case of the two lower classes, it can be a formula for frustration. Promotion comes to be looked on as a right, and the disappointment felt when failing to achieve success even in the difficult limited administrative competition is sometimes out of all proportion to the supposed 'failure'. One of the reasons why I later advocate the untying of the pension scheme is to allow movement out of the Service. I also do not see why the non-industrial Civil Service should be exempt from redundancy as it wrongly is at present.

Service's continuing to attract some very talented youngsters into its ranks. It should be possible for the Service to institute, even on a small scale, at least at first, some sort of Civil Service Scholarship scheme, perhaps on a 'sandwich' basis, whereby serving Civil Servants of talent would have the opportunity of having a university education on full salary. One envisages them dividing a typical year by spending, say, six months at the university and, allowing for annual leave, dividing the remainder of the year between practical work in their departments and private study on their books. The choice of subjects read at the university would have to be restricted in favour of degrees offering either the most valuable background to a Civil Service career, notably the social sciences, or those that include management skills, for example, statistics. The Civil Service Scholars, who would presumably be selected centrally from candidates nominated by departments, would not necessarily subsequently secure swifter advancement than their contemporaries, but they would at least be able to compete with graduate direct entrants on more equal terms. In any case, normal promotion procedures in what are now the three lowest tiers of the Executive Class must be given less of a time-serving emphasis than at present. The restrictive promotion 'fields' in some departments seem almost designed to protect the interests of the mediocre: they need to be drastically amended to make possible swifter advancement for the young men and women of talent. One of the leading aims of the sort of merged Executive–Administrative Class outlined above should be to offer as little as possible to the routineer and the time-server, and to instil a much needed competitive atmosphere into the executive part of the amalgamated hierarchy.

Much depends, of course, on improving what has traditionally been one of the weakest features of the generalist side of the Service – post-entry training. Until very recently, the Service was dominated in this sphere by the 'do-it-yourself' code of 'learning by doing', and this was nowhere more evident than in the ranks of the Administrative Class. Running through this approach was the belief that 'the one qualification essential to the high official' was 'complete familiarity with the working of the machine of government',[1] a familiarity which could only be gained by practical experience and not formal tuition. Few opponents of the 'do-it-yourself' code, however, seriously suggested that training courses could be a complete substitute for practical experience, but what they did doubt was the need to place an exclusive reliance on such an apprenticeship. The establishment of the Centre for Administrative Studies in 1963 represented a move away from the tradition that young administrators should be 'inducted rather than trained',[2] in the direction of the French system, under which both direct entrants and promotees receive the most relevant general education open to the administrator, an education in the social sciences, during a two-and-a-half-year course at the *École Nationale d'Administration*. The aims of the Centre for Administrative Studies were less ambitious: for, besides a brief course in the basic concepts of science given at the Royal Institution in their second year, the Assistant Principals only received a three-week introductory course in the structure of government, together with a twenty-week course concentrating on economics and statistical and mathematical techniques for administration, given in their third year of service. Moreover, even promotees from the Executive Class, the majority of whom have never had a university education of any kind, let alone any instruction in either economics or management skills, did not benefit from these arrangements. Even though the recommendations of the Osmond Committee, which reported in 1964, opened up the prospect of an improvement, the provisions for post-entry training in the Executive Class remained inadequate in relation to the often complex tasks accorded to its members. Even as regards direct entrants to the Administrative Class, it could be doubted if the courses given at the Centre for Administrative Studies were either long enough or extensive enough in their scope, while they also did not provide instruction in the most widely used departmental specialisms. The need was for a much wider approach to post-entry training on the generalist side of the Service, to be signified by the establishment of a Civil Service Staff College or similar institution, preferably not limited

[1] H. E. Dale, *The Higher Civil Service of Great Britain* (1941) p. 219.
[2] C. H. Sisson, *The Spirit of British Administration* (1959) p. 34.

to Civil Servants, and not necessarily aiming to cover the whole field, but which would complement the existing arrangements and serve as a focal point for the professionalisation of the Civil Service.

The major piece of evidence presented to the Fulton Committee about post-entry training was the findings of the Treasury Working Party on Management Training in the Civil Service, which reported in 1967 after having been asked: 'To consider the training needs for middle and higher management in the Civil Service and to submit recommendations on the length, content and organisation of such training, taking account of the long-term future of the Centre for Administrative Studies and the desirability or otherwise of setting up a Civil Service Staff College'.[1] The Working Party made their recommendations on the assumption that some sort of merged Executive–Administrative Class would be created and, after commenting that the present system of early management training was a two-tier system, they observed:

> In principle it does not seem objectionable that an organisation should invest more heavily in the management training of staff who show promise of reaching high posts than in the training of other staff who show less promise. Our criticisms are directed at two features of the present system. Firstly, that neither the longer Centre for Administrative Studies tier nor the shorter departmental tier provide courses of sufficient length to cover in the required depth the full range of subjects relevant to management training in the Public Service. Secondly, that selection for the longer training is determined solely by method of entry to the Service – the courses at the Centre are limited to Assistant Principals.[2]

The Working Party's own plan retained a two-tier basis, but both tiers would provide much more training than at present: 'For middle management, a total of twelve weeks' central training would be provided: for higher management, training lasting about one

[1] H.M. Treasury, *Management Training in the Civil Service. Report of a Working Party* (1967) para. 2.

[2] Ibid. paras 32 and 34. The Working Party made it clear that, because of such factors as late entry recruitment all references 'to the ages at which courses should be taken must be regarded as approximate' (para. 33).

year. Selection for both levels of training would be based on ability rather than on method of entry. And staff would have more than one opportunity to qualify for the longer training during their early years of service.'[1] The Working Party proposed that up to the age of thirty, training arrangements for Civil Servants should be based on two pairs of courses: a four-week and an eight-week course for a substantial number of staff and two twenty-week courses for a smaller number of selected staff.[2] The Working Party recommended: 'central management training should start with a four-week Introduction to Management Course, to be taken at about the age of twenty-five by the whole of the graduate entry and by all who had joined at the age of eighteen unless at this stage their departmental performance had proved unsatisfactory'.[3] The course would be attended by about 1500 general management entrants about 100 of whom go on almost immediately to the first of the twenty-week courses described below:

> Selection of the group of staff regarded as having the greatest potential for higher management would need to be based on departmental assessments of their work. But we consider that the 4-week course could be designed and directed in such a way as to enable reports on the performance and aptitudes of those attending to be submitted to departments to help them in their task of selection. The content of the 4-week course would include a substantial section on the management of a small branch and would be based on practical exercises involving the member of the course in an analysis of problems and in the organisation of work both as an individual and as leader of a small group. The other major section of the course would be on handling quantitative data including an introduction to elementary statistics and to automatic data processing.[4]

All those members of the staff who 'seemed likely to reach middle management posts (i.e., the present Chief Executive Officer level) would take a further eight-week course some five years later, with the exception of the much smaller numbers of staff who showed promise of reaching higher management posts (Assistant Secretary

[1] Ibid. para. 37. [2] Ibid. paras 35, 36 and 47.
[3] Ibid. para. 35. [4] Ibid. paras 39–41.

level and above), who would attend two twenty-week courses separated by an interval of several years'.[1] The eight-week Middle Management Course

> would provide a second opportunity for staff to establish, on the basis of a further series of departmental reports on work and in the light of their performance on this Course, their claims to be selected for a long 20-week course and, on its satisfactory completion, regarded as eligible for accelerated promotion. Those recognised as outstanding at this stage would probably attend the second of the 20-week courses. But if it seemed more appropriate to the career development of the person concerned, a one-year course at one of the Business Schools might be taken as an alternative.[2]

The Working Party said:

> The content of the 8-week Course would include a section on management decisions in the public sector with a study of the allocation of resources and the concept of opportunity cost. The Course would also have a short introduction to decision theory. The preparation and analysis of quantitative data and automatic data processing would be developed in more depth than in the 4-week Course. There would be a section on staff development and on organisation. On 'environment' the Course would cover the economic and social systems, and the structure and operation of industry and commerce.[3]

The Working Party recommended that 'the training in their twenties of staff selected as likely to reach higher management posts should last forty weeks and be divided into two sections each

[1] Ibid. para. 36. [2] Ibid. para. 42.
[3] Ibid. para. 43. The Working Party observed: 'This plan of management training of twelve weeks, rests on the assumption that in any future structure of the Civil Service specialisation would not be so complete or so extensive as to rule out the value of some general training being provided for middle management. But it is also true that our proposals do not rule out a somewhat greater degree of specialisation than at present. Such specialisation might not take the form of being more fully trained and employed for somewhat longer periods than at present on work such as A.D.P., or organisation and methods. It may also take the form of assisting in complex policy or financial work at headquarters. Specialised courses to provide the training needed could be provided externally, or centrally by the Treasury, or within departments.' (para. 44.)

of about twenty weeks'.[1] The first of these courses would be taken
at about the age of twenty-five, and after the successful completion
of the probationary period during which the Working Party
wanted to see the existing system of 'training at the desk', supplemented wherever possible by a regional or out-station assignment,
retained. They said: 'Such assignments, which might usefully
include a period on work involving direct contact with the public,
are already a feature of training in some Ministries and should
in our view form part of the early training in all departments
with regional or local offices and young Civil Servants in many
other departments would benefit from them.'[2] The Working
Party envisaged:

> the first 20-week course should have the same content as the
> present course at the Centre. We are satisfied that the subjects
> studied are relevant to Civil Servants in all departments, for even
> those who spend all their working lives in a department or depart-
> ments with few 'economic' responsibilities can hardly operate
> effectively today without understanding the contribution which
> economics and related disciplines make to the allocation of scarce
> resources, or without understanding the macro-economic environ-
> ment within which all Government departments operate.

The Working Party suggested:

> there should be some flexibility in the timing of the second of the
> 20-week courses, but that normally the graduate selected for quick
> promotion would serve for a period of two or three years in one or
> two jobs before taking the first and taking the second courses,
> and that one of these jobs might be in a private office. The average
> age might, therefore, be about twenty-eight and length of service
> about four to six years, a stage in career corresponding to the time
> when today's direct entry Assistant Principals are promoted to
> Principal.[3]

The Working Party did not consider, however:

> it would be useful, or possible to try to define in great detail the
> syllabus of the second 20-week course. But we envisage that about
> half the time would be spent on general studies taken by all

---

[1] Ibid. para. 47.

[2] Ibid. para. 48. The statement that this first course 'would be taken
at about the age of 25' was made on p. 24 of the Working Party's Report.

[3] Ibid. para. 51.

attending the course, while the remaining half of the time might be more specialised. We envisage the general part including the study in depth of a number of aspects of Government and Public Administration, an introduction to social administration, the study of organisation and management problems, and a section on scientific and technological developments. In suggesting that the remaining half of the time, i.e., about ten weeks, on the second course might be more specialised, we recognise that this recommendation must be related to the future structure of the Civil Service and that the precise form of specialisation would need to be consistent with future policy on staff management in Government departments.[1]

In turning to management training in mid-career and later, the Working Party said:

Although our recommendations give more weight to management training before the age of 30 than has been given in the past by the Civil Service we do so primarily because it seems to us that the best results will be obtained when staff are at an age to benefit from rigorous and intensive training with the maximum use of practical work. But we certainly do not see training as a once-and-for-all process which will be completed, or nearly completed, by that age.[2]

The Working Party emphasised that training for management for staff between thirty and forty must be flexible:

We do not envisage any central Civil Service courses for staff in this age group who have had their appropriate share of management training at an earlier age. We suggest that training in the middle years of service should be related primarily to the career development of the individual in relation to the needs of the jobs to which he is posted. Absence from official duty for a few weeks during which an officer can carry out some study in depth of the background to a job to which he has recently been posted can have most beneficial results. In certain cases this form of training might be of no less importance than general management training. We envisage that more Civil Servants in their middle or late thirties would attend one of the new Business Schools or the Administrative Staff College. Courses of similar quality might in time be developed in other subjects by Universities or research institutions on the lines of those being started in 1967 at the Institute of

---

[1] Ibid. paras 53–4.   [2] Ibid. para. 62.

Development Studies associated with the University of Sussex. These courses might be attended by staff from certain Government departments. Staff in Defence departments would, as now, be eligible for courses at the Services Staff Colleges.[1]

The Working Party also saw this as being 'the period when, if it proves practicable to organise exchanges of staff between the Civil Service and industry, some most valuable widening of experience for Civil Servants would be achieved'. They saw this as possibly being supplemented by a development of the existing Public Service/Private Enterprise courses which have so far affected only a small number of staff each year. Because similar ideas are being discussed in Local Government: 'It might well prove that arrangements for the advanced training of senior Civil Servants could include representatives from Local Government as well as from private enterprise.'[2] If management training was developed on the lines that they recommended, the Working Party believed:

> The main need for staff over the age of forty will be to keep in touch with new developments and have opportunities to study problems with Civil Servants from other departments and with people in other occupations. Short residential seminars, organised centrally by the Civil Service but with some members drawn from outside, could meet part of this need. Seminars on the lines of those now organised by the British Institute of Management would also be available.[3]

For the purposes of management training, the Working Party did not recommend

> any widespread extension of sabbatical leave, at least in its present form in which it is associated with the award of one of the recognised Fellowships and normally lasts a full year. These now serve a valuable purpose but we doubt whether enough applicants of the right quality would be forthcoming to justify a considerable expansion. From the point of view of the best use of limited resources of staff time, it seems to us that sabbatical absences of one year may be less valuable than shorter periods of study leave for a larger number of people.[4]

---

[1] Ibid. paras 63–4.   [2] Ibid. paras 65–6.

[3] Ibid. para. 67.   [4] Ibid. para. 68.

The Working Party also recommended:

> any development of management training in the Civil Service should be based on a far more extensive research programme than at present. Some of this research might be carried out by academic staff but some could be undertaken by Civil Servants released for short periods of, say, three or four months. Although some of this research would have as its primary need the analysis of a problem confronting a Government department, some would be commissioned to provide material on which management training, perhaps through case studies based on actual situations, could be developed. Although these research assignments could not be described as sabbatical leave in the present sense, we believe that they would serve to refresh staff given this change of scene and freedom from pressures of day-to-day work much as do longer periods of sabbatical leave.[1]

After making provisions for staff in mid-career when the training plan was implemented,[2] the Working Party turned to the organisation of their new training plan, in devising which they said:

> we have considered the balance between departmental and central Civil Service training, between internal and external courses such as those at Business Schools or Universities, between courses attended only by Civil Servants and those attended also by people from other occupations and between non-residential and residential training. We believe that a plan for Civil Service management training can and should give the Civil Servant, at various stages of his career, the different advantages of departmental courses, central training and of external courses where he will mix with people from outside the Civil Service.[3]

---

[1] Ibid. para. 69.

[2] Ibid. para. 70. The Working Party said that it considered 'that it would be impracticable to try to apply the new plan retrospectively to staff who had already passed the ages at which the various courses would be taken. But to avoid too great a gap between the training of different generations of Civil Servants, a modified training plan would be needed for such staff for some years. The 20-week course at the Centre for Administrative Studies will have filled part of the need for some who have joined the Service since 1961. Some of the four short management courses, providing in all ten to twelve weeks' training, which the Treasury started in the autumn of 1966, will supplement the training of this group and provide a basic introduction to management training for older staff from all Classes. These will also be eligible for Business School courses and for seminars for senior staff.'

[3] Ibid. para. 72.

About departmental training the Working Party said that it could be

> most valuable, particularly in the larger departments, in bringing together members of the staff who might otherwise have little contact and in enabling the material used on the course to be closely related to the work of the department. The relationship of the new central training plan to departmental training schemes would have to be examined. But we envisage that in the new plan departmental training would be responsible generally for induction training and, apart from the vocational and specialist training of a type which some carry out at present on a large scale, all major departments should develop specialised management courses in particular directions. We believe that this would give departmental training organisations a substantial volume of important work. The smaller departments may need to form themselves into groups for training purposes to organise both the induction and specialised management courses.[1]

The Working Party saw

> the main role for a central Civil Service training organisation in the planning and direction of the management courses which we recommend should be taken by certain staff in their twenties – the two 20-week courses and the 4- and 8-week management courses. At this stage in the career of the Civil Servant we see advantages in the training being provided centrally within the Civil Service, thus bringing together staff from all parts of the service and using case material from the departments. We also see a central Civil Service organisation keeping under review policy on Civil Service training for staff in mid-career and later. But we envisage that, for much of the actual work of training at these later ages, University and Business School courses would be used.

Detailed arrangements for such management training were seen as being the responsibility of the department – to use these external courses to best advantage for the career development of the man in relation to the posts which he is given and to keep the balance right between formal courses and such arrangements as sabbatical leave or research secondments.[2] The Working Party said: 'For older staff over the age of forty the Civil Service would need to run some seminars to inform them of new developments, bringing

[1] Ibid. para. 73.   [2] Ibid. paras 74–5.

in members of the seminar from outside the Civil Service if appropriate. Other seminars would be brought to the attention of Civil Servants when organised by outside bodies like the British Institute of Management or by Universities.'[1]

The Working Party recommended:

the direction of the new plan and the organisation of the two 20-week courses and the 4- and 8-week courses should be developed out of the present Centre for Administrative Studies since all the evidence shows there is merit in the system developed at the Centre for organising very intensive courses which call on teachers of repute from many Universities, Civil Servants from Government departments, and businessmen to combine in taking sessions.[2]

Among the reasons advanced by the Working Party in favour of unified planning and direction of this group of courses was that

the two pairs of courses will cover much the same subjects although the longer pair of courses will naturally be in greater depth. We believe that some of the lessons learned on one course and some of the case material used may well prove appropriate for other courses. And since the courses form part of a single plan and almost everyone who will attend the first of the 20-week courses will shortly before have attended the 4-week 'Introduction to Management' courses, we think it most important that the courses be planned in such a way that no overlapping or omission of essential aspects of a subject occur.[3]

Taking into account these courses and the other arrangements proposed, the Working Party then considered 'whether courses on this scale could best be organised in one place or in more than one place and whether they should be non-residential or at a new residential establishment'. The Working Party observed:

The Centre for Administrative Studies seems to have operated well on a non-residential basis and both the directing staff and those attending the courses believe that there are great advantages in their present quiet location, close to, but not in, the centre of London and with good communications to Whitehall and all the main rail termini. As against this, residential training offers the opportunity of creating a group with team spirit out of individuals drawn from different backgrounds, occupations and parts of the

---

[1] Ibid. para. 76.   [2] Ibid. para. 77.   [3] Ibid. para. 78.

F.S.D.

country. The need for this may be greater on the new management courses than for those now attending the Centre for Administrative Studies who are from the start a fairly homogeneous group.[1]

The Working Party considered:

> there are advantages both in a London centre like the present Centre for Administrative Studies and in a residential establishment which could be out of London, although not so far away that it would not be within convenient reach of the centre of Government. Bearing in mind the substantial scale of training recommended in the new plan, we believe that it may be possible to enjoy the advantages of both types of establishment by dividing the training between a non-residential London centre developed from the present Centre and a residential establishment, which might perhaps be associated with one of the new Universities.[2]

The Working Party were inclined to favour a division between the two centres being made

> on a functional basis with the London Centre specialising in the particular fields in which the Centre for Administrative Studies has acquired experience – economics, economic statistics, decision theory and industry – while the residential centre specialised in the study of Government, social administration and statistics, organisation and staff management. Under this system, the course would divide their time between the two centres according to the subjects under study.[3]

But on whatever basis the courses for staff up to the age of thirty were allocated to the centres, the Working Party envisaged that 'all the short seminars for senior staff would be held at the residential centre which would also house most of research activities which we regard as an important element in the plan. It is for this reason that we suggest that a location associated with one of the new Universities might be particularly appropriate for the residential centre.'[4] The Working Party concluded:

> The new establishment would need a name. We doubt whether the title 'Civil Service Staff College' would be appropriate to the organisation which we recommend should be established with

---

[1] Ibid. paras 81–2   [2] Ibid. para. 84.
[3] Ibid. para. 87.   [4] Ibid. para. 88.

both non-residential and residential parts. It will be fulfilling a different role from that of a conventional staff college and a title emphasising its Management Training responsibilities for the Civil Service would be preferable.[1]

So the Treasury Working Party have recommended to the Fulton Committee 'the development of the existing central management of Treasury training courses in the form of an organisation which, even though perhaps under another name, will give the Civil Service a Staff College, which many have advocated over the last twenty or twenty-five years'.[2] One can add, however, that those who have proposed the establishment of a Civil Service Staff College during that period have not necessarily envisaged its establishment in the form suggested by the Working Party, and a useful comparison can be made between their scheme and that advanced by the Labour Party in their evidence to the Fulton Committee. The Labour Party wanted to see all graduate entrants to the generalist side of the Civil Service given 'a common course of training at a greatly expanded C.A.S. which should have the size and status of a Graduate School of Government'. The Labour Party said that, 'It might even be sensible to develop the Centre primarily as a Graduate School with the mere possibility of recruiting its students into the Government Service'.[3] They recognised that this would 'require a major expansion and will be quite a costly operation, both in terms of money and initially, at least, in manpower, but it can both increase the supply and improve the quality of administrators at all levels in the Service, and should therefore be done'. They recognised also that there would be wastage, although the initial numbers accepted for the course were to be high enough to allow for this. The Labour Party observed that, 'In any case because of existing shortages in the Service, a higher rate of recruitment is desirable, and with the more open Service we should welcome an overspill of well trained people into outside employment. The School would be an important part of administrative/industrial training and we should

---

[1] Ibid. para. 89.   [2] Ibid. para. 96.
[3] *Evidence presented by the Labour Party to the Fulton Committee on the Civil Service* (1967) para. 83.

regard any product of it as a worthwhile investment'.[1] The Labour Party said:

> One of the criticisms of the present system that has most impressed us is the frustration felt by Assistant Principals, both because the main Centre for Administrative Studies training course is delayed until the third year, and because they often feel that they must wait for anything up to seven years before they are entrusted with any responsibility. We feel the present training period would be much better spent in the following fashion. Two years at the Centre of Administrative Studies, a period of two/three years in the department, and a period at a regional centre. Time spent in the regions would vary and we suppose that some might be promoted there; others might return to London on being promoted.[2]

Although they did not go into the details of the curriculum, the Labour Party said of the period of formal post-entry training:

> The course should be designed to last about two years. It should cover the ground at present covered by the C.A.S. courses: the three-week course on the structure of Government; the ten half days on modern science; and the twenty-week course now usually taken in the third year in service. There would, of course, be considerable scope for expanding the syllabus covered by these courses and filling the gaps in them, which are caused, presumably, by the restricted time available at present. A course on the social sciences is, perhaps, the most obvious unfilled need. The course should also include a period in the departments; in local government, if it can be arranged; and a period in industry. It might also be possible to arrange this on a transfer basis. Trainees from the C.A.S. might change places for a time with management trainees in industry to their mutual benefit. We would also recommend to the Committee the suggestion made by the Fabian Society that work in the School should stress the new function of the Civil Service in planning ahead the development not only of the economy but the social structure generally. It would encourage in students constructive thinking on the forward planning of transport, housing, the social services, and so on.[3]

The Labour Party acknowledged:

> In making these suggestions we have naturally been greatly influenced by the success of the French *École Nationale d'Administration*. But we would not want the parallel to be taken too far. There are obvious differences between the two countries

---

[1] Ibid. paras 84–5.   [2] Ibid. paras 91–2.   [3] Ibid. paras 87–9.

which in any case prevent this – we have no equivalent to the provincial 'prefect' and so the nature of the practical training must clearly be different. We feel that it is essentially in its scale that we would wish to recommend the E.N.A.[1]

As the Labour Party say, what is really wanted is a British version of the E.N.A. One can express general agreement with the Treasury Working Party's proposals about management training in mid-career or later: but their recommendations about initial post-entry training are not ambitious enough. The weakness is in the restrictive nature of the Working Party's proposals. The merging of the Administrative and Executive Classes is being proposed because the great increase in the number and variety of governmental jobs which require managerial ability has both destroyed the coherence of the existing system of classes and also necessitated increases in the supply and the skills of managers. It is to be expected that the performance of the new managers will be enhanced by training and it seems likely that the most useful form of training will be intensive instruction on entry. Such obvious professionalisation will have the additional virtue of making the new class attractive to the university graduates for whom it is being designed. The Working Party's recommendations on the one hand do not suggest anything like this for the ordinary graduate entrant, and on the other, by proposing special treatment for a favoured few, effectively downgrade what they do suggest. At the stage of entry there seems no reason why the training provided should not be provided for all. It seems important, moreover, that it should be a thorough training.

As far as the entrants to the generalist side of the Service are concerned, the relevant arrangements could take something like the following general form. All those declared successful in the graduate competition for entry to the Executive–Administrative Class would face the prospect of about two and a half years' training

[1] Ibid. para. 90. The Labour Party added: 'We would not wish to see the C.A.S. entry as restricted or as socially biassed as E.N.A.'s appears to be. We have also noted some criticism of its syllabus, e.g. the weight given to the study of administrative law; and its tendency towards inbreeding. A high proportion of the tutors it is suggested are now *anciens* of the School.'

to be begun immediately after entry. The first nine months would consist of a common course for all entrants given at the Staff College. As much as half of this common course should be devoted to detailed study of the conduct of public administration – the environment in which those successful at the Staff College will, at least at that stage, be hoping to spend much if not all of their working lives. It will be objected that this sort of knowledge can be 'picked up' by entrants as they go along. But this sort of 'learning process' is hardly efficient. The entrants should be taught in considerable detail about the functions of all the government departments, so that they know about their main divisions and branches and what they do and, where applicable, about their regional and/or local office systems. This part of the course should also include instruction in that part of parliamentary procedure which can be formally taught: all entrants must be aware of how the House of Commons works, but not everyone will have the opportunity of learning this during a spell in the private office. This part of the course will also have to include a detailed study of the functions of the local authorities and of the public corporations. Besides this instruction in public administration, entrants would also face courses along the lines of those given at, or in association with, the present Centre for Administrative Studies, similarly aimed at giving them a sound grounding in such subjects as economics, statistics and elementary management techniques. At the end of this first nine-month course there should be an examination, and those who fail to reach the required standard should be invited to retire from the Service. Of course, much will be made by critics about the wastage that this will entail – economy, it seems, being the main reason for the Treasury's timing of the existing C.A.S. course at the Assistant Principals' probationary period of service. But better wastage at this point than in later career, which can be much more expensive to the Service: at least those who go on will have a much better idea of what lies ahead than at present.

The second part of the course should consist of one year of practical experience. The first six months of this should be spent working closely with a Principal in the headquarters of a central government department, devilling for him. It will be objected that this is what Assistant Principals do now anyway, but the present arrangements tend to be haphazard and one envisages a much closer supervision of the graduate entrant's work than is often now the case. The second six months should be spent in either a regional office or a local office of a central government department, or in a local authority, or in a nationalised industry, or in private industry or commerce. In each case the graduate entrant – or, as he might be called, the administrative cadet – should be doing a specific job. There might be some difficulties in making arrangements outside central Government. But one would hope that places could be found for young administrators to work, say, as assistants in Town Clerks' offices, particularly the larger offices. These public and private organisations should recognise the benefit of having this contact with the Civil Service, and it should not be impossible to make suitable permanent arrangements with a number of the larger organisations. At the end of the year reports about the entrants should be made by those who have supervised them: these should be open reports and will give an opportunity of reviewing their progress.

At this point those administrative cadets who have successfully survived the two hurdles of the examination and the report stage would be assigned to a group of departments on the basis of their performance at the Staff College and their own preferences: some attempt would presumably be made in the original selection process by which the administrative cadets had entered the Service to ascertain job aptitudes – in so far as personnel selection procedures as at present developed allow – but allocation to departments, or initially, groups of departments, under the system outlined here would become a function of training. The administrative cadets would then embark upon the last stage of the training course. All cadets would receive a common course developing their knowledge of management techniques, statistics and economics – in the case of economics to the stage where all cadets should be able to discuss the British economy at a professional level. The remainder of the course would be divided into specialisms: for example, those destined for careers in the Ministries administering the social services would have intensive courses in sociology and social statistics as well as social administration. Those assigned to other specialisms would be similarly committed to relevant specialised studies. At the end of this second nine-month course, a further examination would form part of a general final assessment of the administrative cadets and they would then proceed to posts in those departments for the duties in which they had been trained.

The Labour Party's scheme's specific proposal about training seemed to envisage only graduate entrants taking an E.N.A. style course: but if the merged Executive–Administrative Class is to be a reality, and not the fiction of something like the Treasury's 'new management structure', then its non-graduate members must be given a real chance in the competition for advancement that they will face from their formally better educated colleagues. This must mean that the G.C.E. Advanced Level entrants, and those who have achieved a swift escape from the Clerical Class into the Executive Officer grade, should also become administrative cadets and receive the same course of training. They will be well versed in routine, but they will still need a thorough grounding in public administration, and they will certainly need the academic studies. The later promotee from the Clerical Class would present a problem. No doubt by virtue of his lengthy apprenticeship in departmental routine there would still be some jobs that he could do even in the sort of Executive–Administrative Class projected here: perhaps a modified course would be appropriate, but some promotees from below should be given the option of taking the full course. This course would also have to be altered in some cases to suit the needs of those entrants who already had a sound grounding in economics and its related subjects or statistics, including – should such a scheme be instituted – Civil Service Scholars. And, also, the courses would have to be adjusted for those from the Scientific and Professional Classes and the other specialist groups moving into general management. If the Centre for Administrative Studies can be described as a beginning on the road to professionalisation on the generalist side of the Service, then the proposals of the Treasury Working Party would represent a half-way house on the journey away from amateurism. But the Working Party's plan, like the outline scheme presented by the Treasury in its initial evidence to the Fulton Committee, does little more than 'suggest a second class training for those who are not direct entrants to the Administrative Class'.[1] The need is to go the whole way and establish a British form of the E.N.A.: without it professionalism on the generalist side of the Service will remain much less than a reality.

But the Civil Service cannot, of course, be reformed only by unifying the generalist side of the Service and making it more professional. To approach reform only in this way would be to risk perpetuating one of the traditional, and only recently modified, weaknesses of the Service: the inferior status of the specialist. As we have seen, the reasons for this traditional weakness are partly historical in that when the foundations of the modern Service were laid a century or so ago the State employed relatively few specialists so that, compared with the generalists, they tended to be seen as relative newcomers; while, in our society as a whole the cult of the all-rounder has always decreed that those with specialisms are inferior mortals, who must be assigned advisory rather than executive positions, and who, moreover, often disagree among themselves about solutions to problems so that even their advice is suspect. The all-rounder has been supposed to be the ideal umpire in such disputes, having no previous professional commitment, and having acquired during a career emphasising versatility, the ability to pick up the essentials, despite a cursory knowledge of the subject matter. Since the war, with the creation of the major groups, and the steady improvement of their hierarchies, the position of the specialist has been considerably advanced compared with the dark days of the Tomlin Report of 1931. This improvement of hierarchies has been particularly marked since the Priestley Report of 1955. For example, in 1965 the Treasury estimated that 'the number of posts in the Scientific

[1] *Evidence presented by the Institution of Professional Civil Servants to the Fulton Committee on the Civil Service* (1966) 'Comment on H.M. Treasury's note on "The Future Structure of the Civil Service" ', para. 10.

Officer and the Works Group Classes graded at above Under-Secretary level had increased by some 40 per cent over the period since the Priestley Commission, while the total numbers in the Scientific and Works Group Classes had increased by 12 per cent'.[1] Another development – although a slow and, as yet, limited one – has been the move away in some parts of central Government from the traditional separation of the administrator and the specialist and, as in the reorganised structure of the Ministry of Public Building and Works after 1963, to pair specialists and administrators when they are assigned a common group of duties. More recently, as we saw in Chapter 5, the Ministries of Transport and of Technology have developed mixed hierarchies of specialists and administrators over a wide area of their functions. The direction in which these developments seem to point is to the eventual creation of an integrated Higher Civil Service with, as at I.C.I., virtually no boundary between administrative and specialist posts.

The Treasury took note of the recent developments at the Ministry of Technology in their evidence to the Fulton Committee about the future structure of the Civil Service in which they conceded that 'the present Class divisions do put obstacles in the way of cross-postings' which inhibited 'even greater flexibility' than they saw as already existing in the Service. As far as the specialist groups were concerned, the Treasury saw this problem of flexibility as being 'significant only at the senior levels since, in their earlier years in the Service, professional and scientific officers are recruited to undertake specific tasks within their own disciplines, and indeed they wish to be so employed – otherwise they would be candidates for the general management posts which are as open to them as to any other candidates'.[2] Because 'professionals and scientists are recruited to perform specific tasks in their own fields and will wish to operate within their own speciality in the earlier part of their career at any rate', the

---

[1] *Evidence presented by the Institution of Professional Civil Servants to the Fulton Committee on the Civil Service* (1967) para. 40.

[2] H.M. Treasury, 'The Future Structure of the Civil Service', a note submitted to the *Fulton Committee on the Civil Service* (1966) para. 5.

Treasury thought that it was unlikely that there would be much sideways movement between management and specialist classes below the Principal level. But the Treasury did consider that there should be 'a considerable increase in opportunities for training in management' for members of the specialist groups because 'this would facilitate interchange at senior levels'.[1] The Treasury said that further flexibility at these levels 'would not necessarily produce any wholesale changes in the way senior posts are filled. Most scientific and professional officers would still make their careers in their own field and indeed wish to do so; and most senior scientific and professional posts would still need to be filled by men trained in these disciplines'. Nevertheless, the Treasury thought that the Civil Service 'would benefit from increased flexibility of staffing and from public recognition of the fact that senior posts are open to all groups in the Service'.[2] The Treasury hoped: 'In the long run, more scientists and professionals who have the potential for top management might be attracted to the Civil Service if they knew that the highest posts in the general management field were open to them, and that the training courses would be provided to equip them for management and to bring out their aptitudes for it.'[3] The Treasury said that the exact relation between their new management structure and the Scientific and Professional Classes 'would have to be worked out',[4] but they did see difficulties following from the fact that many posts in the professional and specialist field could not be 'telescoped' into the exact pattern of the basic structure of their proposed general management group.[5] The Treasury did think, however, that 'it would be practicable to produce a common structure broadly applicable to the Service as a whole extending from the Permanent Secretary level down to the maximum of the Assistant Secretary (salary) scale'.[6] Below that point the Treasury saw the problem as increasing 'enormously in complexity', because there were 'many specific posts and grades in the Professional and Scientific Classes which have no exact counterpart in the management grades. Any attempt to produce a common

---

[1] Ibid. para. 11.　　[2] Ibid. para. 13.　　[3] Ibid. para. 14.
[4] Ibid. para. 11.　　[5] Ibid. paras 15–16.　　[6] Ibid. para. 17.

structure in the area between the maximum of the Assistant
Secretary scale and the maximum of the Principal scale would be
particularly difficult'.[1] The Treasury admitted:

> We have not so far found any acceptable way of merging the
> scientists, the Works Group, the lawyers and all the rest into
> a common structure at this level. A single scale running from top
> to bottom would be inordinately expensive and also unsatisfactory
> for other reasons. The alternative of having two common scales
> to cover the whole span is also open to objection, mainly because
> of the difficulty of operating two separate grades in the manage-
> ment field now covered by the Assistant Secretary. Our pro-
> visional conclusion is that retention of most of the separate rates of
> pay now existing at this level would not be incompatible with a
> policy of easier movement, free of the rigidities imposed by strict
> Civil Service Class distinctions, between higher management
> posts and professional and scientific posts. Those selected for
> higher management posts would very probably be candidates for
> promotion in their own specialist field and it would not be
> difficult to pay them the management rate while they were doing
> a management job. The return to a professional or scientific post
> might be more difficult: for example, an officer might either have
> to merit promotion within his own discipline to preserve his
> salary, or face – possibly for a limited period – some loss in
> emoluments. But these are not insuperable problems.[2]

The Treasury concluded by saying that the aim of their proposals
was at 'opening up greater opportunities for suitable officers in the
Professional and Scientific Classes to play their full part at the
senior levels of general management'.[3]

The Treasury's evidence was supplemented by that of the
Treasury Working Party on Management Training in the Civil
Service, which framed its proposals for the specialist groups on
the assumption that

> the future structure of the Civil Service might allow the career
> of the professional and scientist to develop in one of three ways.
> For the exceptional scientist who wished to remain personally
> involved in research, there would be opportunities for advance-
> ment. Others would advance, in the way which is most common
> under the present structure, into scientific or professional
> management leading to such appointments as Directors of

---

[1] Ibid. paras 17–18.   [2] Ibid. paras 18–19.   [3] Ibid. para. 20.

Research Establishments or as Directors of Works Services. Some might, from time to time, be associated with central policy making by joining teams working on specific problems with administrators, economists, and others. Other scientists and professional Civil Servants may be integrated in hierarchies with administrators responsible for policy and management. In varying degrees all these people would be working within the bounds of their professional discipline, though also within the management field. There is, perhaps, no very sharp dividing line between them and a third group who might move right into general Civil Service management. But if this latter move is to be made successfully and for the person concerned to have reasonable prospects of further advancement to higher general management, it is essential that the first step should be made about the age of thirty. This was a point on which emphasis was placed by witnesses from industry with experience of such career developments.[1]

For the man who was going to remain primarily a research scientist all his life, the Treasury Working Party said that it might be thought that little or no management training would be needed:

> But, even for these, it seems to us that it would be useful if they were to have, quite early in their careers, some short introduction to the concept of the best allocation of resources, and of the desirable rate of return from investment, and given some understanding of the economic and social environment which affects all Government activity. Since the majority of professional and scientific staff work in relatively few departments, it is suggested that this early training could best be given by the departments concerned.[2]

The Working Party considered:

> For the second group who, as their careers develop, become increasingly involved in management although still in a predominantly scientific or specialised field, we consider that management training of much the same length and intensity is needed as for those in general management. But because of the great range of disciplines and professions represented by this group, the wide age range within which staff are recruited, and the

---

[1] H.M. Treasury, *Management Training in the Civil Service. Report of a Working Party* (1967) para. 57.

[2] Ibid. para. 58.

very different needs of the specialised management work they carry out, we do not think it appropriate in a report of this kind to try to define in detail precisely which courses might be useful at particular stages.[1]

Referring to their general plan for management training, the Working Party did, however, make an attempt to relate it to the specialists' needs, saying that they thought it possible 'for some of them from these Classes who appear to have the highest potential, the first or the second – or even in certain cases both – of the twenty-week courses might prove valuable to their career development. We certainly envisage that some would attend the eight-week "Middle Management" course.' The Working Party also envisaged that in their thirties and forties some specialists would be available for selection for ten- or twelve-week courses at Business Schools or the Administrative Staff College, and that in the seminars for more senior staff they would attend with other senior general managers from government departments. Some specialists, of course, might have had training of this kind before joining the Civil Service.[2] The Working Party concluded its observations about management training for members of specialist groups by considering the needs of the third group of professionals and scientists which consisted of those who

> might be considered at about the age of thirty or even before for transfer to general management. For this group we suggest that there should be at about this age a course lasting about three or four weeks designed to interest those taking it in the possibility of moving into general administration to illustrate the working of Government and to test aptitude for administrative work. This might be followed by the 8-week 'Middle Management' course and on completion of this course, those still interested and showing aptitude for general management might be tried out on a Principal post, preferably one in which their scientific and professional experience would be relevant. If this trial period was successful these officials might attend the second 20-week course or the one-year course at a Business School.[3]

As the General Secretary of the Institution of Professional Civil Servants was a signatory of the Treasury Working Party's

---

[1] Ibid. para. 59.   [2] Ibid. para. 60.   [3] Ibid. para. 61.

Report, one can assume that the institution broadly approves of that report's recommendations about management training for members of the specialist groups. The I.P.C.S. had, however, been rather less happy with the Treasury's own evidence about the future form of the Higher Civil Service. What the I.P.C.S.'s own proposals amounted to was the creation of 'a "one-class" Higher Civil Service' which they considered would be

> relatively easy to implement because, although specialised knowledge is required in many posts, officers are more and more involved in general management. It gives reality to the idea of flexibility, for any post ceases to be considered the preserve of a particular Class. To quote only one absurdity that would disappear, posts in the vast field of general financial management and control are currently restricted to members of the Administrative/ Executive Class. Professional Accountants are not even allowed to apply for these posts – simply because they are members of the Professional Accountant Class. We are not saying that such posts should in future be reserved for Accountants: instead we propose that a man should not be debarred from a middle or higher post of financial control simply because he is a Professional Accountant. He may, or may not, be selected: the point is that he will be considered.[1]

The I.P.C.S. visualised:

> posts will be assessed on the basis of the work to be done and suitable people appointed accordingly. Some of these posts will certainly require specific professional qualifications – as an extreme example, it is impossible to see anyone but a registered medical practitioner filling the post of Treasury Medical Adviser. Other posts will require what is traditionally the expertise of the Administrative Class. But between these extremes, there will be a large number of posts which could be filled by officers from either category: we do not think that all posts are sharply black and white; most are in varying shades of grey.[2]

The I.P.C.S. added:

> This proposal is quite openly designed to open up to professional officers the prospect of promotion to the very top posts in the Service. We see advantages in this beyond those of efficiency in

---

[1] *Evidence presented by the Institution of Professional Civil Servants to the Fulton Committee on the Civil Service* (1967) paras 30–1.

[2] Ibid. para. 32.

the Service and the best utilisation of talent. It will, we consider, make a professional career more attractive and stimulate recruitment. Indeed, it will generally raise the status of professional work and it could result in more young people choosing careers in this field – an aim of national policy appreciated in France and the U.S.A.[1]

That such a structure could operate successfully in practice, the I.P.C.S. considered was demonstrated in the United Kingdom Atomic Energy Authority. After describing its management structure, that authority had told the Fulton Committee:

> This structure for higher management has worked well. It encourages a sense of common status among staff of different disciplines and backgrounds and emphasises the common responsibility and the broader approach which are appropriate at these levels. It also facilitates the selection of those best fitted to fill vacancies at the higher levels. In all these ways it contributes to efficiency in an organisation whose functions require a high degree of integration of the efforts of scientists, technologists and administrators.

The I.P.C.S. agreed with this conclusion and noted: 'most large private organisations operate in this way. Under the spur of competitive conditions, they have found it necessary to organise themselves thus; the Civil Service of other countries have adopted this system. We are confident that a similar approach in the British Civil Service would also contribute to efficiency.'[2]

The I.P.C.S. said that they approved of the general aim of the Treasury's proposals for 'the senior levels' which were 'designed to open up opportunities for suitable officers in all sections of the Service, if they have the capacity'.[3] However, the I.P.C.S. did not think that the Treasury

> have accepted the logic of this desire when they suggest what is, in effect, a one-class Service at and above the Assistant Secretary level. We propose that common entry to the Higher Civil Service should begin above the level of the present Principal and other broadly equivalent grades. We propose this for a number of reasons. Partly it is because we think that it is above the

---

[1] Ibid. para. 33.   [2] Ibid. paras 34–5.
[3] H.M. Treasury, 'The Future Structure of the Civil Service', a note submitted to the *Fulton Committee on the Civil Service* (1966) para. 5.

level of Principal that senior managerial decisions begin to be made; for example, in Whitehall, Assistant Secretaries tend to head separate divisions. Partly it is because we feel that to make the Service common to all Classes above Assistant Secretary sets the level at too late a stage in an officer's career. This is particularly true for professional officers – although it should be noted that the painfully slow progress of those who reach equivalent of Assistant Secretary reflects not lack of capacity but the structure and career prospects as they now are.[1]

The I.P.C.S. said: 'Abolition of Classes in the Higher Civil Service will pose some problems in assimilating a multiplicity of professional grades to the basic structure set out in the Treasury's note. This is, of course, no argument for not doing so. A unified Higher Civil Service means that the same grading structure should apply throughout.' The I.P.C.S. recognised that 'assimilation is not straightforward. But, given a transitional period – which should have a fixed limit of, say, five years – there are no insuperable obstacles. More complicated reorganisations have taken place in the past. In any event, we hope the Committee will not be deflected by transitional problems from a conclusion about the best form of long-term organisation.'[2] The I.P.C.S. did not

> spell out assimilation arrangements in detail at this stage, but we consider that the following factors are relevant. First, as we have indicated, very few posts at this level are narrowly specialist. Practically all of them require a broad range of management considerations to be brought to bear. The higher the level the more this is true. In principle, therefore, it is difficult to see why more grades should be needed in some areas and why some posts in the Higher Civil Service should be treated differently from others.

Secondly, the I.P.C.S. pointed to the improvement in the hierarchies of the Scientific Officer Class and Works Group Classes since 1955 and said that they believed: 'these developments will continue and that they will serve to reduce problems of assimilation'. Thirdly, the I.P.C.S. supported the Treasury's approach to the assimilation of the Principal Executive Officer and Senior

---

[1] *Evidence presented by the Institution of Professional Civil Servants to the Fulton Committee on the Civil Service* (1967) paras 36–7.

[2] Ibid. paras 38–9.

Chief Executive Officer because it pointed the way to similar arrangements on the specialist side, and they said: 'the salaries of the Superintendent Grade of the Works Group and the Senior Principal Scientific Officer, like that of the Principal Executive Officer, come halfway up the Assistant Secretary scale'.[1] The I.P.C.S. concluded:

> We appreciate that what we propose will result in the movement of professional officers into posts which have been occupied exclusively hitherto by officers in the Administrative Class. There will also be some movement of administrators into posts which have been occupied by professionals, but we acknowledge that this is unlikely to be as significant. We believe this is the right and inevitable trend which is already recognised in industry and in other countries. The Atomic Energy Authority provides an apposite example. The alternative course is to maintain the Administrative Class in its present exclusive position. The essential issue is to make a reality of a Higher Civil Service open to all the talents.[2]

The I.P.C.S.'s proposals for reforming the structure of certain of the specialist groups would, if implemented, have implications for the quality of the talents that would eventually be competing for posts in the integrated Higher Civil Service they envisage. For instance, the I.P.C.S. have suggested the establishment of 'a Science Group covering the Scientific Officer, Experimental Officer and Scientific Assistant Classes'. This would be a unified structure which below Assistant Secretary equivalent level would consist of five numbered grades. Grades I and II were described as promotion grades, and presumably would have assigned to them the work at present done by Principal Scientific Officers and Chief Experimental Officers. Grade III was to be 'the entry grade for honours graduates with postgraduate qualifications or experience'. Grade IV would be 'the initial entry grade for the entrant with two "A" levels or equivalent qualifications' who was to be given 'every encouragement' to obtain 'graduate or equivalent qualifications'. The upper part of Grade IV was to 'also provide the entry point for graduates, those with experience or higher qualifications being given incremental advantage over

[1] Ibid. para. 40.   [2] Ibid. para. 41.

others'. Grade V 'would undertake some of the routine work now performed by Scientific Assistants. There would be access to supervisory posts in Grade IV. The grade would cater for the five "O" Level entrant studying for higher qualifications. On acquisition of two "A" levels or equivalent qualifications he would be promoted automatically to Grade IV.'[1] One recalls that the Tennant Report of 1965 on the Scientific Civil Service came down against a suggestion that was made to them that 'the Scientific Officer and Experimental Officer Classes should be merged into one Class'. Arguments in favour had included that

> a reorganisation on these lines could make for greater flexibility, more particularly in the manning and complementing of Research Establishments; also that the image of the Scientific Service might be improved, because the scope for advancement on merit would seem greater in a Class where there was a single promotion ladder. Moreover, increasing numbers of graduates are now entering the Experimental Officer Class. A unified Service might make it easier to make full and proper use of this graduate talent, and might also reduce the effect of the apparent tendency on the part of some Universities to discourage graduate entry to the Experimental Officer Class.

The Tennant Committee thought that 'there must be considerable doubt whether a unified class would succeed in attracting the same number of good scientists as does the present system, and more particularly whether it would attract the really outstanding man', and so the committee came to the conclusion that 'in present circumstances the balance of advantage lies in favour of retaining the present arrangements'.[2] The proposal made to merge the

---

[1] Ibid. para. 55 and appendix III, para. 18.

[2] *Report of a Committee* (chairman: Sir Mark Tennant) *appointed to review the Organisation of the Scientific Civil Service* (1965) paras 19–21. The Tennant Committee produced statistics on recruitment to the Scientific Officer Class to show that 'in general the Service is attracting what might be loosely termed a fair share of the graduates we are setting out to recruit. There is, however, an impression within the Service that we are somewhat less than competitive in the case of the really outstanding men. There is no evidence available either to prove or disprove this conclusively. But the experience of those of us who have been directly concerned with recruiting supports the view that, while some Government Scientific Establishments exercise a greater pull than others, the

Scientific Officer and Experimental Officer Classes made in evidence to the Tennant Committee is not analogous to the proposals that have been made in this book and elsewhere for the amalgamation of the Executive and Administrative Classes. In recruiting to those areas of the generalist side of the Service, with the exception of late-entry recruitment, what is looked for in candidates is crude managerial and administrative potential to be refined or realised by work within the Service. Obviously, in recruiting to the Scientific Civil Service, what one looks for in candidates is scientific knowledge. One could have a single promotion ladder for the Scientific Civil Service if one wished – indeed it might lead to greater flexibility within the Service – but there would have to be differential recruitment to reflect the different levels of scientific knowledge: this suggests different entry points for postgraduates, honours graduates and for those with G.C.E. qualifications. A 'Science Group' could perhaps be created with those separate entry points – which would differ from the I.P.C.S. proposal in not having a common entry point for some graduates and those entering at G.C.E. 'A' Level, and which would differ from the present arrangements in that those with first degrees would enter at the same point – but the changes to be expected will be minimal because the jobs to be done remain specific and demand certain levels of scientific knowledge. Much the same considerations apply to the I.P.C.S.'s suggestion of the creation of a Technology Group covering the functions of 'the Works Group of Professional Classes, the Technical Works Engineering and Allied Classes and the Architectural and Engineering Draughtsman Classes'.[1]

Service as a whole is rather less successful in attracting such people than its competitors.' (Ibid. para. 27.) The Tennant Committee said: 'A limited degree of flexibility in relation to the starting pay of a small number of the most outstanding candidates might improve the Government's ability to attract them. This possibility should be further examined.' (Ibid. para. 34.) Certainly, it should be examined by the Fulton Committee and, at least, tried experimentally.

[1] *Evidence presented by the Institution of Professional Civil Servants to the Fulton Committee on the Civil Service* (1967) para. 54: this proposal was presented in detail in appendix II to that Evidence.

Whether or not the Scientific Civil Service and the classes that the I.P.C.S. would like to see formed into a Technology Group have their structures altered, their members and those of the other specialist groups, given the requisite ability, should have the opportunity of competing with members of the Executive–Administrative Class for advancement in an integrated Higher Civil Service. Probably most of those who have joined the Civil Service as members of specialist groups will wish to continue within their specialism and any reorganisation will have to make available such schemes as that of individual merit promotion in the Scientific Officer Class, whereby the scientist can continue doing the work at which he is a specialist, does not need to assume hierarchical responsibilities, and yet can gain promotion right up to the equivalent of Under-Secretary.[1] Nevertheless, many specialists may wish to move across into general management, and, because the present class divisions inhibit flexibility and may, therefore, prevent senior specialists with administrative potential from securing appropriate opportunities, an integrated Higher Civil Service should be created. This should begin as the I.P.C.S. has suggested, at the level of the Principal salary maximum. One notes that the Society of Civil Servants, like the Treasury, want the integrated Higher Civil Service to begin at Under-Secretary level, in their case because they feared that otherwise the career expectations of management grades entrants would progressively diminish.[2] Admittedly, when they took place, interchanges between the management grades and the specialists would be almost wholly in favour of the latter. But, if those conducting personnel management in the Higher Civil Service consider that in filling particular posts those who had begun their careers in specialist groups were better fitted to undertake the relevant duties, and this tended to happen rather often, then this would be just unfortunate for those drawn from other backgrounds. The integrated Higher Civil Service must start at the level of the

[1] The actual grade reached in this instance being Chief Scientific Officer.

[2] *Supplementary Evidence presented by the Society of Civil Servants to the Fulton Committee on the Civil Service* (1966) paras 12–19.

Principal maximum: it usually takes a specialist longer to reach that point than a generalist, and if he is coming across into general management he must do so at the earliest practicable point in his career in order to learn about general management. Although, even with an integrated Higher Civil Service, it is probable that most of the leading posts would continue to be filled by those who began their careers in the merged Executive–Administrative Class, at least there will be very much less chance than under the present arrangements that administrative talent in the specialist grades will go unnoticed, while on both sides of the present dividing line wider experience will be possible for both administrators and specialists.

But even if the Home Civil Service is reconstructed on the basis of an amalgamated Executive–Administrative Class and a more closely unified Higher Civil Service, it will have, at least to some extent, to lose its present largely self-contained nature and become a more open Service. In their initial submission of evidence to the Fulton Committee, the Treasury, indeed, talked of 'the possibility of increased interchange with employment outside the Service',[1] and this proved to be a theme that was to be found in several of the subsequent pieces of evidence that were presented to the committee. Professor Peter Self said:

> some system of interchange of administrators between Government Departments on the one hand and local authorities and public corporations on the other is now desirable. Obviously there are drawbacks to such an arrangement. The existing clear-cut distinctions of service emphasise the specific loyalty which an administrator owes to his particular employer, and assist a differentiation between national and local (or public enterprise) viewpoints which has its value. Against this it is mistaken to stress differentiation of functions and loyalties too far when a close working partnership (particularly in relation to local authorities) has become the reality. There are many ways by which such an interchange of administrators might be effected. The fullest application would be the creation of an integrated Public Service covering a distinctive sector of administration, such as education, health, transport, power, etc. All employees, whatever level of

---

[1] H.M. Treasury, 'The Future Structure of the Civil Service' a note submitted to the *Fulton Committee on the Civil Service* (1966) para. 15.

government they worked for, would be appointed to this integrated Service. Another approach would be to foster mobility between the various levels of government, through providing contracts of employment for a limited period and stipulating that service at one level should count as a qualification for service at another. A third possibility would be to require all national administrators to spend a period of service, preferably at least three years, within a public corporation, local authority, or other 'outside' organisation: this service might normally be done soon after entry, but in some cases it might come better at a later point of an administrative career.[1]

The Clerk of the Greater London Council, Sir William Hart, talked of the need to develop arrangements 'for the interchange of Civil Servants with staff from industry, commerce, Local Government, the nationalised industries and the like' which he saw as being 'a fruitful means of augmenting the experience available within Government Service'. Sir William said:

> It is the Council's experience that the Civil Service has a good deal to teach as well as to learn in a number of fields so that the benefits of interchange would not lie wholly on one side. Interchange can be of two kinds. The first is by way of short-term secondments and exchanges of staff, or by lending staff for specific purposes and periods, more could be done in this field. The second is by effecting a permanent change of career. The amount of such interchange between the Civil Service and Local Government is, however, limited. A great obstacle is that the Services have no common rank and grading structure. A further barrier to interchange arrangements is the present career structure of the Civil Service. A more flexible policy might enable the first ten years or so of the Civil Servant's life to be spent in industry or commerce, or for his secondment in mid-career, without detriment to his career and retirement prospects.

Sir William also pointed to difficulties regarding pension arrangements.[2] The British Institute of Management favoured 'increased flexibility of movement' between government departments and 'the industrial and commercial world', because 'this would induce

---

[1] *Memorandum of Evidence presented by Professor P. J. O. Self to the Fulton Committee on the Civil Service* (1966) paras 17–18.

[2] *Statement of Evidence made by the Greater London Council to the Fulton Committee on the Civil Service* (1967) paras 10–11.

Conclusion

a cross-fertilisation leading to a broadening of knowledge and understanding on both sides and could have an important effect on livening competition and raising performance standards'.[1] The Confederation of British Industry said: 'It is the policy in some large companies to look for a proportion of their senior men from outside their own ranks in order to prevent in-breeding, to bring in new talent and diverse experience, and to measure their own staff standards against the best available outside. The opening to the outside world of some of the more senior posts in the Civil Service might well bring similar advantages.'[2] More generally, the Confederation said: 'A greater degree of mobility is required so as to create a Civil Service in which men from different specialisations and with varying experiences can play their part more fully', and this meant that Civil Servants had to have 'opportunities for work outside the Service, either temporarily or permanently'.[3]

When asked by the Fulton Committee to elaborate upon the last point, the Confederation of British Industry's subsequent evidence pointed to the difficulties of interchanges between the Civil Service and private industry and commerce. The Confederation said:

Companies we have consulted most believe that the time away from normal work for a promising man that would be involved in seconding him to a Government department would nearly always be better spent from his and their point of view in other ways, for example, at a management or business course. Nor would such secondments contribute much to the better understanding of the Civil Service by industry since only a tiny proportion of rising industrial executives could be involved. The case is different in the other direction, for the numbers of what are at present classed as 'Administrative' Civil Servants in the economic departments are not large; and a systematic programme for giving the younger men some exposure to industry's ways of thinking and working could in a few years have involved a

---

[1] *Memorandum of Evidence presented by the British Institute of Management to the Fulton Committee on the Civil Service* (1966) para. 3.

[2] *Evidence presented by the Confederation of British Industry to the Fulton Committee on the Civil Service* (1966) **para. 15**.

[3] Ibid. para. 8.

significant proportion of the whole. The support and help of industry could be sought and gained on the basis of the benefit to industry of fostering in the Civil Service a better understanding of its problems and attitudes.[1]

The Confederation observed:

In considering secondments to work in industry, different treatment will be required for the specialist and the non-specialist Civil Servant. For the latter the main problem is to find him a worthwhile job while he is in industry. There is a useful place for the short secondment, not exceeding three months at the maximum, designed as a method of acquiring general information about industry with the Civil Servant 'sitting in' as an observer on industry's work. This apart, with some previous schemes it may well have been a mistake to have taken in Civil Servants of too high an age group or seniority group. Some of the companies we consulted feel that much longer, perhaps two years, would be needed before a Civil Servant in his thirties – say of Principal rank – could have acquired enough direct experience of the industry to be entrusted with real responsibility in an equivalent job – before he could in fact be entrusted with 'profit accountability'. Moreover, in the Foreign Office scheme, in which it was intended to exchange officials of about 35 and over, the Foreign Office found the greatest difficulty in sparing men of this level for long. Civil Servants of slightly less seniority, say in their twenties, can much more easily be given responsibilities in industry. Companies gave examples of schemes which acquaint their own trainees with management thinking and methods. The trainees spend about 6 or 8 weeks at company headquarters and they are given a project which involves finding out about the entire operations of the company – for instance, a market research project or a project covering all the different applications of a single raw material. Companies also cited schemes in which they give vacation jobs to people from business schools – usually postgraduates who have already had some experience of industry. Equivalent work would be suitable for Civil Servants after their initial Civil Service training. Such schemes can quickly provide a measure of responsibility as well as general information about industry.[2]

---

[1] *Supplementary Evidence presented by the Confederation of British Industry to the Fulton Committee on the Civil Service about Exchanges between the Civil Service and Industry* (1967) paras 2–3.

[2] Ibid. paras 5–6.

The Confederation said:

> For specialist Civil Servants such as scientists, engineers and
> accountants it will be much easier to provide worthwhile work on
> secondment to industry. We consider that the most useful type of
> exchange will be to give the specialist Civil Servant in industry
> work which is related to his own, but is not an exact replica of it.
> There would, for instance, be little to be gained by a scientist in a
> Government research station taking exactly equivalent laboratory
> work in industry, but much by his undertaking development
> work. The same concept could be applied to non-professional
> specialists – for instance by officials from the Ministry of
> Technology being given experience in industrial marketing, or
> Ministry of Labour officials concerned with safety, health and
> welfare having the opportunity to see these problems being
> tackled from the other end.[1]

The Confederation observed:

> In all these matters we regard systematic career-planning as
> essential if joint training experiences and secondments are to
> make a real contribution to a man's career and not simply be a
> more or less interesting break from his normal work.[2]

So, secondments from the Civil Service to industry would be
difficult for members of the proposed Executive–Administrative
Class except as part of a period of initial training, and if envisaged
at Principal level it would have to be for a fairly substantial period
of time – possibly as long as six years in some cases – if a real job
was to be learnt and done successfully. Those entrants to the
Executive–Administrative Class destined for jobs in the economic
departments should certainly spend a period in an industrial or
commercial enterprise as part of their initial training – perhaps
six months of the year of practical work suggested in the draft
training scheme outlined in this book. Later on in the entrant's
career, unless a real job of work and not just 'sitting in' can be done,
secondments to industry for short periods at any rate seem of
doubtful value compared with the further experience that could
be given within the Service. Administrators with practical
experience of industry and commerce are certainly needed in the
Service, particularly in staffing the economic departments, but

[1] Ibid. para. 8.   [2] Ibid. para. 9.

these could be secured by late-entry recruitment from candidates drawn from such backgrounds and who have been successful managers in those spheres. Professor Self did not attempt 'a detailed assessment of the possibilities' of the schemes that he suggested might be considered for increasing the interchange of staff between local authorities, public corporations and relevant government departments.[1] These schemes cannot, therefore, be fairly evaluated, although, in so far as these possibilities envisage an integrated Public Service for a sector of administration, one can observe that the scale of operations involved could be very large. Exchanges between central and local government staffs have long been favoured by commentators about the Civil Service: one even recalls Professor Laski suggesting that transfer between the two Services 'should be normal and not exceptional'.[2] The eventual development of regional Government may perhaps help to blur the distinction between the work of local authorities and those of central government departments, but at present the former are normally implementing the policies made in legislation mainly prepared by the latter. The local authorities primarily need staff drawn from the professions – and interchanges with central departments could be made here – but they would find it difficult to fit in members of the Executive–Administrative Class. A practicable scheme would be for entrants to the Executive–Administrative Class to have, as part of their initial training, the opportunity of spending six months in either a local authority, or a public corporation, or in a private industrial or commercial enterprise: an alternative to this being six months' service in a regional or local office of a central government department. In each case the entrants must do a real and specific job. This condition must also be applied to secondments outside the Home Civil Service – which would have to last up to six years in some cases. The value of secondments of such length would have to be weighed against the experience that could be gained by working

[1] *Memorandum of Evidence presented by Professor P. J. O. Self to the Fulton Committee on the Civil Service* (1966) para. 19.

[2] Harold J. Laski said this in his introduction to a book by J. P. W. Mallalieu, *Passed to You Please* (1942) p. 11.

in central Government for the same time. Members of the specialist groups should also have opportunities for secondment, but those moving across into general management in the Service will have to learn a good deal about such management and the appropriate training may not leave much time for temporary appointments outside the Service. Late-entry recruitment of a permanent nature from industry and commerce, local authorities and the public corporations and, to some extent, the universities, mainly at Principal level – the level at which most of the wartime intake into the Service entered – would seem an answer to the problem of bringing in relevant outside experience into the Service at above the basic recruitment level. Recruitment to a limited number of specific posts at Assistant Secretary level could continue as now. As noted above, the C.B.I. have made a similar suggestion in their evidence to the Fulton Committee to that once made by Professor Brian Chapman that 'all posts above the rank of Assistant Secretary should be advertised'.[1] This might be a useful idea, provided it was made clear to the applicants that at this level only really outstanding people could be taken in from outside – they would have to be outstanding to do a job at such a level without experience of the Civil Service.

Although the scope for interchanges of staff between the Civil Service and other employment may be more limited than some of those who have given evidence to the Fulton Committee seem to think, movement in and out of the Service should, nevertheless, be made as straightforward as possible. Among other things, this means changing the Civil Service superannuation scheme.[2]

[1] Brian Chapman, *British Government Observed* (1963) p. 60.
[2] A historical background to the Civil Service Superannuation Scheme was secured from Marios Raphael, *Pensions and Public Servants. A Study of the Origins of the British System* (1964). Of particular value is the work of Gerald Rhodes, *Public Sector Pensions* (1964). Some of the complexities of superannuation reform as regards the economy as a whole were made clearer to me by an anonymous article, 'Loosing the Golden Chains', in *The Economist*, 20 June 1964, pp. 1386–8. It is interesting to note that the *Tomlin Report* of 1931, after reviewing the Civil Service pension scheme, concluded: 'A contributory system would be more satisfactory than a non-contributory system in regard to Classes at present established.' (Para. 761.) However, although it felt able to

This scheme is non-contributory (except for widows' and children's benefits) and it is laid down in detail by statute. There is no superannuation fund, the amount required to pay the benefits being voted annually by Parliament. Generally, only established Civil Servants are pensionable; unestablished employees may become eligible for a gratuity on leaving the Service. The main features of the present scheme are that pensions and lump sums are awarded on the basis of the retiring salary and the number of years of service. Pension is awarded at the rate of one-eightieth of retiring salary and pensionable emoluments (averaged over the last three years of service) for each year of reckonable service. In addition, a lump sum or 'additional allowance' is paid at the rate of three-eightieths for each year of reckonable service. Pensions and lump sums cannot be awarded until ten years' reckonable service has been given. In cases of retirement with shorter service, or death in service, gratuities may be payable. Pensions and lump sums are normally awarded only on retirement after the minimum retiring age of sixty.[1] As the Treasury has written about the scheme: 'As it has developed, more particularly in recent years, the Civil Service scheme has acquired a considerable measure of flexibility, so as to provide for the needs of staff who, for one reason or another, do not spend their whole working life in the Civil Service'.[2] For example, as regards movement out of the Service, any Civil Servant over the age of fifty who retires voluntarily may receive the pension and lump sum for which his service qualifies him. The benefits are not paid until he reaches his minimum retiring age except on compassionate grounds.

---

suggest that the introduction of a contributory system might have 'some resultant saving in expenditure' (para. 720), which should have caught the eye of the Treasury particularly at the time, the Tomlin Commission's recommendation was not implemented. Some of the Priestley Commission were 'disposed to believe' that the Civil Service pension scheme should be 'brought into line with the majority of outside schemes and made contributory' (*Report*, para. 706). It does not matter a great deal whether or not the Civil Service scheme is contributory: what matters is to make it fully transferable.

[1] H.M. Treasury, *Introductory Factual Memorandum on the Civil Service presented to the Fulton Committee on the Civil Service* (1966) paras 56–7.

[2] Ibid. para. 58.

Also, reciprocal arrangements exist for transfers of pension rights between the Civil Service and a wide range of other public employments, notably local Government, teaching, police, National Health Service and the public corporations. Even where full transferability is not possible it may be possible to transfer under 'approved employment' arrangements, whereby the Civil Servant receives the benefits for which his Civil Service qualifies him on his retirement from other employment. For those in the Higher Civil Service 'virtually all employment may be approved, including employments of a purely private or commercial nature'.[1] There are also provisions for those moving into the Service which either preserve their existing pension rights, or enable them to maintain membership of other schemes, while, 'as an essential inducement to persons with special qualifications who are recruited to posts, particularly more senior posts', on occasion 'an established Civil Servant who is recruited in mid-career may be allowed to count his service after the age of 40 at 8/5ths of its actual length, any earlier service being ignored'.[2] These developments in the Civil Service superannuation scheme seem to be moving in the direction of full transferability of pension rights and, as a means of making movement in and out of the Service easier than it is at present, the Fulton Committee should recommend this.

The considerable changes that may take place in the Civil Service if even some of the reforms that have been proposed are put into practice has led many of the individuals and organisations who have submitted evidence to the Fulton Committee to consider whether or not the Service's central arrangements for personnel management need to be revised. For example, the Acton Society Trust considered that there were

> good reasons for suggesting that, as in most organisations, recruitment should be merged with other personnel functions and should be administered by one body. This really boils down to a suggestion for a central personnel agency created out of the Civil Service Commission and the Establishment divisions of the Treasury. Apart from being a tidier and more logical arrangement

---

[1] Ibid. para. 59.   [2] Ibid. para. 60.

an agency of this sort, which is self-consciously and solely concerned with Government manpower needs, could carry out the
continuous review of the Civil Service which is required by
modern conditions.[1]

The Liberal Party wanted to see the Civil Service Commission
turned into 'a Public Service Commission concerned with the
general planning of recruitment and training in the Civil Service'.[2]
The Labour Party said: 'the personnel management functions of
the Treasury should be transferred to a strengthened Civil Service
Commission. Its present functions of recruitment and selection
would then comprehend also conditions of service questions and
training. It would also be responsible for some degree of career
planning and for higher appointments in the Service.'[3] Professor
Crick and Mr Thornhill thought: 'The functions of recruitment,
training, and job-study are inter-related, and cannot be carried
out efficiently when different agencies share in their performance.
We suggest, therefore, that these aspects of personnel management
should be brought together in one agency outside the Treasury –
probably a reformed and augmented Civil Service Commission.'[4]
The Society of Civil Servants saw

> no justification for the continued separation of responsibility for
> recruitment from the responsibility of central management of the
> Civil Service. The measurement of recruitment needs, selection
> methods, pay and conditions of service, and career development
> all require to be considered together in relation to both current
> and long-term requirements. The Society favours the creation of
> a central management organisation to embrace all these personnel
> functions and to provide expert assistance to employing depart-
> ments in carrying out their management functions. In essence

---

[1] *Statement of Evidence submitted by the Acton Society Trust to the
Fulton Committee on the Civil Service* (1966) para. 46.

[2] *Evidence presented by the Liberal Party to the Fulton Committee on
the Civil Service* (1966) para. 4.

[3] *Evidence presented by the Labour Party to the Fulton Committee on
the Civil Service* (1966) para. 48. As the Labour Party noted, this suggestion was also made recently by a Fabian Group, *The Administrators.
The Reform of the Civil Service* (1964) p. 33.

[4] *Memorandum on Recruitment and Training presented by Professor
B. R. Crick and Mr. W. Thornhill of the University of Sheffield to the Fulton
Committee on the Civil Service* (1966) para. 29.

this would mean combining the Civil Service Commission and the Management and Pay, etc. divisions of the Treasury. Such a merger has been facilitated by the reorganisation of the Treasury which has made a clear division between the Economic Side on the one hand and the Management and Pay Divisions on the other.[1]

Looking at the question of the location of their proposed central management organisation, the Society said that possibly it could

> either be linked with the Cabinet Office or with the Prime Minister's Office. The head of the combined central management organisation (covering recruitment and personnel management, including pay and conditions) would also be Head of the Civil Service with direct responsibility to the Prime Minister who might be assisted by a Minister of State for Civil Service Affairs. Such an arrangement would ensure that the new central management organisation has sufficient power and authority and the support of the Head of Government. The Society recognises that these changes involve major political decisions and is not wedded to a single solution. The aim should be to bring together under unified control the whole range of Civil Service affairs and to build a strong central leadership which will fight for the resources it requires and provide assistance and firm guidance to employing departments in carrying out their personnel and career management responsibilities.[2]

The C.S.C.A. did not consider that the Treasury should be the central authority for Civil Service personnel management:

> A difficulty in achieving positive personnel policies, under the existing dispensation, is that the first impact on any ideas and proposals is 'What will they cost?' The 'crude' figure of cost is initially calculated. Only at second or later stages do matters of merit, and of 'investment value', enter into the consideration. This we believe is the wrong way round. If the central personnel management work were removed from the Treasury, and placed in a separate department, ideas and proposals could be expected initially to be examined on their overall merits; financial factors would of course be present throughout, but would not dominate the first stage consideration. The Treasury would be involved at second stage.

---

[1] *Evidence presented by the Society of Civil Servants to the Fulton Committee on the Civil Service* (1966) para. 27.

[2] Ibid. para. 29.

The C.S.C.A. favoured 'the establishment of a new department, under a senior Cabinet Minister, to deal with all central personnel management matters other than recruitment' – and other than training which the C.S.C.A. wanted to see made the responsibility of a separate Training Board. The C.S.C.A.'s proposed new department 'would act *vis-à-vis* the Treasury, as the central financial authority, by broadly the same procedures as now obtain between any spending department and the Treasury. Its head should be "Chief of the Civil Service Staff"; and its key staff themselves would be specially trained, drawn in large part from (and interchangeable with) trained departmental management staff.'[1]

Usually accompanied by allegations that staff matters are not being treated 'in the proper spirit' because the Treasury treats them in a manner 'overweighted by financial considerations', there have been several suggestions in the past that the establishments functions of the Treasury should be taken away from it and entrusted to a separate department with its own Minister. When the Tomlin Commission asked Sir Warren Fisher for his views about the creation of such a department, he observed:

> It is a very venerable suggestion (and therefore I suppose one ought to respect it) to have a fifth wheel to the coach. It was looked at by a number of bodies. There was the final report of the Committee appointed to enquire into the organisation and staffing of Government offices; they reported in February 1919, and they examined the matter. I was a member of that Committee; we found no advantage in it. Then the report of the Haldane Committee on Machinery of Government again examined it; they did not see any advantage in it; in fact there is none. Let us look at this new institution with a Minister. He has got to square the Chancellor of the Exchequer; he cannot override the Chancellor of the Exchequer under the English Constitution. Then these Treasury officials come into play, so all you do is to make a much more cumbrous machine, with not a vestige of advantage to anybody.[2]

---

[1] *Supplementary Evidence submitted by the Civil Service Clerical Association to the Fulton Committee on the Civil Service* (1966–7) Part II, para. 3.

[2] *Tomlin Evidence*, question 18,735. One notes that Professor Harold Laski in his introduction to J. P. Mallalieu, *Passed to You Please* (1942)

As for the relationship between the Treasury and the Civil
Service Commission, the remarks made in 1964 by a former
First Civil Service Commissioner, Sir George Mallaby, are of
interest, for he said:

> relations between the Commissioners and the Treasury cannot,
> by the very nature of their respective functions, be automatically
> and continuously smooth and harmonious. In nearly every
> organisation, management comprises recruitment and selection,
> and the Treasury inevitably find it difficult at times to remember
> that while they control everything else in this field they do not
> control the Commissioners and the Commission is not a division
> of the Treasury. The Commissioners for their part sometimes
> feel a little hurt and aggrieved when Big Brother neglects to
> consult them on matters like training and conditions of service
> which must have a direct effect upon their powers of recruitment.
> It is for this and similar reasons that in other Commonwealth
> countries the Public Service Commission comprises the work of
> the Management side of the Treasury and the work of the Civil
> Service Commissioners, and that the Chairman of the Public
> Service Commission is ex officio Head of the Civil Service.
> In this country we shall probably continue to think it wiser to use
> up a little nervous energy in harmonising the discords to which our
> ears have been long attuned rather than to risk the composition of
> perhaps still more discordant sounds.[1]

In this context, Canadian experience may be instructive. In 1946,
a Royal Commission observed:

> It is apparent that the respective functions and responsibilities of
> the Civil Service Commission and the Treasury Board overlap.
> The Treasury has the authority in relation to all matters of
> establishment and organisation but not the immediate responsi-
> bility; the Civil Service Commission has the responsibility but
> not the authority. This division of duties is the outstanding
> weakness in the central direction and control of the Service and
> must be eliminated.

---

said: 'a separation will have to take place between the financial and
establishment functions of the Treasury. A separate Minister of Personnel
is required to whom all questions of recruitment, training, promotion, pay
and other conditions of service will be entrusted. The present fusion of
functions in the Treasury has the undesirable result of making financial
considerations unduly influential in personnel problems' (p. 11).

[1] Sir George Mallaby, 'The Civil Service Commission: its Place in the
Machinery of Government', in *Public Administration* (1964) p. 6.

By a reorganisation in 1961–2 this division, at least, was eliminated, and the powers now given to the Canadian Treasury Board resemble those currently assigned to the Treasury in this country.[1] As for the arrangements in this country, the I.P.C.S. are right when they say that the present division of function between the Treasury and the Civil Service Commission has advantages:

> The divisions concerned with staffing matters could no doubt be separated from the rest of the Treasury. But this would achieve nothing if the new department thus created had then to go to the Treasury to obtain financial approval for the arrangements it wished to implement. There are enough difficulties at present without creating an extra step. It is fundamentally important that departments and staff associations and other bodies should be able to consult and negotiate with a central organisation which has effective power.[2]

The Fulton Committee may well conclude that changes in the Civil Service will require the establishments side of the Treasury to be strengthened, but there seems no advantage to be gained – indeed, a distinct prospect of needless duplication – from putting into effect the institutional changes designed to reduce Treasury control that have been widely proposed in evidence to the committee.

By the time that the Fulton Committee reports it will be almost a century since the process of implementing the Trevelyan–Northcote reforms began in 1870. The reformers of 1853 designed a Service for the Regulatory State, and upon the foundations that they laid the modern Civil Service has largely been constructed. The Fulton Committee have been presented with the task of deciding what form the Civil Service should take in the Positive State. Reviewing recruitment to the Civil Service, the Select Committee on Estimates said in 1965 that they found it 'hard to accept that the task of Government justifies the unique significance attaching to the Administrative Class, and that only a

---

[1] R. MacGregor Dawson, *The Government of Canada* (1963) pp. 284–6.
[2] *Evidence presented by the Institution of Professional Civil Servants to the Fulton Committee on the Civil Service* (1966) 'Civil Service Organisation: Some Issues for Consideration', para. 6.

select few are fitted to undertake this work'.[1] Initially seen as a
class of socially and educationally acceptable and politically anonymous personal advisers to Ministers, recruited from the older
English universities on the basis of general education rather than
any evidence of relevant specialised knowledge, and embracing
an all-rounder tradition of valuing 'versatility' above the acquisition of specialisms, the Administrative Class has retained
its character quite remarkably. Because, under our system of
parliamentary democracy, the Civil Service must always be subject
to political control, even though there are reasons to believe
that the nature of the relevant convention is changing, leading
administrators will always have, to some extent, to exhibit an
'awareness of Ministerial responsibility'. This does not necessarily mean, however, that a separate Administrative Class, seeing
itself as specialising in that 'awareness', should continue to dominate
the Higher Civil Service. Indeed, the Administrative Class's
emphasis upon it having that special role, has led it to give a low
valuation to management, to adopt an order of priorities in which
the technical is subordinated to the political, and to have a
'crisis mentality' in dealing with problems and to scorn preliminary research into their general fields. These are attitudes
more in keeping with the Regulatory State than one in which the
central Government is charged with the management of the
economy and of the Welfare State. The time has now come for the
Administrative Class's separate existence to be ended and for it
to be amalgamated with the Executive Class on the basis of a
more specialist structure: the leading grades of the merged class,
together with the equivalent grades of the specialist groups,
forming an integrated Higher Civil Service which would begin
at the level of the Principal salary maximum. Such changes
might well eventually lead to a more relevant type of administrator emerging than under the present arrangements. But the
new structure would have, to some extent, to be an open hierarchy
in the sense that, whereas a completely closed career Service
may have been appropriate when the State itself largely stood
aside from the rest of society, this is not the case in the era of the

[1] *Sixth Report from the Select Committee on Estimates* (1964–5) para. 37.

Positive State: the Service has to be open for some late-entry recruitment, on a larger scale than at present, from the local authorities, the public corporations, private industrial and commercial undertakings and the universities. Such recruitment, and also movement out of the Service, would be facilitated if, as it should be, the Civil Service pension scheme was made fully transferable.

The above proposals are designed merely as a contribution to a debate: it is not suggested that their implementation would lead to a perfect solution of the problems of the Civil Service. But these proposals are related to the problems that, in the view of the author, either now exist or are likely to present themselves in the foreseeable future. Inevitably, such suggestions and proposals are less stimulating than, for example, the sort of speculative proposals that Mr J. H. Robertson has advanced in evidence to the Fulton Committee about the recasting of the Civil Service and, indeed, the whole machinery of government, along the lines which he expects will be relevant to the role of government at some time in the near future.[1] Mr Robertson's evidence is an essay in social

[1] J. H. Robertson's evidence to the Fulton Committee follows from his premiss: 'An epoch in the history of British Government is ending. The Committee must make a fundamental reappraisal of the tasks of the Civil Service, its environment, and its techniques in order to reach useful conclusions about its future structure, recruitment and management.' Mr Robertson believes: 'The great expansion in the functions of Government over the last hundred years has confused the secretariat role, for which the Civil Service was designed, with a managerial role, for which it was not. As the once separate tasks of Government have become more closely inter-related, the management of the Civil Service has gradually become more unified; but this process has not yet been completed. Our present system of Government, of which the Civil Service forms a part, has not been created by logic or design; it represents the unplanned accumulation of answers to a multitude of different problems which have arisen over the years. As a result of this piece-meal development it is now difficult to discern a logical distinction between the functions of Civil Servants and those of other Public Servants. Finally, the present relationship between Parliament and the Executive – together with the organisation and methods of control of the Civil Service which this relationship involves – is based on the traditional struggle between the parliamentarians and the servants of the monarch, and is unsuited to a people who have now become self-governing.' Mr Robertson continued: 'The system of Government which has thus evolved suffers from a number of

(footnote 1, page 357, continued)

shortcomings. Because of its unplanned growth it contains too many authorities and there is great confusion of responsibility between them. Thus we are burdened with what the Haldane Committee called "lilliputian administration". The present system of financial control in Government, which stems from the traditional relationship between Parliament and the Crown, is out of date and causes much inefficiency. These factors lead to too much centralisation, which leads in turn to too much secrecy. The whole pattern of public administration, including nationalised industries, regional authorities and local government as well as the Civil Service, must be reviewed if these shortcomings are to be removed. Only in the context of such a review can the Committee usefully make recommendations on the future of the Civil Service.' J. H. Robertson believed: 'Current advances in management science and management technology will have a profound impact on Government and therefore on the Civil Service. The application of the new techniques will involve a systemic approach to decision-making and information-handling; and decision-making and information-handling are essentially what government is for. This in turn will encourage the emergence 'out of the scattered fragments' which exist today, of a more integrated system of Government at every level – central, regional and local. Greater use of these techniques in Government will involve a much greater emphasis on management accounting, research and development, and the use of computers in making decisions and handling information. It seems certain, for example, that the 1970s will see the emergence of a country-wide network of inter-linked computers supporting the whole structure of Government. These developments will necessitate, and make possible, more deliberate methods of controlling organisational change than have been thought necessary in the past. In these ways the application of the new techniques will help to solve the problems of fragmentation, confusion of responsibility, and unplanned growth, and thus help to eliminate the other shortcomings of the present arrangements.' Mr Robertson saw the impact of these techniques as being felt 'not just at the level of routine administration. It will also be felt, sooner than many people yet recognise, at the highest policy-making level. The use of these techniques will profoundly affect the nature of Civil Service work and the numbers and types of people who are needed to do it. Not least, they will make redundant many of the administrative and clerical staff required by the present organisation using traditional techniques.' Mr Robertson believed: 'a new pattern of Government – central, regional and local – will emerge under the impact of management technology in response to the shortcomings of the current arrangements. Among other things it will involve the delegation to executive agencies of much of the work for which Ministries are directly responsible today. This pattern will constitute the environment for the Civil Service of the future. It therefore provides the background against which the future structure, recruitment and management of the Service must be considered. The possibility arises that the distinction between the Civil Service and the rest of the Public Service

(*footnote 1, page 357, continued*)
will eventually lapse altogether.' J. H. Robertson then made 'proposals about what needs to be done' in which he included a scheme for the allocation of ministerial responsibilites among eleven Ministries. These were described as follows: Prime Minister's Department; Regional and Local Government, Environmental Planning and Land Use; Economic and Financial Affairs; Manpower and Employment; Industry; Power, Transport and Communications; Education, Science, the Arts and Sport; Health, Housing and Welfare; Law, Public Order and Safety; External Affairs; and Defence. Mr Robertson did not envisage that this division of responsibilities would be permanent: 'It will be the responsibility of the proposed Prime Minister's Department to supervise the continuing process of organisational change by which the structure of Government will adapt itself to technological, economic, social and political change.' Apart from recommendations for other changes in government organisation and procedures, a number of specific proposals were made about such matters as training, recruitment and staff management. Mr Robertson saw himself as having drawn up 'a programme of reform which will take ten or fifteen years to accomplish', and he was confident: 'This programme of reform will provide solutions to our present problems in Government, and will enable us to face the problems of the future. We are entering a phase of history in which, as a people, we shall have to take decisions of kinds which men have never had to take before. These will raise acute moral and political problems. If we are to be able to deal effectively with these problems our political leaders must delegate responsibility for many of the basically managerial and technological problems which occupy their attention today. This will, incidentally, restore the traditional distinction between the secretariat and managerial functions of Civil Servants. Similarly, the professionals and technical men in their turn must delegate to machines as much routine decision-making and information-handling as they can.' Robertson concluded: 'That is the context in which the Committee are considering the future of the Civil Service. This evidence is submitted in the hope that it will help them in their historic task.' (*Evidence submitted by J. H. Robertson to the Fulton Committee on the Civil Service*, 1966, pp. iv–vi, and appendix, paras 1–3.) Robertson conceded that some members of the Fulton Committee might consider that his evidence 'ranges rather more widely than their own interpretation of the Committee's terms of reference'. This seems more than likely because the Fulton Committee has not been assigned the role of some sort of latter-day Haldane Committee on the Machinery of Government: its task is to design a Civil Service for the present and the foreseeable future. To take one example of the difficulties which Robertson's approach could lead to, he writes: 'Mergers between the Administrative and Executive Classes, and between the senior ranks of the Administrative, Scientific and Professional Classes may seem helpful in the short term. But if their effect were to make it more difficult to re-establish the distinction between secretariat work and management work, they could be unhelpful in the longer term.' But the

prediction on a large scale. His particular predictions may or may not turn out to be correct, but the Fulton Committee are unlikely to feel able to go so far. Their task is to design a Civil Service that will be able to run the present functions accorded to the Service, and which will be flexible enough to run those of the foreseeable future. This itself is not an easy task, and it is unlikely to be made easier by the volume of opposition that recommendations for change may well arouse in practice, despite the now widespread recognition in principle of the need for some change. In what one hopes is the unlikely event of the Fulton Committee being tempted to moderate its recommendations because of such opposition, it should recall the example of the Trevelyan–Northcote Report. There are those who always believe that 'the pear is not ripe'[1] for reform, but all established institutions stand in need of periodic change: this is the need of the Home Civil Service at the present time.

(*footnote 1, page 357, continued*)
Fulton Committee can only deal in 'the short term' – solutions for the problems of which will be difficult enough to find – because it must be even less sure of what will or will not be 'unhelpful in the longer term'. The Fulton Committee can only advance proposals which accord either with what it knows or with what it can – at this stage – anticipate with some certainty.

[1] This phrase was, of course, that of Macaulay, who wrote in 1854 that Sir Charles Trevelyan had been too sanguine in proposing the reform of the Civil Service: 'The pear is not ripe. I always thought so. The time will come, but it is not come yet. I am afraid that he will be much mortified.' (Sir George Otto Trevelyan, *The Life and Letters of Lord Macaulay*, 1888, vol. II, p. 374.) However, Sir Charles Trevelyan survived.

Some Observations about the Fulton Report 1968

I INTRODUCTION

THE Fulton Report on the Home Civil Service was published on 26 June 1968; in presenting it to the House of Commons, the Prime Minister described the Report as 'an essential contribution to the modernisation of the basic institutions of this country'. The Prime Minister said that the Fulton Committee had produced a 'wide-ranging and fundamental review' of the Civil Service, that he was confident that the Committee's Report 'will stand comparison with the historic Northcote–Trevelyan Report of more than a century ago', and that the Government had decided 'to accept the main recommendations of the Report and to embark on the process of reform outlined by the Committee'.[1]

The first main recommendation of the Fulton Committee accepted by the Government was that a new Civil Service Department should be set up with wider functions than those now performed by the 'Pay and Management' group of the Treasury, which it would take over. The new department would also absorb the Civil Service Commission. The Committee wanted the new department to be under the control of the Prime Minister, who would retain direct responsibility for senior appointments, machinery of government and questions of security. Outside this area, the Committee suggested that the Prime Minister should delegate day-to-day responsibility to a non-departmental Minister of appropriate seniority who was also a member of the Cabinet. The Committee recommended that the Permanent Secretary of the Civil Service Department should be designated Head of the

[1] House of Commons, *Official Report* (1967–8) vol. 767, cols 454–5.

Home Civil Service.[1] On behalf of the Government the Prime Minister said that 'We accept the proposal to establish a new Civil Service Department on the lines advocated by the Committee and the steps to bring this about will be taken at the appropriate time. Specific and formal arrangements will be made to ensure the continued independence and political impartiality, within the new Civil Service Department, of the Civil Service Commission in the selection of individuals for appointment to the Civil Service.' The Prime Minister announced that the Paymaster-General, a member of the Cabinet with no departmental duties, had been asked 'to supervise the setting up of the new department and to control its day-to-day operations when established'.[2]

The second main recommendation of the Fulton Committee accepted by the Government was that a Civil Service College should be set up which would provide major training courses in administration and management and a wide range of shorter courses. The Committee envisaged the College as having important research functions. The Committee said that the courses provided by the College 'should not be restricted to Civil Servants; a proportion of places should be set aside for men and women from private industrial and commercial firms, local government and public corporations'.[3] On behalf of the Government the Prime Minister said that it had 'accepted the recommendation to set up a Civil Service College to develop the training of Civil Servants broadly on the lines recommended in the Report. The timing of this will, of course, have to be fitted into a programme which takes full account of public expenditure control.'[4]

The third main recommendation of the Fulton Committee accepted by the Government was that 'all classes should be

---

[1] *Fulton Report*, p. 104. The members of the Committee were: Lord Fulton (Chairman); Sir Norman Kipping; Sir Philip Allen; Mr W. C. Anderson; Rt Hon. Sir Edward Boyle, M.P.; Sir William Cook; Sir James Dunnett; Dr Norman Hunt; Mr R. R. Neild; Mr R. Sheldon, M.P.; Professor Lord Simey; and Sir John Wall.

[2] House of Commons, *Official Report* (1967–8) vol. 767, cols 455 and 458.

[3] *Fulton Report*, p. 105.

[4] House of Commons, *Official Report* (1967–8) vol. 767, col. 456.

abolished and replaced by a single unified grading structure covering all Civil Servants from top to bottom in the non-industrial part
of the Service. The correct grading of each post should be determined by job evaluation'.[1] On behalf of the Government the Prime
Minister said that it accepted 'the abolition of classes within the
Civil Service and will enter immediately into consultations with
the staff associations with a view to carrying out the thorough-
going study proposed by the Committee, so that a practicable system can be prepared for the implementation of the unified grading
structure in accordance with the timetable proposed by the Committee'. The Prime Minister added that 'This does not mean that
the professions as such will disappear from the Civil Service, but
it does mean that movement throughout the Service for them and
for all Civil Servants at all levels will be unimpeded. This will
mean that for everyone in the Civil Service, whether from school,
whether from a college of technology, or from a university,
whether he or she comes in from industry or from a profession –
all in future, the school-leaver, the graduate, the accountant, the
engineer, the scientist, the lawyer – for all of them, there will be an
open road to the top which, up to now, has been, in the main,
through the Administrative Class.'[2]

The need for the abolition of the separate Administrative Class
and for related changes in the structure of the Home Civil Service
has been one of the major themes of this book as, indeed, has been
the advocacy of the need for the establishment of a Civil Service
College and for associated improvements in the Service's post-
entry training arrangements. But this observer's general assessment of the Fulton Report is that it by no means constitutes the
'wide-ranging and fundamental review' of the Civil Service that
the Prime Minister said it was. As was said in Chapter 6, the terms
of reference given to the Fulton Committee required it to make
recommendations the implementation of which it was hoped
would eventually lead to an improvement in the quality of the men
manning that part of machinery of Government normally assigned
to the Home Civil Service, whereas, while this might well be

[1] *Fulton Report*, pp. 104–5.
[2] House of Commons, *Official Report* (1967–8) vol. 767, col. 456.

desirable, the overriding need was to reconstruct machinery of Government. The Fulton Committee was charged with a task of partial reform because, except as regards the arrangements for the central management of the Civil Service, it was precluded from proposing changes in machinery of Government. Indeed, as will be seen, the Fulton Committee was forced into the position of having to recommend that a further committee should examine that machinery. As was also indicated in Chapter 6, although given the brief of examining 'the structure, recruitment and management, including training, of the Home Civil Service', the Fulton Committee was precluded by the Government from making recommendations the effect of which would be to change the doctrine of Ministerial responsibility. As is obvious, a consideration of the present working of that constitutional convention should have been an essential activity of a body given the Fulton Committee's terms of reference. The Committee was inhibited from doing much more than cursorily discussing the convention of Ministerial responsibility – instead, it suggested that a proposed committee to examine secrecy in Government should also undertake a full consideration of the present working of that convention – which made incomplete, and diminished the quality of, its Report.

The Fulton Committee seemed to find some compensation for the restrictions placed upon it by expressing some of its criticisms of the Civil Service in a needlessly provocative manner and by presenting its proposals as comprising a more radical programme for the reform of the Service than they in fact amounted to. Even one of the members of the Committee described the first chapter of the Fulton Report as unfair to the Civil Service,[1] and its tone and, indeed, that of the whole Report, was set by its opening paragraph in which the Committee said: 'The Home Civil Service today is still fundamentally the product of the nineteenth-century philosophy of the Northcote–Trevelyan Report. The tasks it faces are those of the second half of the twentieth century. This is what we have found: it is what we seek to remedy.'[2] Some sympathy

---

[1] The member concerned was Lord Simey, and his reservation to chapter 1 of the *Fulton Report* was published on pp. 101–3 of that Report.

[2] *Fulton Report*, para. 1.

can be expressed with the views of a former Head of the Home Civil Service, Lord Helsby,[1] who said of the Fulton Report that it was 'not at bottom a radical report, and perhaps it is natural that the Committee should have been tempted to divert from the relative modesty of its proposals by presenting its criticisms in a somewhat ferocious way that was bound to make headlines. Old-fashioned doctors used to believe that the potency of quite ordinary drugs could be increased by speaking severely to the patient and making the medicine look horrible. A patient who was fundamentally healthy usually did very well.'[2] The Civil Service is 'fundamentally healthy' but, as the Select Committee on Estimates showed in 1965, there both was and is a need for further changes in the Service and the Fulton Committee was established to make appropriate recommendations. However, despite the important task that was charged to the Committee, this observer, at any rate, found the Fulton Report an unimpressive piece of work. Firstly, the Report lacked historical perspective. It contained no study, even of the introductory type contained in Chapter 1 of the development either of the role of the State or of the Civil Service itself over the past century or so. Whatever its supposed dramatic effect, the first sentence of the opening paragraph is historically inaccurate.[3] If the Committee had paid more

[1] Lord Helsby was formerly Sir Laurence Helsby and he was Head of the Home Civil Service from January 1963, when he succeeded Sir Norman Brook, until May 1968, when, on his retirement, he was succeeded by Sir William Armstrong.

[2] Lord Helsby, 'The Fulton Report', in *The Listener*, 18 July 1968, pp. 66–7.

[3] Chapter 1 indicates the historical inaccuracy of the Fulton Committee's opening remarks, and about these one notes that another observer has commented that 'some of the characteristics of the Administrative Civil Service most strongly criticised by Fulton are comparatively new, such as the practice of shunting senior civil servants at great speed from one department to another. The trouble about the higher Civil Service before 1914 was the exact opposite: that officials found it almost impossible to escape from the department to which they had been assigned, or had chosen to go, at the start of their careers. What Fulton blames on the 1850's was the product of Lloyd George and the inter-war years. Northcote–Trevelyan and 19th-century thinking have little to do with it'. (Eric Hobsbawm, 'The Fulton Report: a further view', in *The Listener*, 18 July 1968, p. 67.) Although, ideally, a specific reference to the import-

attention to the history of the Civil Service it would have more easily noted recent improvements in the Service, and if it had included in its Report some description of them it would have produced a better picture of the Service than it did, without lessening its room for manœuvre as regards proposing further changes. Secondly, despite the facilities at its disposal and its own emphasis on the virtues of numeracy, the quantification of its proposals was, unfortunately, not a characteristic of the Fulton Committee. For example, the Fulton Report favoured greater mobility into and out of the Civil Service, without sufficiently indicating the scale at which this was to take place. Thirdly, while its proposals for reshaping the administrative side of the Service had their merits – notably that of proposing the abolition of the separate Administrative Class – the Committee's recommendations about abolishing all classes in the Service and replacing them with a unified grading structure on the American model seems less desirable, particularly because of the probably adverse effects of such a structure as regards recruitment of specialists. The Committee's own analysis seemed to point to a two-tier Service such as that indicated in this book – an integrated Higher Civil Service supported by a range of occupational groups – which would constitute a departure from the existing arrangements, hoping to avoid their failings, and which would probably be easier to present to potential entrants than the Committee's proposed structure. Fourthly, the Committee's treatment of the problems of direct-entry recruitment to the Service was inadequate. It neglected to do more than briefly mention either the problems of recruiting specialists in particular or of non-graduates in general. The Committee also displayed confusion in considering the problems associated with direct-entry recruitment of graduates into the administrative

ance for the development of the Administrative Class of the National Health Insurance episode of 1911–12 would have been preferable, broadly speaking, Dr Hobsbawm's criticism of the Fulton Committee was justified. As it is hoped this book has made clear, the importance of the Trevelyan–Northcote Report for the development of the Civil Service was considerable, but the opening paragraph of the Fulton Report as it stands is too simplistic.

side of the Service, a majority of it favouring policies, one effect of
the implementation of which in the immediate future might well
be to discourage entrants from what has up to now been the main
source of talented administrators in the Service, without making
proposals that would ensure adequate replacements for them.
Fifthly, despite a good deal of talk in its Report about the need for
greater professionalism in the Service, the Fulton Committee gave
surprisingly little attention to post-entry training. The implementation of the Committee's proposals, while they would mean,
at long last, the creation of a Civil Service College, would still
leave the Service without anything comparable with the French
system of post-entry training, which, in my view, for reasons
stated in Chapters 3 and 6, is undesirable. Sixthly, although the
Committee had some interesting observations to make about the
structure of Government departments – the most interesting of
which, as will be seen, its terms of reference did not permit it to
make recommendations about – that of appointing a Senior Policy
Adviser in departments, at the head of a Planning Unit, able to
by-pass the Permanent Secretary, and be guaranteed access to the
Minister, seems misguided. The Permanent Secretary cannot at
the same time have responsibility for 'the day-to-day operations of
the department' and be deprived of it for long-term policy planning and the associated research: he is the Minister's senior policy
adviser. As for the Planning Units themselves, it can be said that
research might be most valuable if conducted in the functional
divisions where it would continually have a practical point of
reference. Seventhly, although the Committee approved of the
practice of making political appointments to the Civil Service, it
neglected to discuss such essentials as numbers, roles, relationships with the Press and with the Official Secrets Act, so it can be
said that the Committee failed adequately to discuss this practice.
Eighthly, despite the popularity that a further clipping of the
Treasury's wings will have in some quarters, this observer considers that the Fulton Committee's recommendation – which the
Government, unfortunately, has chosen to accept – that the
responsibility for central management of the Service should
be handed over from the Treasury to a new Civil Service Depart-

ment both was and is a proposal of doubtful practical value and one which will lead to duplication at the centre of the Service.

The Fulton Committee was, of course, assigned a larger task than that which this observer elected to undertake in writing this book. The Committee was asked to review the whole of the non-industrial Home Civil Service; this observer was concerned with the work of the Administrative Class of that Service. In the summary of some of the Fulton Committee's findings that follows, most attention has been given to those recommendations which have implications for the Administrative Class in particular and which relate to problems considered in this book in general. As will be seen, those aspects of the Fulton Report that have been selected for examination and some discussion are what the Fulton Committee had to say about machinery of Government; the convention of ministerial responsibility; the structure of the Civil Service; direct-entry recruitment to the Civil Service; post-entry training in the Civil Service; mobility, pensions and a career Service; and the central management of the Civil Service.

II   AN EXAMINATION OF SOME ASPECTS OF THE FULTON REPORT

Machinery of Government

Although, according to its Chairman, in framing its recommendations, the Fulton Committee felt obliged to look 'to a period ahead of not less than a quarter of a century',[1] an onerous task in itself, because of its terms of reference the Committee had to make its proposals, if not on the assumption that machinery of Government would be the same as now, then in the knowledge that it could not itself propose changes in that machinery.

The difficulties inherent in this exercise were indicated during the Committee's discussion of the structure of Government

[1] House of Lords, *Official Report* (1967–8) vol. 295, col. 1167.

departments and the promotion of efficiency in them. The Committee said that

> To function efficiently large organisations, including government departments, need a structure in which units and individual members have authority that is clearly defined and responsibilities for which they can be held accountable. There should be recognised methods of assessing their success in achieving specified objectives. The organisation of a government department to-day usually defines with great clarity the area of a civil servant's responsibility; his position within his hierarchy is also clearly established. But it is not easy in the Civil Service clearly and distinctly to allocate to individuals or units the authority to take decisions. There are two reasons for this. Decisions often have to be referred to a higher level than their intrinsic difficulty or apparent importance merits; this is because they involve the responsibility of the Minister to Parliament and may be questioned there. At the same time, many problems overlap departments; they often involve wide consultations at many different levels both between departments and with a variety of interests outside the Service. Decisions, therefore, are frequently collective decisions achieved through a sequence of committees – culminating, if need be, in the collective responsibility of the Cabinet. For these reasons clear delegation of authority is particularly difficult in the Civil Service. This has led well-informed observers, including some who have given evidence to us, to conclude that large-scale executive operations cannot be effectively run by government departments, and that they should be 'hived off' wherever possible to independent boards.[1]

The Committee itself was 'much impressed' by the system operating in Sweden under which small central departments had the main responsibility for policy-making, while the task of managing and operating policies was hived off to autonomous agencies. This system was used not only for activities of a commercial kind, as was largely the case with public corporations in this country, but also for public services in social fields.[2] In the Committee's opinion, Swedish experience suggested that the separation of policy-making from execution worked well, and it considered that there was a wide variety of activities in this country – ranging from

---

[1] *Fulton Report*, paras 145–7.   [2] Ibid. para. 189.

the work of the Royal Mint and air-traffic control to parts of the social services – to which it might be possible to apply the principle of 'hiving off'. The Committee observed:

> We have not been able to make the detailed study which would identify particular cases; but we see no reason to believe that the dividing line between activities for which Ministers are directly responsible, and those for which they are not, is necessarily drawn in the right place to-day. The creation of autonomous bodies, and the drawing of the line between them and central government, would raise parliamentary and constitutional issues, especially if they affected the answerability for sensitive matters such as social and education services. These issues and the related questions of machinery of government are beyond our terms of reference. We think, however, that the possibility of a consideration extension of 'hiving off' should be examined, and we, therefore, recommend an early and thorough review of the whole question.[1]

The large-scale 'hiving off' of what are now part of the activities of Government departments – which work in an atmosphere in which public money is very closely controlled – to bodies that would resemble public corporations – which normally have greater financial freedom of Parliament than departments – would have implications for the Civil Service. It could be argued that, freed from the need for concern about day-to-day Parliamentary control, the Civil Servants charged with 'hived off' activities could more fully concentrate upon managing them, and they could more easily be seen as being responsible for their successful management. Some would argue that it may be the case that only under such conditions can 'accountable management' – as favoured by the Committee – be achieved in the Civil Service. One does not necessarily have to agree with the Committee – and this observer, at any rate, would consider that the public corporations that have been set up in this country have not been successful enough to lead one to want to see more of them created – in order to appreciate the undesirability of the limitations placed upon the Fulton Committee: it was forced to recommend the setting up of a further committee to consider what it needed to consider itself.

[1] *Fulton Report*, para. 190.

The Convention of Ministerial Responsibility

The Fulton Committee's inability to make proposals about 'hiving off' functions from Government departments to semi-independent boards followed not only from its preclusion from conducting a general review of machinery of Government, but also from the rider attached to its terms of reference which prevented it from making recommendations the effect of which would be to alter the constitutional convention concerning the relationship between Ministers and Civil Servants. The Fulton Committee was not, however, barred from discussing the present working of the doctrine of Ministerial responsibility, and it devoted some of its Report to examining the problems of political control of Government departments.

The Committee considered, for example, whether or not it should recommend that Ministers at the head of Departments should be served by a personal *cabinet* on the French model, or alternatively that they should make a substantial number of largely personal and political appointments to positions at the top of their departments as in the United States. The Committee welcomed the introduction in this country of the practice whereby Ministers had the power to make a small number of temporary appointments in their departments, while giving its opinion that it was important that 'Ministers should be free to arrange for the holders of such appointments to be closely associated with the work of many "official" committees (i.e. committees of civil servants without ministerial membership) which make an essential contribution to policy-making'.[1] The Committee also drew attention to its proposals to establish Planning Units in Government departments. Each Unit was to be headed by a Senior Policy Adviser, of not less than Deputy Secretary status, who would have 'direct and unrestricted access to his Minister both personally and in writing', and whose prime job like that of the Unit, would be 'to look to, and prepare for, the future and to ensure that day-to-day policy decisions are taken with as full a recognition as possible of likely future developments'. The Committee said that the

[1] Ibid. para. 285.

Permanent Secretary, whose managerial burdens it thought would be increased if its general proposals were implemented, would still be 'head of the office under the Minister' with 'the main responsibility for the day-to-day service of the Minister and for accounting to Parliament for expenditure'. The Committee believed that the Minister's own methods of working would be one of the main determinants of the pattern of relationships at the top and the precise division of responsibilities between the Permanent Secretary, the Senior Policy Adviser and, in departments where they were appropriate, the holders of the most senior specialist posts.[1] The Committee said that 'these developments should increase the control of Ministers over the formulation of policy in their departments' and it saw 'no need for ministerial *cabinets* or for political appointments on a large scale'.[2]

The Committee also considered the related issue of the extent to which a Minister should be free to change the staff immediately surrounding him, suggesting that it only really arose 'over the positions of the Permanent Secretary, the Senior Policy Adviser and the Private Secretary'. The Committee observed that, 'Because of the nature of the Private Secretary's duties, he must be personally acceptable to his Minister; there should, therefore, in our view, be no obstacle in the way of a Minister's selecting from within the department, or on occasion more widely within the Service, as his Private Secretary the individual best suited to his ways of working; no stigma should attach to a person who is moved out of this job. As far as Senior Policy Advisers are concerned (whether career civil servants or those appointed from outside the Service on a short-term basis), we would hope that, as they will be selected for this job as men of technical competence and vitality, Ministers will not normally wish to replace them. This must, however, be possible when a new Minister finds the current holder of this office too closely identified with, or wedded to, policies that he wishes to change; or when an adviser's capacity for producing and making use of new ideas declines. It should be more exceptional, however, for a Minister to change his Permanent Secretary. Ministers change often, whereas the running of a

[1] *Fulton Report*, paras 172–87.   [2] Ibid. para. 285.

department requires continuity. Even so, Ministers should not be stuck with Permanent Secretaries who are too rigid or tired. Any changes of this kind affecting Senior Policy Advisers or Permanent Secretaries will require the most careful consideration by the Head of the Civil Service and the Prime Minister, whose joint task it is in this context to safeguard the political neutrality of the higher Civil Service'.[1]

In considering the relationship between the Civil Service and Parliament, the Committee stated that it would like to see Members of Parliament

> more purposively associated with the work of government than they are now. The traditional methods of parliamentary scrutiny have often failed to enlarge Parliament's knowledge of what goes on or to secure for it a proper influence; at the same time they frequently impede the efficiency of administration. Even the work of the Public Accounts Committee has not escaped criticism for inducing a play-safe and negative attitude among civil servants (it has been referred to as a 'negative efficiency audit'). We have noted the potential significance of the development of the new specialised Parliamentary Committees on agriculture, science and technology and education. We hope that these will enable M.P.s to be more closely associated with the major business of government and administration, both national and local, in these fields; we hope, too, that their consultations with departments will increasingly include civil servants below the level of Permanent Secretary. It would be deeply regrettable, however, if these committees became an additional brake on the administrative process. We hope, therefore, that in developing this closer association with departments, Parliament will concentrate on matters of real substance, and take fully into account the cumulative cost (not only in time but in the quality of administration) that the raising of minutiae imposes upon them.

The Committee drew special attention in this context to its proposals for accountable management and its recommendation that departments should be organised on the basis of accountable units. The Committee said that these proposals entailed clear delegation of responsibility and corresponding authority, and that it thought that 'in devising a new pattern for a more purposive

---

[1] Ibid. para. 286.

association with government departments, Parliament and its committees will need to give full weight to these changes'.[1]

The Fulton Committee noted the appointment of the Parliamentary Commissioner for Administration, observing that: 'He has not been at work long enough for us to assess the full implications for Ministers and the Civil Service of this new office. It is clear, however, that the office of Parliamentary Commissioner is to be regarded as a further means of ensuring the proper responsibility and accountability of civil servants to Parliament and to the public.'[2]

The Committee recognised that such developments, and any made in the direction – that it favoured – of lessening secrecy surrounding policy making in the Civil Service,[3] had

> important implications for the traditional anonymity of civil servants. It is already being eroded by Parliament and to a more limited extent by the pressures of the press, radio and television; the process will continue and we see no reason to seek to reverse it. Indeed, we think that administration suffers from the convention, which is still alive in many fields, that only the Minister should explain issues in public and what his department is or is not doing about them. This convention has depended in the past on the assumption that the doctrine of ministerial responsibility means that a Minister has full detailed knowledge and control of all the activities of his department. This assumption is no longer tenable. The Minister and his junior Ministers cannot know all that is going on in his department, nor can they nowadays be present at every forum where legitimate questions are asked about its activities. The consequence is that some of these questions go unanswered. In our view, therefore, the convention of anonymity should be modified and civil servants, as professional administrators, should be able to go further than now in explaining what their departments are doing at any rate so far as concerns managing existing policies and implementing legislation.[4]

The Committee did not underestimate the risks involved in such a change because 'It is often difficult to explain without also appearing to argue; however impartially one presents the facts, there will always be those who think that the presentation is biased.

[1] *Fulton Report,* para. 281.   [2] Ibid. para. 282.
[3] Ibid. paras 277–80.   [4] Ibid. para. 283.

It would be unrealistic to suppose that a civil servant will not sometimes drop a brick and embarrass his Minister. We believe that this will have to be faced and that Ministers and M.P.s should take a tolerant view of the civil servant who inadvertently steps out of line.' On balance the Committee thought it best 'not to offer any specific precepts for the progressive relaxation of the convention of anonymity'. It should be left to develop 'gradually and pragmatically', although the Committee thought that an inquiry that it recommended into ways and means of getting rid of unnecessary secrecy in Government departments 'may well result in specific recommendations on this closely related problem'.[1]

So, once more, the Fulton Committee was forced to propose that a field that should have been its to make recommendations about, should be considered by a further committee, and, in this instance, even more so than was the case with the structure of departments, the field that it felt was excluded from its review was intimately connected with its task. The Committee might have managed a fuller discussion of the problems associated with the political control of the Civil Service if it had related its examination of that subject to its consideration of the structure of departments. As was argued in Chapter 6 of this book, proponents of the introduction of ministerial *cabinets* have presented their advocacy of them in an incomplete manner because they failed to discuss satisfactorily the implications of this innovation for the structure of Government departments as they are usually organised in this country. The Fulton Committee not only did not recognise this, but it also made the same mistake regarding its own proposals for Planning Units. Their establishment would seem bound to have a disaggregating effect upon the structure of Government departments in this country: they would represent a move in the direction of the French arrangements. This may or may not be desirable, but the Committee neglected to discuss these implications. The view can also be expressed that research would usually be best conducted not in segregated Planning Units, but in the functional divisions where it would have a practical point of reference. Regarding the Committee's suggested relationship

[1] Ibid. para. 284, the inquiry being recommended in para. 280.

between the Senior Policy Adviser and the Permanent Secretary in departments, it can be observed that formally, at any rate, at present the Permanent Secretary is the Minister's chief policy adviser, and that it is far from clear how the Committee can, on the one hand, accord the Permanent Secretary the day-to-day responsibility for running the department and, on the other, preclude him for responsibility for long-term policy planning and the associated research. The Committee's proposals in this context are impractical and it is to be hoped that the Government will not accept them.

The Fulton Committee's caution about evaluating the effects of the appointment of the Parliamentary Commissioner for Administration upon the Civil Service was understandable, its observations about Ministers' rights to change Permanent Secretaries and some other staff can be broadly agreed with, and it made some useful comments about developments that impinge upon the relationship between Ministers and Civil Servants: but what the Committee was not able to do was to discuss the principle of the doctrine of ministerial responsibility. If it had attempted an adequate historical introduction to its Report, the Committee could have said a good deal more than it did about the development of this convention and related it to that of the Civil Service. In discussing this, Sir Edward Playfair recently wrote that in the period before the Trevelyan–Northcote reforms there were a number of what he called 'super civil servants', such as 'people like Chadwick and Mr. Over-Secretary Stephen, who were terrific men, civil servants far bigger than any contemporary type'. Sir Edward thought that one did not get men of the same type in the Civil Service nowadays because of the effects of what he called 'the great reforms' of 'just over a hundred years ago', after the implementation of which he said

the present concept . . . – Ministers in charge of policy and Civil Servants advising – became very precise; the present theory is in fact the theory of a hundred years ago. It is a rather sound theory and that is why it has lasted so long. The exceptions to it have become rarer. For some decades after the reforms, somebody of the old style would emerge every so often. A lion would jump out

of the jungle – like Morant, and to some extent like Warren
Fisher – but the jungle has now been cut back and the lions are
no more; the capacity of the present generation is no lower, but
they know their place.[1]

But what should that place be in modern circumstances? To this
observer, at any rate, it is a cause for regret that by the inter-war
period 'The pioneering Civil Service tradition of Chadwick, Kay-
Shuttleworth, Simon and Morant was quite extinct.'[2] That
tradition's extinction was needed if the doctrine of ministerial
responsibility was to be universally accepted, but over the lengthy
period that the Trevelyan–Northcote changes were implemented
the range of activities of the State were widened and this process
has continued since. At one stage in its comments the Fulton Committee said that 'Ministers change often' and at another it appeared briefly to recognise that there are now large tracts of Civil
Service work that do not directly depend upon ministerial direction and that it may well not be realistic to see Ministers as being
responsible for them. But the Committee failed to point up the
significance of their observations. The Committee in fact elected
to say as little as practicable about Ministers. Whereas, as will be
seen, it castigated the Civil Service for amateurism, it had little
to say about the tradition that Ministers are all-rounders, supposedly able easily to change between not necessarily related jobs.
Yet, Ministers are supposed to be policy initiators – a task for
which they are usually unfitted – and leading Civil Servants are
'trained' accordingly. If the State has a positive role, must then
Civil Servants be accorded one, too, with appropriate constitutional changes? Such questions have obvious implications for the
Civil Service in the future, but the Fulton Committee either could
not or did not choose to do more than skirt around them. The
doctrine of ministerial responsibility has obvious importance for
the work of the Home Civil Service – for example, the role of its

[1] Sir Edward Playfair, 'Who are the Policy Makers? Minister or Civil
Servant? II. Civil Servant', in *Public Administration* (1965) pp. 261–2.
[2] Robert Skidelsky, *Politicians and the Slump. The Labour Government
of 1929–1931* (1967) p. 391. In Skidelsky's opinion, by that time 'a different attitude reigned, sceptical and ultimately pessimistic'.

governing class, the Administrative Class is seen as being built around it – and any examination of 'the structure, recruitment and management including training' of that Service, unless it is to be incomplete, must include a full consideration of the present working of that doctrine. Given those terms of reference, the Fulton Committee felt precluded from making such a consideration, and its Report suffered in quality in the area it covered as a result of this.

The Structure of the Civil Service

The Fulton Committee's assessment of the existing structure of the Home Civil Service was that

> the present system of classes in the Service seriously impedes its work. The Service is divided into classes both horizontally (between higher and lower in the same broad area of work) and vertically (between different skills, professions or disciplines). There are 47 general classes, whose members work in most government departments and over 1,400 departmental classes. Each civil servant is recruited to a particular class; his membership of that class determines his prospects (most classes have their own career structures) and the range of jobs on which he may be employed. It is true that there is some subsequent movement between classes; but such rigid and prolific compartmentalism in the Service leads to the setting up of cumbersome organisational forms, seriously hampers the Service in adapting itself to new tasks, prevents the best use of individual talent, contributes to the inequality of promotion prospects, causes frustration and resentment, and impedes the entry into wider management of those well fitted for it.[1]

The Fulton Committee severely criticised the Administrative Class for being the main adherent of what it called 'the philosophy of the amateur (or "generalist" or "all-rounder")', which it saw the Service as a whole essentially based upon. The Committee observed: 'The ideal administrator is still too often seen as the gifted layman who, moving frequently from job to job within the Service, can take a practical view of any problem, irrespective of its

[1] *Fulton Report*, para. 16.

subject-matter, in the light of his knowledge and experience of the Government machine.' The Committee believed that 'It cannot make for the efficient despatch of public business when key men rarely stay in one job longer than two or three years before being moved on to some other post, often in a very different area of government activity.'[1] The Committee observed that

> Frequent moves from job to job within the Service or within a department give 'generalist' administrators proficiency in operating the government machine, and in serving Ministers and Parliament. But many lack the fully developed professionalism that their work now demands. They do not develop adequate knowledge in depth of any one aspect of the department's work and frequently not even in the general area of activity in which the department operates. Often they are required to give advice on subjects they do not sufficiently understand or to take decisions whose significance they do not fully grasp. This has serious consequences. It can lead to bad policy-making; it prevents a fundamental evaluation of the policies being administered; it often leads to the adoption of inefficient methods of implementing these policies – methods which are sometimes baffling to those outside the Service who are affected by them; and it obstructs the establishment of fruitful contacts with sources of expert advice both inside and outside the Service.[2]

The Committee also complained that few members of the Administrative Class saw themselves as managers partly because they were 'not adequately trained in management', and partly because they tended 'to think of themselves as advisers on policy to people above them, rather than as managers of the administrative machine below them'.[3] Referring to the members of both the Administrative and the Executive Classes, and their future counterparts as 'administrators', the Committee said that 'fuller professionalism' would be required from them which meant that new principles would have to be applied to their selection, training and deployment. It considered that

> It must be accepted that for the administrator to be expert in running the government machine is not in itself enough. He must

[1] Ibid. para. 15.   [2] Ibid. para. 40.
[3] Ibid. para. 18.

in future also have or acquire the basic concepts and knowledge, whether social, economic, industrial or financial, relevant to his area of administration and appropriate to his level of responsibility. He must have a real understanding of, and familiarity with, the principles, techniques and trends of development in the subject-matter of the field in which he is operating.[1]

As the Committee saw it,

The application of this principle means that an administrator must specialise, particularly in his early years, in one of the various areas of administration. At the same time, since modern administration requires men to have breadth as well as depth, and since civil servants operate in a political environment, it seems to us important that such specialisation should not be too narrowly conceived.[2]

The Fulton Committee also drew attention to what it considered to be the restricted role accorded to specialists in the Civil Service.[3] By specialists the Committee meant

those whose work in government is just one of a number of career opportunities for the exercise of their qualifications and skills. In this category are the architects, lawyers, doctors, engineers, scientists, accountants, economists, draughtsmen, technicians and so on. Some of these, like doctors and scientists, have acquired their professionalism or specialism by recognised training outside the Service. Others, like some draughtsmen and technicians, may acquire and develop their skills after joining the Service. In either event in their early years they do much the same type of work in the public service as if they had gone into private practice, business, the universities or local government.[4]

Although the Service employed large numbers of men and women of this type, the Committee considered that 'it has not always recognised the need for new kinds of specialism quickly enough or recruited enough specialists of the high quality that the public interest demands. In particular it has been slow to recognise the benefits that would flow from a much larger recruitment of particular categories such as accountants, statisticians, economists and Research Officers and their employment in positions of greater

[1] *Fulton Report*, para. 41. [2] Ibid. para. 42
[3] Ibid. para. 17. [4] Ibid. para. 35.

responsibility'.[1] The Committee drew special attention to the position of accountants, saying that 'present practice in the Civil Service severely restricts the role of the Accountant Class and excludes its members from responsibility for financial control. They are limited to the relatively narrow field in which departments themselves keep commercial accounts or are concerned with the financial operations of commercial organisations. Their outlets into other kinds of work and into posts of higher management are severely limited'. It was the Committee's view that 'qualified accountants could make a valuable contribution to the management of several areas of civil service work: for example, in financial forecasting and control, in the whole field of government procurement and in reviewing the financial performance of nationalised industries. These are areas of work similar to those in which accountants are prominent in industry; but they are generally excluded from them in the Civil Service. Further, the skills of the modern management accountant appear to us to be increasingly needed at high levels of policy-making and management. He is trained to evaluate policy options in financial terms, to compare the costs and benefits arising from different uses of resources, and to apply quantitative techniques to the control of expenditure and the measurement of efficiency'.[2] In addition to 'employing specialists

---

[1] Ibid. para. 36. The Research Officer Class has not been discussed in this book. The Fulton Committee described it as being 'employed in the collection, analysis, interpretation and appreciation of information mainly in the field of the social sciences; they prepare studies, reports and surveys. They are principally employed in the intelligence branches of the Ministry of Defence, in the Home Office, in the Ministry of Housing and Local Government, in the Ministry of Technology and in the Board of Trade. They are a graduate class, requiring a first- or second-class honours degree, or a post-graduate or research degree in geography, economics, statistics, sociology or other appropriate subject' (*Report*, appendix D, para. 28). In Chapter 6 the I.P.C.S.'s proposals regarding the creation of a Science Group and a Technology Group – they are reprinted in *Fulton Evidence*, Vol. 5 (1), Memorandum no. 38, pp. 335–45 – were briefly discussed, and it can be noted that the I.P.C.S. subsequently proposed to the Fulton Committee that a Social Scientist Group amalgamating the Research Officer, Economist and Statistician Classes should be created (*Fulton Evidence*, vol. 5 (1) Memorandum no. 39, pp. 347–52).

[2] *Fulton Report*, paras 36–7.

in the right numbers and of the right type and quality', the Committee considered that

> the Service should also allow them to carry more responsibility. Their organisation in separate hierarchies, with the policy and financial aspects of their work reserved to a parallel group of 'generalist' administrators, has manifest disadvantages. It slows down the processes of decision and management, leads to inefficiency, frequently means that no individual has clear managerial authority, and prevents the specialists from exercising the full range of responsibilities normally associated with their professions and exercised by their counterparts, outside the Service.

The Committee said that the obstacles at present preventing specialists from reaching top management must be removed.[1]

The Fulton Committee proposed 'a fundamental change in the structure of the Service'[2] which it thought was needed because the present structure stood in the way of what it considered to be

> the only efficient method of matching men to jobs – rigorously examining what each post demands before selecting the individual who is best fitted to fill it. The structure we recommend will improve the opportunities of civil servants fully to develop their talents and to get the experience they need for jobs of higher responsibility. It will provide a solid foundation for the application of the principles of accountable management and hence for the efficient working of government departments. It will mean that the organisation of a block of work can be determined by the best way of doing the job rather than by the need to observe the traditional hierarchy of particular classes. Since it will enable success in achieving set objectives to become the determining factor in promotion it will be a powerful stimulus to civil servants at all levels. Finally, the opening-up of opportunities, which it will offer to all civil servants, will, we believe, provide the constant competitive challenge needed for the achievement of maximum efficiency.[3]

The Committee believed that it was necessary 'to replace the present multitude of classes and their separate career structures by the creation of a classless, uniformly graded structure of the type that is now being adopted in many large business firms and similar to the system used by the Civil Service in the United

---

[1] *Fulton Report*, para. 38.   [2] Ibid. para. 192.   [3] Ibid. para. 193.

States'.[1] Although what it was proposing was essentially a pay structure that was not designed to determine the precise organisation of each block of work,[2] the Committee said that, by means of job evaluation, all types of job within the Service, whether a scientific job in a research establishment, high level case work in an administrative division, an engineering job, or a line management job in an Executive–Clerical establishment, could all be analysed and ranked within the same grading system.[3] The Committee thought that 'some twenty grades could contain all the jobs from top to bottom in the non-industrial part of the Service'.[4] In recommending a 'single, unified grading-system running across the whole Service,'[5] the Committee recognised that this meant that it was proposing not only the merger of the Administrative, Executive and Clerical Classes, but also mergers of the Scientific Officer, Experimental Officer and Scientific Assistant Classes, and of the Works Group of Professional Classes, the Technical Works, Engineering and Allied Classes and the Architectural and Engineering Draughtsman Classes. The Committee also considered that the supporting grades (e.g. messengers, typists, machine operators) should be brought into this structure.[6]

The Committee said that within the overall structure that it

[1] Ibid. para. 218.   [2] Ibid. para. 221.   [3] Ibid. para. 220.
[4] Ibid. para. 218.   [5] Ibid. para. 214.
[6] Ibid. para. 215. The Treasury's *Introductory Factual Memorandum on the Civil Service*, printed in *Fulton Evidence*, vol. 4, pp. 9–191, contains descriptions of all the classes mentioned above, including, of course, those neither discussed nor described in this book. The Technical Works, Engineering and Allied Classes are linked departmental classes which 'occupy a position between the industrial grades employed on actual production and the professional staff responsible for the initiation of planning, for technical design and development and for the general organisation and direction of all the material construction and working services. Most of the technical grades are complementary to drawing office grades, their function being to translate architectural and engineering drawings into actual production and operation. The technical classes are concerned with building of all kinds, with services such as power, water, heating and lighting, with production, repair and maintenance, with control of contracts on the site or in the factory and with inspection. They are also concerned with apprentice training and with the management of industrial labour. Their concern in these matters is executive and except in some isolated cases, the ultimate responsibility lies with professional officers. The

envisaged there would, of course, continue to be a wide variety of groups of staff. It distinguished what it decided to call the Senior Policy and Management Group which it saw as comprising 'all posts in all grades from the Head of the Civil Service down to, and including, grades that are to-day equivalent to Under Secretary', and it observed that

> Although the work of these grades is not sharply different from those immediately below, nevertheless, the higher one goes in the Service, the more one's work is likely to consist of policy-making and higher management rather than the exclusive practise of a particular skill or discipline. As a civil servant approaches these levels, his responsibilities become heavier and usually less specialist. He begins to share in a real collegiate responsibility to the Minister for the policy and management of the department as a whole; increasingly, too, he has to take interdepartmental considerations into account. At these levels an individual's particular occupational group is thus often of less significance than his range of experience, and personal qualities and qualifications should be the main criteria for filling posts within these wide horizons.

The Committee considered that there came a point, therefore, where promotions became matters affecting the interests of the Service as a whole, and those conducting the central management of the Service should play a part in them. The Committee distinguished the Senior Policy and Management Group in order to define the area to which this should apply.[1]

---

technical staff, however, handle most day-to-day matters connected with technical operations' (ibid. para. 502). The duties of the Architectural and Engineering Draughtsman Classes and the Typist Class are self-evident. The Machine-operator Class is employed 'where blocks of staff are regularly and substantially engaged on the operation of adding, calculating, accounting, punched cards and similar machines' (ibid. para. 367). The Office-keeper, Paper-keeper and Messengerial Classes are worth a note. The various Office-keeper grades are responsible 'for supervising and organising the messengerial and other services in a Government office building'. Paper-keepers are concerned with 'the putting away, custody and getting out of all types of records and any sorting of them that might be required, recording of documents by name and number and associated duties; also duties in stationery stores and post rooms'. Messengers are responsible for 'the carrying of papers and files from one part of an office to another and from building to building, doorkeeping and the escorting of visitors' in most departments (ibid. paras 382–4).

[1] *Fulton Report*, para. 222.

The Committee envisaged that

Below this level, the occupational content of the work is often greater than the managerial content. Thus, occupational group-ings of staff have a greater significance. They vary greatly in kind. The majority of civil servants are employed in supporting grades, where the work has little or no managerial content and its occupa-tional content consists more of the practice of a skill (e.g. typing, filing or operating machines) than the application of a discipline. At higher levels, the development and application of a particular discipline, and the need for specialisation by subject-matter, be-comes much more important, and in many parts of the work its management content steadily increases as a man rises towards the senior levels referred to above. At all levels, however, where the work requires civil servants to specialise (whether in administra-tive, specialist or the various kinds of supporting work), occupa-tional groups will be needed, and civil servants should generally be recruited and trained as members of them.

The Committee said that they should include the supporting grades, the present specialist disciplines, and two groups of ad-ministrative staff.[1]

Although it left to the new Civil Service Department the task of analysing all the administrative jobs in the Service and identifying groups of jobs which provided a field for specialisation on the basis of their common subject-matter, the Committee believed that it could identify two such groups at present.[2] First, it thought that

a broad group of administrative jobs in different departments is concerned with a subject-matter that is primarily economic and financial. Within this broad group the emphasis in some areas of government may be on general economic planning and control; in others, on the problems of international trade or of particular industries; in others, on the financial control of major programmes of capital and current expenditure; in others, (mainly in technical and scientific departments) on the economic and financial aspects of large technological projects. Thus, from a general economic and financial basis, the work develops its own internal specialisms. We think that this pattern should be reflected in the training and deployment of individual administrators for this work.[3]

The Committee also distinguished

[1] Ibid. para. 223.   [2] Ibid. para. 45.   [3] Ibid. para. 46.

a second broad group of administrative jobs where the basis is essentially social; for example, housing, town and country planning, education, race relations, social security, industrial relations, personnel management, crime and delinquency. Again, within a common framework of knowledge and experience, the work develops its own specialisms. Here too the training and deployment of individual administrators should reflect this pattern.[1]

The Committee emphasised that

Though in each department there should be a suitable blend of administrators from both groups, they should not replace those specialists in their departments (e.g. engineers, accountants, economists, sociologists) whose primary concern is the practice of their specialism. Thus, the economic administrators in an economic department would not, for example, generally replace those who are economists by profession. The economic administrators will not have the same depth of expertise, and will be immersed in the day-to-day operations of the department in a way that would be inappropriate for the specialist economist. On the other hand, the employment of specialist economists in a department will not duplicate or make unnecessary the work of economic administrators. Besides making their contribution to policy-making, the economic administrators will be providing a great deal of explanatory information for Ministers, Parliament and the public; they will also be engaged in negotiation with outside interests; many will be involved in the administration of existing economic policies, for example, policies for the distribution of industry. Jobs of this kind do not need to be, nor should they be, handed over to specialist economists. Indeed, a specialist economist who became immersed in these day-to-day problems of administration could not maintain the high degree of economic expertise his work demands. Similar considerations apply to the relationships between social administrators and the specialists with whom they work. Our aim is not to replace specialists by administrators, or vice versa. They should be complementary to one another. It is rather that the administrator, trained and experienced in his subject-matter, should enjoy a more fruitful relationship with the specialist than in the past, and that the Service should harness the best contribution from each.[2]

The Committee said that

---

[1] *Fulton Report*, para. 47.   [2] Ibid. para. 52.

From these groups and from the specialists will also come men and women to specialise in the kinds of government work for which many different kinds of background and experience can be appropriate. Examples are contract work, computers, O. and M., personnel work and so on. Such further specialisation would be encouraged and it should be possible where appropriate for some people to make their careers in one or other of these areas of further specialisation. For example, a social administrator or an accountant might go on to specialise in O. and M. work, moving in this field between departments to jobs of higher responsibility and eventually, perhaps after appropriate experience outside government, rising to the most responsible jobs in this field in the Service.[1]

It was the Committee's belief that

From all these professionals, administrators and specialists alike, will come the future top management of the Service. They will be men and women experienced in running the government machine; they will have a basic expertise in one or more aspects of a department's work; and they will have been broadened by increasing responsibilities and experience to become the fully professional advisers of Ministers and managers of their policies.[2]

The Fulton Committee, therefore, rejected the Treasury's advice about the future structure of the Civil Service for much the same reasons as those advanced in this book, notably that the implementation of the Treasury's proposals would 'to all intents and purposes involve the perpetuation of the present division between the Administrative and Executive Classes' and it thought that to be undesirable.[3] Indeed, although the criticisms about the generalist side of the Service were phrased more moderately than those contained in the Committee's analysis, the Fulton Committee's proposals regarding that part of the Service have their similarities with those developed in Chapters 4 and 6. It was recognised there that, because of the complexity of the work, those employed in those parts of the Service at present the province of the Executive and Administrative Classes would have to lead more specialised careers than was now normally the case, and some possible specialisms were indicated. The Committee left it to the new Civil Service

[1] Ibid. para. 56.   [2] Ibid. para. 57.   [3] *Fulton Report*, appendix F, para. 5.

Department to decide whether or not its two broad groupings of administrators – economic and financial, and social – will be viable. The Committee did 'not preclude further groupings if these are found necessary or desirable',[1] and itself commented on the heterogeneous nature of the latter grouping.[2] However, assuming that career opportunities within these groups will be as comparable as the needs of the work permit, the Committee's emphasis upon the need for greater specialisation on the part of future administrators is to be welcomed, and general agreement can be expressed with the Committee's proposals for recasting the generalist side of the Service.

The Fulton Committee's outspoken attack upon what it termed amateurism in the Civil Service naturally attracted criticism, including some of its conception of professionalism. This the Committee saw as having two main attributes, 'One is being skilled in one's job – skill which comes from training and sustained experience. The other is having the fundamental knowledge and deep familiarity with a subject that enable a man to move with ease among its concepts. Both spring from and reinforce a constant striving for higher standards'.[3] One critic, Eric Hobsbawm, observed that what this meant was 'entirely unclear'. He considered that what the Committee wanted to say, but omitted to express lucidly, was that Civil Servants were either professionals poorly trained (in a formal sense) for their occupation; or that they did not assess the present professional requirements for their jobs correctly; or both. Dr Hobsbawm considered that these were 'quite different criticisms'. He believed that the first of them was undeniable: Administrative Class Civil Servants were poorly trained. But he disputed the need for what he called 'fewer "generalist" and "all-round" administrators (who are quite wrongly identified with "amateurs") and for more specialists. This demand confuses two quite separate things: specialist expertise and a sufficient familiarity (or capacity to familiarise oneself) with a subject to make reasonable judgements about it.' Dr Hobsbawm said that the distinction was important because 'the confusion obscures the crucial point that what is required today

[1] *Fulton Report*, para. 55.   [2] Ibid. para. 51.   [3] Ibid. para. 32.

is more and better "generalists" and "all-rounders" in administration, and not more specialists'. For Dr Hobsbawm believed
that

> the general tendency in all forms of senior administration and
> policy-making has been in precisely this direction. In the high
> ranges of the American corporate world, the Soviet Communist
> Party, the French Civil Service, men do move freely from one
> position of responsibility to others which may be in entirely differ-
> ent technical fields, and are valued according to their ability to do
> so. Doubtless even the most adaptable executive or administrator
> needs to familiarise himself with a new job, and needs a minimum
> period to work himself into it, and the rate of turnover recently
> favoured in both the British Cabinet and the Civil Service is al-
> most certainly too fast, but that is another and less fundamental
> question.[1]

As regards the Civil Service, in this observer's opinion, it is a
fundamentally related question. One notes that, although she
wished that the Fulton Committee had 'chosen their language
more precisely', a former Permanent Secretary, Baroness Sharp,[2]
thought that there was 'a great deal' in what the Committee had to
say about amateurism in the Civil Service. She observed,

> I believe it is true that in the Service we have overdone what
> they call the 'cult of the generalist', and the higher one goes in the
> Service the truer this has been. Far too often, to my way of think-
> ing, Permanent Secretaries have been appointed to take charge of
> departments who have come from some quite different area of
> government and with, inevitably, no real knowledge of the work
> of the department, of the clients of the department or of the con-
> cepts that rule the department. This has been done on the theory
> that administration is an art that can be applied to any subject.
> Sometimes indeed it has been done more to solve a personnel
> problem elsewhere than in the interests of the department con-
> cerned.[3]

---

[1] Eric Hobsbawm, 'The Fulton Report: a further view', in *The Listener*,
18 July 1968, p. 68.

[2] Formerly Dame Evelyn Sharp, the first woman to reach the rank of
Permanent Secretary, a status she attained when made official head of the
Ministry of Housing and Local Government in 1955, a post she held until
1966.

[3] House of Lords, *Official Report* (1967–8) vol. 295, col. 1086.

As was shown in Chapter 1, in some contrast with the period before it, both during and since the Warren Fisher era, the holders of the leading posts in departments have been centrally appointed, by no means necessarily from the ranks of those with experience of the work of the department concerned. Also in contrast with the preceding period, during and since that era, the Administrative Class, whose members have filled most of those leading posts, has organised itself on the basis of being easily interchangeable all-rounders. Although he may well have understated the presence of 'amateur' attitudes in the pre-Warren Fisher Civil Service, Lord Salter's recent comments on the change to the arrangement of the Administrative Class on the basis of the all-rounder have some relevance. He observed about its dangers;

> Much of the work of the different departments is of a highly specialised character. Take, for example, the task of supervising, and subsidising, the complicated legislation under which local authorities carry out housing schemes, or – to take another department – aid is given to farmers. Years of continuous experience may be needed to qualify for such tasks; and without it the personal interest needed to give a sufficient impulse to dispersed and often reluctant local authorities is less likely to be developed. Excessive transfers at the top levels might change the traditional outlook. If the four principal officers in each department had been chosen, not because they had shown interest and ability in the actual work with which it was concerned, but because they had shown 'general administrative ability', administration as such, as distinct from the practical purposes it should serve, might become a fetish. The chief pride of those who rule an office, and set its tone, might come from making the wheels of the machine go round smoothly rather than in securing the right results. Policy, they might say, is for the Minister; ours is the task of providing the machine to execute it. This is of course the orthodox division of function between Minister and Civil Servant. But anyone with experience of actual administration knows that the distinction between policy and execution is not such a simple one. In practice policy is developed gradually by current administrative decisions; and the Minister needs from his principal Civil Servants advice as to the development of policy and not merely an instrument of execution. He needs it more than ever as the range and complexity of governmental action increase. Under the old system he was

assured of receiving it from men who had many years of experience in the actual problems with which his department was concerned, and who were likely to have a strong personal interest in them. Under the new system the principal advisers might be men with as little experience of these problems as himself, and even less interest. The specialists and the enthusiasts of the office would be in subordinate ranks. They would be regarded in the half-appreciative, half-contemptuous, phrase of the Service as 'the pundits'. The great panjandrums would be the administrators, concerned not so much to achieve the best results as to prevent the office machine from becoming clogged, to secure methods uniform with those adopted in other departments, and to avoid trouble – especially to avoid trouble with the Treasury. There might well follow a philistine's attitude towards the more scientific approaches or aids to the problems with which the department was dealing. The specialised officer under the earlier system, with a strong personal interest in the subject matter of his job, would be inclined to use relevant scientific knowledge and personnel, and organisations outside the office. If his life work was in relation to agriculture, for example, he would know the scientists who were doing the relevant work. He would consult experts in fertilisers on one side of his problem, economists on another. He would try to plan ahead, to see the longer-range effects of what was being done in current administrative action. Not so the pure administrator. He would want to 'get on with the job'. He would be one of a little clique of other pure administrators, similarly without specialised knowledge or interest, in other departments, in all of which they occupied the highest posts. He might even take a kind of pride in having neither specialised knowledge nor long-range policies, with which the 'pundits' of subordinate rank were concerned.[1]

Although with more elegance and with the advantage of a good knowledge of the history of the Civil Service, Lord Salter said what the Fulton Committee tried to say about 'the cult of the generalist' that dominates the Administrative Class, and which is also present in the Executive Class. Eric Hobsbawm's suggestion that the leading French Civil Servants are also all-rounders cannot easily be conceded, partly because, as he implied, they change between posts at much less frequent intervals than their British

[1] Lord Salter, *Slave of the Lamp. A Public Servant's Notebook* (1967) pp. 16–18.

counterparts, and also because the French Civil Service draws its senior cadres from the *grande écoles*, to which he rightly said we have no equivalent.[1] Dr Hobsbawm did not relate the deficiencies that still exist, despite recent improvements, in the post-entry training arrangements of the Administrative Class to its view of its role, although they are inextricably linked. He also did not seem to recognise that an Administrative Class which was other than 'poorly trained' and whose 'rate of turnover' between jobs was other than 'too fast' would be a changed entity. That it should be a changed entity has been an argument of this book. A merger of the Administrative Class with the Executive Class has been proposed – because the needs of the work indicate the desirability of this, and because of reasons connected with the recruitment of graduates – on the basis of a more specialised career pattern than at present, because the work that the merged Class would do would usually be complex. Therefore, in this observer's opinion, the Fulton Committee's proposals for recasting the generalist side of the Service have some value, although that was diminished when, as will be seen, the Committee's treatment of post-entry training failed to reflect its emphasis upon professionalism.

The Fulton Committee's proposal, accepted by the Government, that all classes in the Civil Service should be abolished can be examined against the probability that, overall, the freedom for manœuvre for career patterns in the Service of the future may well not be much greater than at present. The lessening of formal divisions may encourage flexibility but, in practice, the increasing complexity of the work may inhibit mobility as much as in the past although perhaps in different ways. Baroness Sharp's observation about the Committee's proposed classless grading structure was: 'Certainly the present class structure ought to go, but the sweeping proposal to have none seems a fine example of what Cardinal Newman called "the bottomless liberality of thought".' She found daunting 'the prospect that in the huge and varied organisation of the Civil Service there should be no classification of staff according to skills, qualifications, aptitudes, no clear idea of career prospects and endless expectation endlessly disappointed. The

[1] Hobsbawm, op. cit. p. 68.

comprehensive system from cradle to grave!'[1] Baroness Sharp's remarks indicated the difficulties of the position of the specialist groups under such an arrangement, a problem of some importance because 'the modern Civil Service contains, and must contain, representatives of practically all the specialist skills that exist in the country, and representatives too, of the few specialist skills of its own – tax inspectors and the like who do not exist in the outside world'.[2] As was shown in Chapter 5, the leading specialist groups are very important within the Service: only just under one-half of the holders of posts of Assistant Secretary status and above are drawn from them.[3] The Fulton Committee said that occupational groups would be retained within the grading structure which it favoured, but it was unclear how well-defined they were to be. If they were distinct groups then the unity of the unified grading structure would be diminished, and if they were not distinct groups – at least as regards the posts likely to be attained in the earlier part of a normal career – then recruitment problems to specialist posts might result. For Lord Helsby may have been correct in believing that 'On the whole, the tendency is for people to pay more attention nowadays to specialist skills than of old, and to say that the scientist is to acquire the label "Civil servant grade 10", or whatever it is, along with the lawyer, doctor, psychologist, agricultural adviser, and a host of others, seems to me to be ignoring differences which might be greatly valued by the people concerned.'[4] Moreover, specialists looking at careers in the Service are not normally going to be impressed by the possibilities offered by the unified grading structure of being able to transfer more easily to other specialist disciplines. Obviously, they are far more likely to be concerned with the opportunities open to them within their specialism – which may be easier to present to them if those practising that specialism form a distinct group, at least as regards

[1] Evelyn Sharp, 'Wide Open in Whitehall', in *The Sunday Times*, 30 June 1968, p. 10.

[2] House of Lords, *Official Report* (1967–8) vol. 295, col. 1099. The speaker was Lord Helsby.

[3] *Fulton Evidence*, vol. 5 (1) Memorandum no. 38, para. 27. This was evidence submitted by the I.P.C.S.

[4] House of Lords, *Official Report* (1967–8), vol. 295, col. 1100.

the earlier part of the career ladder – and, also, whether or not, at an appropriate point in their career, they will have 'the chance of being considered for advancement in the higher management field'.[1] Below that field, as the Committee's own analysis indicated, the practical limits upon interchangeability between the holders of posts tend to be even greater than farther up the structure because, at those levels, although the range of duties as a whole is still very wide, general management comes to play such an important part in most posts that it is sensible to see their holders as being engaged in much the same sort of activity. Where one precisely draws the line between the two areas of the Service is a difficult problem, partly depending upon how one interprets the roles played at and around Assistant Secretary level. But one advantage of drawing the line, at, say, the level of the Principal salary maximum would be that, compared with the Fulton Committee's scheme for a Senior Policy and Management Group, the specialists' opportunities of attaining the very highest posts would be improved. This is because the Committee's Group does not begin until Under Secretary level and as the Committee was told – and it did not suggest that this should necessarily be altered – specialists normally take very much longer than administrators to reach that level.[2] It will be recalled that the proposals developed in Chapters 4, 5 and 6 envisaged the creation of an integrated Higher Civil Service, starting at the level of the Principal salary maximum – the level up to which specialists advance as quickly as administrators – and below which there would be a range of distinct occupational groups. Specialists were to be assured that they could attain very high positions without necessarily having to undertake managerial duties.[3] Such an integrated Higher Civil Service would probably consist of about 6,000 Civil Servants,[4] a manageable total, and it, together with the accompanying structure below, could be more easily introduced than the Fulton Committee's unified grading

[1] House of Lords, *Official Report* (1967–8) vol. 295, cols 1099–1100.

[2] *Fulton Evidence*, vol. 5 (1) Memorandum no. 38, para. 37.

[3] The Fulton Committee indicated that they envisaged similar provisions being made (*Report*, para. 224).

[4] *Fulton Evidence*, vol. 5 (1) Memorandum no. 38, para. 27.

structure, and – subject to the obvious reservation that only a very small minority of the Service can ever even get reasonably near the highest posts – its creation would still mean that there would be 'an open road to the top' in the Civil Service.

Direct-Entry Recruitment to the Civil Service

The Fulton Committee devoted most of its attention regarding direct-entry recruitment to the Civil Service to the problems of the recruitment of graduates, post-graduates and their equivalents to what can at present be called the generalist side of the Service. It said rather less both about the problems of non-graduate recruitment in general and about those of recruitment to the leading specialist groups in particular.

The Fulton Committee did not envisage 'any basic change in the recruitment policy for specialists'.[1] The Committee considered that 'time-consuming formality' would be avoided if it became 'the normal rule' for specialists to be 'recruited direct by the department or establishment that is to employ them'.[2] As we have seen, the Committee wanted the Service to recruit specialists not only 'in the right numbers' but also 'of the right type and quality'.[3] No doubt the Civil Service Commissioners would oblige if they could, for as was shown in Chapter 5 they are aware of the problems of specialist recruitment. The Committee itself recognised that 'there is a national shortage of qualified accountants',[4] and it can also be said that industry and commerce will normally be able to outbid the Service for them. The Committee also said that there is 'a national shortage of lawyers',[5] and it can be observed that it is doubtful if the Civil Service can ever hope to be more than a 'second best' for lawyers, compared with the opportunities available in the profession outside. The Service's difficulties in recruiting statisticians, scientists, engineers, architects and the like perhaps indicate that there is a national shortage of most sorts of specialists and, no doubt, one of the main tasks of the job evaluation exercise

[1] *Fulton Report*, para. 72.   [2] Ibid. para. 73.   [3] Ibid. para. 38.
[4] *Fulton Report*, appendix D, para. 11.   [5] Ibid. para. 23.

to be undertaken by the Civil Service Department will be to pay special attention to the further possibilities of devolving work from those with scarce skills to other, less qualified, staff. It is possible that recent developments which have improved the relative status of some specialists may eventually make the Service more attractive to them. For the moment, however, some of the Service's problems as regards recruitment of specialists seem not readily soluble, and one fears that should the Fulton Committee's general structural reforms be implemented these problems would be added to.

As we have seen, in its recommendations about the future of what are now the Executive and Administrative Classes, the Fulton Committee went further than the Treasury had advocated in their evidence to it, and, in considering direct-entry recruitment to that side of the Civil Service, the Committee also disagreed with the Treasury's view that the graduate intake needed to be increased because the supply of good non-graduates was drying up. Projections of the future output of the educational system supplied to the Committee by the Department of Education and Science suggested that 'the supply of 18-year-olds with two or more "A levels" [the current requirement for entry to the Executive Class] will in fact continue to increase for the foreseeable future, though not steadily and at a slower rate than the output of graduates'. The Committee observed: 'With a steadily enlarging 18-year-old output on to the labour market there is no certain evidence that the quality of this output will be lower than it has been in the past; only if the national pool of ability were *both* fully tapped by the Universities and other institutions of higher education *and* static would there be reason to suppose that the quality of the 18-year-old output would decline.' The Committee considered that the Treasury's case was, therefore, not established.[1] Against the background of the analysis of this subject made in Chapter 4, this observer would suggest that what is lacking is 'certain evidence' either for or against the Treasury's evidence. What is surprising is

[1] *Fulton Report*, appendix F, para. 3. The Department of Education and Science's Memorandum was published in *Fulton Evidence*, vol. 4, Memorandum no. 10, pp. 290–1.

that the Committee did not refer to the evidence submitted to it by those engaged in school-teaching, a conclusion of which was that 'able boys and girls who gain passes at "A" level now want to go on to further education: if possible to a university, if not to teacher training. The majority do not really think of the Civil Service as a possible career at this stage, unless they fail to gain these prior objectives'.[1] In other words, at least as regards those young people whose education reaches the G.C.E. Advanced Level stage, the universities normally have the opportunity to take the cream. Their entrance-selection procedures may well not be particularly efficient at doing this, but it seems reasonable to assume that universities take some advantage of being most sixth-formers' first choice, and, given university expansion, it also seems necessary, therefore, to try to recruit more graduates to those parts of the Service at present assigned to the Executive and Administrative Classes. The Fulton Committee also came to this conclusion because of the larger graduate output from the universities and because – if its structure was changed along the lines preferred by the Committee – the Service would be made more attractive than at present to graduates of less outstanding academic attainments than those usually required for the Administrative Class, and because the changing nature of the Service's tasks and the development of more advanced and sophisticated management techniques increasingly required more highly qualified manpower. For these reasons, the Committee said that 'it would be surprising if the Service did not in the future employ an increased proportion of graduates'.[2]

In considering non-graduate recruitment to the administrative groups it proposed, the Fulton Committee did indicate the possibility of some grading changes and shortening of salary scales which might make the Civil Service more attractive than it is to potential entrants at Clerical Assistant, Clerical Officer and Executive Officer level.[3] Regarding those recruited with G.C.E. Advanced Level qualifications to what would now be the Executive Officer grade, the Fulton Committee – besides expressing its

[1] *Fulton Evidence*, vol. 5 (2) Memorandum no. 110, pp. 744–5.
[2] *Fulton Report*, appendix F, para. 4.   [3] *Fulton Report*, paras. 92–3.

preference for the retention of centralised recruitment – said that those qualifications might be 'pointers to the directions in which the entrants should specialise', that those entrants should be 'given jobs that match and stretch their abilities', and that they should also be given 'the opportunity of developing the skills and specialisms the Service needs, including the ability to use quantitative methods'. The Committee also considered that departments had 'a special responsibility for ensuring that the best of this age-group are picked out for early advancement and for appropriate further training'.[1] The Committee said that those who had shown the highest ability among the non-graduate entrants would join the graduate entry in a training grade, the time spent in which could be anything from two to five years depending on individual circumstances, and the object of which was 'to create a fast promotion route for the most promising young men and women; to test these young civil servants in jobs at different levels of responsibility; and to provide a sufficiently extended period for their training'.[2]

The Fulton Committee wanted all graduate entrants to its proposed administrative groups to be placed in the same training grade 'so that their fitness for different kinds of work can be fully tested after they have entered the Service'. The Committee attached 'great importance' to ensuring that 'the early decisions which may shape a man's career in the Service (e.g. about different kinds of post-entry training or allocation to differently graded jobs at the end of the training period) should be based on post-entry performance rather than pre-entry promise'.[3] However, the Committee considered that to underline the concern of the Service to recruit men and women of the highest calibre 'those judged outstandingly able and well qualified on entry should be given a starting salary two or three increments above the basic for the entry grade', an initial financial advantage which would 'disappear' when such graduates left the training grade. The Committee said that the award of additional increments to some entrants would not carry the implication that senior posts would be reserved to them,[4] but it would be difficult to convince those not awarded such

[1] *Fulton Report*, paras 87–8.   [2] Ibid. para. 95.
[3] Ibid. para. 85.   [4] Ibid. para. 86.

extra increments of this. To the potential recruit the scheme would look much the same as the Treasury's proposals for 'starring' certain graduate entrants to the Service and, therefore, to the present arrangements, which the Committee wanted changed. The likeness to such arrangements would be all the more apparent because, on past experience, unless they were either handicapped in some way during, or precluded from entering, the relevant competition for entry, most of the leading places, which would presumably be those which carried entitlement to additional increments, would mainly be filled by Oxford and Cambridge history and classics graduates.

A majority of the Committee favoured handicapping such graduates – and, indeed, arts graduates generally – when recruiting to the new administrative groupings that the Committee proposed. This view emerged during the Committee's discussion about whether or not the selection process should show some preference to candidates on the basis of 'the relevance to their future work of the subject-matter of their University or other pre-Service studies'.[1] A majority of the Committee believed that

> To give preference for relevance is to adapt to the needs of to-day the old principle that the Service should seek to recruit those it believes best equipped for work in government. When the aim was to recruit men and women to be intelligent all-rounders, the Service naturally drew heavily on courses like classics and history at Oxford and Cambridge, which by their prestige have always attracted young people of the highest abilities. These courses give an insight into the conditions of historical change and because for the most part the material they use is remote from the here and now they provide a 'disinterested' intellectual training. To-day, when the tasks of government have changed, the Service should seek to recruit those equipped for the new tasks. First-degree courses based on the study of modern subjects especially attract many young people with a positive and practical interest in contemporary problems, political, social, economic, scientific and technological. These problems will yield their solutions only to the most concentrated assaults of minds equipped through rigorous and sustained intellectual discipline with the necessary apparatus of relevant ideas, knowledge, methods and techniques. We,

---

[1] Ibid. para. 75.

therefore, wish the Civil Service to attract its full share of young people motivated in this way, with minds disciplined by under-graduate (and post-graduate) work in the social studies, the mathematical, and physical sciences, the biological sciences or in the applied and engineering sciences.[1]

This majority of the Committee observed that

There is also evidence that most undergraduates want jobs in which they can make direct use of their university studies. In recent years the Service has not properly recognised this, giving the general impression that it is more concerned with the quality of a man's degree than its relevance to the work of government. This, in our view, has discouraged applications from graduates whose interests and studies are focused on modern problems. Thus, post-war recruitment to the Administrative Class has run counter to the increased trend in the universities towards the study of the problems of the modern world. Therefore, to be attractive to this growing number of graduates, the Service should declare its special interest in the relevance of their studies. In this way, too, the Service would be attracting its recruits from a wider range of degree subjects than those from which administrators have traditionally been drawn.[2]

This majority of the Committee believed that

Though the ancient universities of Oxford and Cambridge have played their part in this growth in the academic study of the prob-lems of contemporary society, it has been most characteristic of the universities founded in this century. The date and circum-stances of their foundation have ensured that their courses have been mainly designed to prepare their undergraduates for work in a modern industrial society. To draw more fully on this source of manpower, trained in these subjects, would have many ad-vantages for the Civil Service.[3]

As for methods of recruitment, the Committee as a whole agreed that a method broadly along the lines of the present Method II should be retained, involving a procedure based on that of the present Civil Service Selection Board. The Committee, however, proposed changes in the procedure and staffing of the selection process. It said that there should be a larger representation of employing departments among the selectors, and that their age

[1] *Fulton Report*, para. 76.   [2] Ibid. para. 77.   [3] Ibid. para. 78.

distribution should be changed to increase the proportion of younger people. The Committee also recommended 'an inquiry into the methods of selection, to include such matters as the part played by the Final Selection Board and possible ways of making the process of selection more objective in character'.[1] Most of the members of the Committee who recommended 'preference for relevance' thought that the best means of giving effect to the principle, would be

> to give a small but definite advantage to relevance in the selection procedure itself by means of an objective test. One way of doing this might be to include such a test in the written qualifying examination. This is already done to some extent by the inclusion of a statistical-inference section in the general paper. We suggest that this practice might well be extended to provide in each of the papers alternative sections in which one alternative specifically tests the candidate's ability to deal with modern social, political, economic and scientific problems – similar, in effect, to the questions now set in France for entry to the *École Nationale d'Administration.*

These sections would carry higher marks than the 'traditional' sections, with the size of the advantage being 'sufficiently large to indicate clearly the Service's special interest in recruiting those whose studies have already partially equipped them to handle the problems of modern government. At the same time, however, it should not be so great as to discourage the candidature of outstandingly able men and women who have studied other, "irrelevant", disciplines'.[2] A majority of the Committee favoured continuing to have two methods of entry, although that majority did not consider it practicable to retain Method I in its present form. The modified Method I that this majority proposed would remain 'primarily a written examination', but the papers candidates could offer were to be restricted to 'those with a direct relevance to the problems of modern government' which were thought to include 'economics and business studies, social and administrative studies, science and technology'. This majority thought it important to maintain a method of entry by written examination because they

[1] Ibid. para. 82.   [2] *Fulton Report*, appendix E, para. 25.

considered it likely that some good candidates would come forward to compete by it who would not choose to enter if the only method open to them was extended interview procedure. This majority of the Committee, however, envisaged that the proposed modified form of Method I would be introduced on a trial basis and only retained as long as it attracted 'a sufficient number of good candidates'.[1] The minority who opposed the retention of Method I included amongst their arguments that if some potential applicants lacked confidence in their ability to compete in the social atmosphere of Method II, then Method II should be revised accordingly.[2]

It was not stated how this was to be achieved, and, indeed, the Fulton Committee's general analysis of direct-entry recruitment of graduates lacked precision. For example, the majority of the Committee who placed emphasis on 'preference for relevance' did not want this to be read 'as a sign that we wish to discourage applications from those men and women who have studied "irrelevant" disciplines' because 'the Service needs to attract outstandingly able men and women whatever the subject of their University degree'.[3] Given, as the Committee as a whole recognised, that 'the Service will continue to face severe competition for talent',[4] as a minority of it said 'the attractions of the Civil Service as a whole are not so outstanding by comparison with the other employments open to graduates that the Service can afford to discourage any source of supply'.[5] The Service particularly cannot afford to show markedly less interest in what has in the past proved to be its most reliable source of outstanding talent: Oxford and Cambridge liberal arts graduates. For that matter, the Service cannot also afford to appear to repel able graduates from other Universities who have taken similar if less prestigious courses. In Chapter 2 the eventual development of something along the lines of 'preference for relevance' was envisaged, but, as was stated there, as regards the immediate future it would be impractical. The Committee's own proposals for grouping administrators opened the way for a

---

[1] *Fulton Report*, para. 82, and appendix E, paras 13–14.
[2] *Fulton Report*, para. 84.   [3] Ibid. para. 79.   [4] Ibid. para. 69.
[5] Ibid. para. 80.

possible solution to many of the problems of graduate recruitment
to the administrative side of the Service. It would be easier to present such a structure to graduates in the social sciences because
they would be able to see more clearly how their university studies
could prove useful to them within the Service than they can under
the present arrangements. There may be some advantage of having
an additional method of entry reserved for such graduates, perhaps
also being open to graduates in pure and applied science as the
Committee suggested. The latter group would be unlikely to
attract plentiful numbers of able recruits because the best of such
graduates would normally wish to practise their specialisms at
least in their early careers. Nevertheless, more might be encouraged to come into the administrative side than hitherto if such
arrangements were made available, and they would normally
possess the gifts of numeracy which the Committee admired.[1]
This method, whether based on Method I or not, should not be a
soft option. The general standard of quality looked for in successful candidates would be the same as in the main method of entry,
roughly corresponding to Method II, and the starting salaries
awarded to such candidates with additional increments, if any,
being related to age, qualifications and experience. Like a minority
of the Committee,[2] this observer would prefer the Service to pursue a policy of attracting as wide a range of talented graduates to
the Service as practicable, including those from traditional sources,
leaving it to post-entry training to remedy deficiencies in their
professional equipment.

Post-Entry Training in the Civil Service

Although it recognised that 'great efforts have been made in recent
years to increase the amount of training that civil servants receive',[3] the Fulton Committee nevertheless favoured – and built

[1] Ibid. para. 81.   [2] Ibid. para. 80.   [3] Ibid. para. 97.

its discussion of post-entry training around – the creation of a Civil Service College,[1] the establishment of which would contribute to 'the more professional Civil Service of the future'.[2]

The Fulton Committee saw the Civil Service College as fulfilling three main functions. Firstly, it thought that the College should provide major training courses in administration and management. These should include: courses for specialists (e.g. scientists, engineers, architects), who need training in administration and management both early in their careers and later; post-entry training for graduates directly recruited for administrative work in the economic and financial or social areas of government; additional courses in management for those in their thirties and forties moving into top management; refresher courses in the latest management techniques; and courses for the best of the younger entry to help them to compete with the graduates. The Committee said that some of the courses should be wholly or partly residential.[3] Secondly, the Committee considered that

> the College should provide a wide range of shorter training courses for a much larger body of staff. These shorter courses should be in both general management and vocational subjects; they should be designed for all levels of staff and particularly for the more junior. We think it likely that such central courses could train civil servants more economically and to a higher standard in some fields than can be achieved by separate departmental training; we recommend, therefore, a review of the balance between central and departmental training to assess the possible extent of such a change.[4]

Thirdly, the Committee thought that the College should also have two important research functions:

> It will be uniquely placed to conduct research into problems of administration and those of machinery of government. In addition, we hope that the Planning Units in departments, which we recommend . . . , will commission the College to undertake specific research into problems of present or future policy on which they need assistance. Publication and open discussion are

---

[1] *Fulton Report*, para. 99.   [2] Ibid. para. 98.   [3] Ibid. para. 100.
[4] Ibid. para. 101.

important to research; the College should encourage this to the greatest possible extent.[1]

The Committee considered that 'This combination of major teaching and research functions should enable the College to fulfil a role we believe is greatly needed. It should become a focus for the discussion of many of the most important problems facing the Civil Service as a whole – discussion in which we hope that many outside the Service will share.'[2] The Committee did not attempt to prescribe exactly where the two kinds of training courses should be provided, but it thought it important, however, that

> the major courses, including those that are residential, should be concentrated in a single establishment large enough to be the natural centre of training and research within the Service. It need not necessarily, as we see it, be in London – indeed, there would be some advantage in its being outside. But it would be close enough to London to be accessible without difficulty for leaders in many walks of life. The shorter courses for the larger student body on the other hand will need to be provided in London within easy reach of Whitehall and the main range of government offices. A large non-residential centre will be needed. It may well be that this will have to be physically separate from the main establishment, because of the difficulty of providing teaching accommodation for a very large total student-body in one place; unless the residential establishment is quite near the centre of London, the other should in any case be separate.[3]

The Committee envisaged that young graduates recruited into the training grade for the administrative groups it had devised

> should, after an appropriate induction course, spend an initial period of up to two years in their departments, either at headquarters or, wherever possible, for some of the time in local or regional offices. During this period they should be placed in one or two different jobs selected to test their ability and aptitudes and develop their capacity to take responsibility. We attach importance to giving as many as possible the experience – more than can be gained from sight-seeing visits of working in the places and at the levels at which the Civil Service meets and deals with individual members of the public. Once they have passed proba-

---

[1] Ibid. para. 102.   [2] Ibid. para. 103.   [3] Ibid. para. 104.

tion, they should embark upon their main formal training. This should last for up to one year, but it may well be appropriate to divide it into two or three approximately equal parts.

The Committee thought that the course should contain four main elements. Firstly, 'Further training in the subject-matter of the various administrative groups, designed to relate the concepts of the fields concerned (economic and financial or social) to the practical problems of government. The course for Assistant Principals at the Centre for Administrative Studies now gives such training in economics; there should also be courses in the social field. As far as possible, both should be adapted to the needs of the individual, by taking into account the qualifications he already possesses in his chosen field and by providing in whatever way is most appropriate for special study of subjects handled by his particular department.' Secondly, 'The techniques of modern management, including staff organisation and management and the uses of numerate analysis as a tool for dealing with management problems.' Thirdly, 'more advanced and specialised training in the application of an individual's specialism to his particular field of activity.' Fourthly, 'The machinery and practice of government and administration including relations with Parliament, public corporations, and local authorities.' The Committee expected that

the weighting and timing of these four broad elements will vary between individuals. Not all will be of the type to get most benefit from advanced theoretical training. Equally, not all will need to make the same detailed study of the machinery and practice of government. Some will need training at relatively greater depth in management techniques. We do not wish to lay down any rigid pattern in what should essentially be a flexible process designed to meet the needs of the individual, the administrative group in which he is working, and the requirements of his department. Between the parts of his training course, and after it is over, the graduate should spend some further time in his department, still under training but undertaking more responsible work. During this period also, as many as possible should gain experience of work outside the Service – in local government or private or national-ised industry, as is most appropriate. . . . At some stage, too, all should have practical experience in the supervision and control of staff. For some there may also be a spell in a Private Office. The whole process should take up to 5 years, after which the graduate should be posted to the grade and level of job commensurate with the ability he has demonstrated since joining the Service.[1]

The Committee observed that

We are proposing for the graduate entrant to administrative work a crowded programme of training – on the job, in formal courses, and on attachments designed to broaden his outlook. We recognise that this involves the risk of trying to do too much in too short a time and of preventing the young entrants from settling down to a sustained job of work. To counter this, the programme should be flexible. We do not wish to insist that every entrant should go through the whole of the process we have outlined before he leaves the training grade; in some cases it may be appropriate that attachments and loans should take place at a rather later stage. But such variations should not be allowed to upset the general objective of giving the graduate entrant his professional training as soon as possible after he enters the Service, so that he can make a fully effective contribution in the field of his specialisation during the early years of his career.[2]

The Fulton Committee considered that the arrangements for young graduates recruited to the training grade as specialists should not follow any single pattern.

Much will depend on their particular field of expertise – whether, for example, they are scientists, engineers, architects or economists. Much will also depend on the requirements of the job they have been recruited to do. In any event, after an initial introduction to the work of the department or establishment, most will be put on the particular job for which they have been recruited. We think that in most cases they will wish to concentrate on their particular line of specialist activity for some time. It may, however, become clear after a period that an individual is more suited to a different type or level of job; the fact that he is in a training grade will facilitate his transfer to this. It may well be, too, that the requirements of a particular profession involved obtaining further qualifications or experience; some may be obtainable in the Service, some not. In any event, we envisage that many specialist graduates should, after a few years in the Service, go to appropriate management courses at the Civil Service College. For some the emphasis will be on the organisation and control of

---

[1] Ibid. para. 106. [2] Ibid. para. 107.

staff, for others on the techniques of management and financial control. After the completion of such courses, and in any case within three or four years, the specialist should be posted to the grade and level of job commensurate with the ability he has demonstrated since joining the Service. Thereafter we think that many should be selected to return to the Civil Service College at the appropriate stage for longer and more general courses in administration and management to qualify them for the wider role we have proposed they should play.[1]

For 'the 18-year-old entry, both administrative and specialist', the Fulton Committee proposed that they should be encouraged to take advantage of the training and further educational facilities available in the country's general educational system in order 'to take additional qualifications appropriate to their work'. The Committee recommended that bursaries and paid leave should be made available for those attending such courses. The Committee wanted such courses supplemented as necessary through shorter non-residential courses held at its proposed College. It thought that these short courses would be useful in helping to select the best of '18-year-old entry' so that they could join the courses to be attended by the graduates.[2]

The Fulton Committee recognised that the proposals that it had made so far related to the new entrants of the future and that

> The Civil Service College will also need to provide immediately for the present generation of civil servants, many of whom have had little training since they first entered the Service. This constitutes a major transitional problem which must be energetically tackled if the professionalism the Service needs is to be achieved, and to prevent the older and younger members of the Service from being separated by a damaging gap. Besides building up its courses for new entrants, therefore, the College will need to put in hand a rapid and large-scale programme for the further training of the present generation, and especially of those who entered the Service before recent improvements in the training programme began.[3]

The Fulton Committee believed that the facilities of the Civil Service College should not be restricted to Civil Servants. Indeed, it hoped that

[1] *Fulton Report*, para. 108.   [2] Ibid. para. 109.   [3] Ibid. para. 110.

on many of its courses a proportion of the places will be set aside for men and women from private industrial and commercial firms, local government and the public corporations. In our view, the College has an important role to play in laying the foundations for a greater understanding between civil servants and the outside world.[1]

At the same time, the Committee considered that the College

should not attempt to provide the total amount of training required by civil servants. First, departments should continue to run their own courses, though the College will have a part to play in giving advice and guidance. Secondly, we think it most important that more civil servants should attend courses at universities and business schools, not only because of the intrinsic value of their curricula but also again to help ensure that civil servants are not isolated from their counterparts in other employments. Many courses, especially those designed for the particular needs of the Service, must always be mounted internally. But wherever appropriate courses are to be found outside the Service we hope that full advantage will be taken of them.[2]

The Committee recognised that

A College operating on the large scale we propose will obviously need its own full-time teaching and lecturing staff. But in our view the College should also use on a part-time or an *ad hoc* basis civil servants and a substantial number of teachers and instructors drawn from a wide range of institutions of higher education (including the new schools of business administration). They should also come from industry and commerce, nationalised industry, and local government. We hope that the Service will associate with the work of the College the widest possible range of interests that can contribute something of value to the training of civil servants.[3]

The Committee said that

The Civil Service College should be under the general direction of the Civil Service Department which will be responsible for the training policy of the Service as a whole. We consider, however, that the College should have its own governing body, consisting not only of civil servants but also of men and women drawn from a wide range of interests outside the Service – from the Universities, polytechnics and business schools, from private and

---

[1] Ibid. para. 111.   [2] Ibid. para. 112.   [3] Ibid. para. 113.

nationalised industry, and from the trade unions and local government. This will help it to remain outward-looking and keep it in
touch with the needs of the rest of the country.[1]

In its Report the Fulton Committee, rather surprisingly, did not
attempt to evaluate the Report of the Treasury Working Party on
Management Training which was placed in evidence before it. Indeed, the Fulton Committee contented itself with giving 'a broad
outline' of how it saw the future development of training in the
Civil Service, and it did not deal with the exact scope and content
of courses to be provided by the Civil Service College.[2] However,
from what little the Committee had to say, it seemed that it did not
go further than the Working Party's Report. If implemented, the
Committee's recommendations, like those of that Report, would
represent an advance on the existing arrangements which, as was
indicated in Chapter 3, are themselves a considerable improvement on what passed for training as late as the early 1960s. The
Fulton Committee's proposals about post-entry training are open
to much the same criticisms as those made of the Treasury Working Party's Report in Chapter 6. Those criticisms need not be fully
repeated here, but some observations can be made. Firstly, one can
share the Fulton Committee's regret that in this country 'a body
of men with the qualities of the French *polytechnicien* – skilled in
his craft but skilled, too, as an administrator – has not so far been
developed'.[3] The comment can be made, however, that the Committee could have demonstrated its concern more practically by
recommending a more ambitious training programme than it did
for those specialists that are recruited. Secondly, it can be said
that, under the scheme that the Fulton Committee came to favour,
the training needs of all but a small minority of non-graduate
entrants to the administrative side of the Service will continue to
receive little attention. Thirdly, it can also be said that, if the
Committee's 'general objective' was that the graduate entrant
should begin 'his professional training as soon as possible after he
enters the Service', it is not clear why such training is to commence
only after the entrant has been in the Service for at least two years.

[1] *Fulton Report*, para. 114.   [2] Ibid. para. 105.   [3] Ibid. para. 17.

The Fulton Committee said that the Civil Service 'must be staffed by men and women who are truly professional',[1] but – as was argued in Chapter 6 – to achieve that object what is needed is the creation of a British version of the French *École Nationale d'Administration* and in this observer's view, therefore, the Fulton Committee can be condemned for inadequacy as regards its consideration of post-entry training in the Civil Service.

Mobility, Pensions and a Career Service

Having stated early in its Report that 'the public interest must suffer from any exclusiveness or isolation which hinders a full understanding of contemporary problems or unduly restricts the free flow of men, knowledge and ideas between the Service and the outside world',[2] the Fulton Committee included among its proposals that late entry into the Civil Service should be 'considerably expanded'. It considered that 'There are people in business, the professions, nationalised industry, local government and the universities whose experience would be most valuable to the Service. The need is particularly obvious in the specialist disciplines such as engineering, where men are needed with practical experience of kinds that the Service cannot always provide. In these fields there is already some late entry; there should be more.' The Committee also wanted more late entry on the administrative side of the Service as well of which it thought at present there was 'very far from enough', and what there was tended to be 'sporadic and unduly restricted'. In its view 'there should be no restriction on the levels to which suitably qualified and experienced people from outside the Service can be directly appointed. A steady inflow of suitably qualified older entrants with new ideas and relevant experience would, we believe, bring great benefits throughout the Service.'[3] The Committee said that

> At middle and higher levels, there should also be more short-term appointments for fixed periods; this would help to maintain

---

[1] Ibid. para. 31.   [2] Ibid. para. 19.   [3] Ibid. para. 124.

regular movement in and out of the Service. It would be particularly valuable in the case of those specialists, for example some engineers and scientists, whose special contribution would be up-to-date knowledge and practical experience of work outside government. It is also often the best way of using the talents of those, again mainly specialists, who are needed in an advisory capacity. For example, the present system by which professional economists come into the Service from the universities for a few years and then return, perhaps to come back again for further spells later, has been of great value. We think that it should be adopted in other specialist fields. In the various administrative groups similar short-term appointments for those with relevant experience in industry, commerce or the universities could also bring advantages.[1]

The Committee considered that

Determined efforts are needed to bring about the temporary interchange of staff with private industry and commerce, nationalised industry and local government on a much larger scale than hitherto. War-time experience proves beyond doubt the value of such movement in promoting mutual knowledge and understanding. Coming at the right stage, experience in a changed environment can also be of decisive importance in the individual's development. Interchange should be a two-way process (though not necessarily head for head) covering both administrative and specialist staff from the level of Higher Executive Officer and equivalent upwards.

The Committee recognised that efforts were being made to promote these exchanges, and it hoped that these would be continued and developed. The Committee believed that it was

at least as valuable for civil servants to go out for a spell. No doubt there are real obstacles: no doubt it is extremely difficult to spare good civil servants, especially at the level of Principal and upwards. At 1st December 1967 only 30 civil servants were away on secondment to industry, commerce and local government. We cannot believe that this is the most that can be managed.[2]

The Committee noted that

Several times in recent years Ministers have brought in professional experts and advisers of their own. These have been

---

[1] *Fulton Report*, para. 125.   [2] Ibid. para. 128

personal appointments in the sense that they have been individuals known to Ministers concerned, who have judged that their
individual qualities and experience could be of special help to
them in their departments. We welcome this practice as a means of
bringing new men and ideas into the service of the State. We are
satisfied that a Minister should be able to employ on a temporary
basis such small numbers of experts as he personally considers he
needs to help and advise him. They should be men and women of
standing and experience. We consider, however, that this practice
should be put on to a regular and clearly understood basis. We
think it inappropriate to propose any precise limitation of the
numbers of these appointments or any defined procedures. But it
should be made clear that such appointments are temporary and
that the person concerned has no expectation of remaining when
there is a change of Minister.[1]

The Committee said that the corollary of more late entry into
the Service should be a similar flow out of the Service, and it
thought that it should be of three kinds.[2] First, 'however well the
Service is managed, there will always be able men and women who
decide for personal or other reasons that they wish to leave the
Service for another kind of work. At present the pension arrangements make voluntary severance difficult. We do not believe that
restrictive pension arrangements are the right way to keep staff
– even those with scarce skills whose departure is a real loss to the
Service. It would be highly regrettable if civil servants did not
have valuable contributions to make to other areas of our national
life; it should be natural for others to wish to employ them.'[3]
Secondly, the Committee considered that 'the Service should take
the system of probation much more seriously than it appears to do
at present'. The Committee believed that the present almost complete certainty of passing probation successfully was not an
adequate spur to effort.[4] Thirdly, 'The Service should have wider
powers to retire on pension those who have ceased to earn their
keep, and should use them with more determination. Where
culpable inefficiency is in question, the present powers seem adequate, though we suspect that they are not always used as fully as

[1] Ibid. para. 129.   [2] Ibid. para. 130.   [3] Ibid. para. 131.
[4] Ibid. para. 132.

they should be. But wider powers are also needed to deal with the
small minority who, perhaps through no fault of their own, have
unforseeably ceased to be able to give a satisfactory performance
and ought to be retired early in the interests of the Service – on
fair terms.'[1] The Committee wanted the concept of the 'establishment' of Civil Servants to be abolished because it had acquired
'overtones of comfort and complacency', and, as a result, damaged
the reputation of the Service.[2] The Committee recognised that its
proposals to change the terms on which Civil Servants are employed and for greater mobility in and out of the Service meant
that the Service's pension arrangements needed to be changed so
that the scheme was made contributory and more fully transferable
than at present.[3]

Without repeating the appropriate passages in Chapter 6,
general agreement can be expressed with the Fulton Committee's
recommendations about terms of service and pension arrangements for Civil Servants. While in this book it has been envisaged
that greater mobility both into and out of the Service than now
takes place may be beneficial, some doubt has been expressed
about whether the scale of exchange can ever be large. The Fulton
Committee's proposals are difficult to discuss because – as, despite
the facilities at its disposal, tended to be its practice – it did not
quantify them. It can be observed, however, that the Civil Service
will continue to need to employ some specialists, notably economists, on a relatively short-term basis, and it will have some posts
– but probably not many – that can only be satisfactorily filled
from outside the Service. The Committee itself indicated another
consideration when it said that 'if too many of the senior posts
were filled from outside, this would produce frustration among
those already in the Service and discourage recruitment'. The
Committee also appreciated that if its aim was to create a Service
that was truly professional – expert both in the subject matter and
in the methods of public administration – long experience and
accumulated knowledge were essential parts of this concept, so
that while this involved 'a constant inflow of new men and ideas

---

[1] *Fulton Report*, para. 133.   [2] Ibid. para. 142.
[3] Ibid. paras 137–9, and appendix H.

from outside, it must also involve for the majority a professional career in the Service'.[1] Whether or not such a career in the Service should include secondments to posts outside is open to more debate than the Fulton Committee chose to engage in. The Committee received evidence which suggested that, at least as regards some possible areas of exchange, secondments can be difficult to arrange and, where made, should be of lengthy duration.

Lengthy secondments raise the question of whether the time would be better spent gaining experience in the Service, and, generally, this observer would consider this to be likely. As for whether or not there is a need for political appointments in the Service, this observer, unlike the Committee, does not welcome the practice – experience of it so far has not been encouraging – and, while agreeing that governments have the right to make such appointments, one would disagree with the Committee and suggest that more precision about numbers and roles was desirable. One would agree with the Committee that the 'flow of men, knowledge and ideas between the Service and the outside world' should be as free as practicable, but with the rider that in the event, the flow of men, at any rate, will tend to be rather limited.

The Central Management of the Civil Service

The responsibilities of the Treasury, at the time that the Fulton Committee reported, were seen by that Committee as covering 'both financial and economic policy, including the control of public expenditure, and also the central management of the Civil Service'.[2] The Committee described the Treasury as being divided into two parts to carry out its dual task. Its central management functions were discharged by the 'Pay and Management' group under a Joint Permanent Secretary who was designated Head of the Civil Service. The Committee said that this side of the Treasury also had 'important central functions in relation to the pay and pensions of other public services and bodies'. Noting the divided responsibility for recruitment to the Service, the Committee

[1] Ibid. para. 134. [2] Ibid. para. 244.

observed that 'The "Pay and Management" group, however, has never been, and is not to-day, a fully-developed directing body at the centre with complete overall authority to manage the Civil Service'. The Committee said that

> The Treasury has the final responsibility and authority on questions of Civil Service pay (within overall considerations of incomes policy); on pensions; on the number of staff employed and the grading of posts (i.e. determining the level of responsibility demanded by the job), though it delegates certain powers to departments from time to time – in some matters, such as grading, quite extensively. The authority of the Treasury is less in O. and M. work, management services (i.e. the promotion of the best management practices), training and personnel management; in these, its role is mainly guiding and advisory. In machinery of government questions where political considerations are often paramount, the Treasury advises the Prime Minister.[1]

The Committee considered that 'the Treasury has developed its functions most fully in those fields where it has full authority – like pay and numbers of staff. Elsewhere, although its central management role has recently been extended, it has been patchy rather than systematic, with too few staff and too little expertise'.[2] The Committee believed that

> The proposals we are making for the Civil Service as a whole – the abolition of the present system of classes, a system of central recruitment more directly related to the needs of departments, the greater professionalism of administrators and specialists, the better career management, training and deployment of staff, and the promotion of greater departmental efficiency – will all make greater demands than in the past on the central management of the Service to make these proposals fully effective, the role of central management needs to be changed and enlarged.[3]

The Fulton Committee thought that the primary role of central management should be to ensure that the Service is continuously governed by the principle that it should 'constantly review its tasks and the possible ways in which it might perform them; then consider what new skills and kinds of men are needed and how these can be found, trained and deployed'. The Committee said that

---

[1] *Fulton Report*, para. 245.   [2] Ibid. para. 246.   [3] Ibid. para. 247.

this requires that recruitment, training and personnel management and organisation should be regarded as integral parts of a unified process: supplying and developing the talent the Service needs and deploying it to the greatest possible advantage. Clearly this constant adaptation of men and methods to changing tasks must be a joint responsibility, shared between central management and individual departments, but central management must have the appropriate degree of ultimate authority in those questions that affect the interests of the public service as a whole.

The Committee considered that its main responsibilities, including those that are at present discharged by the 'Pay and Management' group of the Treasury, should be: to stimulate and assist departments in reviewing the kinds of skill and forms of organisation needed for their tasks as they change and develop; in the light of this review, to determine manpower requirements both in quantity and quality, agree with departments how these requirements should be met, provide the necessary common services for new recruitment and internal transfer and satisfy itself that departments are efficiently and economically staffed; to specify in consultation with departments the qualities, qualifications and experience required of new recruits to the Service; to determine (after such negotiations as are necessary in each case) pay, pensions and other conditions of service; to determine training policy in consultation with departments, conduct central training courses, arrange external training, and stimulate and guide training within departments; to promote career development throughout the Service, and in particular to co-operate with and guide departments in fostering the promotion, and planning the future development of the most promising members of all disciplines; to promote mobility both between departments and between the Service and outside employments; to discuss with departments (which should be required to consult central management on this matter) all promotions to the Senior Policy and Management Group, and to take the initiative in proposing individual moves between departments both within the group and at lower levels; to advise the Prime Minister on appointments at the salary level of Deputy Secretary and above, and about the most efficient division of responsibility between departments; to study new developments in methods of organising work, in management techniques and in office machinery, and promote their use throughout the Service.[1]

The Fulton Committee considered that for these tasks of central management to be discharged effectively in the Civil Service of the future, two major institutional changes were needed.[2] Firstly, 'the responsibility for recruitment and selection at present carried by the Civil Service Commission should be brought together with the other functions of central management within a single organisation'.[3] Secondly, 'the expanded and unified central management of the Service should be made the responsibility of a new department created specifically for that purpose'.[4] Accordingly, and as we have noted before, the Committee went on to recommend – and the Government have accepted its recommendation – that a new Civil Service Department should be established,[5] the ultimate responsibility for which would be that of the Prime Minister, the day-to-day responsibility for which was to be delegated to 'a non-departmental Minister of appropriate seniority who is also a member of the Cabinet',[6] and the official head of which was to be designated Head of the Home Civil Service.[7]

Although it was recognised that the Treasury's establishments work needed to be extended, it was made evident in Chapter 6 that this observer does not share the widely held view that there is a case for relieving the Treasury of responsibility for management of the Civil Service and handing it over a body such as the proposed Civil Service Department. In my opinion the Fulton Committee did not satisfactorily show why the advances that it thought necessary could not be made within the present structure. For example, the idea of having a Minister for the Civil Service has its attractions for some – although the Committee received evidence which raised doubt about whether the volume of work requiring Ministerial consideration would be sufficient to occupy fully a senior Minister[8] – but this observer would share the view that 'the

---

[1] *Fulton Report*, para. 248.   [2] Ibid. para. 249.   [3] Ibid. para. 250.
[4] Ibid. para. 251.   [5] Ibid. para. 254.   [6] Ibid. para. 261.
[7] Ibid. para. 258.
[8] The Head of the Home Civil Service told the Fulton Committee in 1966: 'It is sometimes claimed that there should be a senior Minister "for the Civil Service" who could speak in Cabinet and elsewhere on behalf of

historic Ministerial structure of the Treasury, in which the Prime Minister is First Lord, happens to fit the needs of Civil Service management very well, although the Financial Secretary might usefully be given a title which more aptly reflected the considerable responsibility that he already carries in this field'.[1] Perhaps the Fulton Committee allowed itself to be unduly worried because the British Civil Service was 'almost alone' in assigning its central management to the central finance department.[2] What was not demonstrated was that other countries' experience of alternative arrangements similar to those which the Committee came to favour worked either better or even as well as our own.[3] The Com-

---

good and economical management. But a Minister with this task would either have very little to do or would find himself interfering in the management functions of his colleagues in relation to their departments, and it is improbable that a strong Minister would long be content with the task' (*Fulton Evidence*, vol. 5 (1) Memorandum no. 14, para. 25). The Royal Institute of Public Administration, in its evidence to the Committee, considered that the idea of having a Minister for the Civil Service had some inherent disadvantages, one of which was that 'it is unlikely that the volume of work requiring Ministerial consideration would be sufficient to occupy fully a senior Minister' (*Fulton Evidence*, vol. 5 (2) Memorandum no. 107, para. 26).

[1] *Fulton Evidence*, vol. 5 (1) Memorandum no. 14, para. 12.

[2] *Fulton Report*, para. 252.

[3] In its evidence to the Fulton Committee about the control and management of the Civil Service, the Royal Institute of Public Administration said that it was 'by no means certain that this can best be done by the country's Ministry of Finance'. It thought that 'as far as the Establishments side of the Treasury is concerned, it is doubtful whether there are now very strong reasons for it to be in close proximity to those responsible for determining financial policy and holding the nation's purse strings'. The Institute thought that 'it would be advantageous to bring together the Civil Service Commission and the Establishment side of the Treasury, so that the interacting problems which each of them encounters can be dealt with under one management and one roof'. The Institute said that 'such an arrangement is understood to be working successfully in other countries' (*Fulton Evidence*, Memorandum no. 107, paras 22–4). The Institute did not indicate which 'other countries' were successfully working with such arrangements, but in an appendix to its evidence to the Fulton Committee (ibid. pp. 735–6) it drew the Committee's attention to the control and management of the Civil Services of Australia, Canada and New Zealand, and to some recent writing on the subject. The book referred to was Gerald E. Caiden, *Career Service. An Introduction to*

mittee failed to rebut satisfactorily the argument that 'under concentrated control the two functions of controlling expenditure and managing the Service can each be more effectively discharged through being combined in one department', and that 'such a single department must be more effective on both sides of its work by reason of the knowledge of departmental organisation and personalities that is derived from its wide range of interest'.[1] The Committee considered that there would be reason to fear too great a concentration of power in one department if the enlarged responsibility for career development, which it envisaged being given to those conducting the central management of the Service, was added to the Treasury's responsibilities for financial and economic policy and for the control of public expenditure.[2] One

---

the *History of Personnel Administration in the Commonwealth Public Service of Australia* 1901–1961 (1965). The articles referred to were: D. C. Rowat, 'Canada's Royal Commission on Government Organization', in *Public Administration* (1963); G. V. Tunnoch, 'The Glassco Commission: did it cost more than it was worth?', in *Canadian Public Administration* (1964); John F. Robertson, 'The Royal Commission on State Services in New Zealand and the State Services Act 1962', in *Public Administration* (1965); and John F. Robertson, 'Efficiency and Economy in the New Zealand Public Service', in *New Zealand Journal of Public Administration* (1965). The articles by Professor Rowat and Messrs Tunnoch and Robertson are remarkably informative, but they do not lend support to the view that the British arrangements should be changed. As for Dr Caiden's fine study of the Australian Public Service, one can note that in his conclusion he observed: 'The intervention of the Government in Service affairs through Cabinet decision, the Treasury Department and the Department of Labour and National Service had limited the Commonwealth Public Service Board's independence of action. Of its three main functions – the overall supervision of personnel administration in the Commonwealth departments, the determination of conditions of employment in the Service, and the maintenance of economy and efficiency in Commonwealth administration – it had been a free (but not the sole) agent only in the first. Even in that limited area the Government had been reluctant to grant it the necessary funds and had maintained a strict scrutiny over its proposals regarding the Commonwealth Public Service Act and Regulations. The departments varied in the extent to which they co-operated with the Board. Only in the 1947–51 period was the Board strong enough to overcome opposition but after that the Government and the permanent heads tended to overrule it' (Caiden, op. cit. p. 433).

[1] *Fulton Evidence*, vol. 5 (1) Memorandum no. 14, para. 24.
[2] *Fulton Report*, para. 252.

notes that the general view among Permanent Secretaries was that a strong and effective combined Treasury improved machinery of Government as a whole,[1] and that they preferred 'to deal with one central controlling department and fear that it would complicate their task of management to have to "clear their lines" with two departments; that in particular the present system enables departments to get central approval of proposals as regards both staff and expenditure in the same operation, and they dislike the prospect of two independent, though overlapping, operations'.[2] It can also be observed that, in view of the importance which the Committee itself placed upon such work, the Fulton Committee's recommendation that the responsibility for 'the development and dissemination of administrative and managerial techniques' should be transferred from the Treasury to the new Civil Service Department[3] was a particularly unfortunate one, because, as the then Joint Permanent Secretary to the Treasury told the Committee: 'The dissemination of knowledge of these techniques, and their application to particular projects or blocks of expenditure call for close collaboration with the divisions dealing with expenditure and the advantages of conducting such a joint operation in a single department are obvious.'[4]

Whether or not it appreciated these advantages, the Fulton Committee did not believe that its general proposals for reform would be implemented in the radical spirit it deemed to be necessary if the central management of the Service remained with the Treasury. The Committee also asserted that 'There is to-day among civil servants a lack of confidence in the Treasury as the centre of Civil Service management'.[5] As no supporting evidence was referred to, this assertion is difficult to examine. The observation can be made, however, that the desire among some staff associations to place the central management of the Service in other hands than those of the Treasury may partly follow from the expectation that 'better' pay deals would result. Even though it is

[1] *Fulton Evidence*, vol. 5 (1) Memorandum no. 14, para. 24.
[2] Ibid. para. 27.   [3] *Fulton Report*, para. 265.
[4] *Fulton Evidence*, vol. 5 (1) Memorandum no. 14, para. 25.
[5] *Fulton Report*, para. 253.

expected to be 'in a position to fight, and to be seen fighting, the Treasury on behalf of the Service',[1] one would think it unlikely that the new Civil Service Department will be able to 'improve' on the present arrangements, which taxpayers may well consider to be generous enough anyway.[2] In 1966, the then Head of the Home Civil Service estimated that the staff costs of the industrial and non-industrial Civil Service, excluding the Post Office, amounted to about £850 millions.[3] It is obvious that the Chancellor of the Exchequer must have a major voice in decisions relating to so large a sum of public expenditure,[4] so the creation of the Civil Service Department seems unlikely to change the present position regarding Civil Service pay. The Treasury may also be unpopular with some Civil Servants because at least during and since the Warren Fisher era, a Permanent Secretary to the Treasury has been designated Head of the Civil Service with power to advise the Prime Minister about leading appointments throughout the Service, and some hopes of advancement will no doubt have been frustrated. In future, as was said earlier, the head of the Civil Service Department will be the Head of the Service, and the Fulton Committee in addition proposed the formalisation of the consultations that the Head of the Service undertakes in advising upon leading appointments.[5] As the Service seems likely always to have

[1] *Fulton Report*, para. 252.

[2] At present Civil Service pay is determined by the principle of 'fair comparison with the current remuneration of outside staffs employed on broadly comparable work' which was established by the Royal Commission on the Civil Service 1953–5 (*Priestley Report*, para. 96). As the Service, at least at present, is virtually immune from redundancy, its existing pay arrangements seem not only generous but inflationary.

[3] *Fulton Evidence*, vol. 5 (1) Memorandum no. 14, para. 22.

[4] Ibid. para. 23.

[5] *Fulton Report*, para. 260. The Committee said that 'At present the Head of the Civil Service makes his recommendations to the Prime Minister after consultation with the Minister and others directly concerned. We have no reason to doubt that all the relevant views are taken into account. We think, however, that this arrangement vests too much responsibility in a single individual and in a way that creates the impression that his recommendations to the Prime Minister are within his sole discretion. Many civil servants criticise this – we think rightly. In future we consider that in putting forward names to the Prime Minister the Head of the Civil Service should be assisted by a committee. The com-

fewer top jobs than ambitious men and women who would like to fill at least one of them, if opprobrium has been heaped on the Treasury about some promotions in the past, it seems probable that this will be the lot of the Civil Service Department in the future.

Without denying either that the Treasury's past record as regards its management of the Service has not been without its blemishes, or suggesting that further improvements in its performance in that sphere were not needed, it does seem to this observer that the Fulton Committee attached insufficient importance either to the effects of the 1962 reforms of its organisation upon the Treasury's attitudes to its managerial duties, or to the arguments presented to it about the advantages of having the management of the Service and finance within one department. The Fulton Committee did not show why its programme of reform could not have been entrusted to an expanded Treasury, perhaps one even including the Civil Service Commission enjoying the status that the Committee saw it having in the Civil Service Department.[1] While the creation of that Department may well have 'some presentational advantage',[2] at least at first, it seems probable that practice

---

mittee should have a variable composition, depending on the appointments and candidates under consideration. It should be drawn from a panel. The panel should have a rotating membership, appointment to it being for a term of, say, two or three years. Normally the committee would consist of two or three Permanent Secretaries, an approximately equal number of scientists or other specialists and not more than two eminent people from outside the Service. The "outsiders" might have no personal knowledge of the candidates, but their wide experience of business or other outside activity could in our view help to avoid an inbred and purely Civil Service attitude to these appointments. The Head of the Civil Service, after consulting the Ministers concerned and this Committee, should put forward recommendations to the Prime Minister. We recommend that this procedure should cover all appointments at the salary-level of Deputy Secretary and above.'

[1] *Fulton Report*, para. 64. The Committee did not wish to make a detailed recommendation, but it did envisage an individual senior officer in the Civil Service Department as First Civil Service Commissioner with 'the formal responsibility for final decisions on the selection of recruits'. The Committee said that 'It should be accepted no less clearly than in the past that the First Commissioner would not be subjected to ministerial or parliamentary questioning over individual appointments'.

[2] *Fulton Evidence*, vol. 5 (1) Memorandum no. 14, para. 28.

will eventually show that the Committee's ill-considered recommendation has led to needless duplication at the centre of the Service.

III   FINAL COMMENTS

Since the present Government took office in 1964 there has been a good deal of activity in the sphere of institutional reform. Changes have been made in Central Government machinery – notably the establishment of the Ministry of Technology and the Department of Economic Affairs; and the amalgamations which led to the creation of the Ministry of Health and Social Security, and the Foreign and Commonwealth Office – and some regional bodies have been established. One can also point to the attempts that have been made to modernise Parliamentary procedure; the appointment of a Parliamentary Commissioner for Administration; the Seebohm Committee's review of Local Authority Personal Service; the then Ministry of Health's Green Paper about the structure of the National Health Service; and the investigations of the Maud and Wheatley Commissions into the English and Scottish Local Government systems. To this list one can add the Fulton Committee's Report on the Civil Service. However, the Prime Minister's claim that this activity constitutes 'a strong start' towards achieving 'the modernisation of the basic institutions of this country'[1] cannot easily be conceded. What has taken place has been unco-ordinated. No synoptic view of machinery of Government has been taken. In the absence of such a general reappraisal what we have had is a series of piecemeal reappraisals – such as those listed above – one of which has been conducted by the Fulton Committee on the Civil Service.

The Fulton Committee pointed out that there has been no systematic examination of the machinery of Government by an outside body since the Haldane Committee reported in 1918, and it said that its suggested review of the possibilities of 'hiving off'

[1] House of Commons, *Official Report* (1967–8) vol. 767, col. 455.

some more Government activities to autonomous boards recommended substantial changes, this would 'also provide the opportunity for simultaneous consideration to be given to a general review of the machinery of Government'.[1] Baroness Sharp recently observed that 'both Ministers and Civil Servants suffer acutely from the present confusion of responsibilities and multiplicity of departments', and that 'unless we tackle this problem of the machinery of Government, whatever changes are made in the Civil Service, it will still work under appalling handicaps'.[2] As the Fulton Committee did not do it, a detailed consideration of the working relationship between Ministers and their departments needs to be undertaken, and would be most appropriately done as part of a review of machinery of Government. In this observer's opinion, this task would be best assigned, not to an 'outside body' such as the Haldane Committee – the practical achievements of which were not numerous[3] – but to a body similar to the Plowden Committee on the Control of Public Expenditure of 1958–61, although in this instance the membership would have to include

[1] *Fulton Report*, para. 293.

[2] House of Lords, *Official Report* (1967–8) vol. 295, col. 1090. Another former Permanent Secretary, Lord Sherfield (formerly Sir Roger Makins), observed that 'A practice seems to have developed of setting up two departments in a field of activity which had hitherto been the province of one department. The Department of Economic Affairs and the Treasury, the Ministry of Technology and the Board of Trade, are examples. This policy establishes an interface between departments in the same field which inevitably generates friction and therefore increases the strain on the machine and on the civil servants who have to work it' (Ibid. cols 1122–1123.) The creation of the Civil Service Department seems to be another exercise in needless duplication and in some contrast with the present Government's attempts to rationalise other parts of the machinery of Government, notably the mergers of the Foreign and Commonwealth Relations Office, and of the Ministries of Health and of Social Security. The administrative advantages of the latter merger are not obvious. What is obvious is that this activity as regards institutional change is uncoordinated.

[3] As the Warden of Nuffield College, Oxford, once commented: 'The Haldane Committee on the Machinery of Government is often cited as an outstanding document in the field of public administration, but how many of its recommendations were implemented?' (D. N. Chester, 'The Plowden Report: I. Nature and Significance', in *Public Administration*, 1963, p. 6.)

not only serving or former Civil Servants but also those with Ministerial experience.

Ideally, such a review should have preceded the recent activity concerning institutional reform and, as has been shown, the Fulton Committee's examination of the Home Civil Service was handicapped because it had to consider proposals for changing machinery of Government, except as regards the central management of the Service as being outside its terms of reference. However, as has been shown, and allowing for its preclusion from being able to make a full consideration of the present working of the convention of Ministerial responsibility, even in the sphere that was indisputably its to review, the Fulton Committee all too often displayed a lack of imagination in making its proposals, and when it did demonstrate that quality realism was frequently absent. Yet, contemporary observers spoke equally harshly about the Trevelyan–Northcote Report. The Fulton Committee has had the satisfaction of having its major recommendations accepted by the Government of the day. Should great things follow from the effects of their implementation, the Fulton Report, for all its shortcomings, may, by historical provenance, still come to be ranked as one of the landmarks in the development of the British Constitution.

The Structure and Relative Size
of the Administrative Class

TABLE I: THE STRUCTURE OF THE
ADMINISTRATIVE CLASS, 1966

	Numbers as at 1 January 1966		
Grade	*Permanent*	*Temporary*	*Total*
Joint Permanent Secretary to the Treasury and Secretary to the Cabinet	3	–	3
Permanent Secretary	26	–	26
Second Permanent Secretary	4	–	4
Deputy Secretary	65	1	66
Under Secretary	256	1	257
Assistant Secretary	759	5	764
Principal	1004	69½	1073½
Assistant Principal	244	2	246
TOTAL	2361	78½	2439½

Source: H.M. Treasury, *Introductory Factual Memorandum on the Civil Service presented to the Fulton Committee on the Civil Service* (1966) para. 97. The halves in the statistics denote part-time staff.

Note: These figures differ from those given for 1 Jan 1966, in the publication by H.M. Treasury, *Civil Service Manpower* (1966), table 19. This is of importance because the next two Tables in this Appendix are taken from that collection of statistics. The structure of the Administrative Class as shown there was Permanent Secretaries (32), Deputy Secretaries (71), Under-Secretaries (256), Assistant Secretaries (732), Principals (1013) and Assistant Principals (240), giving a total of 2344.

TABLE 2: THE ADMINISTRATIVE CLASS BY METHOD OF ENTRY, 1966

Grade	Direct Entrants	Indirect Entrants	Entry According to			
			A	B	C	D
Permanent Secretary	26	6	20	4	–	8
Deputy Secretary	59	12	39	10	–	22
Under-Secretary	182	74	144	28	5	79
Assistant Secretary	414	318	295	68	64	305
Principal	528	485	352	127	62	472
Assistant Principal	204	36	204	–	20	16
TOTAL	1413	931	1054	237	151	902
Percentages	60	40	46	10	6	38

Notes: (1) The source was H.M. Treasury, *Civil Service Manpower* (1966) table 20: the figures being for 1 Jan 1966.
    (2) A = Open Competition to Assistant Principal.
         B = Open Competition, Assimilation or Nomination to Principal or Assistant Secretary.
         C = Limited Competition to Assistant Principal.
         D = Promotion from other classes.

TABLE 3 : UNIVERSITY GRADUATES IN THE
ADMINISTRATIVE CLASS, 1966

	Known to be graduates	Not known to be graduates
Permanent Secretary	30	2
Deputy Secretary	67	4
Under Secretary	231	25
Assistant Secretary	561	171
Principal	686	327
Assistant Principal	222	18
TOTAL	1797	547
Percentages	77	23

Notes: (1) Figures derived from the Administrative Class Register at 15 Mar 1966: excludes C.R.O., Trade Commission and staff loaned to the Foreign Office.
    (2) Published in H.M. Treasury, *Civil Service Manpower* (1966) table 20.

TABLE 4: SIZE OF THE NON-INDUSTRIAL
CIVIL SERVICE

Year	Numbers employed excluding Post Office	Numbers employed including Post Office
1939	191,171	387,377
1950	434,930	684,799
1960	382,455	637,374
1961	389,198	650,201
1962	396,939	669,825
1963	412,440	688,074
1964	415,394	689,635
1965	419,520	803,327
1966	426,077	821,551

Notes: (1) The source was H.M. Treasury, *Civil Service Manpower* (1966) table 1; the figures for all years but 1966 relate to 1 Apr, the last figures being for 1 Jan 1966.

(2) An idea of the relative size of the Administrative Class to the total of non-industrial staff can be secured by looking at the totals as at 1 Jan for the following years, as given in H.M. Treasury, *Civil Service Manpower* (1966) table 20:

1961: 2381	1962: 2435	1963: 2444
1964: 2483	1965: 2534	1966: 2344

Recruitment to the Administrative Class: the Post-War Record

TABLE I: DIRECT-ENTRY RECRUITMENT TO THE
ADMINISTRATIVE CLASS, 1948–66

Year	Vacancies	Applications	Effective applications	Number declared successful	Number certificated for appointment
1948	–	446	–	50	–
1949	60	513	–	50	–
1950	60	889	–	77	–
1951	60	1050	–	75	–
1952	60	873	–	63	–
1953	65	838	660	51	49
1954	52	829	650	54	49
1955	65	593	470	31	30
1956	62	553	450	40	33
1957	68	627	500	43	40
1958	69	622	520	43	35
1959	66	700	570	46	41
1960	80	732	600	52	47
1961	75	864	690	61	56
1962	74	842	680	53	39
1963	80	869	680	67	51
1964	88	835	660	75	48 (12)
1965	100	955	740	107	80 (5)
1966	90	1036	824	96	59 (22)

Notes: (1) These statistics were supplied by the Civil Service Commissioners: the figures in brackets denoted open cases.

(2) The number declared successful in 1953 differed from that given in the *Priestley Report* (p. 93) because 5 candidates successful for the Administrative Class were also successful for and preferred other appointments, i.e., 3 House of Commons Clerkships and 2 Northern Ireland Civil Service.

TABLE 2: THE PROBATION RECORD OF
SUCCESSFUL CANDIDATES

One method of measuring the subsequent performance of successful candidates is by probation reports, and those received up to 1961 covering 445 entrants who were still serving at the end of the normal two-year probationary period gave the following picture.

Confirmed after normal probation	394
Confirmed after extended probation	38
Appointments terminated (inc. medical causes)	8
Still serving extended probation	2
Resigned during extended probation	3
TOTAL	445

Notes: (1) The source was the *Sixth Report from the Estimates Committee* (1964–5) p. 28.

(2) Appendix 10 (p. 260) of that publication showed that in addition to the 11 indicated in the table, besides 2 deaths, 23 entrants had resigned before the end of normal probation thus making total wastage 34 out of a gross original entry of 470 or 7 per cent.

TABLE 3: DEPARTMENTAL ASSESSMENTS OF
SUCCESSFUL CANDIDATES

Departmental assessments of performance on the 363 entrants for whom full reports are available show the following results:

Grading	Passed by Method II	Passed by Method I	Method I passes who had failed Method II
Very good indeed	18 (13·6%)	12 (5·2%)	2 (2·7%)
Distinctly above average	60 (45·5%)	69 (29·9%)	18 (24·6%)
Well up to standard	45 (34·1%)	117 (50·6%)	39 (53·4%)
Total with good reports	123 (93·2%)	198 (85·7%)	59 (80·7%)
Rather below standard	8 (6·1%)	27 (11·7%)	10 (13·7%)
Unsatisfactory	1 (0·7%)	6 (2·6%)	4 (5·6%)
GRAND TOTAL	132 (100%)	231 (100%)	73 (100%)

Source: *Sixth Report from the Estimates Committee* (1964–5) p. 28.

TABLE 4: ADMINISTRATIVE RECRUITMENT, APPLICATIONS
AND SUCCESSES, 1948–63

| | Method I | | | | Method II | | | |
Year	Appli- cations (a)	Com- pleted Candi- datures (b)	Suc- cesses (d)	Assign- ments to Adm. Class (e)	Appli- cations (a)	Com- pleted Candi- datures (c)	Suc- cesses (d)	Assign- ments to Adm. Class (e)
1948–56	3319	1720	319	n.a.	3165	2746	208	n.a.
1957	277	128	20	20	350	327	26	23
1958	254	129	22	19	369	332	24	18
1959	329	155	27	22	371	336	33	19
1960	331	131	32	27	400	355	42	24
1961	353	131	25	22	515	448	60	37
1962	312	114	16	10	529	431	53	33
1963	361	153	27	15	508	420	56	36
TOTALS	5536	2661	488	n.a.	6207	5395	502	n.a.

Source: Sixth Report from the Estimates Committee (1964–5) p. 29.

Notes: (a) Includes withdrawals before any stage. There are more applications than candidates because of candidates who entered for both methods.

(b) Includes candidates compulsorily eliminated at any stage.

(c) Includes candidates who took the qualifying papers.

(d) Covers successes in respect of all 'dual' candidatures which included candidatures for the Administrative Class.

(e) Excludes candidates covered by (d) who in fact went to the Foreign Service, Northern Ireland Administrative Class, or to Clerkships in the House of Commons, or who either declined appointment or were ineligible.

TABLE 5: ADMINISTRATIVE RECRUITMENT:
UNIVERSITIES OF CANDIDATES, 1948-63

	Method I				Method II			
	Competitors		*Successes*		*Competitors*		*Successes*	
University	'48–'56	'57–'63	'48–'56	'57–'63	'48–'56	'57–'63	'48–'56	'57–'63
Oxford	503	359	137	87	993	1030	114	150
Cambridge	322	164	93	48	589	719	64	110
	825	523	230	135	1582	1749	178	260
London	348	166	34	13	476	245	17	14
Scottish	181	68	35	11	208	140	8	9
Others: U.K. and Eire	322	168	20	10	460	455	5	9
Overseas	4	4	–	–	2	1	–	1
No University	40	12	–	–	18	59	–	1
TOTALS	1720	941	319	169	2746	2649	208	294

Source: Sixth Report from the Estimates Committee (1964–5) p. 29.
Notes: (1) The classification refers to gross successes, i.e., those shown in the columns covered by Note (*d*) of Table 4, and this is also the case with the following tables about the degree subjects, degree classes, schools and father's occupation of candidates.

(2) In the above table, the candidates admitted to Method II competitions with no degree are former regular members of H.M. Forces and of H.M. Overseas Civil Service, who are not subject to that method's normal degree requirements.

TABLE 6: ADMINISTRATIVE RECRUITMENT:
CANDIDATES' DEGREE SUBJECTS, 1948–63

Degree Subjects	Method I				Method II			
	Competitors		Successes		Competitors		Successes	
	'48–'56	'57–'63	'48–'56	'57–'63	'48–'56	'57–'63	'48–'56	'57–'63
Classics	212	167	59	48	248	363	51	63
Economics and Politics	197	77	31	11	340	174	24	18
P.P.E.	81	40	27	13	187	171	23	19
English	128	54	21	5	195	164	9	18
History	557	272	121	57	757	690	50	94
Law	35	32	9	5	130	138	12	14
Mathematics	61	10	10	1	50	18	2	4
Modern Languages	232	163	21	20	558	423	25	17
Science and Technology	16	13	2	3	42	57	4	7
Other subjects	161	98	–	6	221	384	8	37
No University	40	15	–	–	18	67	–	3
TOTALS	1720	941	319	169	2746	2649	208	294

Source: Sixth Report from the Estimates Committee (1964–5) p. 30.
Note: Most of the category described as 'Other subjects' were candidates who took two different subjects at university, neither of which was clearly the dominant one. P.P.E. refers to the Philosophy, Politics and Economics honours course at Oxford.

TABLE 7: ADMINISTRATIVE RECRUITMENT:
CANDIDATES' DEGREE CLASSES, 1948–63

	Method I				Method II			
	Competitors		Successes		Competitors		Successes	
Class of Degree	'48–'56	'57–'63	'48–'56	'57–'63	'48–'56	'57–'63	'48–'56	'57–'63
	231	92	130	48	312	271	77	92
II	529	312	115	60	915	816	74	104
II (1)	363	210	60	53	601	578	41	67
II (2)	324	147	8	5	568	389	10	16
III	152	97	5	3	248	223	4	7
IV	57	6	1	–	54	7	2	1
None	64	29	–	–	48	82	–	3
War degree	–	–	–	–	–	3	–	2
Not known	–	48	–	–	–	280	–	2
TOTALS	1720	941	319	169	2746	2649	208	294

Source: Sixth Report from the Estimates Committee (1964–5) p. 30.

Notes: (1) Those shown under Method II successes as having 3rd and 4th Class Honours degrees were only provisionally declared successful, on failing to obtain at least 2nd Class Honours degrees.

(2) As noted earlier, certain candidates – former regular members of H.M. Forces and of H.M. Overseas Civil Service – are not subject to the normal degree requirements for Method II.

(3) Information about the degree classes of unsuccessful candidates is incomplete for recent years.

TABLE 8: ADMINISTRATIVE RECRUITMENT:
CANDIDATES' SCHOOLS, 1948–63

	Method I				Method II			
	Competitors		Successes		Competitors		Successes	
	'48–'56	'57–'63	'48–'56	'57–'63	'48–'56	'57–'63	'48–'56	'57–'63
British Boarding Day:	261	247	74	53	693	905	91	120
(a) Independent and direct grant	470	308	86	54	737	838	54	91
(b) L.E.A.-maintained or -aided	980	375	157	60	1298	877	62	80
Foreign	9	11	2	2	18	29	1	3
TOTAL	1720	941	319	169	2746	2649	208	294

Source: Sixth Report from the Estimates Committee (1964–5) p. 31.

TABLE 9: ADMINISTRATIVE RECRUITMENT:
FATHER'S OCCUPATION, 1948–63

	Method I				Method II			
	Competitors		Successes		Competitors		Successes	
Group	'48–'56	'57–'63	'48–'56	'57–'63	'48–'56	'57–'63	'48–'56	'57–'63
I	434	338	103	60	918	1042	99	152
II	754	355	131	72	1169	1011	74	104
III	479	181	76	25	590	487	29	30
IV	34	40	5	7	40	63	1	6
V	13	4	4	–	16	9	3	2
Unknown	6	23	–	5	13	37	2	–
TOTAL	1720	941	319	169	2746	2649	208	194

Source: Sixth Report from the Estimates Committee (1964–5) p. 31.
Note: The occupational groups are those defined by the Registrar-General:
- I   Administrators, managers, senior professional and scientific occupations.
- II   Intermediate professional, managerial and technical occupations.
- III   Highly skilled workers, foremen, supervisors, clerks.
- IV   Skilled and semi-skilled.
- V   Unskilled.

TABLE 10: ANALYSIS OF METHOD II, 1960–6

Year	No. of Applications		No. qualified in written exam		No. qualified at C.S.S.B.		No. qualified at F.S.B.	
	Ox-bridge	Non-Ox-bridge	Ox-bridge	Non-Ox-bridge	Ox-bridge	Non-Ox-bridge	Ox-bridge	Non-Ox-bridge
1960	269	132 (5)	130	16 (1)	108	14 (1)	39	3 (1)
1961	315	196 (10)	153	47	109	24	50	10
1962	315	214 (18)	139	57 (3)	91	29 (2)	42	11 (1)
1963	284	224 (19)	156	68 (4)	103	28 (2)	48	8
1964	269	250 (22)	146	66 (1)	120	39	53	12
1965	303	272 (8)	176	95 (1)	131	57 (1)	67	26 (1)
1966	281	444 (16)	169	175 (4)	127	108 (2)	59	35

Source: Information supplied by the Civil Service Commissioners.
Note: The figures in brackets denote candidates who did not attend university and have been included in the main figure.

*The Executive and Clerical Classes
and their Opportunities*

TABLE 1: THE GENERAL EXECUTIVE CLASS, 1966

	Numbers as at 1 January 1966		
Grade	*Permanent*	*Temporary*	*Total*
Heads of Major Executive Establishments	57	–	57
Principal Executive Officer	105	–	105
Senior Chief Executive Officer	323	–	323
Chief Executive Officer	1284	5	1289
Senior Executive Officer	3727	18½	3745½
Higher Executive Officer	11,563	72	11,635
Executive Officer	29,519	167½	29,686½
TOTAL	46,578	263	46,841

Source: H.M. Treasury, *Introductory Factual Memorandum on the Civil Service presented to the Fulton Committee on the Civil Service* (1966) para. 303. The halves in the statistics refer to part-time staff.

TABLE 2: THE SOURCES OF ENTRANTS TO THE
EXECUTIVE OFFICER GRADE, 1965

Source of Entrants	*Percentage of total*
(i) Promotion	59·7 (60·2)
(ii) Competitions, except (iii)	
(a) Existing Permanent Officers 9·8 (8·4)	
(b) Existing Temporary Officers 4·8 (4·6)	33·1 (32·9)
(c) New Direct Entrants 18·7 (20·1)	
(iii) Limited Competition (existing Permanent Officers)	5·7 (4·7)
(iv) Other means, e.g., assimilation (existing Permanent Officers)	1·5 (2·2)
TOTAL	100 (100)

Note: The figures in brackets refer to the General Executive Class only: the source of the statistics being H.M. Treasury, *Civil Service Manpower* (1966) table 27.

TABLE 3: THE GENERAL CLERICAL CLASS, 1966

| | *Numbers as at 1 January 1966* | | |
Grade	*Permanent*	*Temporary*	*Total*
Higher Clerical Officer	1734	13	1747
Clerical Officer	75,818	11,907	87,725
TOTALS	77,552	11,920	89,472

Source: H.M. Treasury, *Introductory Factual Memorandum on the Civil Service presented to the Fulton Committee on the Civil Service* (1966) para. 125: the natural promotion outlet for the Clerical Officer is to Executive Officer.

TABLE 4: DIRECT-ENTRY RECRUITMENT TO THE
EXECUTIVE CLASS, 1950–66

Year	No. of vacancies	No. of applications	No. declared successful	No. certificated for appointment
1950	583	5747	564	482
1951	505	4663	565	473
1952	500	4253	539	484
1953	465	4088	515	451
1954	477	3757	536	438
1955	578	3082	635	575
1956	712	3387	720	645
1957	739	3552	786	698
1958	1140	3386	911	774
1959	1431	5513	1406	1198 (8)
1960	1489	5089	1419	1248 (8)
1961	1417	5663	1582	1207 (208)
1962	1350	6410	1555	1177 (241)
1963	1366	6460	1560	957 (466)
1964	1836	4463	1743	1438 (5)
1965	2575	5451	2486	2113 (19)
1966	4078	7132	3274	2714 (55)

Source: For the years 1950–4 the source was the *Priestley Report* (1955) p. 103, and the remaining statistics were supplied to me personally by the Civil Service Commissioners.

Note: The figures in brackets denote undecided cases.

APPENDIX FOUR

The Major Specialist Groups

TABLE I: THE SCIENTIFIC OFFICER CLASS, 1966

Grade	Permanent	Temporary	Total
Posts above Chief Scientific Officer	16	$5\frac{1}{2}$	$21\frac{1}{2}$
Chief Scientific Officer	82	$3\frac{1}{2}$	$85\frac{1}{2}$
Deputy Chief Scientific Officer	194	1	195
Senior Principal Scientific Officer	628	30	658
Principal Scientific Officer	1395	$115\frac{1}{2}$	$1510\frac{1}{2}$
Senior Scientific Officer	222	$322\frac{1}{2}$	$544\frac{1}{2}$
TOTAL	3411	708	4119

Source: H.M. Treasury, *Introductory Factual Memorandum on the Civil Service presented to the Fulton Committee on the Civil Service* (1966) para. 467: the halves in the statistics represent part-time staff.

TABLE IA: EXPERIMENTAL OFFICER CLASS, 1966

	Numbers as at 1 *January* 1966		
Grade	*Permanent*	*Temporary*	*Total*
Chief Experimental Officer	226	2	228
Senior Experimental Officer	1512	37	1549
Experimental Officer	3504	$504\frac{1}{2}$	$4008\frac{1}{2}$
Assistant Experimental Officer	1149	545	1694
TOTAL	6391	$1088\frac{1}{2}$	$7479\frac{1}{2}$

Source: H.M. Treasury, *Introductory Factual Memorandum on the Civil Service presented to the Fulton Committee on the Civil Service* (1966) para. 314: the halves in the statistics represent part-time staff.

TABLE IB: THE SCIENTIFIC ASSISTANT CLASS, 1966

Grade	*Permanent*	*Temporary*	*Total*
Senior Scientific Assistant	1035	92	1127
Scientific Assistant	1673	2916	4589
TOTAL	2708	3008	5716

Source: H.M. Treasury, *Introductory Factual Memorandum on the Civil Service presented to the Fulton Committee on the Civil Service* (1966) para. 457.

TABLE 2: THE WORKS GROUP OF PROFESSIONAL CLASSES, 1966

Grade	Numbers as at 1 January 1966		
	Permanent	Temporary	Total
Top posts	24	–	24
Directing grades	251	3	254
Superintending grades	622	2	624
Senior grade	2078	60	2138
Main grade	4241	406	4647
Basic grade	3174	555	3729
TOTAL	10,390	1026	11,416

Source: H.M. Treasury, *Introductory Factual Memorandum on the Civil Service presented to the Fulton Committee on the Civil Service* (1966) para. 564.

TABLE 3: THE LEGAL CLASS, 1966

Grade	Numbers as at 1 January 1966		
	Permanent	Temporary	Total
Top posts	2	–	2
Head of Legal Department or Branch	15	–	15
Deputy Head	7	–	7
Principal Assistant Solicitor	19	3	22
Assistant Solicitor	126	$1\frac{1}{2}$	$127\frac{1}{2}$
Senior Legal Assistant	351	15	366
Legal Assistant	159	50	209
TOTAL	679	$69\frac{1}{2}$	$748\frac{1}{2}$

Source: H. M. Treasury, *Introductory Factual Memorandum on the Civil Service presented to the Fulton Committee on the Civil Service* (1966) para. 350: the halves in the statistics represent part-time staff.

TABLE 4: THE MEDICAL OFFICER CLASS, 1966

Grade	Numbers as at 1 January 1966		
	Permanent	Temporary	Total
Chief Medical Officer			
Deputy Chief Medical Officer	15	2	17
Senior Principal Medical Officer			
Principal Medical Officer	35	–	35
Senior Medical Officer	112	57	169
Medical Officer	366	$69\frac{1}{2}$	$435\frac{1}{2}$
TOTAL	528	$128\frac{1}{2}$	$656\frac{1}{2}$

Source: H.M. Treasury, *Introductory Factual Memorandum on the Civil Service presented to the Fulton Committee on the Civil Service* (1966) para. 376: the halves in the statistics represent part-time staff.

TABLE 5: THE STATISTICIAN CLASS, 1966

Grade	Numbers as at 1 January 1966		
	Permanent	Temporary	Total
Higher Directing Staff	7	1	8
Chief Statistician	34	1	35
Statistician	85	13	98
Assistant Statistician	21	3	24
TOTAL	147	18	165

Source: H.M. Treasury, *Introductory Factual Memorandum on the Civil Service presented to the Fulton Committee on the Civil Service* (1966) para. 483.

P

TABLE 6: THE PROFESSIONAL ACCOUNTANT CLASS, 1966

	Numbers as at 1 *January* 1966		
Grade	*Permanent*	*Temporary*	*Total*
Director	7	–	7
Assistant Director	21	–	21
Chief Accountant	80	1	81
Senior Accountant	148	47	195
Accountant	19	11	30
TOTAL	275	59	334

Source: H.M. Treasury, *Introductory Factual Memorandum on the Civil Service presented to the Fulton Committee on the Civil Service* (1966) para. 81.

TABLE 7: THE ECONOMIST CLASS, 1966

	Numbers as at 1 *January* 1966		
Grade	*Permanent*	*Temporary*	*Total*
Top posts	7	$6\frac{1}{2}$	$13\frac{1}{2}$
Senior Economic Adviser	5	$16\frac{1}{2}$	$21\frac{1}{2}$
Economic Adviser	7	$28\frac{1}{2}$	$35\frac{1}{2}$
Economic Assistant	3	35	38
TOTAL	22	$86\frac{1}{2}$	$108\frac{1}{2}$

Source: H.M. Treasury, *Introductory Factual Memorandum on the Civil Service presented to the Fulton Committee on the Civil Service* (1966) para. 291: the halves in the statistics represent part-time staff.

APPENDIX FIVE

Select Bibliography

I OFFICIAL REPORTS

The evidence presented to and the reports produced by official committees charged with inquiry into and reporting on either the Civil Service as a whole or various aspects of its working, have proved the most valuable source of information in the preparation of this book. The major reports consulted are listed below in alphabetical order of the Chairmen's names. Unless stated otherwise, and with the obvious exceptions of Royal Commissions, the reports are those of Treasury Committees.

Anderson Committee on the Pay of State Servants (1923).

Asquith Committee to advise as to the Salaries of the Principal Posts in the Civil Service, B.P.P. 1921, IX.

Assheton Committee on the Training of Civil Servants, B.P.P. 1943–4, III.

Barlow Committee (Civil Service National Whitley Council) on Recruitment to Established Posts in the Civil Service during the Reconstruction Period, B.P.P. 1943–4, VIII.

Barlow Committee on the Organisation, Remuneration and Conditions of Service of Officers employed in Government Legal Departments (1944).

Barlow Committee on the Scientific Civil Service, B.P.P. 1945–6, XVIII.

Bradbury Committee to Inquire into the Organisation and Staffing of Government Offices, B.P.P. 1918, VII and 1919, XI.

Bridgeman Committee of Inquiry on the Post Office, B.P.P. 1931–2, XII.

Bridges–Day Joint Committee (Civil Service National Whitley Council) to consider the Political Activities of Civil Servants (1953).

Carpenter Committee on the Staffs of Government Scientific Establishments (1931).

Childers Committee on Civil Service Expenditure, B.P.P. 1873, VII.

Chorley Committee on Higher Civil Service Remuneration, B.P.P. 1948–9, XII.

Fulton Committee on the Civil Service (1966–8).

Gardiner Committee on the Organisation, Structure and Remuneration of the Works Group of Professional Classes (1952).

Gardiner Committee on the Organisation, Structure and Remuneration of the Professional Accountant Class (1952).

Gladstone Committee on Recruitment for the Civil Service after the War, B.P.P. 1919, XI.

Haldane Committee (Ministry of Reconstruction) on the Machinery of Government, B.P.P. 1918, XII.

Heath Sub-Committee of the Inter-Departmental Committee on the Application of the Whitley Report to the Administrative Departments of the Civil Service, B.P.P. 1919, XI.

Howitt Committee on the Pay and Organisation of Civil Service Medical Staffs (1951).

Kennet Committee on the Calling-up of Civil Servants, B.P.P. 1940–1, IV.

Leathes Committee to consider the Scheme of Examination for Class I of the Civil Service, B.P.P. 1917–18, VIII.

Lytton Committee on the Appointment of Ex-Service Men to Posts in the Civil Service (1920–1).

Macaulay Committee on the Indian Civil Service, B.P.P. 1855, XI.

Macdonnell Royal Commission on the Civil Service, B.P.P. 1912–13, XV; 1913, XVIII; 1914, XVI; 1914–16, XI and XII.

Masterman Committee on the Political Activities of Civil Servants, B.P.P. 1948–9, XII.

Patten Committee on Official Salaries, B.P.P. 1850, XV.

Playfair Commission of Inquiry on the Selection, Transfer and Grading of Civil Servants, B.P.P. 1875, XXIII.

Priestley Royal Commission on the Civil Service, B.P.P. 1955–6, XI.

Ramsay National Provisional Joint Committee on the Application of the Whitley Report to the Administrative Departments of the Civil Service, B.P.P. 1919, XI.

Ramsay Reorganisation Committee of the Civil Service National Whitley Council (1920–1).

Ridley Royal Commission on Civil Establishments, B.P.P. 1887, XIX; 1888, XXVII; 1889, XXI; and 1890, XXVII.

Southborough Committee on the Appointment of Ex-Service Men to Posts in the Civil Service (1923–4).

Stanley Committee on Civil Service Appointments, B.P.P. 1860, IX.

Tennant Committee on the Organisation of the Scientific Civil Service (1965).

Tomlin Royal Commission on the Civil Service B.P.P. 1930–1, X.

Trevelyan–Northcote Committee on the Organisation of the Permanent Civil Service, B.P.P. 1854, XXVII: and also Papers about their proposals in B.P.P. 1854–5, XX.

The Annual Reports of the Civil Service Commissioners between 1856 and 1967 have provided an invaluable record of direct-entry recruitment to the Civil Service over that period.

The following reports of the Select Committee on Estimates have also proved particularly valuable:

(i) Ninth Report, 1947–8: the Civil Service Commission.
(ii) Sixth Report, 1957–8: Treasury Control of Expenditure.
(iii) Fifth Report, 1963–4: Treasury Control of Establishments.
(iv) Sixth Report, 1964–5: Recruitment to the Civil Service.

The following individuals and organisations were kind enough to make available to me their written evidence to the Fulton Committee on the Civil Service:

Acton Society Trust
British Institute of Management
Mr R. G. S. Brown
Civil Service Clerical Association
Civil Service Union
Confederation of British Industry
Professor B. R. Crick and Mr Thornhill
Dr A. F. Earle
Engineers' Guild
First Division Association
Greater London Council
Institute of Chemistry
Institute of Heating and Ventilating Engineers
Institution of Professional Civil Servants
Labour Party
Liberal Party
Rating and Valuation Association
Mr J. H. Robertson
Professor Peter Self
Society of Civil Servants
Trades Union Congress
H.M. Treasury

II BOOKS ABOUT THE CIVIL SERVICE AND ITS ENVIRONMENT

What follows is a list of books specifically read in connection with the preparation of this book. As is evident from the footnotes, a considerable number of articles have also been consulted. Having read all of its issues from 1923 to 1967, I will make clear my debt to the valuable fund of information available in *Public Administration*, the Journal of the Royal Institute of Public Administration: the *Political Quarterly*, to a lesser extent, has also proved of value. The Journals of the Staff Side of the National Whitley Council, *Whitley Bulletin*; of the I.P.C.S., *State Service*; the C.S.C.A., *Red Tape*; and especially, the Society of Civil Servants' admirable *Civil Service Opinion*, have been very valuable sources of information. I also acknowledge the debt I owe to the various contributors to *The Sunday Times*, *The Observer*, *The Times*, *The Guardian*, *The Daily Telegraph* and, above all, *The Economist* for their continual flow of informed comment about public affairs. The list of books which follows is a record of reading about the Civil Service and its environment.

Abramovitz, Moses, and Eliasberg, Vera, *The Growth of Public Employment in Great Britain* (1957).

Abbotson, Martin, *Bureaucracy Run Mad* (1940).

Abbott, Evelyn, and Campbell, Lewis, *The Life and Letters of Benjamin Jowett* (1897).

Allen, Bernard M., *Sir Robert Morant. A Great Public Servant* (1934).

Allen, Sir Carleton K., *Bureaucracy Triumphant* (1931).

— *Law and Orders* (1956).

Anderson, Sir John, *The Machinery of Government* (1946).

— *The Organisation of Economic Studies in Relation to the Problem of Government* (1947).

— *Administrative Technique in the Public Service* (1949).

Anonymous, *Letters from a Civil Servant to his Son* (1947).

Appleby, Paul H., *Public Administration for a Welfare State* (1961).

Ashton-Gwatkin, Frank, *The British Foreign Service* (1950).

Ashworth, William, *An Economic History of England 1870–1939* (1960).

Aylmer, Gerald E., *The King's Servants: The Civil Service of Charles I, 1625–1642* (1961).

Barker, Sir Ernest, *The Development of Public Services in Western Europe 1660–1930* (1944).

Bauchet, Pierre, *Economic Planning: the French Experience* (1964).

Baxter, Stephen B., *The Development of the Treasury 1660–1702* (1957).

Beer, Samuel, *Treasury Control* (1957).

Beloff, Max, *New Dimensions in Foreign Policy: A Study in British Administrative Experience 1947–1959* (1961).

Beloff, Nora, *The General Says No* (1963).

Benham, F. C., *Great Britain under Protection* (1939).

Beveridge, Sir William (later Lord), *The Public Service in War and in Peace* (1920).

Beveridge, Lord, *Power and Influence* (1953).

Birkenhead, Lord, *The Prof. in Two Worlds: the Official Life of Professor F. A. Lindemann, Viscount Cherwell* (1964).
Blair, Leo, *The Commonwealth Public Service* (1958).
Blau, Peter M., *Bureaucracy in Modern Society* (1956).
Bowley, A. L., *Some Economic Consequences of the War* (1931).
Boyle, Andrew, *Montagu Norman* (1967).
Bridges, Sir Edward (later Lord), *Treasury Control* (1950).
— *Portrait of a Profession* (1950).
— *The Elements of Any British Budget* (1956).
Bridges, Lord, *The State and the Arts* (1958).
— *The University and the Public Service* (1960).
— *The Treasury* (1964).
Briggs, Asa, *Public Opinion and Public Health in the Age of Chadwick* (1946).
Brittan, Sir Herbert, *The British Budgetary System* (1959).
Brittan, Samuel, *The Treasury Under the Tories 1951–1964* (1964).
Brown, R. Douglas, *The Battle of Crichel Down* (1955).
Brown, William J., *So Far* (1943).
— *The Civil Service. Retrospect and Prospect* (1943).
Brown, Sir William Robson, and others, *Change or Decay* (1963).
Bruce, Maurice, *The Coming of the Welfare State* (1961).
Bunbury, Sir Henry, *Officials and the Public* (1947).
— (ed.), *Lloyd George's Ambulance Wagon* (1957).
Butler, Sir Harold, *The Confident Morning* (1950).
Caiden, Gerald E., *Career Service. An Introduction to the History of Personnel Administration in the Commonwealth Public Service of Australia 1901–1961* (1965).
Callaghan, L. James, *Whitleyism: A Study of Joint Consultation in the Civil Service* (1953).
Campbell, G. A., *The Civil Service in Britain* (1965).
Campion, Lord, and others, *Parliament. A Survey* (1952).
Cardwell, D. S. L., *The Organisation of Science in England* (1957).
Carr-Saunders, Sir Alexander, *The Professions* (1928).
Carswell, John, *The Civil Servant and His World* (1966).
Caves, Richard E., *Britain's Economic Prospects* (1968).
Chapman, Brian, *The Prefects and Provincial France* (1955).
— *The Profession of Government* (1959).
— *British Government Observed* (1963).
Chester, D. N. (ed.), *Lessons of the British War Economy* (1951).
— and Willson, F. M. G., *The Organisation of British Central Government 1914–1956* (1957).
— and Bowring, Nona, *Questions in Parliament* (1962).
Chubb, Basil, *The Control of Public Expenditure* (1952).
Clarke, Sir Richard, *The Management of the Public Sector of the National Economy* (1964).

Clark, Ronald W., *Tizard* (1965).

Clay, Sir Henry, *Lord Norman* (1957).

Cohen, Emmeline, *The Growth of the British Civil Service 1780–1939* (1941).

Cole, Margaret (ed.), *Beatrice Webb's Diaries 1912–1924* (1952).

Colvin, Ian, *Vansittart in Office* (1965).

Conan, Arthur R., *The Rationale of the Sterling Area* (1961).

Coombes, David, *The Member of Parliament and the Administration: The Case of the Select Committee on Nationalised Industries* (1966).

Craig, Sir John, *A History of Red Tape* (1955).

Crick, Bernard, *The Reform of Parliament* (1964).

Crisp, L. F., *Australian National Government* (1965).

Critchley, Thomas A., *The Civil Service Today* (1951).

Crombie, Sir James, *Her Majesty's Customs and Excise* (1962).

Cross, Colin, *Philip Snowden* (1966).

Crozier, Michael, *The Bureaucratic Phenomenon* (1964).

Daalder, Hans, *Cabinet Reform in Britain 1914–1963* (1964).

Dale, Harold E., *The Higher Civil Service of Great Britain* (1941).

— *The Personnel and Problems of the Higher Civil Service* (1943).

Davies, Ernest, '*National*' *Capitalism* (1939).

Davison, R. C., *British Unemployment Policy Since 1930* (1938).

Dawson, R. MacGregor, *The Government of Canada* (1963).

Demetriadi, Sir Stephen, *A Reform for the Civil Service* (1921).

— *Inside a Government Office* (1921).

Devons, Ely, *Essays in Economics* (1961).

Dicey, Albert Venn, *Lectures on the Relation Between Law and Public Opinion in England* (1905: 1962 ed.).

Douglas, J. W. B., *The Home and the School* (1964).

Dow, J. C. R., *The Management of the British Economy 1945–1960* (1964).

Du Sautoy, Peter, *The Civil Service* (1957).

Dunnill, Frank, *The Civil Service. Some Human Aspects* (1956).

Dunsire, A. (ed.), *The Making of an Administrator* (1956).

Eaglesham, Eric, *From School Board to Local Authority* (1956).

Edmonds, E. L. and O. P. (eds.), *I Was There: The Memoirs of H. S. Tremenheere* (1965).

Emmerson, Sir Harold, *The Ministry of Works* (1952).

Evans, Dorothy, *Women and the Civil Service* (1934).

Faber, Sir Geoffrey, *Jowett. A Portrait with Background* (1957).

Fabian Society, *The Reform of the Higher Civil Service* (1947).

— *The Administrators* (1964).

Fairlie, John A., *British War Administration* (1919).

Finer, Herman, *The British Civil Service* (1937).

— *Municipal Trading* (1941).

Finer, Samuel E., *A Primer of Public Administration* (1950).

Finer, Samuel E., *The Life and Times of Sir Edwin Chadwick* (1952).

Floud, Jean, Halsey, A. H., and Martin, F. M., *Social Class and Educational Opportunity* (1957).

Flynn, Sir J. Albert, *Problems of the Civil Service* (1928).

Franks, Sir Oliver, *The Experiences of a University Teacher in the Civil Service* (1947).

— *Central Planning and Control in War and Peace* (1947).

Gerth, H. H., and Mills, C. Wright, *From Max Weber: Essays in Sociology* (1961).

Gilbert, Bentley, *The Evolution of National Insurance in Great Britain: The Origins of the Welfare State* (1966).

Ginsberg, Morris (ed.), *Law and Opinion in England in the Twentieth Century* (1959).

Gladden, E. N., *Civil Service or Bureaucracy?* (1956).

— *An Introduction to Public Administration* (1961).

— *British Public Service Administration* (1961).

— *Approach to Public Administration* (1966).

Greaves, H. R. G., *The Civil Service in the Changing State* (1947).

Gretton, Richard H., *The King's Government* (1913).

Grier, Lynda, *Achievement in Education. The Work of Michael Ernest Sadler* (1952).

Griffith, J. A. G., *Central Departments and Local Authorities* (1966).

Griffith, Wyn, *The British Civil Service 1854–1954* (1954).

Grigg, Sir James, *Prejudice and Judgment* (1948).

Grove, J. W., *Government and Industry in Britain* (1962).

Guillemard, Sir Laurence, *Trivial Fond Records* (1937).

Hackett, John and Anne-Marie, *Economic Planning in France* (1963).

Hagen, Everett, and White, Stephanie, *Great Britain: Quiet Revolution in Planning* (1966).

Halsey, A. H., Floud, Jean, and Anderson, C. A., *Education, Economy and Society* (1961).

Hamilton, Sir Horace, *Sir Warren Fisher and the Public Service* (1951).

Hankey, Sir Maurice, *The Development of the Higher Control of the Machinery of Government* (1942).

— *Government Control in War* (1945).

— *Diplomacy by Conference* (1946).

— *Politics, Trials and Errors* (1949).

— *The Science and Art of Government* (1951).

Hanson, A. H., *Parliament and Public Ownership* (1962).

— (ed.), *Nationalisation: A Book of Readings* (1963).

Harris, John S., *British Government Inspection as a Dynamic Process* (1955).

Harris, Richard W., *Not So Humdrum* (1939).

Harrod, Sir Roy, *The Life of John Maynard Keynes* (1951).

Harrod, Sir Roy, *The Prof. A Personal Memoir of Lord Cherwell* (1959).

Headlam, Sir Cuthbert, and others, *Some Proposals for Constitutional Reform* (1946).

Heath, Sir Thomas, *The Treasury* (1927).

Henderson, Sir Hubert, *The Inter-War Years and Other Papers* (1955).

Heussler, Robert, *Yesterday's Rulers: The Making of the British Colonial Service* (1963).

Humphreys, B. V., *Clerical Unions in the Civil Service* (1958).

Hurwitz, Samuel J., *State Intervention in Great Britain 1914–1919* (1949).

Ince, Sir Godfrey, *The Ministry of Labour and National Service* (1960).

Jackson, Brian and Marsden, Dennis, *Education and the Working Class* (1962).

Jeffries, Sir Charles, *The Colonial Office* (1956).

Jenkins, Sir Gilmour, *The Ministry of Transport and Civil Aviation* (1959).

Jennings, Sir Ivor, *The Law and the Constitution* (1959).

— *Parliament* (1961).

— *Cabinet Government* (1961).

Jewkes, John, *Ordeal by Planning* (1947; new edn., 1968).

Johnson, Nevil, *Parliament and Administration. The Estimates Committee 1945–1965* (1966).

Johnston, Sir Alexander, *The Inland Revenue* (1965).

Jones, J. Harry, *Josiah Stamp, Public Servant* (1963).

Jones, Thomas, *Lloyd George* (1951).

— *A Diary with Letters* (1954).

Jones, W. H. Morris, *Socialism and Bureaucracy* (1949).

Junz, Alfred J. (ed.), *Present Trends in American National Government* (1960).

'Justice', *The Citizen and the Administration* (1961).

Kahn, Hilda R., *Salaries in the Public Services of England and Wales* (1963).

Kalder, Nicholas, *Causes of the slow rate of economic growth of the United Kingdom* (1966).

Keith-Lucas, Bryan, *The History of Local Government in England* (1958).

Kekewich, Sir George, *The Education Department and After* (1920).

Kelf-Cohen, R., *Nationalisation in Britain. The End of a Dogma* (1961).

Kelsall, R. K., *Higher Civil Servants in Britain* (1955).

Kempe, Sir John A., *Reminiscences of an Old Civil Servant, 1846–1927* (1928).

Keynes, John Maynard (later Lord), *The Economic Consequences of Mr. Churchill* (1926).

— *General Theory of Employment, Interest and Money* (1936).

King, Sir Geoffrey, *The Ministry of Pensions and National Insurance* (1958).

Kingsley, John D., *Representative Bureaucracy* (1944).

Lambert, Royston, *Sir John Simon and English Social Administration* (1963).

Lang, Andrew, *Life, Letters and Diaries of Sir Stafford Northcote* (1890).

Laski, Harold J., *Democracy in Crisis* (1933).

— *Parliamentary Government in England* (1938).

— *Reflections on the Constitution* (1951).

— Jennings, W. Ivor (later Sir), and Robson, William A., *A Century of Municipal Progress* (1935).

Laver, F. J. M., *Introducing Computers* (1965).

Lee, Sir Frank, *The Board of Trade* (1958).

Lee, John, *The Attitude of the Press to the Civil Service* (1921).

Legge-Bourke, Sir Harry, *Master of the Offices* (1950).

Lewis, R. A., *Edwin Chadwick and the Public Health Movement 1832–1854* (1952).

Lewis, W. A., *Economic Survey 1919–1939* (1949).

Liberal Party, *Civil Service Reform* (1942).

Lipson, Ephraim, *The Growth of English Society* (1949).

Lloyd, Edward M. H., *Experiments in State Control at the War Office and the Ministry of Food* (1924).

Lockwood, David, *The Blackcoated Worker* (1958).

Lowell, A. Lawrence, *The Government of England* (1926).

MacDonagh, Oliver, *A Pattern of Government Growth 1800–1860* (1961).

Mackenzie, W. J. M., and Grove, J. W., *Central Administration in Britain* (1957).

Mackintosh, John P., *The British Cabinet* (1962).

Macrae, Norman, *Sunshades in October* (1963).

Mallalieu, J. P. W., *Passed to You Please* (1942).

Markham, Violet, *Friendship's Harvest* (1956).

Marris, Peter, *The Experience of Higher Education* (1964).

Marshall, Geoffrey, and Moodie, Graeme C., *Some Problems of the Constitution* (1961).

Martin, Arthur P., *The Life and Letters of Robert Lowe, Viscount Sherbrooke* (1893).

Martindale, Hilda, *Women Servants of the State* (1938).

Marx, F. Morstein (ed.), *Elements of Public Administration* (1946).

McLean, Joseph E. (ed.), *The Public Service and University Education* (1949).

Melville, Sir Harold W., *The Department of Scientific and Industrial Research* (1962).

Merton, Robert K. (ed.), *Reader in Bureaucracy* (1952).

Meyer, Poul, *Administrative Organisation. A Comparative Study of the Organisation of Public Administration* (1957).

Miller, J. D. B., *Australian Government and Politics* (1966).

Milne, Sir David, *The Scottish Office* (1957).

Mises, Ludwig Von, *Bureaucracy* (1944).

Mitchell, Joan, *Crisis in Britain 1951* (1963).

Monck, Bosworth, *How the Civil Service Works* (1952).

Morley, John, *The Life of William Ewart Gladstone* (1903–5).

Morton, W. A., *British Finance 1930–1940* (1943).

Moses, Robert, *The Civil Service in Great Britain* (1914).

Mowat, Charles Loch, *Britain Between the Wars 1918–1940* (1956).

Muir, J. Ramsay, *How Britain is Governed* (1930).

Munro, C. K., *The Fountains in Trafalgar Square* (1952).

Murray, Lady Mildred, *The Making of a Civil Servant. Sir Oswyn Murray* (1940).

Murray of Elibank, Lord, *Reflections on Some Aspects of British Foreign Policy Between the Wars* (1946).

Mustoe, Nelson E., *The Law and Organisation of the British Civil Service* (1932).

Newman, Bernard, *Yours for Action* (1953).

Newman, Sir George, *The Building of a Nation's Health* (1939).

Newsam, Sir Frank, *The Home Office* (1955).

Newsholme, Sir Arthur, *The Ministry of Health* (1925).

— *Fifty Years in Public Health* (1935).

Nicholson, Max, *The System. The Misgovernment of Britain* (1967).

Nigro, Felix A., *Modern Public Administration* (1965).

Normanton, E. L., *The Accountability and Audit of Government* (1966).

Northedge, F. S., *British Foreign Policy: The Process of Readjustment 1945–1961* (1962).

Ogilvy-Webb, Marjorie, *The Government Explains. A Study of the Information Services* (1965).

Parker, Charles S., *Life and Letters of Sir James Graham* (1907).

Parkinson, Sir Arthur, *The Colonial Office from Within 1909–1945* (1947).

Parkinson, C. Northcote, *Parkinson's Law or the Pursuit of Progress* (1958).

Parris, Henry, *Government and the Railways in Nineteenth Century Britain* (1965).

Peacock, A. T., and Wiseman, J., *The Growth of Public Expenditure in the United Kingdom* (1961).

Pigou, A. C., *Aspects of British Economic History 1918–1925* (1947).

Pilgrim Trust, *Men Without Work* (1938).

Pilmott, John A. R., *Toynbee Hall. Fifty Years of Social Progress 1884–1934* (1935).

Polanyi, Karl, *Origins of Our Time* (1945).

Polaschek, R. J., *Government Administration in New Zealand* (1958).

P.E.P., *A Civil General Staff* (1943).
— *Recruiting Civil Servants* (1947).
— *Government and Industry* (1952).
— *Growth in the British Economy* (1960).
— *Economic Planning in France* (1961).
— *French Planning: Some Lessons for Britain* (1963).
Price, Don K., *Government and Science* (1962).
— *The Scientific Estate* (1965).
Prouty, Roger, *The Transformation of the Board of Trade 1830–1855* (1957).
Raphael, Marios, *Pensions and Public Servants: A Study of the Origins of the British System* (1964).
Reid, Sir George, *The Origin and Development of Public Administration* (1913).
Reid, Gordon, *The Politics of Financial Control: The Role of the House of Commons* (1966).
Rhodes, Gerald, *Administrators in Action* (1965).
— *Public Sector Pensions* (1965).
Rhodes, H. V., *Setting Up a New Government Department* (1949).
Richardson, H. W., *Economic Recovery in Britain 1932-9* (1967).
Ridley, F. and Blondel, J., *Public Administration in France* (1964).
Riper, Paul P. Van, *The History of the United States Civil Service* (1958).
Robbins, Lionel (later Lord), *The Great Depression* (1934).
— *The Theory of Economic Policy in English Classical Political Economy* (1952).
Robbins, Lord, *Politics and Economics: Papers in Political Economy* (1963).
Roberts, David, *The Victorian Origins of the British Welfare State* (1960).
Robinson, Howard, *The British Post Office* (1948).
Robson, William A., *From Patronage to Proficiency in the Public Service* (1922).
— (ed.), *Public Enterprise* (1937).
— (ed.), *The British Civil Servant* (1937).
— *The Development of Local Government* (1948).
— *Justice and Administrative Law* (1951).
— (ed.), *The Civil Service in Britain and France* (1956).
— *Nationalised Industry and Public Ownership* (1960).
— *The Welfare State* (1962).
— *The Governors and the Governed* (1964).
— *Local Government in Crisis* (1966).
Rogow, A. A. and Shore, P., *The Labour Government and British Industry* (1955).
Rowat, Donald C. (ed.), *The Ombudsman: Citizen's Defender* (1965).

Rowse, Alfred L., *The End of an Epoch* (1947).
Roy, Naresh Chandra, *The Civil Service in India* (1958).
Sadleir, Michael T. H., *Michael Ernest Sadler 1861–1943. A Memoir by his Son* (1949).
Salter, Lord, *Memoirs of a Public Servant* (1961).
—*Slave of the Lamp. A Public Servant's Notebook* (1967).
Sampson, Anthony, *Anatomy of Britain* (1962).
Saunderson, F. W., *Government Service. An Essay Towards Reconstruction* (1920).
Sayre, Wallace S. (ed.), *The Federal Government Service* (1965).
Scarrow, H. A., *The Higher Public Service of the Commonwealth of Australia* (1957).
Scott, Sir Harold, *Your Obedient Servant* (1959).
Selby, Sir Walford, *Diplomatic Twilight 1930–1940* (1953).
Self, Peter, and Storing, H. J., *The State and the Farmer* (1962).
— *Bureaucracy or Management?* (1965).
Shanks, Michael, *The Stagnant Society* (1961).
— (ed.), *The Lessons of Public Enterprise* (1963).
Sheahan, John, *Promotion and Control of Industry in Postwar France* (1963).
Shonfield, Andrew, *British Economic Policy Since the War* (1959).
— *Modern Capitalism. The Changing Balance between Public and Private Power* (1965).
Shore, Peter, *Entitled to Know* (1966).
Skidelsky, Robert, *Politicians and the Slump. The Labour Government of 1929–31* (1967).
Sisson, C. H., *The Spirit of British Administration* (1959).
Smellie, Kingsley B., *A Hundred Years of English Government* (1954).
Smith, Adam, *An Inquiry into the Nature and Causes of the Wealth of Nations* (1776; 1937 ed.).
Snow, Sir Charles P., *The Two Cultures and the Scientific Revolution* (1959).
— *Science and Government* (1961).
— *Recent Thought on the Two Cultures* (1962).
— *The Two Cultures and a Second Look* (1964).
Society of Civil Servants, *The Civil Servant and His Profession* (1920).
— *The Development of the Civil Service* (1921).
Spann, R. N., *Public Administration in Australia* (1959).
Stanley, David T., *Changing Administrations. The 1961 and 1964 Transitions in Six Departments* (1965).
— *The Higher Civil Service. An Evaluation of Federal Personnel Practices* (1965).
Stokes, Eric, *The English Utilitarians and India* (1959).
Strang, Lord, *The Foreign Office* (1955).
— *The Diplomatic Career* (1962).
Strauss, Erich, *The Ruling Servants* (1961).

Street, Harry, *Freedom, the Individual and the Law* (1963).

Taylor, A. J. P., *English History 1914–1945* (1965).

Taylor, Sir Henry, *The Statesman* (1832: 1957 ed.).

Thomas, Hugh (ed.), *The Establishment* (1959).

— (ed.), *Crisis in the Civil Service* (1968).

Thomas, M. W., *The Early Factory Legislation* (1948).

Titmuss, Richard M., *Problems of Social Policy* (1950).

— *Income Distribution and Social Change* (1962).

Tizard, Sir Henry, *A Scientist in and out of the Civil Service* (1955).

Trevelyan, Sir George Otto, *The Life and Letters of Lord Macaulay* (1888).

Utley, T. E., *Occasion for Ombudsman* (1961).

Vansittart, Lord, *The Mist Procession* (1958).

Vernon, Philip, and Parry, J. B., *Personnel Selection in the British Forces* (1959).

Vickers, Sir Geoffrey, *The Art of Judgment: A Study of Policy Making* (1965).

Walker, Sir Charles, *Thirty-Six Years at the Admiralty* (1934).

Walker, Harvey, *Training Public Employees in Great Britain* (1935).

Walker, Nigel, *Morale in the Civil Service* (1961).

Wallas, Graham, *Human Nature in Politics* (1938 ed.).

Ward, Charles H. D., and Spencer, C. B., *The Unconventional Civil Servant. Sir Henry H. Cunynghame* (1938).

Watt, D. C., *Personalities and Policies: Studies in the Formulation of British Foreign Policy in the Twentieth Century* (1965).

West, Sir Algernon, *Recollections 1832–1886* (1899).

— *Contemporary Portraits. Men of My Day in Public Life* (1920).

— *Private Diaries* (1922).

Wheare, Kenneth C., *The Civil Service in the Constitution* (1954).

— *Government by Committee* (1955).

Wheeler-Bennett, Sir John, *John Anderson, Viscount Waverley* (1962).

White, Leonard D. and others, *The Civil Service Abroad. The British Civil Service* (1935).

— *Introduction to the Study of Public Administration* (1955).

Williams, David, *Not in the Public Interest* (1965).

Willson, F. M. G., *Administrators in Action* (1961).

— *The Organisation of British Central Government 1955–1961* (1962).

Wilson, Sir Charles Rivers, *Chapters from my Official Life* (1916).

Winnifrith, Sir John, *The Ministry of Agriculture, Fisheries and Food* (1962).

Woodruff, Philip, *The Men Who Ruled India* (1954).

Worswick, G. D. N. (ed.), *The British Economy 1945–1950* (1952).

— and Ady, P. H. (ed.), *The British Economy in the 1950s* (1962).

Young, D. M., *The Colonial Office in the Early Nineteenth Century* (1961).

Youngson, A. J., *The British Economy 1920–1957* (1960).

Index

Abell, Sir George (quoted), 102 n.
Acton Society Trust, 302, 306
Addison, Christopher, 1st Viscount, 22–3
Addison Act (1919), 22–3
Administrative Class, *passim*; degree classes of candidates, 437; degree subjects of candidates, 436; development since 1853, 33–6; dominance of, 56; direct-entry recruitment (1948–66), 432; departmental assessments of successful candidates, 433; and Higher Civil Service in Positive State, 257–360; occupations of candidates' fathers, 439; post-war recruitment to, 83–110, 431–40; pre-Fulton proposals for fusion with Executive Class, 171–97; probation record of successful candidates, 433; promotion from below, 157–71; schools of candidates, 438; structure and relative size of, 427–30; universities of candidates, 435; university graduates in, 305, 429, 435. *See also* Executive–Administrative Class
Administrative Staff College, Henley, 139–45, 151
Admiralty, 13; promotions, 162
Agricultural Land Commission, 258, 259 n.
Agricultural Land Service, 258
Agriculture, Board of, 38; patronage in, 82
Agriculture, Fisheries and Food, Ministry of: and Crichel Down, 258–64; professionals in, 217 n., 224
Agriculture and Fisheries for Scot-land, Department of, 214; professionals in, 217 n.
Allen, Sir Philip, 362 n.
American Civil Service, 281, 366, 371, 382–3
Anderson, Sir John (Viscount Waverley), 44 n. 74, 101; and introduction of Executive Class, 41 n.; on promotion from below, 164
Anderson, W. C., 362 n.
Annual Abstract of Statistics, 232
Anson, Sir William, on older universities, 75 n. 91 n.
Arbuthnot, Sir George: on duties of Civil Servants, 44–5; on departmentalised Service, 47
Architectural and Engineering Draughtsman Classes, 383, 384 n.
Armed Forces, 220; entry into Executive Class, 186 n.; ex-members in Principal grade, 108, 109 n.
Armstrong, Sir William, 153 n., 365 n.
Asquith Committee on salaries (1920–21), 56 n.
Assheton, Sir Ralph, 113 n.
Assheton Report on training (1944), 112 n., 113–19, 131, 136–7, 138 n., 146–7, 150, 152
Assistant Clerks Class, 39, 40, 41
Assistant Experimental Officer, 447
Assistant Principals, 287, 290; and Centre for Administrative Studies, 149–50, 312, 324; compared with Scientific Officer hierarchy, 216; graduates as, 429; method of entry, 429; numbers, 428; post-entry training, 111–36,